About Island Press

Island Press is the only nonprofit organization in the United States whose principal purpose is the publication of books on environmental issues and natural resource management. We provide solutions-oriented information to professionals, public officials, business and community leaders, and concerned citizens who are shaping responses to environmental problems.

In 2006, Island Press celebrates its twenty-first anniversary as the leading provider of timely and practical books that take a multidisciplinary approach to critical environmental concerns. Our growing list of titles reflects our commitment to bringing the best of an expanding body of literature to the environmental community throughout North America and the world.

Support for Island Press is provided by the Agua Fund, The Geraldine R. Dodge Foundation, Doris Duke Charitable Foundation, The William and Flora Hewlett Foundation, Kendeda Sustainability Fund of the Tides Foundation, Forrest C. Lattner Foundation, The Henry Luce Foundation, The John D. and Catherine T. MacArthur Foundation, The Marisla Foundation, The Andrew W. Mellon Foundation, Gordon and Betty Moore Foundation, The Curtis and Edith Munson Foundation, Oak Foundation, The Overbrook Foundation, The David and Lucile Packard Foundation, The Winslow Foundation, and other generous donors.

The opinions expressed in this book are those of the author(s) and do not necessarily reflect the views of these foundations.

THE
ENDANGERED
SPECIES ACT
AT
THIRTY

Volume 1

Volume 1
Renewing the Conservation Promise

Volume 2
Conserving Biodiversity in Human-Dominated Landscapes

THE
ENDANGERED
SPECIES ACT
AT
THIRTY

Renewing the Conservation Promise
Volume 1

Edited by

Dale D. Goble · J. Michael Scott
Frank W. Davis

ISLANDPRESS

Washington • Covelo • London

Library of Congress Cataloging-in-Publication Data
The Endangered Species Act at thirty / edited by Dale D. Goble, J. Michael Scott, and Frank W. Davis.
    p. cm.
   Includes bibliographical references and index.
   ISBN 1-59726-008-8 (cloth : alk. paper) — ISBN 1-59726-009-6 (pbk. : alk. paper)
   1. Endangered species—Law and legislation—United States. 2. Endangered species—United States. 3. Wildlife conservation—United States. I. Goble, Dale. II. Scott, J. Michael. III. Davis, F. W. (Frank W.), 1953-
   KF5640.E482 2005
   346.7304'69522—dc22

                                                        2005026419

British Cataloguing-in-Publication Data available.

Book design by Brighid Willson

Printed on recycled, acid-free paper

Manufactured in the United States of America
09 08 07 06 05 04 03 02   8 7 6 5 4 3 2 1

Contents

Preface

This book grew out of a multidisciplinary, multi-interest evaluation of the Endangered Species Act that coincided with the act's thirtieth anniversary. The project—known informally as the Endangered Species Act at Thirty project—began in the winter of 2001 when Dale Goble (University of Idaho College of Law) and J. Michael Scott (U.S. Geological Survey and University of Idaho College of Natural Resources) began an in-depth evaluation of the act. Frank Davis (University of California, Santa Barbara, Donald Bren School of Environmental Science and Management) and Geoffrey Heal (Columbia University, Graduate School of Business) joined as organizers the following spring and fall. With the generous support of Dennis J. Aigner, dean of the Bren School, the project was housed there.

Two principles guide the project. First, all analyses of the act should be scientifically rigorous. Thus, papers that form the basis for subsequent discussion have been through multiple peer reviews. Second, discussion should engage the full spectrum of perspectives on the act. To that end, the project has involved groups as diverse as the American Farm Bureau Federation, the National Cattlemen's Beef Association, Plum Creek Timber Company, Environmental Defense, the National Wildlife Federation, and the Center for Biological Diversity.[1] The organizers also have benefited from the ongoing involvement of four individuals who have played significant roles in the evolution of the Endangered Species Act: Michael J. Bean (director of wildlife program, Environmental Defense), James L. Caswell (administrator, Office of Species Conservation, State of Idaho), William J. Snape III (chairman of the board, Endangered Species Coalition), and Steven P. Quarles (attorney, Crowell & Mooring, LLP). Others who have been generous with their time are Holly Doremus (University of California, Davis), Peter Kareiva (The Nature Conservancy), and Buzz Thompson (Stanford University); they have led author groups and chaired topic sessions for the November 2003 conference, solicited additional contributed papers, and prepared substantial papers of their own.

The Endangered Species Act at Thirty project began in mid-November 2002 with a gathering of a select group of nearly thirty scholars and practitioners—biologists, economists, geographers, land use planners, natural resource lawyers, philosophers, and policy analysts[2]—for a two-day discussion of the Endangered Species Act. Following this initial meeting, the attendees drafted some forty papers that examined the act from multidisciplinary perspectives. After an initial round of peer review, these papers served as the analytical basis for a two-day conference held in Santa Barbara in mid-November 2003. A group of nearly a hundred individuals representing a diverse cross section of the interests affected by the act—nongovernmental organizations from both the conservation and development communities as well as federal, state, and local government representatives—met to discuss the papers and share ideas. The group was addressed by Bruce Babbitt (secretary of the interior in the Clinton administration), Dirk Kempthorne (governor of Idaho and then-chair of the National Governors Association), and Craig Manson (assistant secretary for fish and wildlife and parks, Department of the Interior).

The discussions produced a remarkable degree of consensus on potential avenues for increasing the act's effectiveness. These ideas have been further refined at a series of workshops convened by Goble and Scott with the guidance of an ad hoc steering committee composed of Michael Bean, Sharon Oxley (National Center for Housing and the Environment), and Bill Snape. Participants were again chosen to provide a multi-interest perspective. In addition to agency personnel with managerial responsibility for workshop topics, representatives from a full range of the impacted community were involved. In the workshops, participants developed detailed proposals for implementing the points of consensus. To date, workshops have been held on diverse topics such as identifying species that could be delisted quickly (hosted by Environmental Defense, in Washington, D.C.), conservation-reliant species (hosted by the U.S. Fish and Wildlife Service, in Arlington, Va.), recovery management agreements (hosted by the National Cattlemen's Beef Association, in Washington, D.C.), streamlining habitat conservation plans (hosted by the National Center for Housing and the Environment, in Washington, D.C.), state-based programs (hosted by the National Center for Housing and the Environment, in Atlantic City, N.J.), creating a single source of permitting information (cohosted by the University of Idaho and the Center for Research on Invasive Species and Small Populations [CRISSP], in Moscow, Idaho), and landowner incentives (hosted by Defenders of Wildlife, in Washington, D.C.). An additional workshop is planned on large-area, multiparty conservation agreements (hosted by Soulen Livestock Company and CRISSP, in Boise, Idaho).

The organizers have also presented preliminary findings to a variety of involved groups, including several groups of U.S. Fish and Wildlife Service directors and staff; the staff of Senate Committee on Environment and Public Works; the Western Association of Fish and Game Agencies; and the Nature Conservancy–Smith Fellows. The results of the workshops and consultations were presented at a senate policy briefing in the Dirksen Senate Office Building in Washington, D.C.; the assistant secretary of the interior and his staff were briefed the following day. We have benefited from the discussions that these presentations stimulated.

The Environmental Species Act at Thirty project has produced two books. The book you hold in your hands, *The Endangered Species Act at Thirty: Renewing the Conservation Promise*, emphasizes the policy issues; the second book, *The Endangered Species Act at Thirty: Conserving Biodiversity in Human-Dominated Landscapes*, which Island Press will publish in 2006, will examine several key issues in more detail. For example, there is no discussion here of the role that science should play in decision making. That topic is, however, examined at length in the second volume (*Doremus forthcoming*; Ruckelshaus and Darm forthcoming; Waples forthcoming).

The project has been assisted at every stage by many people and institutions. The sponsors of the preconference authors meeting, the conference, and the postconference workshops were very generous in their support; they include the National Center for Housing and the Environment, Defenders of Wildlife, Donald Bren Foundation, Idaho Office of Species Conservation, National Wildlife Federation, Turner Endangered Species Fund, Donald Bren School of Environmental Science and Management, and the colleges of law and natural resources at the University of Idaho.

Our host institutions, the University of California, Santa Barbara; University of Idaho; and U.S. Geological Survey, have provided both financial and in-kind support. They have also fostered the project by providing supportive working environments. We would like particularly to thank our deans, Dennis Aigner, Donald L. Burnett (University of Idaho College of Law), and Steven Daley Laursen (University of Idaho College of Natural Resources).

To Jennifer L. Purcell, fund-raiser extraordinaire, a special thanks for her enthusiasm for our effort. We could not have completed the project without B. J. Danetra, a one-woman tactical team. And we are in debt to Gina Wilson, computer whiz extraordinaire, for rescuing the figures. Graduate students, as always, played indispensable roles in handling the myriad details—none more than Leona Svancara and Durward Bagley. Thanks also to Andrew Fricker, who compiled the references.

This project has worked only because of the willing participation of individuals who have played major roles in the implementation of the act. Our thanks to the Honorable Dirk Kempthorne, the Honorable Craig Manson, and the Honorable Bruce Babbitt. These individuals provided a policy context for our endeavor that was essential to its success. Employees of the U.S. Fish and Wildlife Service were generous with their time and information. Michael Franz was particularly helpful in tracking down information in the Fish and Wildlife Service endangered species database and explaining the vagaries of its Web site. Others were incredibly helpful in explaining subtle issues of policy and law: thanks to John Fay, Claire Cassell, Gary Frazer, Michelle Morgan, Donna Brewer, Elizabeth H. Stevens, Debby Crouse, Wendi Weber, and Laverne Smith. Jim Tate (senior science advisor to Secretary of the Interior Gale Norton) was helpful in many ways.

Our steering committee has provided wise counsel on a number of issues. We owe its members, Michael Bean, James Caswell, Steve Quarles, and Bill Snape, a particular debt of gratitude for helping to ensure the participation of well-informed individuals from all points of view on the Endangered Species Act and helping us to identify the issues and frame the questions for participants.

The publication of a book with as many authors as this one has presents special challenges. We had a great editorial team from Island Press. Barbara Dean, a professional's professional and a truly nice person to boot, has guided us through the complexities of publication starting with writing the prospectus; from the project's beginning, she has been unfailingly encouraging. Our thanks as well to Barbara Youngblood for guiding us through the production process and Erin Johnson for her vigilant eyes and pesky questions.

Finally, to all of the participants, a special thanks for your participation and your candor.

D.D.G.
J.M.S.
F.W.D.

Part I   What Have We Protected?

One measure of the Endangered Species Act can be captured in numbers: the number of species listed; the number of species recovered, improving, stable, declining, extinct; the number of consultations completed, biological opinions delivered, jeopardy decisions made; the number of conservation agreements. The chapters in part 1 examine the numbers and the processes that have produced them. Together, they are one report card on the first thirty years of implementing the act.

I   Introduction

J. Michael Scott, Dale D. Goble, and Frank W. Davis

Conserving the biological infrastructure that makes life possible is crucial to the survival of the human species. Providing the material requirements of the human population is a fundamental imperative. This is the dilemma of our time: how do we reconcile the preservation of nature with increasing human population and consumption?

This book examines one legislative effort to resolve the dilemma, the Endangered Species Act of 1973 (ESA 1973). The ESA was an idealistic and perhaps naive attempt to preserve humanity by preserving other species in the ecological support system that makes life possible. In the words of the House report accompanying the bill:

> A certain humility, and a sense of urgency seem indicated. . . . One might analogize the case to one in which one copy of all the books ever printed were gathered together in one huge building. The position in which we find ourselves today is that of custodians of this building, and our choice is between exercising our responsibilities and ignoring them. If these theoretical custodians were to permit a madman to enter, build a bonfire and throw in at random any volume he selected, one might with justification suggest that others be found, or at least that they be censored and told to be more careful in the future. So it is with mankind. Like it or not, we are our brothers' keepers, and we are also keepers of the rest of the house. (U.S. Congress 1973, 4–5)

Species conservation was already a difficult challenge in 1973. The human population of the United States had increased from less than 4 million in the first census of 1790 to roughly 212 million by 1973 (Census Bureau 2000). This increase was accompanied by even more dramatic increases in per capita consumption of resources. The combination of population growth and increased consumption has driven a precipitous loss of nonhuman species that continues today: more than five hundred species formerly found in the United

States are presumed to be extinct and an additional 47 percent of the species unique to this country are at risk (Master et al. 2000).

It has been thirty years since the ESA was signed into law on December 28, 1973, and the task of conserving at-risk species is more complex than ever. Societal pressures on wildlife habitat have increased. The U.S. population has increased nearly 40 percent since 1973 to 293 million (Doremus, this volume), and our gross domestic product is nearly eight times greater (Census Bureau 2004a). These increases have resulted in additional habitat loss and increased numbers of invasive, nonnative species, the two biggest threats to endangered species (Wilcove et al. 1998; Wilcove et al. 2000; Cox 1999).

The thirty years have produced a record that allows a preliminary evaluation of the extent to which the act's goals have been achieved. This book begins with an examination of what the Endangered Species Act has protected, focusing on species listed as either threatened or endangered. The second part, "Achieving On-the-Ground Conservation," examines the act's record viewed through the lenses of different land use systems and institutional actors. The third part, "Prospects," offers several perspectives on how the ESA could be strengthened while reducing its negative social impact.

First, however, we briefly review the evolution of at-risk species conservation and the legal requirements of the ESA.

The Evolution of the Conservation of At-Risk Species

The Endangered Species Act stands at the confluence of two strands of wildlife protection law. The first is nearly a millennium of common and statutory law intended to conserve game species. This is the traditional "hook-and-bullet" wildlife management that relies on take restrictions, such as closed seasons and bag limits, to maintain huntable populations of game species (Goble and Frey-fogle 2002; Bean and Rowland 1997). The second strand of law—habitat protection—is equally ancient. Both the king in Parliament and colonial American legislatures routinely restricted land uses to conserve wildlife habitat (Goble and Freyfogle 2002). Although the tools—take restrictions and habitat protection—are ancient, the act's objectives are not. Indeed, the idea that it is important to save all the pieces is, in the sweep of things, a new perspective—and one that remains intensely contested.

From Game Protection to Endangered Species Preservation

Although legal protection of wildlife in the United States dates back to the colonial period (Goble and Freyfogle 2002), the post–Civil War period—with the near-extermination of the American buffalo (*Bison bison*) and the looming extinction of the passenger pigeon (*Ectopistes migratorius*)—produced a new urgency (Hornaday 1889). The massive, often-wasteful slaughter of wildlife that characterized the end of the nineteenth century produced a coalition of scientists, Audubon societies, and hunters that sought to conserve wildlife by closing down markets (Barrow 1998; Dorsey 1998; Doughty 1975; Dunlap 1988). Congress responded by enacting the Lacey Act, the first federal wildlife protection statute, in 1900 (Act of May 25, 1900). When that proved insufficient, the federal government negotiated a treaty with Great Britain (acting for Canada) to protect migratory birds (Dorsey 1998). Congress ratified the treaty (Convention with Great Britain for the Protection of Migratory Birds 1916) and enacted the Migratory Bird Treaty Act (Act of July 3, 1918), imposing a federal regulatory scheme for hunting migratory birds, and the Migratory Bird Conservation Act (Act of February 18, 1929), authorizing the creation of a refuge system for migratory birds. Apart from migratory birds—and a 1940 statute nominally protecting the bald eagle (*Haliaeetus leucocephalus*) (Act of June 8, 1940)—the federal government remained largely uninvolved in wildlife conservation; the wildlife management system created during the Progressive Era lasted until the 1960s.

This wildlife management system was focused primarily on game species. There was, however, some recognition that species threatened with extinction also required special management. In 1936, Aldo Leopold—as always, at least a step ahead—published a short article entitled "Threatened Species" in which he argued that preservation of species such as the grizzly bear (*Ursus arctos horribilis*) and the ivory-billed woodpecker (*Campephilus principalis*) was "a prime duty of the conservation movement" (Leopold 1936, 230). In 1937, the Bureau of Biological Survey—enjoying a brief golden age of funding under the leadership of J. N. "Ding" Darling—acquired the Aransas National Wildlife Refuge in Texas to protect the wintering grounds of the critically imperiled whooping crane (*Grus americana*) (Allen 1952; McNulty 1966). And in 1942, a committee drawn from the U.S. Fish and Wildlife Service (USFWS) and the National Park Service produced a book entitled *Fading Trails: The Story of Endangered American Wildlife*. The book was written

> to show how certain forms of wildlife have approached the brink of extinction. . . . It attempts to explain the poor economy of allowing any wildlife species to pass completely from being, if it is possible for such disaster to be averted. All forms of animal life, whether they be game species, fur bearers, predators, or what, are valuable in nature's enduring battle for perfection. Each form of life does its bit to help maintain the elusive "balance" between all living things. (Beard et al. 1942, ix)

A gangly looking but graceful bird emerged as a potent symbol of a species on the brink. The whooping crane had been in trouble since the end of the nineteenth century as a result of agriculture, drainage, settlement, and hunting: by 1912 its population numbered fewer than ninety birds; ten years later it was less than half that number; by 1938, when the Aransas Refuge was established, there were fewer than twenty remaining (Allen 1952, 80; Lewis 1995). Only then did the whooping crane's perilous situation catch the attention of the public, symbolizing what America stood to lose by ignoring the growing numbers of endangered native species. By the middle of the 1950s, the USFWS was holding press conferences and newspapers were reporting the annual count of whooping cranes (McNulty 1966), which gradually rebounded to 325 birds in the summer of 2005 (Tom Stehn, USFWS whooping crane coordinator, pers. comm.). The cranes contributed to the broadly based environmental consciousness that was beginning to stir in the United States.

Two decades after the publication of *Fading Trails*, the Department of the Interior created the Committee on Rare and Endangered Wildlife Species (Yaffee 1982). Two years later in 1966, the committee published a preliminary list of 331 species divided into three categories of concern: 130 species considered either rare or endangered; 74 species at the edge of their range (and therefore at risk); and 127 species of "undetermined" status (Committee on Rare and Endangered Wildlife Species 1966). This list, known as the Redbook, lacked any legal force; indeed, it contained one species, the Utah prairie dog (*Cynomys parvidens*), that another federal agency was trying to eradicate. The Redbook did, however, increase awareness of the risk of extinction.

The first legislative response to increasing public concern for endangered wildlife came in 1963. Acknowledging that habitat loss was a significant cause of extinction, Congress included a provision in the Land and Water Conservation Fund Act (Act of May 28, 1963) allowing monies to be used in "the acquisition of land, waters, or interests in land or waters . . . [f]or any national area which may be authorized for the preservation of species of fish or wildlife that are threatened with extinction" (Act of May 28, 1963, sec. 460*l*-9(a)(1)). This language embodied two fundamental changes that reflected the increased scientific and popular awareness of ecology: first, it provided for the *preservation* of wildlife rather than the *management* of game species and, second, it specified that protection was to be accomplished through *habitat preservation* rather than *take regulation*. Zoo specimens—like the Victorian curio cabinet—were no longer sufficient: wildlife was to be preserved in the wild.

The first federal endangered species act was the Endangered Species Preservation Act of 1966 (ESPA 1966). As with the Land and Water Conservation Fund, the ESPA focused on habitat protection. This focus on habitat, however, ignored the impact of taking and commercial activities on wildlife populations. It also ignored the international aspect of extinction: the American market was often the cause of problems elsewhere in the world. The failure to regulate these activities was partially remedied in 1969 when Congress extensively supplemented the ESPA and renamed the combined statute the Endangered Species Conservation Act (ESCA 1969). The ESCA provided a more comprehensive but still limited program that emphasized the regulation of interstate and foreign commerce in species listed by the secretary of the interior as endangered.

In the ESCA, Congress instructed the secretaries of the interior and state to call an international conference on protecting endangered species. The conference finally convened in Washington, D.C., in February 1973 and drafted the Convention on International Trade in Endangered Species of Wild Fauna and Flora (CITES 1973), a multilateral treaty that was signed in March 1973. CITES established an international system of import and export permits that created a control structure to regulate international commerce in species designated for protection.

The enactment of the ESA reflected a broad consensus that existing federal law was inadequate to preserve at-risk species. In his 1972 environmental message, President Richard Nixon concluded that federal law "simply does not provide the kind of management tools needed to act early enough to save vanishing species" (Nixon 1972, 223–24); congressional leaders offered a similar analysis (Dingell 1973). The act was among the least controversial bills enacted by Congress in 1973: the bill was passed by the Senate 92–0; an even more stringent bill passed the House 390–12. Following a conference to resolve the differences, the Senate passed the bill without dissent on a voice vote and the House adopted it by an overwhelming 355–4 (Yaffee 1982).

The Endangered Species Acts

The central substantive and procedural requirements of the Endangered Species Act are set out in five sections:

- *Section 4* establishes procedures for listing species as either threatened or endangered, for designating critical habitat, and for preparing recovery plans for listed species.
- *Section 7* requires federal agencies that authorize, fund, or carry out an action—"federal action agencies"—to consult with the U.S. Fish and Wildlife Service in the Department of the Interior or with the National Marine Fisheries Service in the Department of Commerce—the "federal fish and wildlife agencies"—to "insure that actions authorized, funded or carried out by them do not jeopardize the continued existence" of listed species.
- *Section 9* prohibits any person from taking or engaging in commerce in endangered species.

- *Section 10* provides exemptions, permits, and exceptions to section 9's prohibitions.
- *Section 11* specifies the civil and criminal penalties applicable to the violations enumerated in section 9.

As this outline suggests, the ESA envisions a linear process: when a species is at risk of extinction, it is listed as either endangered or threatened and its critical habitat is designated. The USFWS prepares a recovery plan for the species that specifies how the threats to its continued existence will be removed or mitigated so that the species no longer requires protection under the act. In the interim, the species is protected under the provisions of sections 7 and 9 from all activities not exempted or permitted pursuant to sections 10 and 11.

The act also includes a "cooperative federalism" provision in section 6(c) that authorizes the secretary to enter into a cooperative agreement with any state that established "an adequate and active program for the conservation of" listed species that is "in accordance with" the act and a list of criteria (ESA sec. 6(c)). Despite the breadth of the provision, it has had little impact on the evolution of the protection at-risk species. In part, this reflects state reticence, since most species that reach the point of being listed have been subject to long periods of state management. In part, it also reflects the continuous underfunding of conservation in this country.

The ESA in its first incarnation embodied "prohibitive policy"—in Steve Yaffee's apt phrase (Yaffee 1982). For instance, in *Tennessee Valley Authority v. Hill* (1978, 74), the Supreme Court noted that the prohibitions on jeopardizing a listed species "admit to no exception"; the Court could have written the same phrase about the prohibition against "take," which was defined far more expansively than "kill" (ESA sec. 3(18)). While people continue to speak of the "Endangered Species Act of 1973," the current version of the act is markedly different than the original. It is useful to think of these changes as embodying four ESAs—the original 1973 version, the ESA that emerged from the 1978 and 1979 amendments, the ESA of the 1982 amendments, and the fourth version, the product of the administrative amendments of the 1990s. This combination of legislative and administrative amendments has transformed the act from a prohibitive law into a flexible, permitting statute (Houck 1993; Fischman and Hall-Rivera 2002; Greenwald et al., this volume; Suckling and Taylor, this volume), as demonstrated by the following three examples.

In 1978, the Supreme Court's decision *Tennessee Valley Authority v. Hill* made the snail darter (*Percina tanasi*) a national symbol that was assigned diametrically different meanings by different groups. Congress responded to the ensuing controversy by amending the ESA. While leaving the act's substantive standards generally intact, Congress significantly modified its procedures to increase its flexibility. "No," in another words, became "maybe."

The 1978 amendments to the listing process clearly show the act's transformation from prohibitive to permissive. Congress amended—or, perhaps more accurately, burdened—the listing process by substantially expanding the procedural requirements to list a species: it imposed additional notice provisions, required local hearings, and mandated the designation of critical habitat as part of the listing determination. While increasing the complexity of the listing procedures, the amendments also placed a two-year time limit on the process: listings that had not been completed within two years were to be withdrawn. The effect of these legislative changes was dramatic: less than 5 percent of the more than two thousand species that had been formally proposed for listing in November 1978 were listed; and on December 10, 1979, the USFWS withdrew proposals to list 1,876 species (USFWS 1979).

In the 1978 amendments, Congress focused on procedure: what had been a relatively simple statute became procedurally complex. Much of an administrative lawyer's craft is focused on procedure because an agency is far more likely to err procedurally than substantively. Procedure, in other words, empowers those opposed to an agency's decisions. By modifying the procedures, Congress was able to restructure the act without changing its substantive standards. In the process, the statute's original prohibitive severity was substantially softened.

The second example is drawn from the amendments of 1982. If the theme of the 1978 and 1979 amendments was "flexibility," the dominant concern in 1982 was "discretion." Congress again tinkered with the listing procedures. When James Watt became secretary of the interior in 1981, listing virtually ceased after the Reagan administration added a requirement that listings be economically justified (Executive Order 12291 1981; Greenwald et al., this volume). Congress responded by restricting the secretary's discretion, specifying that the listing determination was to be made "*solely* on the basis of the best scientific and commercial data available"; economics were not to be considered in determining whether a species was threatened or endangered.

But the most significant amendments in 1982 were to section 10. Before 1982, the ESA's take prohibition (in section 9) applied to all "persons"—a term defined broadly to include not only individuals but also all business organizations and agencies of the federal and state governments (ESA sec. 3(8)). As a result, prohibited takes could occur both within the context of an agency action subject to consultation under section 7 (which includes "private" actions that require a federal permit) and on private lands whose owner had no need of a federal permit and who thus was not required to consult. In 1982, however,

Congress amended the act to permit "incidental" takes in both situations. For actions requiring consultation under section 7—actions that have some federal involvement, such as the issuance of a permit—Congress added a provision authorizing the wildlife agency to include an "incidental take statement" permitting take as long as it would not jeopardize the continued existence of the species (ESA sec. 7(b)(4)). And, to "addres[s] the concerns of private landowners who are faced with having otherwise lawful actions not requiring Federal permits prevented by section 9 prohibitions against taking," Congress adopted an "incidental take permit" under section 10 (U.S. Congress 1982a, 29). It authorized the issuance of the permits in conjunction with the development of a "conservation plan" prepared by the applicant (ESA sec. 10(a)(2)(A)); the secretary was required to find that the take incidental to the plan would not "appreciably reduce the likelihood of the survival and recovery of the species in the wild" (ESA sec. 10(a)(2)(B)).

The third example comes from the chaotic nineties. Much of the transformation of the ESA from prohibitive to permitting is a result of administrative rather than legislative actions. Following Republican congressional victories in 1994, ideologically divisive politics increased debate on the ESA. In response to the hostility to endangered species that was openly expressed by some members of Congress and to several bills that would have fundamentally reduced protection for at-risk species (Goble, forthcoming), Secretary of the Interior Bruce Babbitt "resolve[d] to save the Endangered Species Act by implementing a series of reforms on the implementation of the Act from top to bottom, particularly as it applied to private lands" (Barry 1998, 131). To achieve this objective, the secretary advocated "incentive-based strategies to try and reconcile endangered species conservation with economic development" (Barry 1998, 131). The centerpiece of this incentive-based initiative was a series of permits— habitat conservation plans (HCPs) (USFWS and NOAA 1996), candidate conservation agreements (CCAs) (USFWS and NOAA 1999), and safe harbor agreements (SHAs) (USFWS 1999a)—that were available to private landowners and included assurances from the USFWS and the National Marine Fisheries Service that the agencies would impose no additional restrictions on land uses—the "no surprises" policy (USFWS and NOAA 1998; *Spirit of the Sage Council v. Norton* 2003). Although details of the agreements varied, the agreements and assurances were intended to make the ESA more developer friendly by balancing two competing goals: flexibility (to adapt to changing biological circumstances and new information) and certainty (to allow the permittee to make economic decisions) (Thompson, this volume).

The combination of legislative amendments and administrative revisions has produced a dramatically different ESA than that of thirty years ago. The absolute take prohibition of the 1973 statute has been conditioned by the flexible incidental take permit that—in J. B. Ruhl's phrase—authorizes a landowner to kill endangered species, legally (Ruhl 1999).

Proponents have justified each successive revision of the act by citing its increased efficiency. The first part of this book examines the statistical record behind these claims.

What Have We Protected?

The ESA's linear process begins with the listing of a species at risk of extinction as either endangered or threatened. Listing triggers the act's safeguards, the taking prohibition, and the consultation requirements. What has been listed?

The original list of endangered species named only 78 species (Wilcove and McMillan, this volume), all vertebrates. Thirty years later, the list has increased more than sixteenfold to 1,260 domestic species (USFWS 2003a), including 516 animals (179 of which are invertebrates) and 744 plants (USFWS 2003a). Even so, the list is still not representative of the taxonomic diversity of the country (Kareiva et al., this volume; Scott, Goble, et al., this volume) nor of the diversity of at-risk species (Master et al. 2000). For example, as Armsworth and his colleagues (this volume) note, relatively few marine species have been listed (70 of 1,855 taxa worldwide) despite severe population reductions for many. Greenwald and his coauthors provide a detailed history of the listing program.

Listing is only the beginning of the process; recovery—"conserving" a species so that "the measures provided by this Act are no longer necessary" (ESA sec. 3(3))—is the goal. One of the recurring criticisms of the Endangered Species Act is that it has failed to adequately recover species (National Wilderness Institute 1994). To date, only thirty-six U.S. species have been delisted, and only thirteen due to recovery; the USFWS recently proposed delisting eastern populations of gray wolves (*Canis lupus*) (Scott, Goble, et al., this volume). Another twenty-one species have been reclassified from endangered to threatened (Scott, Goble, et al., this volume).

There are questions, however, of whether recovery is the proper measure of success (avoiding extinction is an apparent alternative) (Schwartz 1999), whether three decades has been sufficient time to recover species that have been declining for decades or centuries (Doremus, this volume), and whether recovery is even possible for some species (Doremus and Pagel 2001). It is also apparent that some risks (such as overharvest) are more remediable than others (such as habitat loss or invasive species) (Scott, Goble, et al., this volume). Wilcove and McMillan (this volume) put a more specific face on these questions with their examination of the fates of the members of the first endangered species list. Of the seventy-eight species in the "Class of '67," two have recovered, one population of a third species has been delisted, four have been reclassified from endangered to threatened, three are extinct and were removed from the list, and, with the recent sighting of the ivory-billed woodpecker (*Campephilus principalis*) (Gallagher 2005), eight others are presumed extinct but remain on the list. These statistics do not bode well for the current list of species.

DeShazo and Freeman provide different perspective on recovery; based on their research they conclude that extinction may turn more on the preferences of members of Congress than on the statute's criteria.

On-the-Ground Conservation

A second metric for evaluating the Endangered Species Act is its on-the-ground outcomes: Does the ESA work in a variety of landscapes? How well does it bring together the various potential actors, such as states, local governments, tribes, private landowners, and nongovernmental organizations?

Again, the data are mixed. Several authors suggest that we are not taking advantage of conservation tools now available. Suckling and Taylor, for example, see a positive correlation between designating critical habitat and a species status. Davison and his colleagues argue that the national wildlife refuge system could play a larger role in the conservation of at-risk species. Thompson and Tarlock examine the use of HCPs, the former on working landscapes and the latter on urbanizing landscapes. Finally, Swain—who directs both the Archbold Biological Station and the MacArthur Agro-ecology Research Center in Florida and its associated orchards and grazing lands—provides a reality check that comes from having worked with a number of regulatory tools. Three common themes emerge from these diverse perspectives. First, we have failed to develop tools that are useful to many different types of land users; for example, while HCPs work well for land developers, they are of little use to ranchers. Second, the assumptions built into the different tools are largely untested; we simply do not know if they are really accomplishing what is intended. Finally, the tools are too complex and time consuming to implement.

On-the-ground conservation involves not only tools but also actors. The authors of these chapters are generally hopeful. Niles and Korth summarize state wildlife conservation programs; Behan reports on the Sonoran Desert Conservation Plan developed by Pima County, Arizona, to create ecologically based land use planning; Rodgers discusses three Indian tribes that have played dynamic roles in conserving at-risk species; Kareiva and his colleagues suggest that nongovernmental organizations can potentially play a significant role. These authors paint a picture of a growing constituency for at-risk species in the states and counties—where the decisions are made about land use practices.

Prospects

It is clear that the thirty years since the passage of the Endangered Species Act have changed the way we think about and manage wildlife. Where once the focus was on single species of recreational or commercial value, today management is concerned with the full range of species. States have written endangered species laws reflecting these new interests and responsibilities (Goble et al. 1999; Center for Wildlife Law and Defenders of Wildlife 1996, 1998). At the same time, however, the act continues to be a lightning rod—particularly for those opposed to restrictions on the use of land.

The authors in the final part are in broad agreement on at least two points—the act is successful in preventing extinctions, but it could be made more efficient. Doremus introduces these recurrent themes, providing a concise overview of several of the key lessons from the history of implementing the act, focusing on the interface of law and biology; her conclusions counsel against simplistic approaches, noting for example the complex relationship between flexibility and accountability. Rosenzweig also urges the reader to look beyond the current reserve-based strategies for species conservation. Noting that reserves can slow but not prevent the loss of species, he argues that we must better reconcile human activities with native species through more deliberate planning and management. This will require a change in popular beliefs and attitudes toward nature. Yaffee believes that the ESA has broadly changed natural resource decision making by creating new processes, influencing existing processes, and changing the dynamics of negotiations by empowering new participants. He concludes with an analysis of several collaborative approaches that he finds encouraging. The chapters by Clark and Wallace and by Burnham and his colleagues from the Peregrine Fund also advocate increased collaboration, although they differ on the details. Clark and Wallace draw upon several case studies to support their proposal for the use of an adaptive management approach that relies on iterative, practice-based, and structured decision making. Burnham and his colleagues also reflect a hands-on perspective to species recovery. They offer perhaps the most radical restructuring proposal, arguing that stakeholder groups should be the primary recovery managers.

One recurrent debate is over the relative merits of incentives versus command. Parkhurst and Shogren provide a catalogue of incentives and a discussion of their strengths and weaknesses. Bean, who favors an incentive-based approach, argues that we must find simpler and more expeditious agreements if "second-generation" tools such as habitat conservation plans, candidate conservation agreements, and safe harbor agreements are to fulfill their potential. Shaffer and his colleagues also focus on next-generation options beyond the current ESA. They outline the scientific, political, and economic lessons to be learned from the ESA implementation record and conclude that the necessary degree of habitat conservation cannot be achieved through regulation alone. Instead, they propose a proactive, state-based incentive policy that could be incorporated into comprehensive state wildlife conservation plans currently being developed.

Some Preliminary Conclusions

For over three decades the Endangered Species Act has transformed the conservation of nature in America, preventing the extinction of hundreds of species and directly or indirectly protecting millions of acres of terrestrial and aquatic ecosystems. At the same time, the ESA has imposed high costs and forced marked changes in the design and practice of economic activities such as housing, transportation, farming, ranching, logging, and fishing. Not surprisingly, debate over the efficacy of the law remains polarized, with environmental groups touting its successes and industry and property rights groups emphasizing its costs. The authors in this volume provide a more measured analysis of "the Endangered Species Act at thirty." A surprising degree of consensus emerges from their chapters, although contentious issues remain. There are three pervasive themes: the role of the federal government, the emergence of new actors and institutional relationships responding to the challenges of ESA and reshaping conservation of the American landscape, and the limits of the ESA as a biodiversity conservation policy.

Despite many conservation successes, the federal government is not meeting the intent of the ESA. To do so would take significantly increased federal funding along with some limited administrative and perhaps regulatory reforms. If increased funds are not forthcoming, the act could still be operated more effectively with expedited listing procedures, clearer guidelines and priority setting for species recovery, greater consultation and coordination with state and local agencies, and more attractive incentive programs for private landowners.

The political geography of conservation under the ESA continues to evolve. The act has exposed gaps and shortcomings in state conservation laws and practices, and in doing so it has catalyzed reforms at all levels of government. The act has also affected the daily lives and livelihoods of many private landowners; in response, property rights groups have organized effectively to limit the reach of the act. Nonetheless, new political relationships and processes have emerged in many areas of the country in response to the challenges posed by the ESA. These relationships and the new planning processes they have created are producing viable local and regional conservation solutions.

The act has done some things very well. Most notably, it has reduced extinctions substantially (Scott, Goble, et al., this volume). But the ESA is an at-risk *species* act—it is not a comprehensive *biodiversity preservation* act. It is also a statute from the 1970s with that decade's emphasis on command and control. Although the act has been amended to provide limited incentives—primarily through limiting its take prohibition—it has not been brought forward into the twenty-first century. One of the surprising areas of consensus at the discussions in Santa Barbara was not only the need to do so but also the need to maintain powerful restrictions on actions that put species at risk.

Ultimately, however, the ESA is a tool of last resort that can slow but not prevent the accelerating loss of biodiversity from the American landscape. Simply put, it comes into play too late. To prevent species from becoming endangered and thereby conserve our nation's biological infrastructure, we must look beyond the ESA and craft ways to accommodate more native species in the areas where we live, work, and recreate.

2   By the Numbers

*J. Michael Scott, Dale D. Goble, Leona K. Svancara,
and Anna Pidgorna*

The current endangered species list has its administrative beginnings in 1964 when the Department of the Interior's Committee on Rare and Endangered Wildlife Species published a preliminary list of 62 species at risk of extinction (Goble, forthcoming). Following the enactment of the Endangered Species Preservation Act of 1966 (ESPA), the secretary of the interior in 1967 published the first official list of 78 "native fish and wildlife threatened with extinction" (ESPA sec. 1(c); U.S. Department of the Interior 1967; Wilcove and McMillan, this volume). By the time the Endangered Species Act (ESA) was adopted in 1973, there were 392 species on the list (Yaffee 1982). These first lists included only vertebrate species. On the thirtieth anniversary of the ESA, the number stood at 1,260 domestic species and 558 foreign species (USFWS 2003a), with plant and invertebrate species outnumbering vertebrates.

This chapter presents a graphical summary encapsulating thirty years of species protection and restoration under the ESA. The summary reveals both gains and losses. For some species, such as the Aleutian Canada goose (*Branta canadensis leucopareia*), the process worked as it was meant to, reversing decline and restoring populations to healthy levels (USFWS 2001a); for others, such as the dusky seaside sparrow (*Ammodramus maritimus nigrescens*), the process failed, and despite being listed the species continued to spiral toward eventual extinction (USFWS 1983; Walters 1992).

What follows is an assessment of the state of species protection as it has evolved under the ESA. This includes the taxonomic and demographic distribution of listed species, and the number of critical habitat designations. We also examine newer legal tools for conserving habitat on private land (such as habitat conservation plans), various measures of the act's success, and funding levels for species protection.

The Endangered Species List

The first step in recovery of a threatened and endangered species is listing it under the Endangered Species Act. The growth of the endangered species list from 78 species in 1967 to 1,260 at the end of 2003 is in part the result of expansion of the range of taxa that could be included on the list and in part the result of nonbiological factors such as litigation (Greenwald et al., this volume). An additional point should be noted: the number of listed species (1,260) is misleading. For example, the list groups together separate populations of a species listed as both endangered and threatened, infers that several species represent entire genera or families, and leaves out distinct population segments of some species. These assumptions about taxonomic diversity and species categorization, definition, and distribution are explained below.

Taxonomic Diversity

The most significant reason for the increase in the number of species listed has been an increase in the species eligible for listing (figs. 2.1 and 2.2). The 1967 list was compiled under the Endangered Species Preservation Act, which covered only "native fish and wildlife" (ESPA sec. 1(c)). In 1969, Congress expanded

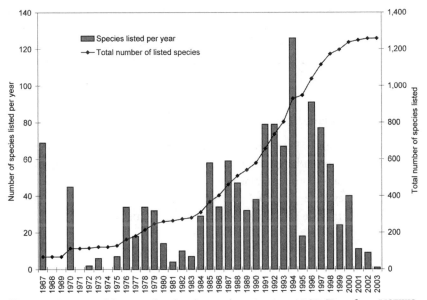

Figure 2.1. Listings of threatened and endangered species since 1967. (Data from USFWS 2004a.)

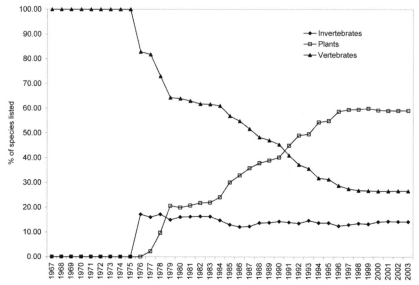

Figure 2.2. Taxonomic breakdown of listed species over time. (Data from USFWS 2004a.)

coverage in the Endangered Species Conservation Act (ESCA) to include mollusks, crustaceans, foreign species, and subspecies (ESCA secs. 3(a), 12(a)). Finally, in 1973, Congress expanded the definition of "species" to include plants, insects, "or smaller taxa." The ESA also created a new category of risk, "threatened" (ESA secs. 3(5), (11), (15), (4)(a)). At the end of 2003, there were 923 species of plants and invertebrates listed (73.3 percent); plants alone accounted for 59 percent of listed species.

Species Categorization

At the end of 2003, 78.2 percent of listed species were categorized as endangered. The ratio of endangered to threatened species has varied over time (fig. 2.3) and also varies among major taxa (table 2.1). Because species are threatened before they are endangered, the fact that most species are listed as endangered suggests that we are failing to get ahead of the risk curve.

Species Definition

As originally enacted, the ESA defined "species" as "any subspecies or smaller taxa." In 1978, the act was amended to include "any distinct population segment of any species of vertebrate." This allows the listing of three taxonomic categories only for vertebrates: species, subspecies, and *distinct population seg-*

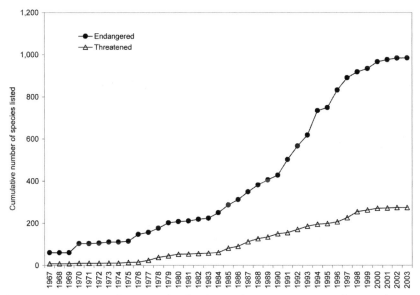

Figure 2.3. Proportion of threatened and endangered species over time in the United States. (Data from USFWS 2004a.)

TABLE 2.1. Number and percentage of threatened and endangered listings by taxonomic groups

Group	Threatened	Endangered
Vertebrates	94 (27.65)	246 (72.35)
Invertebrates	31 (17.32)	148 (82.68)
Plants	147 (19.76)	597 (80.24)

Note: Percentages given in parentheses.

ments. Species comprise 75.5 percent of the list, subspecies 21.1 percent, and distinct population segments 5.6 percent (table 2.2).

The listing of subspecies and distinct population segments is not consistent with their occurrence within taxa. Wilcove and his colleagues (1993) found that approximately 80 percent of taxa added to the list were full species. They also found, however, that more subspecies and populations than full species were listed for birds and mammals.

Logic suggests that the lower-ranking taxonomic units would be at risk earlier than higher-ranking units. Thus, individuals are lost from populations and populations from subspecies, and subspecies are extirpated prior to the loss of a species (Lomolino and Channell 1995; Hughes et al. 1997; Channell and Lomolino 2000; Cebellos and Ehrlich 2002). This process is well documented

TABLE 2.2. Number and percentage of threatened and endangered species, subspecies and distinct population segments (DPS) among different taxonomic groups

Taxonomic group	Number listed	Number DPS	Number species	Number subspecies	% dps	% species	% subspecies
PLANTS							
Conifers and cycads	3	N/A	2	1	N/A	66.7	33.3
Ferns and allies	26	N/A	23	3	N/A	88.5	11.5
Flowering plants	713	N/A	593	120	N/A	83.2	16.8
Lichens	2	N/A	2	0	N/A	100.0	0.0
Subtotal	744	N/A	620	124	N/A	83.3	16.7
INVERTEBRATES							
Arachnids	12	N/A	12	0	N/A	100.0	0.0
Clams	70	N/A	61	9	N/A	87.1	12.9
Crustaceans	21	N/A	21	0	N/A	100.0	0.0
Insects	44	N/A	20	24	N/A	45.5	54.6
Snails	32	N/A	30	2	N/A	93.8	6.3
Subtotal	179	N/A	144	35	N/A	80.5	19.6
VERTEBRATES							
Amphibians	21	5	15	2	23.8	71.4	9.5
Birds	91	16	44	35	17.6	48.4	38.5
Fishes	114	30	83	21	26.3	72.8	18.4
Mammals	78	13	28	40	16.7	35.9	51.3
Reptiles	36	7	20	10	19.4	55.6	27.8
Subtotal	340	71	190	108	20.9	55.9	31.8
Total	1,263	71	954	267	5.6	75.5	21.1

for the passenger pigeon (*Ectopistes migratorius*) (Schorger 1955) and is likely occurring with other species (e.g., greater prairie chicken [*Tympanuchus cupido*]). Although listing a species protects all biological units beneath it, most species are not listable until they have lost a substantial portion of their population, and thus it is likely that some lower taxa have already been lost. To the extent that the act's objective is to conserve the genetic potential of the species, such losses are evolutionarily significant.

Species Distribution

Geographically, listed species are not distributed uniformly across the United States. Instead, some 72 percent occur in just six states: California, Hawaii, Florida, Alabama, Tennessee, and Texas (fig. 2.4).

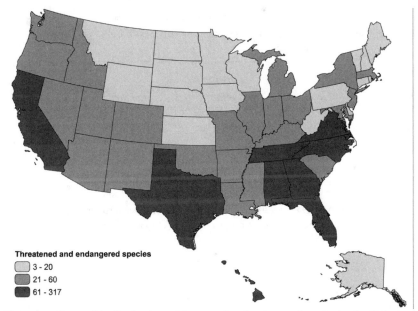

Figure 2.4. Geographic distribution of threatened and endangered species in the United States as of April 1, 2004. (Data from USFWS 2004a.)

Demographics

The Endangered Species Act specifies that a species is "endangered" when it is "in danger of extinction throughout all or a significant portion of its range"; a species is "threatened" when it "is likely to become an endangered species within the foreseeable future throughout all or a significant portion of its range." These definitions do not specify demographic guidelines; thus, the act lacks explicit criteria for determining population thresholds (individuals and populations), risk of extinction, and demographic trends. This is reflected in the published listing decisions. Wilcove and colleagues (1993) found that the median population size at the time of listing was fewer than 1,075 individuals for vertebrates, 999 for invertebrates, and fewer than 120 for plants. Population sizes at the time of listing varied by more than two orders of magnitude, even for species in the same taxonomic group (Wilcove et al. 1993).

Other groups identify species at risk of extinction with more quantitative thresholds. The World Conservation Union maintains a global "red list" that is based on population size, number of populations, trends, and threats (Mace and Lande 1991; IUCN 2003). NatureServe uses similar standards with emphasis on species in the United States (Master et al. 2000). Using the data of Master et al. (2000), we found that 3,122 species were identified in 1999 as either "criti-

TABLE 2.3. Comparison of threatened and endangered listings with NatureServe G1 and G2 species

Group	Threatened and endangered	G1 or G2
Vertebrates	324	324
Invertebrates	159	387
All animals	483	711
Plants	721	2,411

Source: Data for G1 and G2 species are taken from Master et al. (2000); those from the endangered species list are from the December 31, 1999, boxscore (USFWS 1999b).

cally imperiled" (G1) or "imperiled" (G2) within the United States. This is nearly three times more than the 1,204 species listed by the federal government as endangered or threatened species that year. More plants and invertebrates categorized as G1 or G2 were listed than were vertebrates in the same categories (table 2.3) (Stein et al. 2000). Although the same number of vertebrates were listed as were characterized as imperiled (324), mammals, birds, and reptiles were more likely to be listed than characterized as imperiled (table 2.4).

Assuming all G1 and G2 species in the United States are endangered or threatened, the backlog of unlisted species is a minimum of 6,029 (the number of unlisted G1 and G2 species as of November 2003). The number, however, is likely even larger since 35 percent of listed species (as of November 2003) were not ranked as G1 and G2 by NatureServe. Thus, an additional 2,552 species may be at risk. This would bring the number of potentially listed species to more than 9,000—a daunting number and one that suggests the workload for endangered species biologists will not lighten in the near future.

There is concern that species are listed unnecessarily or that species which should be listed are ignored because nonbiological factors are introduced into listing decisions (GAO 1993, 2003; Scott et al. 1995; National Wilderness Institute 1994). But the small numbers of individuals and populations at the time of listing suggest not that we list species without biological justification but rather that we face a backlog of unlisted at-risk species. That 78 percent of species are characterized as endangered at the time of listing supports this conclusion. Bluntly stated: we are not getting ahead of the extinction curve.

TABLE 2.4. Comparison of threatened and endangered listings with NatureServe G1 and G2 listings of vertebrate groups

Group	Threatened and endangered	G1 or G2
Mammals	69	29
Birds	89	47
Reptiles	36	21
Amphibians	17	49
Total	324	324

Source: Data for G1 and G2 species are taken from Master et al. (2000); those from the endangered species list are from the December 31, 1999, boxscore (USFWS 1999b).

Critical Habitat Designations

Although the Endangered Species Act requires that critical habitat be designated concurrent with the decision to list a species (ESA sec. 4(b)(6)(c)), often, this does not happen (Suckling and Taylor, this volume). The number of designations per year since 1973 varies from 0 to 25, except for a single large increase (278) that occurred in 2003. As of April 2004, critical habitat has been designated for 450 species (35.6 percent of all listed species), but these designations are taxonomically (table 2.5) and geographically (fig. 2.5) uneven. For instance, critical habitat has been designated for nearly half of all fish species but for only 0.2 percent of insect species, and most designations are in Hawaii and California. These patterns are explained elsewhere in this volume (Suckling and Taylor).

Despite the statutory requirement for designation at the time of listing, there have been significant delays in designating critical habitat for species (Greenwald et al., this volume). The time between listing and critical habitat designation was greatest for plants and least for reptiles and invertebrates (fig. 2.6).

Critical habitat designations have been controversial (USFWS 2003b; Williams 2001). Suckling and Taylor (this volume) found a positive relationship between critical habitat designation and recovery status. The reasons for this positive relationship are uncertain and the data suggest that critical habitat designation is but one of many possible factors accounting for a species' improved population status. Hoekstra et al. (2002b) concluded that critical habitat provided no positive effects in the recovery planning process. They did

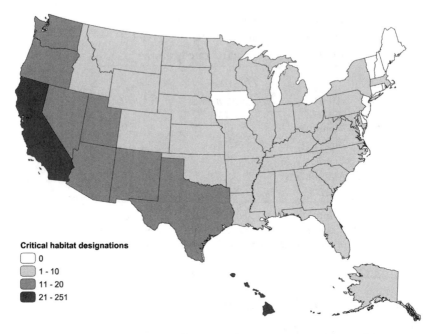

Figure 2.5. Geographic distribution of critical habitat designations in the United States as of April 1, 2004. (Data from USFWS 2004a.)

TABLE 2.5. Critical habitat designations for major taxonomic groups

Taxonomic group	Species with critical habitat	Percentage of listed species
Mammals	14	17.9
Birds	19	20.6
Amphibians	5	16.1
Reptiles	14	38.9
Fish	56	48.7
Crustaceans	4	19.0
Clams	2	2.9
Snails	2	6.3
Insects	1	0.2
Arachnids	6	8.3
Flowering plants	273	33.6
Ferns and allies	11	39.3

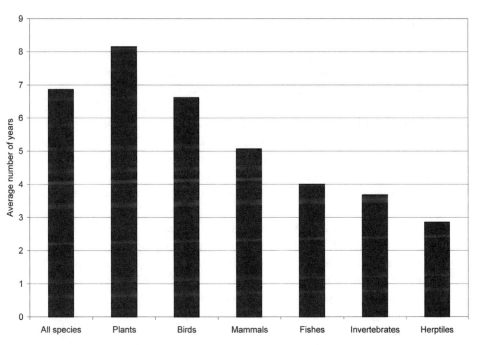

Figure 2.6. Average number of years between listing and designation of critical habitat. (Data from USFWS 2004a.)

not address the question of its influence in species recovery. Thus, in-depth species-by-species assessments may be required.

Conservation Tools for Nonfederal Lands

The U.S. Fish and Wildlife Service (USFWS) has developed three instruments intended to facilitate the conservation of species while providing greater certainty for nonfederal landowners. The statutory authority for these instruments is found in 10(a) of the Endangered Species Act, which authorizes the secretary to issue permits for the incidental taking of listed species (ESA sec. 10(a)(1)(B)) when the secretary has approved a "conservation plan" that meets enumerated criteria (ESA sec. 10(a)(2)). The USFWS has embroidered on the "conservation plan" provisions to create three categories: (1) candidate conservation agreements (*Code of Federal Regulations* 50:17.22(d)); (2) habitat conservation plans (*Code of Federal Regulations* 50:17.22(b)); and (3) safe harbor agreements (*Code of Federal Regulations* 50:17.22(c)).

Candidate Conservation Agreements

A *candidate conservation agreement* (CCA) is a voluntary agreement between the USFWS and a landowner under which the landowner agrees to specified actions to conserve "[p]roposed or candidate species [or] other unlisted species that are likely to become a candidate or proposed species" (USFWS 1999a). CCAs reflect the idea that implementing conservation measures before a species is listed may provide sufficient conservation to make it unnecessary to list the species. CCAs may be issued "with assurances," that is, with a promise that a nonfederal landowner will not be subjected to future regulatory obligations in excess of those agreed to at the time the landowner enters into the agreement.

As of April 1, 2004, there were 104 CCAs nationwide; only 7 CCAs included assurances. CCAs were distributed unevenly geographically (fig. 2.7) and taxonomically. The most commonly included taxa was vertebrates (71), followed by plants (66) and invertebrates (13); 14 CCAs were proposed with no candidate species specified. Of the 104 approved agreements, one addressed more than 25 species and one addressed 117 of the 133 species covered by CCAs, but most (97 plans, or 93 percent) addressed only a single species.

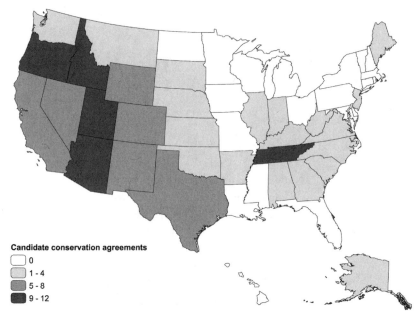

Candidate conservation agreements
- 0
- 1 - 4
- 5 - 8
- 9 - 12

Figure 2.7. Geographic distribution of candidate conservation agreements (CCAs) in the United States as of April 1, 2004. (Data from USFWS 2004a.)

Habitat Conservation Plans

A *habitat conservation plan* (HCP) is a mitigation plan for activities that take listed species; an HCP is required for the issuance of an incidental take permit. Although Congress authorized HCPs in 1982, they remained little used until the Clinton administration: only fourteen HCPs were approved from 1983 to 1992, but by April 1, 2004, there were more than four hundred approved HCPs covering more than 38 million acres (USFWS 2004b). HCPs vary widely in size, ranging from less than 2.5 acres to more than a million acres (fig. 2.8). They also vary widely in the coverage of both the number of species and their taxa. Reptiles as a group have the highest percentage of species addressed by HCPs (44 percent); plants are least represented (5 percent). Of the 356 HCPs in the USFWS ECOS database, 273 (77 percent) addressed a single species; 10 addressed twenty or more species. Geographically, HCPs are unevenly distributed (fig. 2.9).

HCPs have been the focus of a number of studies. Kareiva and colleagues (1998) called for increased efforts to use explicit scientific standards and summaries of available data on the ecology of a species in plans as well as to create centralized databases that are generally accessible and include monitoring data.

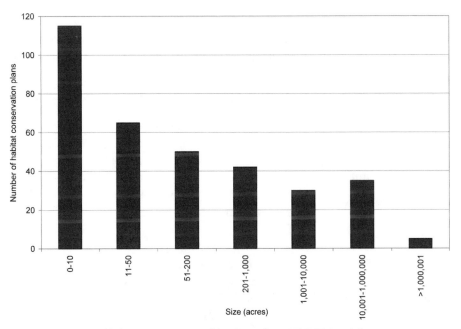

Figure 2.8. Size of habitat conservation plans. (Data from USFWS 2004a.)

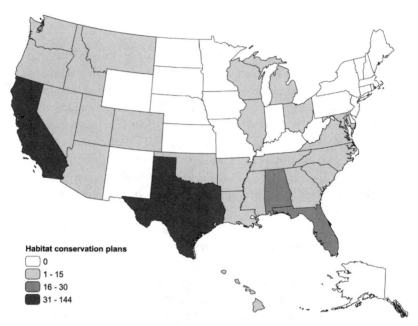

Figure 2.9. Geographic distribution of habitat conservation plans (HCPs) in the United States as of April 1, 2004. (Data from USFWS 2004a.)

Watchman et al. (2001) characterized HCPs as tools of compromise whose benefits to endangered species are yet untested. For a detailed examination of HCPs, see Thompson (this volume).

Safe Harbor Agreements

Safe harbor agreements (SHAs) are based on the principle that people who do good deeds on behalf of endangered species should not be penalized. To that end, a SHA may be issued when it "will provide a net conservation benefit to the affected listed species by contributing to the recovery of the listed species" (*Code of Federal Regulations* 50:17.22(c)(2)). The example most frequently cited activity is "restoring and enhancing habitat for endangered species."

As with CCAs and HCPs, these agreements are unevenly distributed both geographically and taxonomically. Twenty-three SHAs have been approved as of April 1, 2004, that cover twenty-six listed species and range in size from 0.2 to 161,173,776 acres. The number of species covered in SHAs range from one to five; of the twenty-three agreements, fourteen address a single species.

TABLE 2.6. Status of species with experimental populations

Status	Percentage of all listed species	Percentage of experimental species
Stable	30	8.9
Increasing	9	23.0
Unknown	24	8.9
Declining	34	47.0
Captive	<1	2.9
Presumed extinct	2	8.9

Experimental Populations

Experimental populations are a tool to reestablish threatened or endangered species in their former range (Goble 2002). An experimental population is a population released into an area that is "wholly separate geographically" from all other populations of the same species (ESA sec. 10(c)(j)). Members of an experimental population are treated as threatened even though nonexperimental populations of the same species may be endangered. This allows the USFWS to write less-restrictive rules under section 4(d) of the act. For example, gray wolves (*Canis lupus*) in Yellowstone are classified as an experimental population and depredating animals may be killed—something that would be illegal but for their classification.

Thirty-five experimental populations have been established for thirty-one species of animals. Only the gray wolf, the whooping crane (*Grus americana*), and the yellowfin madtom (*Noturus flavipinnis*) have multiple experimental populations. The statistical data on experimental populations is mixed. Species with experimental populations had higher percentages of both increasing and declining populations than did listed species in general (table 2.6).

Measures of Success

A consistent criticism of the Endangered Species Act is that it has not accomplished its purpose of recovering populations of listed species.

One correlate of recovery is the type of risk facing a species. Recovering species had easily identifiable threats and/or occupied major parts of their historic range (Abbitt and Scott 2001); none of the recovered species were primarily threatened by habitat loss. This suggests that we are recovering species with specific, easily remediable threats but are less successful when confronted with

Table 2.7. Changes in percentage of U.S. species by status over time

Status	Species listed 5 years or less		Species listed 6–10 years		Species listed 11 years or more	
	As of 09/30/98	As of 09/30/00	As of 09/30/98	As of 09/30/00	As of 09/30/98	As of 09/30/00
Stable	15	17	32	27	36	40
Improving	2	3	6	7	15	14
Declining	41	48	23	32	32	27
Uncertain	41	31	39	30	13	15
Captivity	<1	<1	0	<1	<1	<1
Presumed extinct	<1	<1	<1	3	4	3

Source: USFWS 2003c.

habitat loss. Habitat loss, however, is the major cause of endangerment (Wilcove et al. 1998). Abbitt and Scott (2001) found a positive correlation between percentage of historical range occupied at time of listing and achieving recovery. This suggests that targeting habitat for conservation may be a cost-effective way to reduce future listings while also protecting currently listed species (Shaffer et al., this volume). Similarly, targeting at-risk ecosystems (Noss et al. 1995) for conservation efforts before they deteriorate to the point where associated species are at risk is another proactive approach to the endangered species problem.

Beginning in 1990, the secretaries of the interior and commerce have provided biennial status reports to Congress for species under their jurisdiction. The most recent USFWS report covers the period October 1, 2000, to September 30, 2002 (USFWS 2004c); it states that 30 percent of listed species had stable populations, 6 percent were characterized as improving, 21 percent were declining, and 39 percent were characterized as uncertain (USFWS 2004c). Generally, the longer a species was listed the better its status (table 2.7).

The most recent National Marine Fisheries Service (NMFS) report covers the period from October 1, 2000, to September 30, 2002 (NMFS 2002). At the end of that period, NMFS had sole (forty-three species) or joint (seven species) responsibility for fifty species (NMFS 2002). Of these species, 30 percent are increasing, 4 percent have stable populations, 10 percent are "mixed," 34 percent are declining, and 22 percent have an uncertain status (NMFS 2002).

In addition to status trends in biennial reports, there are several other potential measures of the success of the ESA. These include extinctions, prevention of extinctions, reclassifications, and delistings.

Species Presumed Extinct

By the end of 2003, the USFWS (2004a) had delisted nine species presumed extinct. In addition, the agency reported that twenty-eight species (2 percent) were considered extinct as of September 30, 2000. This number was subsequently reduced to twenty-six species after two Hawaiian plants were rediscovered. These numbers are consistent with two other independent estimates of extinction for the same time period (B. Czech, pers. comm. [estimated twenty-seven species]; K. Suckling, pers. comm. [estimated thirty-one species]).

Prevented Species Extinctions

Based on the risk of extinction, Schwartz (1999) found that 192 U.S. species could have been expected to go extinct between passage of the act in 1973 and 1999. Using his logic that 67 percent of species characterized as threatened or endangered would be expected to go extinct in one hundred years, 262 currently listed species could be expected to have gone extinct in the thirty years since passage of the act. Subtracting the 9 species declared to be extinct and 26 assumed to be extinct by the USFWS, we are left with 227 species that the ESA arguably prevented from going extinct.

TABLE 2.8. Downlisted species

Common name	Date downlisted	Status change From	To
American alligator	1/10/1977	E	T
Virginia round-leaf birch	11/16/1994	E	T
Missouri bladderpod	10/15/2003	E	T
Siler pincushion cactus	12/27/1993	E	T
Maguire daisy	06/19/1996	E	T
Snail darter	07/05/1984	E	T
Bald eagle (lower 48 states)	07/12/1995	E	T
Arctic peregrine falcon	3/20/1984	E	T
MacFarlane's four-o'clock	03/15/1996	E	T
Alentian Canada goose	12/12/1990	E	T
Tinian monarch	04/06/1987	E	T
Louisiana pearlshell	09/24/1993	E	T
Small whorled pogonia	10/06/1994	E	T

(continues)

TABLE 2.8. *Continued*

		Status change	
Common name	Date downlisted	From	To
Utah prairie dog	05/29/1984	E	T
Large-flowered skullcap	01/14/2002	E	T
Apache trout	07/16/1975	E	T
Greenback cutthroat troat	04/18/1978	E	T
Lahontan cutthroat trout	07/16/1975	E	T
Paiute cutthroat trout	07/16/1975	E	T
Gray wolf (western DPS*)	04/01/2003	E	T
Gray wolf (eastern DPS)	03/09/1978, 04/01/2003	E	T

*Distinct population segment.

Downlisted Species

A species is downlisted when its status changes from endangered to threatened. Twenty-two species had been downlisted (table 2.8) by the thirtieth anniversary of the Endangered Species Act. The USFWS has identified twenty-seven species it considers to be on the brink of recovery. Five species are identified as nearly ready to downlist and twenty-two to delist (D. Crouse, pers. comm.).

Delisted Species

A species is delisted when it meets recovery goals and is no longer threatened, that is, no longer "likely to become an endangered species in the foreseeable future" (ESA sec. 3(20)). At the thirtieth anniversary of the ESA, thirty-seven species had been delisted, thirteen due to recovery (fig. 2.10). In addition, the USFWS recently proposed delisting of eastern populations of gray wolves (*New York Times* 2004).

Abbitt and Scott (2001) examined factors associated with delisted species that had been recovered and found a positive relationship between population status and percentage of historical range occupied at the time of listing, as well as with percentage of recovery goals achieved. This suggests that the management actions set out in recovery plans are biologically relevant and, when implemented, can improve the status of the species.

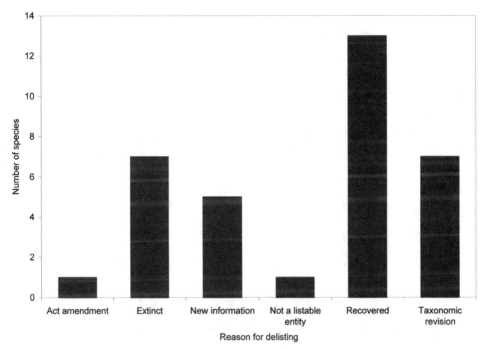

Figure 2.10. Delisted species in the United States and reasons for delisting as of December 31, 2003. The reason for delisting Rydberg milk-vetch (*Astragalus perianus*) has subsequently been changed to "original data in error (new information discovered)." (Data from USFWS 2004a,b.)

Funding

Funding for the endangered species program has varied dramatically since 1973 (fig. 2.11). The expenditure per listed species for all activities—administration, law enforcement, recovery, and others—was greatest four to six years after the act was passed, when it reached $241,000 per species. Figure 2.11 understates total funds because it does not include expenditures by the private sector; such funding often substitutes for direct federal funding (Kareiva et al., this volume). Nonetheless, this funding history suggests a diminished commitment to meeting the act's objectives.

Another measure of the adequacy of funding is to evaluate the percentage of the funds identified in recovery plans as needed to recover a species. Miller and colleagues (2002) found a positive relationship between funding and species recovery. Their findings suggest that recovery plans are identifying tasks that, when implemented, make a difference in the population status of the species. Thus, it would seem that large gains in the number of recovered species

Figure 2.11. Expenditures per listed species in constant 2003 U.S. dollars. (Data from USFWS 2004a.)

could be obtained by increasing recovery expenditures for plants, a group of which only two species have been delisted due to recovery. Restani and Marzluff (2002) also suggested that improving the correlation between USFWS spending and species ranks would increase the number of recovered species.

Conclusion

A review of the numbers generated by thirty years of implementing the Endangered Species Act reveals a checkerboard pattern. Increasing numbers of listed species, with endangered species far outnumbering threatened species in 1973 and in 2003, suggest that listing and recovery planning are implemented when extinction risks have already reached critical levels. This message is reinforced by the number of species that have gone extinct while listed and by the existence of six thousand or more unlisted but apparently imperiled species. Our biggest challenge may lie not in the recovery of endangered species but in preventing imperiled species from becoming endangered.

Reinforcing these conclusions is the fact that, although full species are most often listed, subspecies and populations are likely at risk earlier. These conclusions are also supported by the fact that only a small number of populations and individuals are present at the time of listing (Wilcove et al. 1993).

A recurring question is, how are we to measure success? Our findings suggest that success is a continuum (J. M. Scott et al., forthcoming) but that delisting or downlisting are widely accepted measures. Our view is that success is incremental: an increase, however small, in the number of individuals, in the number of populations, or in the distribution of a listed species indicates success, as does any reduction in the number or intensity of threats to a listed species. Although each increase by itself may not signal full ecological recovery for a species or restore it to an ecological and evolutionarily viable level, combined they nonetheless are signs that progress is being made. That there is a demonstrated correlation between number of years since a species is listed and improvement in its status (USFWS 2004c) also gives reason for optimism. But it also suggests that it may be several more decades before we can fully assess the success of the Endangered Species Act in preventing the loss of species on this planet.

3   Marine Species

Paul R. Armsworth, Carrie V. Kappel, Fiorenza Micheli,
and Eric P. Bjorkstedt

The 4.1 million square miles of ocean inside the 200-mile *exclusive economic zone* around the United States surpasses the 3.6 million square miles total land area within federal jurisdiction (Lindholm and Barr 2001). The coastal oceans contain a great diversity of habitat types and ecosystems. These habitats are associated with particular substrate features such as coral reefs, sea grass beds, rocky shores and soft-bottom habitats, and also with persistent oceanographic features such as frontal convergence zones and upwelling regions.

Our marine ecosystems contain unique and rich biotas. At higher taxonomic levels, biodiversity is much richer in the marine environment than it is on land or in freshwater. For example, thirty-six out of thirty-seven animal phyla are represented in the sea (Groombridge and Jenkins 2002), and 64 percent of animal phyla are found exclusively there, whereas only 3 percent are confined to land and none are exclusive to freshwater (May 1994; Reaka-Kudla 1997). Marine ecosystems appear relatively less diverse at the species level—roughly 15 percent of all described species are marine (Reaka-Kudla 1997).

Consistent national accounting of marine ecosystems is constrained by a lack of data, but the available indicators are worrying. As of 2002, of 237 domestic stocks managed by the National Marine Fisheries Service (NMFS) whose current status are known, 86 are overfished and overfishing continues for 66 stocks (NMFS 2003). The overfished status of the remaining 695 managed stocks, which are mostly of lesser commercial importance, is unknown (NMFS 2003). Two comprehensive national reviews of the state of marine ecosystems, the first in over thirty years, report that marine ecosystems are "in crisis" (Pew Oceans Commission 2003) and "in trouble" (U.S. Commission on Ocean Policy 2002).

The views or opinions expressed or implied are those of the authors and do not necessarily reflect the position of the National Marine Fisheries Service.

In this chapter, we review the role of the Endangered Species Act in protecting endangered marine species. Although our main focus is on those populations whose ranges fall primarily within the exclusive economic zone, we include both U.S. and foreign listed species in our analyses. Elsewhere (Armsworth et al., forthcoming), we review threats and conservation strategies for endangered marine species.

Extinct Marine Species

Relatively few species extinctions have been documented in marine ecosystems (Roberts and Hawkins 1999; Dulvy et al. 2003), but local extirpations of populations are more common (Dulvy et al. 2003; Musick et al. 2000; Powles et al. 2000). "Ecological" or "functional" extinctions are more common still and occur when species, such as top predators, that determine key ecosystem properties are diminished to a size at which fundamental ecosystem characteristics are altered (Jackson et al. 2001). Local extirpations and severe population reductions may be "the first steps on the road to global extinctions" (Dulvy et al. 2003).

That more marine extinctions have not been reported might be interpreted as support for a commonly stated view that marine species are less vulnerable to extinction than are terrestrial or freshwater species (Malakoff 1997; Roberts and Hawkins 1999; Hutchings 2001). This view is premised on the fact that some well-known marine species have large range sizes, high fecundities, and significant dispersal potential. The small number of documented extinctions may, however, reflect a paucity of data for marine ecosystems (Malakoff 1997; McKinney 1999). We have hardly begun to catalogue marine biodiversity, and the number of cryptic species is unknown. Without better stocktaking of marine biodiversity, it is not possible to evaluate with confidence the risk or frequency of human-induced extinctions. For example, Carlton et al. observe that the extinction of the eelgrass limpet (*Lottia alveus*), which was once abundant on New England shores, went unnoticed by the scientific community for over fifty years (Carlton et al. 1991). A recent review of 130 local to global extinctions of marine populations found that the median delay in reporting was fifty-three years (Dulvy et al. 2003).

Contrary to the perception that "typical" marine life histories render species less vulnerable to extinction, many marine species show a high degree of endemism and habitat specialization, and many others are long lived, have low fecundities, and mature slowly (Musick et al. 2000). Among vulnerable species on the World Conservation Union's red list, the proportions of species whose ranges are restricted that are (1) terrestrial and freshwater, (2) strictly marine, or (3) use marine habitats at some point in their life cycles are comparable (2.4

percent, 3.2 percent, and 2.2 percent respectively). Even species with large range sizes and high dispersal ability may not realize their full dispersal potential and can display significant local differentiation (Taylor and Hellberg 2003). There is also little evidence that highly fecund species enjoy greater reproductive success than species that invest more heavily in a small number of offspring (Hutchings 2001). Myers et al. found similar maximum reproductive rates across a variety of marine fish with a broad range of fecundities, and these maximum reproductive rates were comparable to those of terrestrial vertebrates (Myers et al. 1999).

Endangered Marine Species

Responsibility for ESA listing decisions and for the conservation and management of endangered and threatened marine, estuarine, and diadromous species resides primarily with the NMFS's Office of Protected Resources. For seabirds, this responsibility lies with the U.S. Fish and Wildlife Service (USFWS), as it does for a number of coastal, brackish-water fish.

The first step in determining whether a species will be listed as endangered or threatened under the Endangered Species Act (ESA) is to determine whether it meets the definition of a "species" under the statute. The act is not restricted to full biological species but can be used to protect any species or subspecies of fish, wildlife, or plant, and, for vertebrates only, the act can protect distinct population segments (DPSs) of a species (see Waples [forthcoming] for a review of the DPS and ESU [Evolutionarily Significant Unit] concepts and their application to Pacific salmon). The inclusion of DPSs allows vertebrate species to receive differing levels of protection in different parts of their range and can serve to guard against local extirpations.

To date, marine species have been listed as DPSs more frequently than their terrestrial counterparts (Scott, Goble, et al., this volume). The 39 marine, estuarine, or diadromous species listed as endangered or threatened are represented by 70 species, subspecies, and DPSs. The five salmon and steelhead species alone account for 26 listings. Only 25 marine species are listed across their entire range. By contrast, of the 1,855 listed species, subspecies, or DPSs reported by the USFWS, 98 percent represent full biological species. This disparity could reflect a real difference in population structure of marine and terrestrial species, or it could simply be an historical artifact of different listing processes used by the agencies.

The vulnerability of a species (including subspecies and DPS) that is being considered for listing under the ESA is assessed by NMFS or USFWS in a twelve-month scientific review process. The species appears on a candidate species list during this year. At the end of the formal assessment period, the species can be listed in the *Federal Register* as being endangered or threatened, or it can be removed from the candidate list if it is not foreseeably imperiled. In some circumstances, a species may not be listed as threatened or endangered but may be retained as a species of concern for future reappraisal. This designation was created by NMFS in 2004 to identify species for which "significant concerns or uncertainties remain regarding their biological status and/or threats," though they may not be currently considered for listing under the ESA.

Marine species are being listed under the ESA with increasing frequency (NMFS 2002), although they still make up only a tiny fraction of total listings (70 of 1,855 U.S. and foreign endangered and threatened listings). Early marine applications of the act focused on marine mammals and turtles (Wilcove and McMillan, this volume). Gradually, the emphasis in listings has shifted toward fish, but it has also diversified to include other taxonomic groups, including gastropods, corals, and marine plants. The current list of species of concern reflects this increased focus on other taxonomic groups. The majority of recent listings have been for Pacific salmon (*Oncorhynchus* spp.) and steelhead (*Oncorhynchus mykiss*) ESUs. Diadromous species feature prominently, both because obligate habitat specializations render them vulnerable to degradation of freshwater and estuarine environments and because diadromy lends itself to differentiation of local population units, which can sometimes be listed individually. Also noteworthy are the growing numbers of fully marine species listed as endangered, threatened, candidate species, or species of concern (see boxes 3.1 and 3.2).

Of the seventy marine species examined here that were once assessed as being endangered or threatened, only one, the eastern North Pacific population of the gray whale (*Eschrichtius robustus*), has recovered to the point at which its removal from the list was warranted (USFWS and NOAA 1994a). A second species, the Caribbean monk seal (*Monachus tropicalis*), has most likely gone extinct since it was listed. Nevertheless, NMFS reports that the status of marine species under ESA is "encouraging" (NMFS 2002). In its September 2002 report to Congress, the agency stated that of the endangered and threatened species with recovery plans in place, 36 percent "had been stabilized or were improving," 31 percent were declining, and 33 percent were "unknown or mixed in their status" (NMFS 2002). These trends are comparable to those for listed terrestrial and freshwater species, of which 39 percent were stable or improving, 34 percent were declining, 24 percent were uncertain, and 3 percent were extinct or found only in captivity in 2000 (USFWS 2003c).

Ocean Governance and the Role of the Endangered Species Act

Governance of our oceans is extremely fragmented, and the ESA must mesh with many other statutes, the implementation of which involve multiple agencies. Waters up to 3 miles offshore are managed by states, while those from 3 to 200 miles offshore are the responsibility of the federal government. Over 140 statutes govern exploitation of marine environments of which 43 are considered to be major. Regulation of our oceans spans sixty congressional committees overseeing nearly twenty agencies and permanent commissions. "Individuals who work and live on the water . . . face a Byzantine patchwork of federal and state authorities and regulations" (U.S. Commission on Ocean Policy 2002, 4). There are increasingly vocal calls for a reorganization of national ocean policy, one that would consolidate and integrate across these disparate management schemes (Cicin-Sain and Knecht 2000; Pew Oceans Commission 2003; U.S. Commission on Ocean Policy 2002).

We feel it is time for discussion on how the ESA might most effectively support sustainable management and conservation of marine species. Discussions on the future of the ESA, as reviewed elsewhere in this book, are occurring in parallel with the first comprehensive reviews of ocean policy in over thirty years (Pew Oceans Commission 2003; U.S. Commission on Ocean Policy 2004). Therefore, we find it disappointing that the role of the ESA, of extinction processes in the marine environment, and of the need for a fuller stocktaking of marine biodiversity have not appeared more prominently in these discussions on ocean policy. For example, while the Pew report repeatedly calls for crosscutting and integrative regulations and provides a comprehensive suite of recommendations for improving marine conservation and management in general, it only discusses the ESA in passing and as a minor theme.

The remit of the ESA overlaps in marine systems with other key regulations. For example, rebuilding depleted populations is also a central goal of the Sustainable Fisheries Act (SFA) (Act of October 11, 1996) and of the Marine Mammal Protection Act (MMPA) (Act of October 21, 1972), a goal that has resulted in regulation of and moratoria on take of depleted species under these statutes. For both of these acts, however, the goal of rebuilding is not merely to prevent full extinction, as it is under the ESA, but rather to restore a species to some "optimal" abundance level. For the SFA, the goal under national standard 1 is to rebuild species to abundance levels that will provide "on a continuing basis . . . optimal yield for the US fishing industry." The major objective of the

BOX 3.1. White Abalone

The white abalone (*Haliotis sorenseni*), a gastropod, was listed as endangered under the ESA on May 29, 2001; it is the first marine invertebrate to be listed (NOAA 2001). The species is a broadcast spawner and adults are highly fecund and produce millions of eggs or sperm during spawning. However, fertilization success depends on the density of adults and may fall off sharply when adults are sparsely distributed (Leighton 1972; Babcock and Keesing 1999; Hobday and Tegner 2000). White abalone undergo a free-swimming larval stage of nine to ten days during which they are thought to have relatively limited dispersal potential (Hobday and Tegner 2000). Abalone grow slowly, do not mature until four to six years of age, and have a lifespan of thirty-five to forty years.

Over the last thirty years, abalone abundance is thought to have declined by 99.9 percent from approximately 2.22–4.24 million individuals to 1,613–2,540 animals (NOAA 2001). The decline was driven by overfishing. Commercial fishing of white abalone began in 1967 and landings peaked at 86,000 individuals in 1972 (NOAA 2001). The commercial fishery collapsed within ten years of first opening.

In California, white abalone are now restricted to a few localized populations, mostly within the Channel Islands. The sedentary nature of adults (movements on the order of meters or less) means that it is possible to delineate these localized populations. However, the National Marine Fisheries Service declined to specify critical habitat for abalone because of concerns that publicly identifying remaining habitats could encourage poaching. Hobday and Tegner estimated that 3.7 square miles of suitable habitat for white abalone exist within its historic range, but much of this area remains unoccupied (Hobday and Tegner 2000).

The white abalone population is not expected to recover without human intervention. Recruitment failure is believed to be recurrent and the remaining population may constitute aging adults, surviving offspring from the last known successful recruitment in 1966 before the population collapsed (Hobday and Tegner 2000). Current densities, estimated at 0.0002 per meter, are well below the threshold of 0.15 per meter at which fertilization success for abalone in the field drops by 50 percent (Babcock and Keesing 1999; Hobday and Tegner 2000). Restoration efforts based on captive breeding are under way (Western Ecological Research Center 2002), but the science of marine restoration ecology is very much in its infancy.

BOX 3.2. Bocaccio

On January 30, 2001, the National Marine Fisheries Service (NMFS) received a petition to list the central/southern population of bocaccio (*Sebastes paucispinis*), a species of rockfish, as a threatened species (Natural Resources Defense Council et al. 2001). Bocaccio ranges from Baja California to Stepovak Bay, Alaska. The species is separated into northern and southern segments by an area of low abundance off northern California and southern Oregon. NMFS ruled that the two subpopulations constitute distinct population segments (MacCall and He 2002) and that therefore the central/southern subpopulation could be considered for listing. However, at the end of the review process, NMFS announced that a listing was not warranted.

Bocaccio are ovoviviparous and females give birth to 20,000 to 2,298,000 larvae (Love et al. 2002). Recruitment is highly variable in bocaccio. Individuals mature after about five years and can live up to forty years (MacCall and He 2002; Love et al. 2002). Adults are widely distributed and are often found over rocky reefs or boulder fields.

Bocaccio abundance has decreased steadily since 1969. Current abundance is estimated to be 1.6 million fish of age one or older, or 3.6 percent of estimated unfished spawner abundance (NOAA 2002). Stock assessments since 1996 indicate that the population is in severe decline and it was formally declared overfished in 1999. The decline of bocaccio has been driven by directed fishing and bycatch and has been exacerbated by a string of poor recruitment years. The published ruling by NMFS catalogues a sequence of problems with the scientific advice provided to the Pacific Fishery Management Council and repeated management failures on the part of the council to take action (NOAA 2002).

The decision not to list the population was based on recent conservation measures that have been adopted by the council and the State of California. These measures include the prohibition of directed fishing or retention of the species, measures to reduce bycatch of bocaccio, large catch reductions, with allowable catch rates less than 5 percent of their average over the previous fifty years, marine reserve creation, and time-area closures. Bocaccio remain on the agency's list of species of concern.

MMPA is to ensure that marine mammal species remain a "significant functioning element in the ecosystems of which they are a part," in other words, to prevent functional extinctions. Therefore, each of these statutes sets more conservative rebuilding targets than are required under the ESA for the suite of species that they protect.

If interpreted and applied judiciously, the ESA can play important roles in marine management. These roles will vary somewhat across taxonomic groups, however, because of the interaction of the act with other statutes. For species that receive protection under complementary regulations, such as the SFA and MMPA, the ESA provides an extra layer of protection and can serve as a strong safety net should other, perhaps more flexible, regulatory instruments fail to prevent a species from becoming imperiled. However, not all species receive protection under other statutes, many of which like the MMPA have a narrow taxonomic or other focus. Therefore, the ESA also has a crucial role to play in ensuring that species, like Johnson's seagrass (*Halophila johnsonii*) or the tidewater goby (*Eucyclogobius newberryi*), receive at least some measure of protection and do not fall between the regulatory cracks.

The laws that protect marine species differ not only in the species they cover but also in the burdens they place on regulators and when they are binding. The ESA is only binding when there is a credible threat of extinction to a species, subspecies, or vertebrate DPS. In contrast, the SFA and other laws confer protection to species regardless of their current plight. When the ESA is applicable, it can provide substantial security to a species and place a heavy burden of responsibility on managers. To illustrate, suppose some species of conservation concern is caught as unwanted bycatch in a fishery. If the vulnerable species is listed, then NMFS must ensure that any continued operation of the fishery is "not likely to jeopardize the continued existence" of the listed species under section 7 of the ESA. In contrast, if the species is not listed, then the agency must implement management measures under national standard 9 of the SFA that "to the extent practicable, (A) minimize bycatch and (B) to the extent that bycatch cannot be avoided, minimize the mortality of such bycatch."

We anticipate that listings and listing petitions for marine species will continue to increase in frequency and that therefore the profile of the ESA in marine management discussions will grow. An increase in listing attempts could reflect the continuing decline of species that are already intensely impacted by human activities as well as more accurate reporting of these declines as additional data become available. An increase in listings could also reflect a broadening of the suite of marine species confronting anthropogenic impacts as human influences propagate further within and across marine ecosystems. Marine taxonomy is relatively underdeveloped and an increase in listings will result from improvements in taxonomic resolution, which are certain to reveal more cryptic species and subspecies. Frustrated stakeholder groups may turn to listing attempts in light of the growing scarcity of marine resources and increasing conflicts over marine ecosystems. This outcome seems particularly likely given the growth in the marine conservation lobby.

It is important that managers and stakeholders strive to find the statute that provides the best available tool for the issue at hand. When trying to prevent the final extinction of an already critically depleted species like white abalone (*Haliotis sorenseni*), the ESA is the appropriate regulatory instrument. Implementation of the act will likely be most effective when the species in question has a spatially restricted and easily demarcated range; when the listing only impacts a small and concentrated number of resource users; and when a taking can be clearly defined and a "no takings" policy can be efficiently enforced. When trying to alter exploitation practices to stem the flux of additional species into endangerment, however, other regulations like the SFA provide more suitable tools.

If more general resource conflicts can be managed successfully under the suite of other marine statutes, then the ESA could be freed to fulfill its role as a species safety net; it could then serve as a powerful tool for preventing further marine extinctions. Provided it is not expected to carry the weight of broader marine biodiversity conservation, we perceive much potential for applying the ESA to improve the status of threatened marine species.

4   THE CLASS OF '67

David S. Wilcove and Margaret McMillan

Before 1967, the U.S. Department of the Interior was monitoring several imperiled species and even acquiring important habitats for them, but it lacked an explicit mandate from Congress to spend money to conserve these species. In 1966, Congress remedied the problem by directing the secretaries of the interior, agriculture, and defense and the heads of all federal agencies "to protect species of native fish and wildlife, including migratory birds, that are threatened with extinction" (ESPA sec. 1(c)). The secretary of the interior was also directed to publish in the *Federal Register* the names of all species found to be in danger of extinction (Bean and Rowland 1997). Thus, on March 11, 1967, the Interior Department released its official list of endangered species in the United States, totaling seventy-eight species. Six years later, Congress passed the Endangered Species Act (ESA), greatly expanding the responsibilities and powers of the federal government with respect to protecting imperiled wildlife. Given the important and controversial role the ESA has played in American environmental history, it seems only fitting in this chapter to look back at the first cohort of listed species and ask, what became of the Class of '67?

Compared to the approximately 1,265 species that comprise the current list of endangered species, the Class of '67 is striking in its lack of diversity (table 4.1). It consists entirely of vertebrates (fourteen mammals, thirty-six birds, three reptiles, three amphibians, and twenty-two fish), reflecting a decision at that time by the Interior Department to define "native fish and wildlife" as encompassing vertebrates only. Invertebrates would not become eligible for protection under the ESA until 1969; plants would have to wait until 1973. The first listing of invertebrates and plants would not occur for several years (see Scott, Goble, et al., this volume). Today, vertebrates account for only 27 percent of the species on the list, with plants and invertebrates comprising 59 and 14 percent, respectively (USFWS 2004d). In another respect, however, the Class of '67 is curiously similar to today's cohort of endangered species. Nine-

Table 4.1. The Class of '67: Species listed by the U.S. Fish and Wildlife Service on March 11, 1967

Species	Current USFWS status
Akiapolaau (*Hemignathus munroi*)	E
Aleutian Canada goose (*Branta canadensis leucopareia*)	delisted; recovered
American alligator (*Alligator mississippiensis*)	delisted; recovered
American ivory-billed woodpecker (*Campephilus principalis principalis*)	E
Apache trout (*Oncorhynchus apache*)	T
Attwater's greater prairie-chicken (*Tympanuchus cupido attwateri*)	E
Bachman's warbler (*Vermivora bachmanii*)	E
Bald eagle (*Haliaeetus leucocephalus*)	T
Big Bend gambusia (*Gambusia gaigei*)	E
Black toad (*Bufo boreas exsul*)	never listed
Black-footed ferret (*Mustela nigripes*)	E; also EXPN
Blue pike (*Stizostedion vitreum glaucum*)	delisted; extinct
Blunt-nosed leopard lizard (*Gambelia silus*)	E
California condor (*Gymnogyps californianus*)	E; also EXPN
Cape Sable seaside sparrow (*Ammodramus maritimus mirabilis*)	E
Caribbean monk seal (*Monachus tropicalis*)	E
Clear Creek gambusia (*Gambusia heterochir*)	E
Colorado squawfish (*Ptychocheilus lucius*)	E; also EXPN
Columbian white-tailed deer (*Odocoileus virginianus leucurus*)	delisted (recovered) in Douglas County; E elsewhere
Comanche Springs pupfish (*Cyprinodon elegans*)	E
Crested honeycreeper (*Palmeria dolei*)	E
Cui-ui (*Chasmistes cujus*)	E
Delmarva Peninsula fox squirrel (*Sciurus niger cinereus*)	E; also EXPN
Desert dace (*Eremichthys acros*)	T
Devil's Hole pupfish (*Cyprinodon diabolis*)	E
Dusky seaside sparrow (*Ammodramus maritimus nigrescens*)	delisted; extinct
Eastern timber wolf (*Canis lupus lyacon*)	E; T; also EXPN
Eskimo curlew (*Numenius borealis*)	E
Everglade snail kite (*Rostrhamus sociabilis plumbeus*)	E
Florida panther (*Felis concolor coryi*)	E
Florida (=West Indian) manatee (*Trichechus manatus*)	E
Gila topminnow (*Poeciliopsis occidentalis*)	E
Gila trout (*Oncorhynchus gilae*)	E
Greenback cutthroat trout (*Oncorhynchus clarki stomias*)	T
Grizzly bear (*Ursus arctos horribilis*)	T; also EXPN
Guadalupe fur seal (*Arctocephalus townsendi*)	T
Hawaiian common moorhen (*Gallinula chloropus sandvicensis*)	E
Hawaiian crow (*Corvus hawaiiensis*)	E

Species	Current USFWS status
Hawaiian goose (nene) (*Branta sandvicensis*)	E
Hawaiian dark-rumped petrel (*Pterodroma phaeopygia sandwichensis*)	E
Hawaiian duck (*Anas wyvilliana*)	E
Hawaiian hawk (*Buteo solitarius*)	E
Humpback chub (*Gila cypha*)	E
Indiana bat (*Myotis sodalis*)	E
Kauai akialoa (*Hemignathus procerus*)	E
Kauai nukupu`u (*Hemignathus lucidus hanapepe*)	E
Kauai `o`o (*Moho bracatus*)	E
Key deer (*Odocoileus virginianus clavium*)	E
Kirtland's warbler (*Dendroica kirtlandii*)	E
Laysan duck (*Anas laysanensis*)	E
Laysan finch (*Telespyza cantans*)	E
Little Colorado spinedace (*Lepidomeda vittata*)	T
Longjaw cisco (*Coregonus alpenae*)	delisted; extinct
Masked bobwhite (*Colinus virginianus ridgwayi*)	E
Maryland darter (*Etheostoma sellare*)	E
Maui parrotbill (*Pseudonestor xanthophrys*)	E
Mexican duck (*Anas platyrhynchos diazi*)	delisted; hybridization
Moapa dace (*Moapa coriacea*)	E
Montana westslope cutthroat trout (*Oncorhynchus clarki lewisi*)	never listed
Nihoa finch (*Telespyza ultima*)	E
Nihoa millerbird (*Acrocephalus familiaris kingi*)	E
`O`u (*Psittirostra psittacea*)	E
Owens pupfish (*Cyprinodon radiosus*)	E
Pahrump killifish (*Empetrichthys latos*)	E
Paiute cutthroat trout (*Oncorhynchus clarki seleniris*)	T
Palila (*Loxioides bailleui*)	E
Puerto Rican parrot (*Amazona vittata*)	E
Red wolf (*Canis rufus*)	E; also EXPN
San Francisco garter snake (*Thamnophis sirtalis tetrataenia*)	E
San Joaquin kit fox (*Vulpes macrotis mutica*)	E
Santa Cruz long-toed salamander (*Ambystoma macrodactylum croceum*)	E
Shortnose sturgeon (*Acipenser brevirostrum*)	E
Small Kauai thrush (*Myadestes palmeri*)	E
Sonoran pronghorn (*Antilocapra americana sonoriensis*)	E
Texas blind salamander (*Typhlomolge rathbuni*)	E
Tule white-fronted goose (*Anser albifrons gambelli*)	never listed
Yuma clapper rail (*Rallus longirostris yumanensis*)	E
Whooping crane (*Grus americana*)	E; also EXPN

Source: U.S. Department of the Interior 1967.
The current federal status of each species is given (T = threatened; E = endangered; EXPN = experimental population(s) of reintroduced individuals).

teen members or 24 percent of the Class of '67 were Hawaiian species, compared to approximately 25 percent of the current list.[1]

With respect to the threats facing the Class of '67, 76 percent of the members were imperiled by habitat destruction, 38 percent by alien species, 27 percent by overharvest, 13 percent by disease, and 8 percent by pollution. (The summed percentages exceed 100 because individual species may be threatened by more than one factor.) The primacy of habitat destruction as a threat to biodiversity, followed by alien species, mirrors the situation still facing endangered species today (Wilcove et al. 1998).

There is an unfortunate element of familiarity to the Class of '67. No fewer than sixty-nine of its members are still on the endangered species list, including such well-known animals as the California condor, whooping crane, and red wolf (for scientific names, see table 4.1). That most of the members of the Class of '67 are still on the endangered list has been taken as evidence that the ESA itself isn't working but, in fact, the truth is more complicated.

Two members of the Class of '67—American alligator and Aleutian Canada goose—recovered fully and were removed from the list in 1987 and 2001, respectively. Both species were threatened primarily by single factors (overharvest in the case of the alligator, an introduced predator in the case of the goose), and once those problems were addressed, the species quickly rebounded. Another species, the Columbian white-tailed deer, has been declared recovered in a portion of its range but remains protected elsewhere. Four others—Apache trout, Paiute cutthroat trout, bald eagle, and eastern timber wolf—have been "downlisted" from endangered to threatened, reflecting the fact that significant progress has been made in restoring their populations to healthy levels. Both the eagle and wolf are likely to be declared recovered and removed from the list in the near future. (Protection for three species—black toad, Montana westslope cutthroat trout, and tule white-fronted goose—was not continued beyond 1973, when the ESA was passed, apparently because the Interior Department felt listing was no longer warranted.)

Counterbalancing these success stories are the three members of the Class of '67 that were removed from the list because they are now extinct: blue pike ("delisted" in 1983), longjaw cisco (1983), and dusky seaside sparrow (1990). To these we may add an additional eight species that still remain on the list but are almost certainly extinct, too: Bachman's warbler, Caribbean monk seal, Eskimo curlew, Kauai `o`o, Kauai akialoa, Kauai nukupu`u, Maryland darter, and `o`u. As we have noted elsewhere (McMillan and Wilcove 1994), most of these species were either extinct or beyond the point of rescue by the time the ESA was passed in 1973.[2] Their demise is not a reflection of problems with the ESA. The dusky seaside sparrow, however, would surely be alive today had the federal government been more vigilant in administering the ESA, and perhaps the `o`u, Kauai `o`o, and Maryland darter as well.

Most of the other members of the Class of '67 fall somewhere in between the broad categories of recovered and extinct, reflecting a mixed record of progress and setbacks. The whooping crane, for example, is still accorded endangered status, but few people would consider the steady growth of its population from fewer than twenty-five individuals in 1941 to over four hundred today as anything less than a success story (see Scott, Goble, et al., this volume). The Key deer is another species that, while still classified as endangered, has rebounded significantly, from approximately one hundred individuals in 1942 to over seven hundred by 2003. The Kirtland's warbler, Gila trout, red wolf, and Delmarva Peninsula fox squirrel fall into the same category.

The California condor, on the other hand, presents a more complicated story. When it was added to the endangered list in 1967, a small and declining population remained in the mountains of Southern California. That population continued to dwindle despite protection under the ESA until 1985, when the Interior Department made the risky decision to bring all remaining individuals into captivity. The captive breeding program, in turn, proved remarkably successful, enabling federal and state officials to begin reintroducing birds into the wild by the start of 1992. In 2003, a pair of captive-reared condors successfully fledged a chick in the Grand Canyon, marking another important milestone in the species' history. It is still too early to judge whether the reintroduction program will succeed and, thus, depending upon the time frame one chooses, the effort to save the condor can be seen as either a success or a failure.

The population of Puerto Rican parrots has followed its own roller-coaster ride, from twenty-four individuals at time of listing to only thirteen by 1975. Alarmed by the prospect of its imminent extinction, federal and Commonwealth of Puerto Rico agencies launched an ambitious captive-breeding and habitat-enhancement program on behalf of the parrot, thereby boosting the wild population to nearly fifty individuals. In 1989, however, these recovery efforts were dealt a severe blow when Hurricane Hugo reduced the wild parrot population by nearly half. Once again, federal and Commonwealth agencies managed to rebuild the wild population to nearly fifty individuals, but the captive population suffered its own blow in April 2001, when thieves broke into the captive-breeding facility and removed an undisclosed number of birds.

The question naturally arises as to the how the Class of '67 has fared relative to other cohorts of endangered species. The simple comparison in table 4.2 suggests that greater progress has been made in recovering the Class of '67 than with other endangered and threatened vertebrates. We must be careful, however, not to read too much into such a comparison. Our analysis does not take

Table 4.2. Recovery progress of the Class of '67 relative to other listed vertebrates in the United States. Numbers in each category refer to species.

	Recovery objectives achieved (%)	
	0–50	51–100
Class of '67	47	20
Other listed vertebrates	225	26

Source: USFWS (2003c).
Note: Species are divided into two categories: those for which 0–50 percent of recovery objectives have been achieved and those for which 51–100 percent have been achieved. All delisted species, whether for reasons of recovery, extinction, or listing error, are excluded. The proportion of Class of '67 species for which more than half of the recovery objectives have been achieved is significantly greater than for other listed vertebrates (chi-square = 16.24, df = 1, p < .001).

into account those species (from the Class of '67 or other cohorts) that were removed from the federal list due to recovery, extinction, or listing error. Moreover, the determination of the percentage of a given species' recovery goals that have been achieved is itself a somewhat subjective decision (USFWS 2003c).

The Class of '67, in short, defies easy categorization. Its history reflects the complicated history of the ESA itself, a mixture of success and failure, hope and disappointment—just like any high school or college reunion.

5   The Listing Record

D. Noah Greenwald, Kieran F. Suckling, and Martin Taylor

The effectiveness of the Endangered Species Act (ESA) is often evaluated in terms of the recovery status of listed species. Reviews typically attempt to determine whether recovery plans, critical habitat, consultation procedures, and habitat conservation plans are scientifically adequate and measurably beneficial to listed species. The greatest weakness in ESA implementation, however, has been the lengthy delays in listing at-risk species. Unlisted species are at great risk of extinction because species are protected only after they are formally listed. For example, in 1977 the U.S. Fish and Wildlife Service (USFWS) determined that the Valdina Farms salamander (*Eurycea troglodytes*) warranted review for listing (USFWS 1977a). The USFWS placed the species on the candidate list in 1982 (USFWS 1982a), but it still was not listed in 1987 when the Edwards Underground Water District drove it to extinction by channeling flood water into the only cave it inhabited (Elliot 2000). The alani (*Melicope quadrangularis*) fared no better. It was listed as endangered in 1994—twenty years after the Smithsonian Institution petitioned to have it listed, nineteen years after the USFWS officially proposed listing, fifteen years after the species was placed on the candidate list, and two years after it went extinct (USFWS 2000a).

These are not exceptional cases. At least forty-two species have become extinct during delays in the listing process (Suckling, in preparation). As our analysis details, hundreds of species have suffered lengthy delays between the time they were first identified as being at risk and when they were actually protected under the ESA. Many declined during these delays, making their recovery more difficult, more expensive, and in some cases, impossible.

Management of the listing process by the USFWS appears inconsistent with the intent of the ESA and has been a constant point of criticism. Congress (U.S. Congress 1982c), the Government Accounting Office (GAO 1979), the U.S. Department of the Interior Inspector General (U.S. Department of the Interior Inspector General 1990), academic scientists, environmentalists, and the agency's own biologists (Sidle 1998) have repeatedly documented and criticized listing delays. Yet the annual listing rate has steadily declined since 1996.

To better understand the ESA listing program, in this chapter we analyze trends in the annual listing rate, funding levels, and speed and taxonomy of individual listings from January 1974 to December 2003. We correlate these trends with changes in legislation, administrative policies, political pressure, and citizen enforcement efforts. Recommendations to improve the process depend upon an understanding of how it has actually functioned.

Introduction and Background

The Endangered Species Act includes a provision allowing individuals to petition to list species. In 1982, Congress amended the ESA to impose deadlines for listing decisions. The amendments also established two listing pathways: a discretionary pathway allowing the agency to initiate listing, and a nondiscretionary pathway requiring that citizen petitions be reviewed within the statutory timelines.

On the discretionary pathway, the USFWS can initiate the listing process either by placing a species on the candidate list or by issuing a proposed listing rule. Until the agency issues a proposal, there is no required timeline. Once listing is proposed, however, the agency has twelve months to make a final decision. On the petition pathway, on the other hand, the agency is required to complete the review within two years.

We obtained data on the listing history of all species listed as threatened or endangered since passage of the ESA, including the dates species were made candidates, proposed for listing, and listed as threatened or endangered, and whether a petition or lawsuit had been filed. This information was obtained from final listing rules, from candidate notice of reviews periodically published in the *Federal Register*, through Freedom of Information Act requests to the agencies for petitions and litigation documents, by surveying environmental groups and law firms known to be active in ESA listing issues, and by searching LexisNexis, an online legal database. All information was entered into a database along with the common and scientific name of the species, range by state, and taxonomic class (i.e., herpetofauna, plants, mammals, birds, fish, and invertebrates).

To analyze trends in the listing rate over time, we tabulated annual numbers of species listed 1974–2003 and whether they were listed following petitions or lawsuits, or solely by agency action. Because policies often change with administrations, we used the presidential administrative year (January 23–January 22 of the following year) rather than the calendar year when tabulating the annual number of species listings. We identified differences in the number of species listed per year and attempted to relate these differences to the listing budget, government policies, and numbers of species listed in response to lawsuits and petitions. ANOVA (analysis of variance) was used to test for significant differences in listing rate between time periods.

To quantify the length of time required by agencies to list species, we calculated times between the various actions and findings (e.g., candidate to proposed rule, petition to proposed rule, etc.). We quantified the overall time to listing using the earliest date of initiation, whether it was the filing of a petition, designation of candidate status, or issuance of a proposed rule. Using these data, we tested three hypotheses in relation to the 1982 amendments. First, we expected species petitioned after 1982 to take less time to be listed than species petitioned before 1982. Second, we expected species listed entirely under agency discretion (discretionary pathway) to take longer to be listed than species listed as a result of petitions after 1982 (petition pathway). Third, we expected that lawsuits would tend to expedite listing of species.

A challenge to testing these hypotheses is time-horizon or econometric effects. Our database is limited to species that were listed, biasing our data in two ways. First, the data do not include the thousands of species petitioned for listing from 1974 to 1978 that have yet to be listed; if we included these species, our estimate of average time to listing would increase substantially. Second, and conversely, our data do not include the far fewer number of species that were initiated post-1982 that have yet to be listed, potentially underestimating delays for species initiated in this latter period. For each of the various tests, we took measures to reduce these effects.

To test the first hypothesis, we compared the time from filing of a petition to issuance of a proposed rule between species petitioned pre- and post-1982 using a *t*-test. We did not test the time from filing of a petition to listing (issuance of a final rule) because many of the species petitioned prior to 1982 were proposed for listing after 1982, when they then became subject to the timelines, thus confounding our ability to test for an effect of the timelines. We controlled for time-horizon effects by limiting the analysis to species petitioned prior to 1992 thus reducing underestimation of delays for species petitioned more recently.

To test the second hypothesis, we used a *t*-test to compare time from filing of a petition to listing versus time from initiation by the agency to listing. We limited the analysis to species initiated after 1982 to avoid time-horizon effects.

For the third hypothesis, we performed two tests. First, we compared time from initiation to proposed rule for species without a lawsuit to time from filing of a lawsuit to proposed rule, limiting the analysis to the period after 1989 when the first lawsuits to obtain proposed rules were filed. Second, we compared time from issuance of a proposed rule to listing without a lawsuit to time from filing of a suit to listing, again limiting the analysis, in this case to after 1992 when the first suits to obtain listing were filed. In both cases, limiting the analysis to species initiated after the first suits were filed avoided bias related to time-horizon effects.

We obtained data on the USFWS listing budget from 1979 forward by reviewing annual requests to Congress by the Department of the Interior, and congressional appropriations. There were no line-item distinctions prior to 1979. We compared the unadjusted annual budget to annual requests from the Department of the Interior to Congress to determine the latter's responsiveness to administrative budget requests.

To determine the influence of petitions and lawsuits on the overall composition of listed species, we calculated the proportions of each taxonomic class (i.e., birds, fish, herpetofauna, invertebrates, and plants). We compared differences in time to listing between taxonomic classes using ANOVA.

Listing Species: 1974–2003

In enacting the ESA, Congress assumed that all imperiled plants and animals would be listed. It was known from the beginning that this would require a substantial effort. In 1975, for example, the director of the USFWS estimated that full implementation of the act would involve listing 7,000 species; Keith Schreiner, an associate director of USFWS, stated that listing had been initiated for 3,606 species, the vast majority of which were domestic species (U.S. Congress 1975). Between January 1974 and December 2003, just 1,229 domestic species were listed, an average of 41 species per year. Based on an estimated 9,206 critically imperiled or imperiled species in the United States (Nature-Serve 2003), it will take approximately 177 years to list all species in need of protection. During this time, many of these species may become extinct.

To understand why the listing program has performed so poorly, we reviewed the history of all domestic listings, all listing petitions submitted to the USFWS, all policy and legislative developments affecting the program, and the changing nature of nongovernmental organization (NGO) interaction with the program. The first pattern that we noted is the contribution of state governments, scientists, and conservation NGOs, who attempted to jumpstart the program by submitting petitions to list species. For example, the USFWS reported to Congress in 1975 that it had received nineteen petitions to list a total of 23,962 domestic and foreign species (U.S. Congress 1975). In addition, the Smithsonian submitted a list that had been requested by Congress of 3,187 plants warranting listing (Smithsonian Institution 1974). Thus, a large number of potentially endangered species were identified shortly after enact-

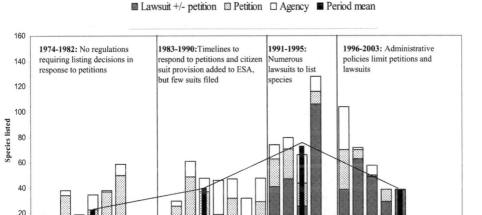

Figure 5.1. Species listed by year following petitions, lawsuits, and agency action, 1974–2003.

ment of the ESA. Of all species listed in the United States, 54 percent were petitioned by conservation NGOs. Furthermore, when lawsuits are taken into account, 71 percent of all listings are attributable to conservation interests. To a large degree, therefore, the history of the listing program is a history of the laws and policies governing the relationship of conservation interests to the program and the listing agencies.

Four distinct listing periods are evident: 1974–82, 1983–90, 1991–96, and 1997–2003 (fig. 5.1).[1]

Period One—1974–82

Listings steadily increased from 1974 to 1980, then collapsed to near zero in 1981 and 1982. The average listing rate was just twenty-three species per year (SD = 20.3) (fig. 5.1). Despite the low listing level, the great majority of listing petitions (at least 4,123) were actually filed during this period. Furthermore, the USFWS published listing proposals for over two thousand species (a feat not matched in any other period).

In 1978, Congress substantially amended the listing program requiring withdrawl of all proposed listings if they had not been finalized within two years. In addition, listings could not be reproposed unless new information was obtained. A one-year grace period was allowed for proposals in existence at the time of the amendment. The USFWS had begun a massive listing push in 1976 and had active listing proposals for approximately two thousand species when the amendment was passed. It had one year to complete most of these listings and two years to complete all of them. Failure to do so could delay listing for many years due to the "new information" requirement. This was the first test of the USFWS's resolve to prioritize the listing program and swiftly protect imperiled species. The agencies did not rise to the challenge. The annual listing rate did increase in 1979 and 1980, but not dramatically or beyond the increasing trend from 1974 to 1978.

The agency withdrew proposed listing rules for 1,876 species on November 10, 1979 (USFWS 1979). The USFWS promised to swiftly repropose and list the species, but in most cases did not do so. As of December 2003, only 512 of the 3,187 plants identified by the Smithsonian Institution had been listed. A USFWS biologist stated at the time that the agency did not mount an aggressive listing response to the looming deadline due to "incompetence and ineptitude" and because administrators were "afraid to take the bull by the horns because they worried what would happen politically to the Endangered Species Act itself. We have been so busy saving the act that we are not saving plants and animals" (*New York Times* 1979). The deadline was withdrawn by Congress in 1982; thus it did not establish a permanent legal barrier. The agencies, however, never again attempted a mass listing program.

Another provision of the 1978 amendments that is often cited as impacting the listing program is a requirement that critical habitat be designated concurrently with listing. Bean and Rowland, for example, suggest that amendments to the ESA enacted in 1978 placed a "near stranglehold" on the listing program and that the requirement to designate critical habitat concurrently with listing "posed a major barrier to listing" (Bean and Rowland 1997, 205). The USFWS concurs, asserting that the amendment caused an "enormous workload" from which the listing program "has never fully recovered" (USFWS 2001b). Had the 1978 critical habitat amendment been implemented, a stranglehold might well have occurred. The empirical record, however, shows that in the two years following the 1978 amendments, the annual rate of listing increased slightly. The decrease predicted by reading the law did not occur because the amendments were only marginally implemented. Between 1979 and the modification of the amendments in 1982, only 16 percent of listings contained a concurrent critical habitat designation. Similarly, critical habitat was not designated for most of the proposed species that were listed in the two years following 1978. Thus, the critical habitat amendment was so routinely ignored that it had little effect on the listing program.[2]

A second major effect on listing in Period One was the election of Ronald Reagan as president in 1981. Shortly after entering office, Reagan suspended issuance of federal rules (including listing rules) and later issued an executive order requiring an economic impact analysis prior to issuance of proposed rules (Executive Order 12291 1981; Tobin 1990). Additional reviews by Interior's Office of the Solicitor and by the Office of Management and Budget were used as a tool to shut down the listing program; 1981 stands out as the only administrative year after 1974 in which no species were listed. The chief of the U.S. Fish and Wildlife Service's Office of Endangered Species complained that "legitimate policy decisions" were being "precluded, circumvented, or subordinated by pseudolegalistic ploys being used as excuses for delay" (Tobin 1990).

Period One is characterized by a lack of laws or policies requiring the agencies to list threatened and endangered species systematically. For example, there was no requirement that the agencies process the listing petitions they received—petitions were not even tracked. When the GAO audited the USFWS in 1978, it found that 41 percent of petitions submitted before June 30 were lost (GAO 1979).

Political pressure and inertia thrive in the completely discretionary legal environment that characterized Period One. According to the GAO, politically motivated listing delays and refusals were common during this period, especially when species protection potentially conflicted with major federal projects or otherwise generated controversy. The GAO also found that the administration failed to request sufficient funds, dedicate adequate staffing for the listing program, or implement consistent listing procedures. "[T]hese deficiencies," it warned, "could jeopardize the existence of some species or result in the selective extinction of others" (GAO 1979, 9). The GAO audit and the Reagan administration's shutdown of the listing program set the stage for legislative reforms to increase NGO involvement and ensure that listing actions—especially the processing of listing petitions—be completed.

Period Two—1983–90

Congress amended the ESA in late 1982, establishing strict timelines for processing petitions and completing listing decisions. Its intent, to speed up the listing program, assure petitions were fully processed, reduce agencies' discretion to delay action, and increase the ability of NGOs to enforce the law, was clear:

> [T]he Secretary should make considerably more progress in the listing process than he has during the past 14 months. (U.S. Congress 1982c)

> The listing process under section 4 is the keystone of the Endangered Species Act. The bill further amends the Act to . . . speed up the process by which species are added to or subtracted from the endangered and threatened species lists. (U.S. Congress 1982b)

> The amendments will force action on listing and delisting proposals. (U.S. Congress 1982a)

The amendments did allow the agencies to delay final action on listing petitions by declaring that listing is "warranted but precluded"—that is, that sufficient information exists to warrant a listing proposal, but the proposal is precluded by other, higher-priority listing actions. The deferral was allowed only if the agencies were making "expeditious progress" on other listings:

> [T]he Secretary must determine and present evidence that he is, in fact, making expeditious progress in the process of listing and delisting other species. . . . In cases challenging the Secretary's claim of inability to propose an otherwise warranted petitioned action, the court will, in essence, be called on to separate justifications grounded in the purposes of the Act from the foot-dragging efforts of a delinquent agency. (U.S. Congress 1982a)

Congress also required that listing decisions be based "solely" on the best scientific and commercial information, thus banning the Reagan administration's economic reviews.

The amendments increased the mean listing rate to forty species per year in Period Two. Nonetheless, the listing rate remained well below that needed to address the large backlog of at-risk species. Most of the more than three thousand species on the candidate list were not reviewed for listing, and most petitions resulted in "warranted but precluded" findings rather than listings. The use of this loophole was not challenged; indeed, there were very few lawsuits filed by NGOs during this period. In essence, Period Two shows how the agencies implement congressional reforms in the absence of NGO enforcement: the listing rate increased but remained low—well under that required by law.

In 1990, the USFWS listing program was again audited, this time by the Interior Department's inspector general. The conclusions were much the same as the 1979 GAO investigation:

> Timely progress has not been made toward officially listing and protecting endangered and threatened plant and animal species. . . . During the last 10 years, at least 34 animal and plant species have been determined to be extinct without ever having received the full benefit of the Act's protection, and those species currently known to merit protection, as well as those candidate species eventually determined to need protection, are similarly in jeopardy of extinction. (U.S. Department of the Interior Inspector General 1990, 5)

To overcome these deficiencies, the inspector general recommended "en masse" listing of all species known to be imperiled, maximum use of multiple-species listing packages, and a large increase in funding for the listing program. He also urged the development of a "national plan to prioritize and survey all candidate species on which conclusive knowledge is lacking" and the immediate listing of those species that are determined to be imperiled. The inspector general's report is striking because it expresses an urgency that we find entirely lacking in the agency. It recommends not just better, more efficient work, but dramatic action to increase the listing rate by orders of magnitude. Perhaps the most important phrase in the report, however, was the conclusion that the "length of time to list and protect endangered species is not indicative of the 'expeditious progress' specified in the Act."

Period Three—1991–95

In this period, NGOs begin to rigorously enforce the 1982 amendments. Beginning in 1991, the number of species listed increased dramatically (an average of seventy-three species per year, SD = 39.9, contrast after ANOVA F1, 27 = 8.28, P = 0.008) (fig. 5.1). This increase occurred despite a twelve-month listing moratorium in 1995–96. A primary factor in this change was a series of lawsuits that forced the agency to move more quickly on listing the backlog of candidate species. Prior to 1991, only eight species were listed due to lawsuits—and six of those occurred in 1990. From 1991 to 1995, however, 237 species were listed following litigation. The upsurge in litigation was largely driven by three lawsuits, which covered 89 percent of all species listed following litigation (*California Native Plant Society v. Lujan* 1991; *Conservation Council for Hawaii v. Lujan* 1990; *Fund for Animals v. Lujan* 1992). These species had been determined to warrant listing, but the agency had failed to do so. Many other suits were filed to list individual or groups of species. According to our data, during this period 66 percent of all species were listed following lawsuits; overall, 39 percent of all species listed from 1974 to 2003 were listed as a result of litigation.

The NGOs multiple-species suits and detailed settlement agreements advanced the multispecies approach recommended by the inspector general. Indeed, the director of USFWS specified that "ecosystem clusters" of species be listed in single rules to comply with the terms of the Hawaiian plant litigation (USFWS 1990a). Greater numbers of multispecies rules were issued and more species were listed in such rules from 1991 to 1995 than in any previous period. The years in which the most species were listed were significantly correlated with years in which the greatest proportion of species were listed in multispecies rules (p = 0.0012, R = .58).

Following the peak listing year in the history of the ESA, the Republican-dominated Congress of 1994 placed a twelve-month moratorium on the listing program from April 1995 to April 1996. Although the USFWS has asserted that the moratorium "caused" a backlog of endangered species listing (USFWS 1999c), the backlog existed for many years prior to the moratorium. The moratorium, however, has had a profound political effect. In 1995, Secretary of the Interior Bruce Babbitt stated that he would not have approved the legal settlements of the early 1990s that led to the tremendous increase in listings (*Wall Street Journal* 1995). To slow the listing process, he developed a series of administrative policies that eliminated the primary stimulus of listing: NGO participation in the listing process (USFWS 1995a).

Period Four—1996–2004

In this period, administrative policies were adopted to limit petitions and lawsuits that had been successfully used to increase listings. Period Three had the greatest annual listing rate in the history of the ESA in part because NGOs went to court to enforce the timelines established by the 1982 amendments. To stop the flood of listings, the Interior Department needed to stop the actions that produced justifiable deadlines. As noted, there are two paths to listing. On the petition pathway, a petition is submitted and must be processed according to legally enforceable timelines; on the discretionary pathway, the agency may issue a proposed listing rule at its own discretion, but the final rule must be finalized within twelve months. Interior's strategy was to eliminate the petition pathway and use its discretion not to initiate listings along the discretionary pathway.

In 1995, Interior issued a policy prohibiting petitions to list species that were included on the candidate list (USFWS 1995a). The policy asserted that listing a species as a candidate was equivalent to a "warranted but precluded" finding in response to a petition. A petition to list a candidate species is, therefore, by definition a "second" petition, and as such did not have to be processed under the statutory timetables. The policy not only shielded existing candidate species from the petition pathway but also encouraged the agency to head off petitions in progress by moving the species onto the candidate list:

> If petitioned, the Service would have to consider listing the sage grouse and within a year would make a finding on a listing decision. . . . [T]he Service decided that placing the Gunnison sage grouse on candidate list now is the best option. Placement of the Gunnison sage grouse on the candidate list now will likely allow for continuation of the working groups as they are currently operating for several years. In contrast, if we receive a petition, legal charges may result in a threatened or endangered listing in the near future. . . . If any petitions are received after Director approval of the candidate form, they will be treated as a second petition, which does not initiate the standard petition process by the Service. (USFWS 2000b)

Although the policy nullified many petitions, there were still many imperiled noncandidates that could be petitioned. To address these, the USFWS employed a previously little-used statutory provision that permitted the agency to delay issuing initial findings (i.e., the ninety-day findings) on petitions if it was "not practicable" to do so. Beginning in 1997, the USFWS routinely issued "not practicable" findings to avoid the otherwise-applicable listing deadlines. In 1996, for example, the agencies listed thirty-one petitioned species without having to be sued. From 1997 to 2003, however, they listed a total of only six petitioned species. With few listing petitions being accepted, few enforceable deadlines were established, and few new lawsuits could be filed.

The Clinton and Bush administrations also dramatically reduced the number of species listed at the agencies' discretion. In 1996, the agencies listed forty species through this pathway. Between 1997 and 2003, they listed eleven species, ten of which occurred in 1997 and 1998.

The impact of these policies was dramatic. Of the 232 listings during Period Four, all but 24 were driven by petitions, proposals, and lawsuits initiated prior to the 1996 policies; 11 listings were initiated by the agency, 9 of which were part of a single negotiated settlement (*Center for Biological Diversity v. Norton* 2001); 4 others were subject to individual lawsuits. With the USFWS listing few species on its own and most petitions being rejected as duplicitous or delayed, the annual listing rate steadily declined as the backlog of court orders, listing proposals, and petitions was slowly processed.

Although the USFWS has suggested that NGO involvement needs to be eliminated in order to implement its own listing priorities, the empirical record demonstrates that agency-initiated listings decreased after the policies were issued. With both listing pathways blocked, the annual listing rate declined dramatically in Period Four after having reached a historic high in Period Three.

After 1999, an increase in critical habitat designations also contributed to the declining listing rate by absorbing a significant portion of the listing/critical habitat designation budget. The listing rate had, however, already been declining steadily between 1994 and 1999. The increase in critical habitat designations only contributed to an existing trend.[3]

It is also important to note that the increased workload created by critical habitat designation is only a problem if the budget is not increased in relation to the new workload. The Department of the Interior, however, not only failed to request sufficient funds from Congress to keep up with its workload but in 1998 also requested that Congress legislatively limit the amount of money available for listing and critical habitat decisions. That cap has been renewed at the request of the secretary of the interior in every year from 1999 to 2004 (OMB 2003).

Trends in the Annual Listing Rate

This history demonstrates the impact of regulation, administrative policies, petitions, and lawsuits on the listing rate. One of the primary ways these factors influence the listing rate is by lengthening or shortening the time required to list a species. President Reagan's 1981 executive order, for example, lengthened the time and delayed listing of species. Petitions and lawsuits, on the other hand, increase the rate of listing by forcing agency action. Because of the importance of listing delays in determining the rate of species listings and, ultimately, how many species receive protection, the following discussion details factors that cause listing delays and demonstrates that the 1982 amendments reduced listing delays.

The majority of species listed today experienced substantial delays in the listing process. On average, the agencies took nearly eleven years to list species (fig. 5.2). Such delays have important consequences for species conservation, reducing the likelihood of recovery by allowing continued population decline or further loss of habitat. Often by the time species are listed, their populations are near extinction: "Early intervention is critical to the success of endangered species recovery efforts. Yet our analysis indicates that most species, subspecies, and populations protected under the Endangered Species Act are not receiving that protection until their total population size and number of populations are critically low" (Wilcove et al. 1993). Waiting until species are on the brink of extinction increases the eventual cost of recovery and in some cases may even

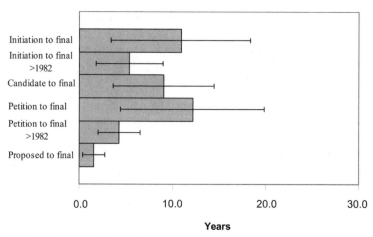

Figure 5.2. Mean time to listing from various starting points. Error bars show one standard deviation.

lead to extinction. The U.S. Department of the Interior Inspector General (1990) documented that at least thirty-four species went extinct waiting for protection from 1980 to 1990, and Ando (1999) documented that the longer listing is delayed, the less likely it is that a species will be listed.

The GAO (1993) examined the specific factors delaying the listing of six species and found that uncertainty about the status of the species and concern over the economic and other impacts of listing were the primary contributing factors. Ando (1999) found that both opposing public comments and the presence of a legislator on one of the committees charged with authorizing or funding the ESA who opposed the listing significantly slowed time to listing (see also DeShazo and Freeman, this volume). Ando (1999, 48) concluded, "Public pressure, whether direct or indirect, can have big effects on bureaucratic delay, and those effects can translate into nontrivial changes in the likelihood that a species is thwarted completely from being proposed for listing."

The effect of political opposition on listing delays is also supported by statements from agency officials. One former listing biologist with the USFWS, for example, concluded, "The Department of Interior consistently missed statutory deadlines for listing and deliberately allowed politics to influence listing decisions. . . . Listing species has been a controversial process for a long time. When I was writing proposed and final listing decisions in the early 1980s, U.S. Fish and Wildlife administrators rarely were interested in the biology of species, only the political repercussions of a proposed listing" (Sidle 1998).

One means of countering the effects of outside political pressure is to reduce agency capacity for delay through mandatory timelines and outside enforcement. Congress did just this in 1982, adding mandatory listing timelines in response to petitions and a citizen suit provision. These statutory requirements were effective in reducing delay. The USFWS took an average of 13.8 years (SD = 7.5) to list species prior to 1983, but only 4.3 years (SD = 2.2) after 1982 ($p < 0.001$). Moreover, species for which a petition was filed after 1982 (petition pathway) were listed in less time (4.3 years, s = 2.2) than species where listing was initiated by the agencies (the discretionary pathway) after 1982, for which there are no timelines (5.0 years, s = 3.6, $p = 0.011$).

Lawsuits also reduced listing delays. In the absence of litigation, the USFWS took an average of 7.1 years (SD = 5.9) to propose species for listing after initiation. Following a lawsuit, however, a proposed rule was issued in an average of 2.4 years (SD = 1.9, $p = 0.004$). Similarly, it took the agency an average of 1.4 years (SD = 1.1) to list species after issuance of a proposed rule in the absence of a lawsuit, but only 0.7 years (SD = 0.5, $p < 0.001$) following filing of litigation. Thus, both the statutory timelines enacted in 1982 and lawsuits reduced listing delays. The findings also demonstrate that legal mandates are an effective means to force action in the face of political opposition.

Trends in Program Funding

Lack of funding is frequently cited as a cause for listing delays by officials in the Department of the Interior (USFWS 2003b), and indeed both the GAO (1979) and Interior's Inspector General (1990) observed that lack of resources was a perennial problem for the listing program. The lack of funding, however, is not simply a function of resource scarcity or congressional unwillingness to fund the listing program; rather, it reflects the low priority placed on listing species by the Department of the Interior. The Inspector General (1990) estimated that $144 million was necessary to address listing backlogs. More recently, the USFWS estimated that $153 million was necessary (Frazer 2003). Despite the clear need for more money, however, Interior has typically asked for less than $9 million per year for listing; in fiscal years 1998–2003, it asked Congress to cap spending on listing.

Congress has appropriated an average of 97 percent of the amount requested by the Department of the Interior from 1979 to 2003. In ten of the last nineteen years (including 2002 and 2003) Congress appropriated 100 percent or more of what was requested (fig. 5.3). At the request of Interior, Congress has also dramatically increased funding for other ESA programs such as consultation (up 1,791 percent since 1983) and recovery (up 1,240 percent since 1983). In contrast, the listing budget has increased only slightly and if adjusted for inflation is nearly flat (fig. 5.4) (see also Scott, Goble, et al., this volume). As a result, the listing budget has declined from 18 to 22 percent of the budget in the mid-1980s to 3 percent of the budget in 2002.

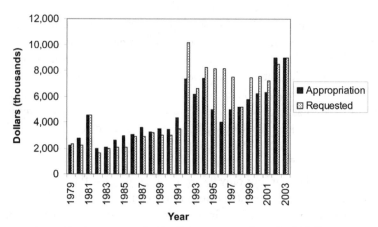

Figure 5.3. Annual budget requests for the listing program from the U.S. Department of the Interior compared to annual budget appropriations from Congress.

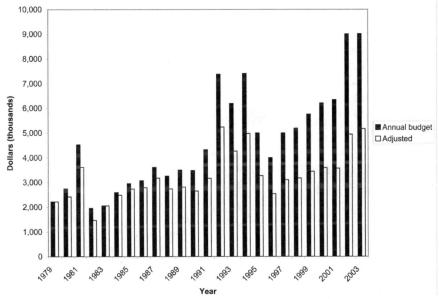

Figure 5.4. Annual listing budget, 1979–2002: unadjusted and adjusted for inflation to 1979 dollars.

Trends in the Taxonomy of Listed Species

Many factors that influence listing also influence the types of species that are listed. Species that are perceived to have less value to society, such as invertebrates or plants, often engender greater opposition. Over the history of the ESA, such opposition has translated into administrative policies and practices that favor some groups of species over others.

When it enacted the ESA, Congress required the USFWS to review all vertebrate animals that had been listed under the earlier Endangered Species Preservation Act and the Endangered Species Conservation Act. The agency retained 131 vertebrate species on the new list. Although the ESA allowed listing of plants and invertebrates, the USFWS was slow to do so, and the list of threatened and endangered species therefore retained an imbalance toward vertebrate animals for much of its history (Kareiva et al., this volume; Scott, Goble, et al., this volume). By the end of the 1970s, the USFWS had listed just thirty-nine invertebrates and fifty-seven plants (fig. 5.5).

The agency has often been hesitant to list "lower" life forms, particularly if protection of the species conflicted with federal projects (GAO 1979). In 1981, the Reagan administration proposed a priority system that favored "higher life forms" over other species, prioritizing vertebrate animals and vascular plants over invertebrates and nonvascular plants (Tobin 1990). Although the proposal

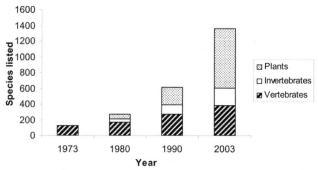

Figure 5.5. Number of plants, invertebrates, and vertebrates listed by years: 1973, 1980, 1990, and 2003.

was never finalized, only twenty-seven invertebrates were listed during the eight years of the Reagan presidency—suggesting that the USFWS carried the policy forward informally.

Plants did make large gains during the 1990s in large part because of litigation. The three suits previously noted, for example, resulted in proposed listing of 381 plants. Petitioners also focused on plants; 68 percent of species listed following petitions were plants. In contrast, only 10 percent of species listed solely by the agencies were plants. Lawsuits and petitions thus helped to correct the historic imbalance in the list toward vertebrate animals. According to Nature-Serve, plants comprise 51 percent of known critically imperiled and imperiled species; plants today comprise a comparable 55 percent of all U.S. listed species.

In contrast, however, invertebrates remain severely underrepresented on the threatened and endangered lists. This group of species comprises only 16 percent of all threatened or endangered species, compared to 37 percent of all imperiled or critically imperiled species recognized by NatureServe (2003).

An analysis of listing delays found that plants experienced significantly longer delays than other species ($p < 0.001$), primarily because the Smithsonian plants experienced such long delays in obtaining protection. We did not find significant differences between groups of animals in time to listing, suggesting that although agencies exhibited bias in the number of invertebrate species listed, they did not overly delay those that did make it onto the list. These findings, however, must be tempered by the fact that we did not include the many species petitioned or otherwise considered for listing that were never listed. Invariably, such a list would be heavily weighted toward plants and invertebrates and would thus greatly increase estimates of delay.

Conclusion and Recommendations

In summary, the U.S. Fish and Wildlife Service has failed to list thousands of at-risk species and has exhibited bias in the species that it has listed. These problems stem from the agency's timidity in the face of political opposition and its chronic failure to request sufficient resources to list all species recognized to be in need of protection. The listing program has proven vulnerable to changes in administrative policies, such as those enacted by the Reagan administration in 1981 and the Clinton administration in 1996. Improvements in the listing rate were correlated with enactment of statutory mandates governing processing of petitions to list species and later enforcement of these mandates through litigation, indicating that strict enforcement is necessary to improve the listing rate. Based on these results, we recommend the following:

- Given the failure of the USFWS to list species in a timely manner, establish an independent scientific body, possibly under the National Academy of Sciences, to prepare listing rules for all imperiled and critically imperiled species recognized by NatureServe. We recommend that these species be listed en masse.
- If the agencies retain control over listing of species, provide them with sufficient funds and staffing to list all candidate species; in the next five years they should be given sufficient funds to list all imperiled and critically imperiled species.
- Strengthen existing regulations to include timelines for agency-initiated species as well as petitioned species.
- Remove the ability of the agencies to declare species "warranted but precluded."

6 Congressional Politics

J. R. DeShazo and Jody Freeman

The Endangered Species Act (ESA) specifies that its central decisions are to be made "solely on the basis of the best scientific . . . data available" (ESA sec. 4(b)(1)(A)). Our study demonstrates, however, that members of Congress use their positions on oversight and appropriations committees to prevent the U.S. Fish and Wildlife Service (USFWS) from complying with the specific provisions of the ESA (DeShazo and Freeman 2003). Listing and funding decisions are influenced to a greater extent by a member's "institutional identities"—party affiliation, committee jurisdiction, and chamber—than by the act's evidentiary requirements.

Moreover, when these institutional identities are combined, their cumulative impact is even more dramatic, strongly influencing the likelihood a species will be listed and how much money will be allocated for its recovery. These combined institutional identities are political considerations that have nothing to do with a species' endangerment ranking or its genetic uniqueness, which are the statutory criteria most relevant to whether species should be listed. The agency's attentiveness to member influence, therefore, contradicts the statute, which requires that science be determinative.

We also find that different committees may affect different aspects of USFWS decision making. Members on the appropriations committee affect USFWS spending decisions more than do oversight committee members. Conversely, oversight members affect the USFWS species listing decisions far more often than do members on the appropriations committee. Our results are striking given the clear choices made in the statute that political considerations should not count. And yet they do: extinction may turn on the preferences of members of oversight committees, not on the criteria established by law.

To make this point more concrete, imagine for a moment that you are an endangered species. The best-case scenario for your survival and recovery would be that your geographic range falls within states with exclusively Democratic representation; that your elected members of Congress—especially your

68

senators—sit on committees with oversight and appropriations authority over the implementation of the ESA; and that you are a mammal (or at least not a mollusk, arachnid, or reptile). As it turns out, who you are matters, but who you know—who represents you on committees—might matter more.

Of course, there is room for discretionary judgment—we do not claim that Congress makes the listing decision mechanically. We merely assert that by mandating that scientific criteria determine listing and funding, and by clarifying this mandate over time, Congress has ruled out political considerations—such as the number of representatives on oversight committees with species in their districts, or party affiliation of those members, or whether those members sit on a House versus a Senate committee—as determinants of agency decision making. We believe that in its preference for scientifically grounded listing decisions, the ESA is unusually clear.

Oversight measures do in fact affect listing decisions (table 6.1). As Democratic representation on oversight committees goes up, so does the statistical chance of species being listed. As Republican representation goes up, the chance of listing declines. For those species with one or more representatives, Democratic representation is associated with 37 percent of all organisms being listed as species while Republican representation is associated with only 26 percent of all organisms being listed as species—a statistically significant differ-

TABLE 6.I. Percentage of organisms listed as a subspecies by number of committee members who are Republican or Democrat[a]

No. of members	Democratic representation		Republican representation	
	Listed as subspecies (%)	No. of organisms	Listed as subspecies (%)	No. of organisms
0	17[b]	523	25	694
1	34	233	28	142
2	47	89	23	22
3+	28	40	15	27

[a]When species listed with one or more representatives are compared, Democratic representation is associated with a higher percentage of subspecies listings (37 percent), while the Republican representation is associated with a lower percentage (26 percent); this is a significant difference at the 5 percent level.

[b]Comparing species listed with no representation to those with one or more representatives shows that under Republican representation, there is no statistical difference in the percentage listed as subspecies ($Z = 0.67$; for a more rigorous test of this hypothesis, see table 6.2.); under Democratic representation, however, there is a significant increase in the percentage listed as subspecies ($Z = 3.93$).

TABLE 6.2. Total expenditure (in $1,000s) for listed species between 1989 and 1993 by number of committee members who are Republican or Democrat[a]

No. of members	Democratic representation ($)	No. of species	Republican representation ($)	No. of species
0	207[b]	523	356	694
1	962	233	2,138	142
2	1,710	89	1,826	22
3+	10,015	40	10,899	27

[a]When species listed with one or more representatives are compared, Democratic representation is associated with lower per-species spending ($2,146), while Republicans are associated with higher per-species spending ($3,341); this is a significant difference at the 1 percent level.

[b]When species listed with no representation are compared to those with one or more representatives, both Democratic and Republican representation are associated with significantly higher average spending at the 1 percent level.

ence. These data suggest that more Democrats than Republicans supported USFWS's discretion to list species.

In addition, funding levels rise with greater geographic representation by either party (table 6.2). The more members a listed species can claim as "its" representatives, the more money the appropriations committee allocates for its recovery. This is true regardless of party affiliation; everyone, it seems, wants to appropriate funds (see Kareiva et al., this volume). While such a result might seem surprising in light of Republican opposition to listing in the first place, upon closer analysis, bipartisan enthusiasm for funding makes perfect sense. Money appropriated for species recovery funnels substantial resources into the locations that constitute the listed species' range, especially when critical habitat is in danger. Not only do expenditures on a species go toward "pure" recovery efforts but also they are likely to be perceived by committee members as reducing compliance costs, both economically and politically, at the local level.

For example, species perceived by the USFWS as being in conflict with development are allotted by Congress a relatively larger share of financial resources. A portion of this money directly funds consultation and planning with local landowners, which may reduce the political opposition and transaction costs associated with recovery efforts. State agencies might also receive federal allocations in the form of matching grants that can be spent broadly on habitat conservation. This money can help private landowners significantly defray the costs associated with implementing recovery plans. Federal appropriations thus help to minimize the overall direct cost to landowners of the initial listing decision. Finally, funding that successfully helps to move a species toward recovery can produce two valuable political benefits: the elected member can claim credit for progress, and, if the species recovers sufficiently, the USFWS might delist it and free the affected lands of restrictions.

Our results would suggest that a senator or representative's institutional identities largely determine his or her relative influence over ESA implementation. Together, these political considerations strongly affect the fate of endangered species.

We did find some support for the claim of a "charismatic mega-fauna" bias explains USFWS noncompliance with the statutorily required priority system. Our data, however, go further, supporting our claim that an internal competition exists among rival congressional principals for control of delegated power. As it turns out, the USFWS is not acting on its own when it deviates from statutory criteria. Rather, the agency's listing and resource allocation decisions respond to legislative principals whose preferences simply contradict what the enacting majority intended when it passed (or reauthorized) the law.

Part II Achieving On-the-Ground Conservation

Numbers are not the sole metric by which to evaluate the Endangered Species Act. Recovery of at-risk species is a complex process that seeks to reverse decades or centuries of decline. How well does the act work in the variety of habitats that characterize modern America? How well does it facilitate the interaction of the various potential actors—federal, state, and local government agencies, tribes, private landowners, and nongovernmental organizations? The chapters in part 2 examine the utility of available conservation tools such as habitat conservation plans and the experiences of a diverse group of stakeholders.

7 Critical Habitat and Recovery

Kieran F. Suckling and Martin Taylor

The Endangered Species Act (ESA) has three fundamental goals: to prevent the extinction of imperiled species, to secure their eventual recovery, and to protect the ecosystems upon which those species depend. As a survival tool, it has been very successful. Only 22 of 1,370 species have become extinct after being listed (Suckling et al. 2004), while 227 would have been expected to become extinct (Scott, Goble, et al., this volume).

The recovery record is less impressive. Just fifteen species have recovered and been removed from the list.[1] Although the short time most species have been listed makes any expectation of hundreds of recoveries unrealistic (see Doremus and Pagel 2001), few would disagree that more species should have been recovered. This slow recovery rate is significantly influenced by a tendency on the part of agencies to manage for minimum viable populations rather than recovery. For example, the National Marine Fisheries Service (NMFS) explained its decision to cease considering the removal of four salmon-threatening dams on the Snake River by saying, "The Endangered Species Act does not mandate recovery, it mandates a recovery plan. That's different from recovery" (Clarren 2004).

Ecosystem protection also lags. Although difficult to quantify, it is notable that most of the fourteen recovered species were primarily threatened by hunting, pollution, or exotic species. Thus, although habitat loss is the primary cause of imperilment (Wilcove et al. 1998), recovery efforts have been most successful at recovering nonhabitat threatened species.

The ESA's success in preventing extinctions is linked to the act's language clearly forbidding extinction. Recovery and ecosystem protection do not enjoy such clear marching orders. Although recovery is listed as the goal of the ESA, it is a goal without specific legal requirements. Similarly, federal agencies are admonished to recover species, but the language is so broadly cast that several decades of case law have not resulted in a clear standard (Bean and Rowland 1997).

Congress understood that stemming habitat loss would not be easy: the "most significant [threat to endangered species] has proven also to be the most difficult to control: the destruction of critical habitat" (U.S. Congress 1973). It thus required that critical habitat be designated for species (with some exceptions) and managed for the species' recovery. Critical habitat would shift focus from species to the habitat upon which they depend:

> It is the Committee's view that classifying a species as endangered or threatened is only the first step in insuring its survival. . . . If the protection of endangered and threatened species depends in large measure on the preservation of the species' habitat, then the ultimate effectiveness of the Endangered Species Act will depend on the designation of critical habitat. (U.S. Congress 1976, 3)

Initially, the implementing agencies embraced the concept of critical habitat as a tool for saving imperiled species. In 1977, for instance, Jimmy Carter issued a presidential directive requiring all federal agencies to identify in "the shortest possible time" those lands under their control that should be designated as critical habitat (Carter 1977). By early 1978, the U.S. Fish and Wildlife Service (USFWS) and the National Marine Fisheries Service had developed a prioritized list of 190 critical habitats to be designated (USFWS and NMFS 1978). The program was never carried out. Twenty-six years later, critical habitat has been designated for only sixteen of these species, four of them under court order. The highest priority had been assigned to forty-one species facing "imminent threats which will essentially destroy all or a major part of their habitat. Extinction is likely in the immediate future.²" (USFWS and NMFS 1978) Only five of these species received critical habitat. Seven of the remaining thirty-six are extinct, two are possibly extinct, and two are probably extirpated from the wild (Center for Biological Diversity 2004).

As of January 1, 2000, critical habitat had been designated for only 10 percent of listed species (Center for Biological Diversity 2004). Due to litigation, the percentage climbed to 37 percent by August 23, 2005. Rather than celebrate the revival of the program, the Department of the Interior opposed every designation and drafted a lengthy "disclaimer" that appears in every critical habitat proposal, designation, and press release. The disclaimer states that critical habitat is wholly redundant to other protections and that "in 30 years of implementing the ESA, the [Fish and Wildlife] Service has found that the designation of statutory critical habitat provides little additional protection to most listed species" (U.S. Department of the Interior 2003).

The Interior Department cites no scientific studies to support its surprising claims. In response to a Freedom of Information Act request, it acknowledged possessing no evidence (U.S. Department of the Interior 2004). The lack of empirical support was emphasized by a USFWS review of an unpublished study demonstrating a positive correlation between species' recovery trends and presence of critical habitat:

> I think the authors are dead-on correct to criticize the DOI and/or current administration for drawing conclusions regarding the value or lack thereof of critical habitat designations without any real data or science to back up such conclusions. As flawed as the authors' approach might be, they have more science behind their position than DOI and/or current administration has behind theirs. (Skorupa 2003)

The Interior Department position lacks empirical support because it is a legal theory, not a factual conclusion. At best, it states what critical habitat *should* do, but says nothing about what it *has* done.

This chapter reviews the Interior Department's legal theory, showing that it has been rejected by numerous federal courts. It also reviews case studies demonstrating that critical habitat improves habitat management through a diverse array of mechanisms. Finally, it concludes with a statistical analysis of USFWS data on 1,049 species showing a strong correlation between positive recovery trends and presence of critical habitat.

Legal Analysis

The Interior Department argues that critical habitat "does not result in any benefit to the species that is not already afforded by the protections" in other provisions of the Endangered Species Act (U.S. Department of the Interior 2003). The agency's argument relies primarily upon the statutory prohibition against jeopardizing species' existence or taking an endangered species.

Jeopardy and Adverse Modification

Section 7 of the ESA prohibits federal agencies from authorizing, funding, or carrying out actions likely to "jeopardize the continued existence of any [listed] species or result in the destruction or adverse modification" of critical habitat (ESA sec. 7(a)(2)). Although state and private parties are not directly regulated by these prohibitions, they do, nonetheless, apply to many state and private lands due to the broad scope of federal permitting (authorizing) process. Most large-scale land modification projects, for example, require a federal Clean Water Act permit and thus are also subject to the standard. Similarly, the issuance of a section 10 incidental take permit is a federal action, ensuring that all habitat conservation plans come under the adverse modification standard.

Jeopardy is the outer limit of permissible action under the ESA. Interior has used this to make the argument that critical habitat does not provide additional protection not available via the jeopardy prohibition. This assertion faces two obvious hurdles. First, the ESA has separate jeopardy and critical habitat standards. Interior argues, however, that in creating the ESA in 1973 and amending it in 1978, Congress did not intend to establish different standards (U.S. Department of the Interior and U.S. Department of Commerce 1986). Second, the assertion is plainly contrary to other portions of the ESA. The ESA defines critical habitat as all lands, air, or water "essential to the conservation of the species" (ESA sec. 3(5)(A)). "Conservation" is defined as all the actions necessary to recover and delist species (ESA sec. 3(3)).

By citing its own regulations, the Interior Department justifies conflating the ESA's distinction between protections aimed at recovering species and those that seek merely to prevent extinction. The ESA does not define either "jeopardy" or "adverse modification." In 1986, the Reagan administration defined the latter as an "alteration that appreciably diminishes the value of critical habitat for both the survival and recovery of a listed species" (U.S. Department of the Interior and U.S. Department of Commerce 1986). "Jeopardy" was defined to mean "reduc[ing] appreciably the likelihood of both the survival and recovery of a listed species in the wild" (U.S. Department of the Interior and U.S. Department of Commerce 1986). Having defined both terms in identical language, Interior asserts that critical habitat is redundant to the jeopardy protection. The Interior Department's argument is fundamentally circular: "it doesn't protect species because we refuse to protect critical habitat."

The argument is also contrary to the agency's prior practice. Throughout the 1970s, the Interior Department managed critical habitat under a standard that did not allow federal agencies to appreciably reduce the capacity of critical habitats to support recovery of endangered species. (USFWS and NMFS 1975; USFWS 1976; U.S. Department of the Interior 1978). The 1986 Reagan regulation changed course dramatically.[3] The regulation's conflation of critical habitat and jeopardy eliminated the recovery standard from critical habitat. To adversely modify critical habitat, it was henceforth necessary to appreciably reduce a critical habitat's ability to support "both the survival and recovery of a listed species"; injury to recovery potential alone was no longer adverse modification (U.S. Department of the Interior and U.S. Department of Commerce 1986). Lest there be any confusion, the administration explained that

> the word "both" was added by the proposed rule to emphasize that, except in exceptional circumstances, injury to recovery alone would not warrant the issuance of a "jeopardy" biological opinion. . . . [Several commenters] argued that injury to recovery for an already depleted species would require the issuance of a jeopardy opinion. They also remarked that the Service's position disregarded the conservation

requirements of the Act, failed to adequately protect critical habitat, operated to weaken or nullify recovery efforts. . . . These commenters misconstrued the Service's role in conducting consultations. . . . [C]onsultation is to identify conflicts between proposed Federal actions and the "jeopardy" standard of section 7(a)(2). The "continued existence" of the species is the key to the jeopardy standard, placing an emphasis on injury to a species' "survival." . . . There can be no doubt that Congress considered the jeopardy standard of section 7(a)(2) as being the substantive cornerstone of section 7. . . . The commenters' argument would require Federal actions to halt if they failed to conserve listed species, a result clearly not intended by Congress. (U.S. Department of the Interior and U.S. Department of Commerce 1986)

This remarkable passage may have done more to undermine species recovery than any other legislative or regulatory action of the past thirty years. It allows federal agencies to continue reducing endangered species' populations and habitats, even if doing so appreciably diminishes the species' ability to recover. Indeed, it prohibits the USFWS and NMFS from stopping them.

Most legal scholars (e.g., Darrin 2000; Hicks 2000; Armstrong 2002; Senatore et al. 2003) opine that the Interior Department regulation is illegal and its arguments specious. The judiciary agrees. Between 1998 and 2004, at least eight courts (including three different circuit courts of appeals) judged the regulation illegal. Two struck it down. None upheld it. In the most recent appeals court decision, the Ninth U.S. Circuit Court of Appeals stated: "This can not be right. If the [USFWS] follows its own regulation, then it is obligated to be indifferent to, if not to ignore, the recovery goal of critical habitat" (*Gifford Pinchot Task Force v. United States Fish and Wildlife Service* 2004).

The Interior Department's assertions notwithstanding, critical habitat establishes a higher protective standard than is available to species without critical habitat. The higher standard prohibits federal agencies from undermining recovery when critical habitat is present. As one federal court succinctly stated: "Critical habitat is the area 'essential' for 'conservation' of listed species. Conservation means more than survival; it means recovery. . . . [T]he proper definition of 'destruction or adverse modification' is: 'a direct or indirect alteration of critical habitat which appreciably diminishes the value of that habitat for either the survival or the recovery of a listed species'" (*Center for Biological Diversity v. Bureau of Land Management* 2004).

Take and Critical Habitat

Section 9 prohibits "take" of any endangered species; "take" is defined to include "harm" (ESA sec. 3(18)). Although this gives the definition an expansive reach, it is nonetheless less protective than critical habitat because critical habitat directly protects habitat regardless of the presence of the listed species. The take provision, on the other hand, only applies to actions that actually impact individual animals. Although habitat destruction can in some instances qualify as take, it does so only if it is likely to harm animals present at the location (*Babbitt v. Sweet Home* 1995). The destruction of unoccupied habitat, even if it limits or precludes recovery, is not take because an individual cannot be harmed if it is not present (*Arizona Cattle Growers Association v. U.S. Fish and Wildlife Service* 2001; *Defenders of Wildlife v. Bernal* 2000). Even if an animal is present and likely to be affected by the habitat loss, further proof of harm is necessary to establish a taking (*United States v. West Coast Forest Resources Limited Partnership* 2000).

Critical habitat also differs in the level of protection it provides. Although the act prohibits adverse modification of critical habitat, it does not prohibit take; it only regulates it. All parties are permitted to take endangered species as long as they do not jeopardize the species' survival (ESA secs. 7(a)(2), 10(a)(2)(B)). Nonfederal parties have an additional requirement to "minimize and mitigate [take to] the maximum extent practicable" (ESA sec. 10(a)(2)(B)). But actions that degrade important habitat or cause population declines are permitted as long as the species is not jeopardized. For example, the USFWS asserts that the southwestern willow flycatcher (*Empidonax traillii extimus*) is declining toward jeopardy (USFWS 1997), yet it authorized the take of approximately 25 percent of all birds because the jeopardy threshold had not been reached. This prompted a USFWS biologist to complain that "the southwestern willow flycatcher is being piecemealed to extinction; the [U.S. Fish and Wildlife] service is turning a blind eye to the aggregate effects of its own consultation process" (see Greenwald 1998).

Case Studies

Although critical habitat should be managed for recovery to be consistent with the act's goals, it is less clear how it is actually managed. Reviews of critical habitat have generally focused on the language of the act and its implementing regulations. Very few studies have attempted to examine how critical habitat actually works on the ground. And those that have tend to rely almost exclusively on court orders requiring the protection of critical habitat areas (e.g., Paulson 2003). While such orders are important, they provide a very narrow line of sight.

The following case studies illustrate the ways in which critical habitat has improved land management. Some involve the courts and/or section 7 consultation; others are entirely voluntary with little if any involvement by the USFWS or NMFS. These case studies indicate not only that the Interior Department is wrong when it says critical habitat has no legal effect, but that it is also wrong when its says critical habitat has no on-the-ground effect. Perhaps most important, it is wrong when it characterizes critical habitat as an exclusively regulatory tool whose only role is to operate within the confines of section 7 consultation. Like regulation of take, prohibition of jeopardy and recovery plans, critical habitat is a broad conservation tool that has been implemented in diverse ways.

Voluntary Protection

The designation of critical habitats does not in itself establish a preserve or specify management actions. Those decisions are left to land managers. In subsequent sections, we describe how the USFWS and courts have used the regulatory power of critical habitat to impose management regimes advocated by agency biologists but stalled by higher-level decision makers. Most of these cases involve the section 7 consultations because consultation is the venue for resolving federal habitat management disputes. But consultation is only one avenue through which critical habitat improves land management. In addition, private and governmental land managers have responded to critical habitat by voluntarily adopting habitat management plans. These actions may be regulatory, but the regulations come from the land manager rather than NMFS or the USFWS. Indeed, NMFS and the USFWS are often completely absent from the process. These actions are invisible if, as Interior Department suggests, we only look for critical habitat effects through the prism of consultation.

For example, the Osgood Mountains milk-vetch (*Astragalus yoder-williamsii*) was emergency listed as an endangered species with critical habitat in August 1980 due to the threatened destruction of the largest remaining population by mining operations (USFWS 1980). The action came at the urging of the U.S. Bureau of Land Management (BLM), which had filed a listing petition in 1979 and in July 1980 warned that "recent changes in ownership of mining claims within the recommended critical habitat" required emergency measures (BLM 1980a). Responding quickly to the designation, BLM informed the USFWS of a series of habitat-protection actions

> by which we feel the critical habitat of the species will receive additional protection. First we are proposing to designate the critical habitat in the Osgood Mountains as an "Area of Critical Environmental Concern" . . . to insure special management attention. . . . However, final designation of an ACEC may be two to three years away. We are therefore proposing . . . the withdrawal of the area of the critical habitat from mining activity [to] insure that the critical habitat would receive protection from mining activities pending ACEC designation. (BLM 1980b)

Because the BLM's permanent protection of the critical habitat area eliminated the primary reason for the species' listing, the USFWS allowed the emergency listing to expire in 1981 since the species was no longer at risk.

Similar agency, private sector, or local government actions to protect critical habitat have taken place with regard to Robbins' cinquefoil (*Potentilla robbinsiana*) (USFWS 2002a), the large-flowered fiddleneck (*Amsinckia grandiflora*) (U.S. Department of Energy 2000), the southwestern willow flycatcher (Van Clothier, pers. comm.), the cactus ferruginous pygmy-owl (*Glaucidium brasilianum cactorum*) (DeBonis 2000), the Borax Lake chub (*Gila boraxobius*) (Williams and Macdonald 2003), and the Plymouth red-bellied turtle (*Pseudemys rubriventris bangsi*) (USFWS 2005).

Consultation Avoidance

In most cases, section 7 consultation occurs because a federal agency proposes to harm a species or its critical habitat. When an agency instead chooses to restore, prohibit, or reduce harm to critical habitat, it rarely consults. Thus, Interior Department's insistence that the value of critical habitat be measured by the number of consultations misses those situations in which critical habitat has proved most effective: when it spurs actions that obviate the need for consultation. Again, case studies demonstrate that federal agencies take action to protect critical habitats in order either to avoid consultation or to ensure the consultation will not result in an adverse modification determination.

The Peninsular bighorn sheep (*Ovis canadensis* pop.) inhabits the arid, lower elevations of the Peninsular Mountain Ranges in Southern California. It has declined dramatically due to habitat loss, disease, predation, and disturbance. Domestic sheep grazing is a factor in all of these threats. It was listed as an endangered species in 1998, and 844,897 acres of critical habitat were designated in 2001 (USFWS 2001c).

Conservationists sued the U.S. Forest Service (USFS) and the BLM for failing to consult over impacts to the bighorn and other listed species (*Center for Biological Diversity v. Sprague* 1998). A settlement was reached requiring the Forest Service to consult and to prohibit sheep grazing on all critical habitat under its jurisdiction. Responding to complaints from the permittee, the Forest Service explained that "[t]he closure of a portion of the allotment is a direct result of the settlement agreement and the designation of Bighorn sheep habitat by the U.S. Fish and Wildlife Service" (USFS 2001). Sheep grazing was allowed to continue on portions of the allotment outside critical habitat. A similar agreement was reached requiring the BLM to consult and to prohibit sheep grazing on all 34,850 acres of critical habitat within its jurisdiction. Grazing was allowed to continue on the portions of the allotments outside the critical habitat. Both agencies also agreed to conservation measures to eliminate or pro-hibit other actions that would adversely modify critical habitat (BLM 2001). With these measures in place, neither the BLM nor the Forest Service consulted on these aspects of critical habitat management when they did eventually enter into consultation with the USFWS over the programmatic effects of their land management plans on multiple endangered species.

The difference between the presence and absence of designated habitat is starkly demonstrated in a case involving the southwestern willow flycatcher and two fish—the loach minnow (*Tiaroga cobitis*) and spikedace (*Meda fulgida*). The lawsuits claimed that the Forest Service had failed to consult over the impact of 160 grazing allotments in the Gila River basin (*Southwest Center for Biological Diversity v. U.S. Forest Service* 1997; *Forest Guardians v. U.S. Forest Service* 1997). A settlement was reached requiring the Forest Service to consult with the USFWS and remove cattle from virtually all occupied and critical habitat. The agreement and the rapid riparian restoration that followed have been called "one of the largest, if not the largest, single exodus of cattle in the post–Taylor Grazing Act history of federal land management" (Davis 2001), but its benefits were not equally distributed. For the flycatcher, it meant removal of cattle from over two hundred miles of streams within its critical habitat even though most of the area was unoccupied. The loach minnow and spikedace lacked critical habitat, and thus the areas protected centered on iso-lated areas the species still occupied. Due to the presence of critical habitat, the Forest Service agreed to manage the flycatcher for recovery, while the noncriti-cal habitat species were managed only for survival.

Similar effects can be seen in the case of the desert tortoise (*Gopherus agas-sizii* pop.). Before the designation of critical habitat, the BLM chose not to remove cattle from the habitat; after designation, recovery management was required, and BLM agreed to prohibit grazing (USFWS 1994). As a result, sig-nificant portions of the species' recovery plan were finally implemented, but only due to the regulatory link to critical habitat. The sweeping scope of the agreement led a member of the desert tortoise recovery team to state that more had been done to protect the tortoise and its habitat in a single year than in all the years since the species was listed (David Morafka, pers. comm.).

Consultation

If federal agencies choose to conduct actions that are likely to harm critical habitat, section 7's adverse modification prohibition can exert a powerful regu-latory force on behalf of species conservation. In most cases, the consultation process results in the land management agency agreeing to a USFWS alterna-tive in order to avoid an adverse modification determination. Thus the absence of an adverse modification determination is not an indication that critical habitat did not affect the outcome.

The primary threats to the palila (*Loxioides bailleui*), a Hawaiian honeycreeper, has been grazing by exotic sheep, goats, and cattle; increased fire activity associated with exotic grasses and weeds; and the vulnerability of the single population to stochastic events. Although 96 percent of the species occurs on the southwestern slope of Mauna Kea (USFWS 2003d), more than 30,000 acres of critical habitat were designated in a ring surrounding the peak to provide for its expansion and recovery (USFWS 1977b). In the 1990s, the Federal Highway Administration and the Department of Defense proposed to realign an existing road so that it would pass through 102 acres of the southeast east corner of this habitat. Although the area had not been used by palilas in over twenty-five years, USFWS advised the other agencies that the realignment would be prohibited as adverse modification unless it was fully mitigated. An agreement was eventually reached, requiring the contribution of $14 million to palila conservation, the removal of cattle and feral ungulates from 10,000 acres of palila habitat, extensive fire-risk reduction measures, and the creation of new populations through reintroduction of wild and captive-bred birds. With the agreement in place, the USFWS declared that the project would not only not harm critical habitat, it would "enhance the likelihood of survival and recovery of the palila" (USFWS 1998a).

The critical habitat of another species, the Hawaiian cotton tree (*Kokia drynarioides*), was also threatened by an alternative location of Saddle Road. The highway administration dropped the alternative from consideration rather than proceed with formal consultation. Other species without designated critical habitat in the project area—Hawaiian goose (*Nesochen sandvicensis*), Hawaiian hawk (*Buteo solitarius*), Hawaiian hoary bat (*Lasiurus cinereus semotus*), Hawaiian dark-rumped petrel (*Pterodroma phaeopygia sandwichensis*), Newell's Townsend's shearwater (*Puffinus auricularis newelli*), and several listed plants—did not receive mitigation for impacts to unoccupied habitat.

Regulation by the Courts

Critical habitat has also played an important role in litigation where land managers choose to harm endangered species and the USFWS or NMFS either ignore or facilitate the violation. But even here the role is complex. Although some courts have straightforwardly enforced the adverse modification standard, others have used critical habitat to define the geographic boundaries of injunctive relief even if critical habitat was not the central issue of litigation.

The northern spotted owl (*Strix occidentalis caurina*) is threatened by logging of mature forests in the Pacific Northwest. The USFWS listed the owl only in response to a court order. The agency also initially refused to establish critical habitat, but again as a result of a court order (*Northern Spotted Owl v. Lujan* 1991) designated 6.9 million acres on federal lands in 1992 (USFWS 1992a). Since then, the USFWS has issued over two hundred biological opinions permitting the take of 1,080 spotted owls and the destruction or degradation of 82,000 acres of habitat (*Gifford Pinchot Task Force v. United States Fish and Wildlife Service* 2004). Conservationists sued over six of the opinions, arguing that the USFWS erred in declaring that timber sales would neither jeopardize the owl nor adversely modify its critical habitat (*Gifford Pinchot Task Force v. United States Fish and Wildlife Service* 2004). The Ninth U.S. Circuit Court of Appeals upheld the no-jeopardy decision but overturned the no-adverse modification decision stating that according to the Reagan regulation,

> the FWS could authorize the complete elimination of critical habitat necessary only for recovery, and so long as the smaller amount of critical habitat necessary for survival is not appreciably diminished, then no "destruction or adverse modification," as defined by the regulation, has taken place. This cannot be right. If the FWS follows its own regulation, then it is obligated to be indifferent to, if not to ignore, the recovery goal of critical habitat. (*Gifford Pinchot Task Force v. United States Fish and Wildlife Service* 2004, 1069–70)

The court struck down the regulation, overturned the six biological opinions, and ordered the USFWS to reassess the logging plans in a manner that did not allow the destruction or adverse modification of critical habitat.

The same issue was at stake, and the same decision was reached, in a suit challenging a USFWS determination that BLM actions would neither jeopardize the desert tortoise nor adversely modify its critical habitat (*Center for Biological Diversity v. Bureau of Land Management* 2004). Other examples include the palila (*Palila v. Hawaii Department of Land and Natural Resources* 1979), the cactus ferruginous pygmy-owl (*Defenders of Wildlife v. Ballard* 1999), and the Steller sea-lion (*Eumetopias jubatus*) (*Greenpeace v. National Marine Fisheries Service* 2002).

Statistical Analysis

Case studies are sufficient to show that the Interior Department's assertion that critical habitat provides no benefit is both incorrect and conceptually blind to the ways that critical habitats actually work. But case studies cannot establish the magnitude of the effect across all endangered species. Several authors have done this by correlating species recovery trends as reported by the USFWS and NMFS with the presence or absence of critical habitat. In biennial reports to Congress spanning the years 1989–2002, the USFWS and NMFS have scored every listed species as declining, stable, improving, unknown, extinct, or extinct in the wild.

Clark et al. (2002) reviewed 128[4] of the 683 species with a known trend in the 1995–96 report. They observed that those species with critical habitat were more likely to be improving or stable, and less likely to be declining, than those without critical habitat. The difference, however, was not statistically significant, which the authors suggest may have been an artifact of the small sample size. They are correct. Our analysis of the entire 1995–96 dataset demonstrated a significant correlation (see below). We also note that the sample was biased (i.e., it only involved species with recovery plans) and the authors did not account for the confounding effects of recovery plans and length of time species were listed under the ESA, factors that are independently correlated with recovery trends (see below).

Rachlinski (1997) reviewed 560 of the 612 species with a known trend in the 1993–94 USFWS report. He found that species with critical habitat were 11 percent less likely to be declining and 14 percent more likely to be stable than species without it. The correlations were statistically significant even when the presence/absence of recovery plans and the length of time listed were controlled for. The author, however, excluded mollusks, virtually all of which were declining and none of which had critical habitat. He also did not account for species that were delisted prior to the report or that became extinct prior to or after listing.

Taylor et al. (2003) reviewed all species with known scores in USFWS and NMFS reports of 1995–96 ($n = 701$), 1997–98 ($n = 803$), and 1999–2000 ($n = 915$) while also accounting for species delisted prior to the reports, extinct prior to listing, or extinct after listing. After documenting and controlling for the independent effects of recovery plans and length of time listed, they reported a statistically significant trend within each report whereby species with critical habitat were approximately twice as likely to be improving as species without critical habitat.

The consistent correlation between critical habitat and positive recovery trends across differing datasets and methodologies is a strong indication that species with critical habitat are in fact recovering faster than those without it. Nonetheless, these studies have a limited perspective because they rely on individual congressional reports that span only two years. They suggest, but do not demonstrate, long-term trends. Nor do they adequately account for temporal directionality. For example, if two species are scored as "stable" in the 1999–2000 report, they are treated in the same manner regardless of their previous trend history. But if one species was declining in the previous three reports while the other was improving, the meaning of its current "stable"

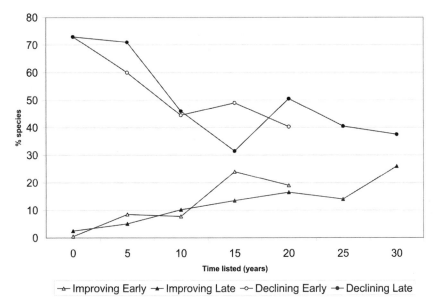

Figure 7.1. Proportions of species declining or improving in early- and late-period reports, in five-year intervals from the date of listing (see Taylor et al. 2005).

condition would be very different from that of the other species. Taylor et al. (2005) address these problems by combining the trend scores of all 1,095 species with a known trend score in at least one of the ten NMFS and USFWS reports covering the years 1989–2002. They found that the longer species were listed, the more likely they were to be improving and the less likely they were to be declining (see fig. 7.1), indicating that the ESA is placing species on a recovery trajectory. The correlation was statistically significant and independent of the separate effect of critical habitat and recovery plans.

The rate of improvement, however, was lower in the late period. Consistent with the observation of the USFWS (2003b), the proportion of species declining appeared to level off after ten years in the late period (see fig. 7.1). Taylor et al. concluded that these results may indicate that rapid early progress in reducing known or easily addressed threats was followed by slower progress, possibly due to threats being less well known or more intractable due to biological or political factors.

After controlling for length of time listed and the presence or absence of recovery plans, Taylor et al. (2003) found that in the early period, species with-

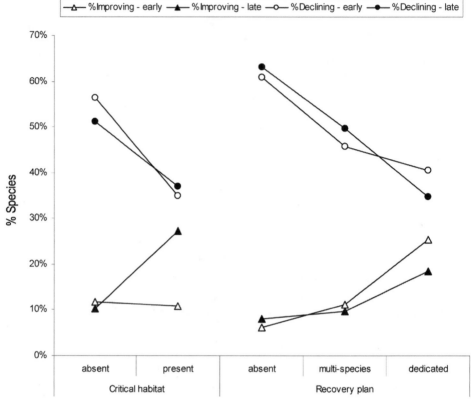

Figure 7.2. Proportions of species improving or declining in early- and late-period reports with and without critical habitat and with and without multispecies or dedicated recovery plans (see Taylor et al. 2005).

out critical habitat were more than twice as likely to be declining as species with critical habitat (see fig. 7.2). In the late period, species with critical habitat were more than twice as likely to be improving as species without critical habitat.

To account for the possibility that the correlation was influenced by species that have critical habitat but are not habitat limited, Taylor et al. (2003) repeated the analysis on a group of 985 species classified as habitat limited by Wilcove et al. (1998), Clark et al. (2002), and Miller et al. (2002) and 77 additional habitat-limited species without recovery plans added to balance the dataset. The results were still highly statistically significant.

Species with dedicated recovery plans were less likely to be declining and more likely to be improving in both the late and early periods regardless of length of time listed and presence or absence of critical habitat (see fig. 7.2). Consistent with Boersma et al. (2001), Taylor et al. (2003) found that multispecies plans were not correlated with recovery trends. This is disturbing because the USFWS is increasingly emphasizing multispecies plans. The apparently lower success rate may be due to the multispecies plans being less specific in their biological descriptions and management recommendations (Clark and Harvey 2002).

Conclusion

The Endangered Species Act establishes clear prohibitions and processes to prevent extinction. The clarity of these provisions is undoubtedly responsible for the ESA's extraordinary success saving endangered species from the ultimate cataclysm. Of the 105 recorded extinctions since 1974, only 22 occurred to species under the ESA's protection (Suckling et al. 2004) and virtually all of these species were at such low population levels by the time of listing that there was little that could be done.

Unfortunately, the recovery and habitat protection mechanisms of the ESA are not as clearly expressed. It is disturbing that critical habitat is the most underused provision of the ESA because it is also the only provision that establishes a clear regulatory link between habitat protection and recovery. Although most of the ESA's regulatory provisions focus on effects to individuals and species and the regulation of harm, critical habitat requires the identification and protection of all lands, water, and air necessary to actually recover endangered species. Nonetheless, the USFWS and NMFS have systematically refused to establish critical habitat areas. As of January 1, 2000, just 10 percent of listed species had critical habitat (Center for Biological Diversity 2004). Due to conservation lawsuits, the rate increased dramatically to 37 percent by August 23, 2005. But the essential recovery habitats have still not been identified for the vast majority of species.

To help speed and ensure the recovery of endangered species, we recommend that the critical habitat provision of the ESA be fully implemented and funded, and that the Interior Department and NMFS expand their view of the mechanisms through which critical habitat influences land management.

8 The National Wildlife Refuge System

Robert P. Davison, Alessandra Falcucci, Luigi Maiorano,
and J. Michael Scott

The National Wildlife Refuge System (NWRS) has played a key role in conserving at-risk species from its beginnings in 1903 when President Theodore Roosevelt established a preserve to protect Pelican Island, in Florida, as a breeding ground for an imperiled population of brown pelicans (*Pelecanus occidentalis*) (Fischman 2003). Today, the Atlantic coast population of the brown pelican is no longer in need of protection under the Endangered Species Act (ESA), but Pelican Island National Wildlife Refuge provides protection for nine threatened and endangered species.

Management of the refuge system has changed significantly since the presidency of Teddy Roosevelt, evolving from the creation of "inviolate sanctuar[ies]" (Act of February 18, 1929, sec. 715d) through a period in which conservation of wildlife and natural communities was balanced with public uses, often to the detriment of conservation (Curtin 1993), to the current period in which the refuge system is to be managed to protect biological integrity, diversity, and environmental health, the management mandates enacted in the National Wildlife Refuge System Improvement Act of 1997 (Act of October 9, 1997; Gergely et al. 2000).

This chapter describes the role the National Wildlife Refuge System plays in conserving species listed under the ESA, identifies factors that limit the refuge system's effectiveness in achieving that objective, and identifies opportunities to increase imperiled species conservation within the refuge system.

The Role of Refuges in Species Conservation

The National Wildlife Refuge System consists of more than 37 million hectares (91.4 million acres) in 542 units that host more than seven hundred species of birds, eight hundred other vertebrate species, and many hundreds of species of plants and invertebrates (Butcher 2003).

Fifty-seven NWRS units have been established solely under authority of the ESA (table 8.1). These units were established to aid in the conservation of some of the best-known as well as some of the most obscure imperiled species. James River National Wildlife Refuge in Virginia, for example, provides habitat for the threatened bald eagle (*Haliaeetus leucocephalus*), while Ash Meadows National Wildlife Refuge in Nevada protects at least twenty-four plants and animals found nowhere else in the world, including twelve listed species. Many other units were established in part using the acquisition authority of the ESA. Blackwater National Wildlife Refuge in Maryland, for example, consists of lands and waters acquired under the authority not only of the ESA, but also of the Migratory Bird Conservation Act (Act of February 18, 1929), Land and Water Conservation Fund Act (Act of May 28, 1963), the Emergency Wetlands Resources Act (Act of November 10, 1986), the North American Wetlands Conservation Act (Act of December 13, 1989), and through the withdrawal of other public lands. In addition, some units—such as Pelican Island National Wildlife Refuge—initially established for other purposes, currently provide habitat for listed species. Indeed, more than 80 percent of the NWRS units provide habitat for one or more species listed under the ESA. This high rate of occurrence is misleading, however, since a few relatively common listed species, such as the bald eagle, account for it. Most endangered species that occur in the refuge system are found on fewer than three

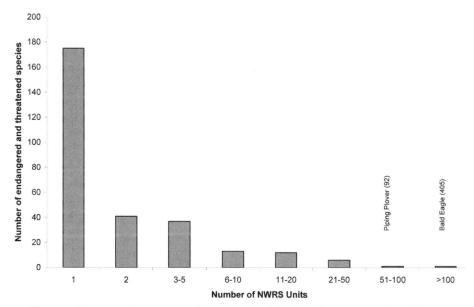

Figure 8.1. Number of occurrences of endangered and threatened species on units of the National Wildlife Refuge System.

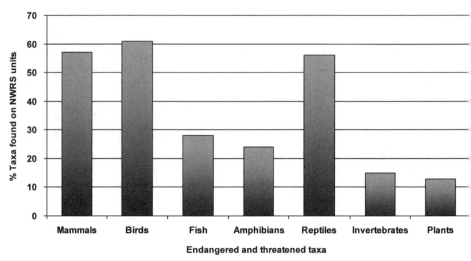

Figure 8.2. Percentage of endangered and threatened taxa found on National Wildlife Refuge System units.

refuges (fig. 8.1). Furthermore, most listed species are not found within the refuge system: approximately 75 percent of listed fish and amphibians and roughly 85 percent of listed plants and invertebrates are not present on NWRS units (fig. 8.2).

Czech (forthcoming) found that units of the National Wildlife Refuge System are able to support evolutionarily viable populations for 44 percent, demographically viable populations for 52 percent, and outbreeding viability for 58 percent of the threatened and endangered vertebrate species he studied. One would expect that larger percentages of viable populations would be found for invertebrates and plants because they have smaller area requirements. Nonetheless, the fifty-seven NWRS units established under the authority of the ESA are relatively small; median size is just 415 hectares (1,025 acres). Seventeen are smaller than 100 hectares (247 acres), and thirty-one are smaller than 500 hectares (1,236 acres). Only two are larger than 10,000 hectares (24,711 acres) (fig. 8.3). As a consequence, these units could be expected to support fewer viable populations of threatened and endangered species than reported by Czech (forthcoming) for all refuges.

Unit size is also relevant because the effectiveness of the refuge system in conserving endangered and threatened species is affected by activities that occur on adjacent properties. Although some of the NWRS units established for listed species are an integral component of larger conserved landscapes, oth-

TABLE 8.1. National Wildlife Refuge (NWR) System units established for one or more species under the authority of the Endangered Species Act

State	Unit name	Unit size Hectares	Unit size Acres
Alabama	Blowing Wind Cave NWR	107	264
	Fern Cave NWR	81	199
	Key Cave NWR	429	1,060
	Watercress Darter NWR	3	7
Arkansas	Logan Cave NWR	50	124
Arizona	Buenos Aires NWR	47,217	116,585
	Leslie Canyon	1,120	2,765
	San Bernardino NWR	960	2,369
California	Antioch Dunes NWR	22	55
	Bitter Creek NWR	5,692	14,054
	Blue Ridge NWR	363	897
	Castle Rock NWR	6	14
	Coachella Valley NWR	1,455	3,592
	Don Edwards San Francisco Bay NWR	8,717	21,524
	Ellicott Slough NWR	56	139
	Hopper Mountain NWR	1,001	2,471
	Sacramento River NWR	3,193	7,884
	San Diego NWR	745	1,840
	San Joaquin River NWR	663	1,638
	Seal Beach NWR	369	911
	Sweetwater Marsh NWR	128	316
	Tijuana Slough NWR	414	1,023
Florida	Archie Carr NWR	12	29
	Crocodile Lake NWR	2,708	6,686
	Crystal River NWR	32	80
	Florida Panther NWR	9,469	23,379
	Hobe Sound NWR	397	980
	Lake Wales Ridge NWR	267	659
	National Key Deer Refuge	3,460	8,542
	St. Johns NWR	2,533	6,260
Hawaii	Hakalau Forest NWR	13,256	32,730
	Hanalei NWR	371	917
	Huleia NWR	98	241
	James C. Campbell NWR	66	164
	Kakahaia NWR	18	45
	Kealia Pond NWR	280	691
	Pearl Harbor NWR	25	61
Iowa	Driftless Area NWR	211	521

(continues)

TABLE 8.1. *Continued*

State	Unit name	Unit size	
		Hectares	Acres
Massachusetts	Massasoit NWR	75	184
Michigan	Kirtland's Warbler WMA	2,647	6,535
Mississippi	Mississippi Sandhill Crane NWR	7,984	19,713
Missouri	Ozark Cavefish NWR	17	42
	Pilot Knob NWR	37	90
Nebraska	Karl E. Mundt NWR	8	19
Nevada	Ash Meadows NWR	5,374	13,268
	Moapa Valley NWR	13	32
Oklahoma	Ozark Plateau NWR	894	2,208
Oregon	Bear Valley NWR	1,701	4,200
	Julia Butler Hansen Refuge for Columbian White-tail Deer	1,114	2,750
	Nestucca Bay NWR	185	457
South Dakota	Karl E. Mundt NWR	423	1,044
Texas	Attwater Prairie Chicken NWR	3,243	8,007
	Balcones Canyonlands NWR	5,728	14,144
Virgin Islands	Green Cay NWR	6	14
	Sandy Point NWR	132	327
Virginia	James River NWR	1,680	4,147
	Mason Neck NWR	922	2,276
Washington	Julia Butler Hansen Refuge for Columbian White-tail Deer	1,125	2,777
Wyoming	Mortenson Lake NWR	719	1,776

ers are isolated and poorly connected with other lands and waters managed for conservation purposes (Scott et al. 2004). The fact that NWRS units generally are far smaller than the areas over which large-scale ecological processes operate and too small to maintain viable populations of many species presents significant challenges for long-term maintenance and recovery of imperiled species (Gergely et al. 2000; Scott et al. 2001a, Scott et al. 2001b; Scott et al. 2004).

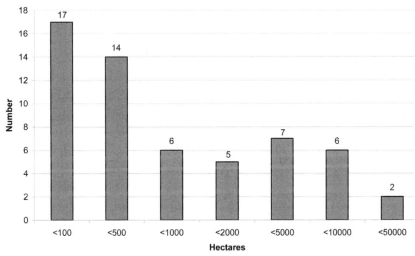

Figure 8.3. Sizes of National Wildlife Refuge System units established under Endangered Species Act authority.

The Role of Refuges in Species Recovery

A key objective for those NWRS units established pursuant to the ESA is to assist in achieving the act's recovery goal. As might be expected, recovery plans generally identify management or research actions on ESA-established units. Of the ninety listed species for which NWRS units have been established under ESA authority, two-thirds (sixty) have recovery plans that specifically cite all of the NWRS units established for those species (table 8.2). Twenty-three percent (twenty-one) of the species have recovery plans that cite only the general area in which the NWRS unit is found or fail to cite one or more of the NWRS units established for the species. For example, although the recovery plan for the Hawaiian hoary bat (*Lasiurus cinereus semotus*) (USFWS 1998c) mentions refuges in general, it does not mention Hakalau Forest National Wildlife Refuge, where it is commonly found (Kepler and Scott 1990).

Although recovery plans usually cite those NWRS units that were established for the species in question, the link with recovery planning may be more tenuous to NWRS units that report occurrences of listed species but that were not established solely for ESA purposes. The recovery plan for the endangered least tern (*Sterna antillarum*), for example, addresses limited management and monitoring actions on four NWRS units but does not mention any of the other thirty-three NWRS units on which the species occurs (USFWS 1990b).

Table 8.2. Citation of National Wildlife Refuge (NWR) System units in Endangered Species Act recovery plans

	NWR cited	General area cited	One or more NWR not cited	Unknown	Total
Mammals	5	0	1	2	8
Birds	10	4	7	4	25
Reptiles	6	2	1	2	11
Amphibians	0	1	0	0	1
Fish	9	1	2	0	12
Invertebrates	4	2	0	0	6
Plants	26	0	0	1	27
Total	60	10	11	9	90

Similarly, the recovery plan for the threatened Atlantic coast population of the piping plover (*Charadrius melodus*) mentions only six of the twenty-one NWRS units within the population's breeding range on which the species is found (USFWS 1996a). None of the approximately twenty-four NWRS units within the species' wintering range are mentioned. Such examples could be multiplied, particularly for lesser-known species such as the endangered American burying beetle (*Nicrophorus americanus*) (USFWS 1991a).

Refuge Acquisition and Funding

Although the National Wildlife Refuge System is being expanded at an increasing rate, clearly there are also limits on how much land can be set aside for species conservation. In the twenty-one years from fiscal year 1982 through fiscal year 2002, 5,147,319 acres were added to the refuge system. Over the first seven years of this period the annual average number of acres added was 104,205; over the next seven years the yearly average was 235,931; and over the last seven years, NWRS additions averaged 395,196 acres annually.

Of the lands added since 1982, relatively little (229,738 acres, or 4.5 percent) has been for ESA purposes. More revealing is the fact that only 13 percent of the 1.75 million acres that were purchased were acquired under the authority of the ESA. In addition, unlike the overall rate of acquisition, the rate at which ESA additions were made did not increase from fiscal year 1982 through fiscal year 2002. In the same period, the number of threatened and endangered species increased from 243 to 1,261 (USFWS 1982b, 2002b). These facts probably understate the benefits to listed species. In all likelihood, much of the more than 4.9 million acres added to the refuge system since fiscal year 1981 is providing benefits for listed species.

Funding limitations constrain not only acquisition but also management of NWRS units. The General Accounting Office (GAO 1994a) found that available funding was insufficient to meet established objectives for refuges because the level of funding had not kept pace with the increasing costs of managing new or existing refuges. The GAO found that at fourteen of the fifteen locations visited, refuge managers and staff said that funding limited their ability to enhance habitat and to facilitate the recovery of listed species.

Expanding the Role of Refuges in Species Conservation and Recovery

Although NWRS units play an important role in species conservation, this role could be expanded. In fact, it may be that the affirmative duty imposed by section 7(a)(1) of the ESA to take actions to conserve species actually requires priority to be given to refuge projects that would recover a listed species or prevent its extinction.

As noted, although many recovery plans use NWRS units to perform recovery objectives, it is not clear how frequently a recovery plan fails to mention NWRS units utilized by (rather than established specifically for) the species. Similarly, it is not known how commonly recovery plan strategies fail to incorporate management actions on these non-ESA units that are used by listed species. The failure of recovery plans to integrate NWRS units into their conservation strategies may mean that refuges are not engaged in any specific activities to conserve the species addressed in the recovery plan, or that those preparing the recovery plans are not aware of opportunities on the refuges. In any case, there is an opportunity for some—perhaps many—NWRS units to play a greater role in the recovery of listed species.

Overall, federal lands support at least one example of nearly three-fifths (59 percent) of species listed under the ESA and about one-third of the populations for both listed and at-risk species (Groves et al. 2000). Lands within the National Wildlife Refuge System, however, provide shelter for just 6 percent of federally listed species populations and 13 percent of listed species—fewer ESA-listed species populations and species than the lands of any other federal land management agency (Groves et al. 2000). The role of the refuge system in endangered and threatened species conservation could be enhanced by increasing the relatively infrequent use of ESA authority in acquiring NWRS lands and by allocating a greater proportion of NWRS acquisition funding to that purpose. In particular, highest priority could be given to land acquisition projects that score 200 in the Land Acquisition Priority System (LAPS) endangered and threatened species category because they either would recover a species or prevent its extinction. Opportunities also exist to increase funding to meet costs of enhancing habitat and to facilitate the recovery of listed species.

Given that private lands support at least one population of more than half of the species listed under the ESA, conservation of these lands is essential to recovering listed species. Limited resources and opposition to further acquisition of private lands by the federal government (particularly in the West) constrain acquisition of private lands for addition to the refuge system and prevent the system from becoming a functioning network of fee title lands that meet the needs of at-risk species. Acquisition of fee title to specific parcels may not, however, be necessary to achieve conservation objectives. Thus, there is value in determining precisely the objective of the land conservation effort. In at least some cases, the objectives for listed species can be met as effectively, or perhaps more effectively, by other means, such as keeping the land in ranching or forestry (Thompson, this volume). A broad, long-term view may well argue against efforts to exert absolute control over the landscape and in favor of alternative approaches such as conservation easements (Parkhurst and Shogren, this volume). This fact has not gone unrecognized by the USFWS. On average over the past two decades, approximately 40,000 acres have been added to the National Wildlife Refuge System through leases or easements (USFWS, unpublished data).

Even less direct control may be necessary in order to achieve more ambitious objectives such as conserving watersheds, habitat types, or ecosystems. Maintaining biological diversity at the landscape level requires the participation of many people and a broad array of interests. The Silvio O. Conte National Wildlife Refuge in New England is a good example of such an approach. The refuge seeks to conserve the natural resources of the 7.2-million-acre Connecticut River watershed largely by involving the public—especially landowners and land managers—in environmental education programs and cooperative management projects. Fostering partnerships among public agencies, conservation organizations, and private landowners continues to be one of the most successful models for encouraging private lands conservation, as evidenced by the North American Waterfowl Management Plan and the USFWS's Partners for Fish and Wildlife Program.

To achieve the land conservation necessary to recover listed species, the use of all available conservation programs must be integrated and focused on those habitats upon which at-risk species depend. This means that research, monitoring, and management of NWRS units must be integrated with ESA recovery planning. It suggests that the LAPS could be a highly effective tool to promote protection of threatened and endangered species' habitat through the National Wildlife Refuge System.

It is unlikely that there ever will be a single comprehensive program to conserve biological diversity. Congress and the executive branch think in terms of specific programs for particular constituencies. The result is programs to establish NWRS units to recover endangered and threatened species, to conserve North American wetlands and migratory birds, to promote conservation practices on agricultural lands, and to acquire and manage national forests, public lands, and national parks. These programs are neither comprehensive nor integrated. Indeed, they often conflict because of the manner in which congressional committees and executive agencies are organized and operate. Whether in Congress or in the executive branch, it often is easier and more highly rewarded to create a new program than it is to integrate new objectives into an existing program.

The reality of independently created programs makes habitat conservation more challenging. It means that habitats for species conservation need to be identified and prioritized. It suggests that all available programs to achieve that conservation must be identified. Identifying government programs that could benefit listed species and informing landowners and land managers of these resources can complement habitat conservation efforts in the refuge system. The North American Waterfowl Plan and Joint Ventures efforts provide possible models for such multiparty partnerships.

Given greater resources, there would be more opportunities for the National Wildlife Refuge System to play a central role not only in identifying and prioritizing lands for acquisition and managing those lands for conservation purposes but also in serving as a resource for other landowners. Additionally, the refuge system, through the example of its management practices, plays a significant role as a catalyst for improved management on other lands. Finally, greater integration of the refuge system's activities with those of other federal and nonfederal landowners and with regional land conservation efforts would further enhance recovery efforts. These actions could substantially elevate the already important role the refuge system plays in the conservation of endangered and threatened species.

Conclusion and Recommendations

The relationship between recovery planning and management of NWRS units requires more thorough investigation. For example, the citation of NWRS units in recovery plans may indicate that those units are involved in the recovery of listed species, but more research is needed to determine the implications of such citations: are the plans used to establish land acquisition priorities, to determine management actions on the unit, or to guide other actions? Moreover, monitoring is needed to verify how often the conservation actions included in the recovery plans have been implemented on NWRS units. If these units are not cited in recovery plans, further investigation can ascertain why and assess their potential for protecting listed species.

The low priority given to LAPS projects essential to listed species should also be investigated to determine whether the scoring is valid or if administrative or other hurdles give insufficient priority to land acquisition projects that could recover a species or prevent its extinction. Examining projects that receive maximum scores in the endangered species portion of LAPS would help to determine how many would aid recovery or prevent extinction.

An important but perhaps more difficult issue is the relationship between NWRS acquisition funding and ESA-related grants to states for endangered species habitat acquisition under approved habitat conservation plans. Investigations are needed to assess whether the two are inversely related—as land acquisition grants to states under section 6 of the ESA increase, NWRS land acquisition funding decrease (Robert Davison, unpublished data). Investigation is needed to explore the relative efficacy and costs of these two means of acquiring habitat for ESA-listed species.

9   Managing the Working Landscape

Barton H. Thompson Jr.

The nation's efforts to protect and promote biodiversity will be successful only to the degree that those efforts ensure that private landowners, in managing their lands, take into account the needs of the other species that live or could live there. Private parties control almost 70 percent of the land in the United States, with the proportion of private lands exceeding 90 percent in some eastern and midwestern states (Koch 2002). Public lands, moreover, tend to be those lands at higher elevations and with less productive soils that no one else wanted; they therefore underrepresent many of the types of ecosystems upon which the nation's fish, wildlife, and flora depend (Scott et al. 2001b). Not surprisingly, almost 80 percent of the species listed by the United States as endangered or threatened depend on private land for some or all of their habitat needs (GAO 1994b).

The management of farms and ranches, or what I will refer to as the "working countryside," is of particular importance to the survival of many listed species. Agricultural and ranch lands constitute more than two-thirds of all private land in the nation (National Governors Association 2001). The working countryside is also active habitat for a sizable number of listed species (Brosi et al., forthcoming). Many farming and ranching activities, moreover, can benefit listed species (Pauli 1999; Vickerman 1998a, 1998b). Choices of agricultural practices, protection of wetlands and riparian area, and other actions on the working countryside can affect the habitat potential of that land and of neighboring lands, both private and public.

Although a variety of federal, state, and local laws attempt to protect and foster biodiversity on private lands, sections 9 and 10 of the Endangered Species Act (ESA) are currently the regulatory centerpiece of such efforts (Thompson 2002a). Section 9 of the ESA prohibits private landowners from modifying or degrading the habitat of a listed species to a degree that would actually injure or kill the species. Section 10 permits private landowners whose land use plans would otherwise violate section 9 to obtain *incidental take per-*

mits, so long as they are willing to develop and implement acceptable *habitat conservation plans* (HCPs).

As discussed below, the U.S. Fish and Wildlife Service (USFWS) has used sections 9 and 10 primarily to establish reserves and other areas of protected habitat while permitting the development of remaining land. The USFWS has paid far less attention to ensuring that most of the nation's working land-scapes—the nation's farms, ranches, and cityscapes—are as supportive of listed species as possible. The major exception to this approach has been the USFWS's regulation of timberlands (or *working forests*), which have been the subject of a number of major habitat conservation plans and legal challenges under section 9.

The USFWS's pro-reserve bias continues a tradition in wildlife conservation in the United States. The national government has long tried to protect wildlife and other environmental amenities by establishing national wildlife refuges and other public reserves. Much like zoos, national wildlife refuges and similar reserves provide a spatial enclosure that protects, isolates, and restricts the target species. And much like zoos, these reserves often see humans and other species as needing to reside in separate geographic domains rather than coexisting in the same territory.

This may be the best or only workable approach for ensuring the survival and restoration of many, if not most, species. Some species, however, can live and thrive on both native habitat and the working landscape (Brosi et al., forthcoming; Germano et al. 2001; Noss et al. 2002; Rosenzweig 2003a, this volume). For these species, management of the working landscape may be an important supplement to the creation and maintenance of reserves. In a few cases, management of the working landscape may be a sufficient conservation measure in and of itself.

Managing working landscapes for their habitat values is important for several reasons. First, reserves often cannot protect a species without the additional habitat and interconnectivity that the working landscape, if managed properly, can provide (Noss et al. 2002). Reserves, moreover, cannot be isolated from the lands surrounding them. The actions of neighboring landowners can undermine the effectiveness of reserves by introducing predators or competing species or by taking, or failing to take, other steps that have an external impact on the reserves.

Second, reserves can be economically costly. Reserves preclude potentially valuable commercial uses of the protected land. For this reason, and because reserves often do not produce local tax revenue, local communities, landowners, and various commercial interest groups, such as farm bureaus, tend to oppose large reserves. As a result, reserves are often significantly smaller than biologists believe is necessary to protect and restore species. In these cases, well-managed working landscapes can provide additional, needed protection. Where working landscapes can substitute for reserves, moreover, they can protect species while keeping land in economic use.

Third, and more speculatively, some reserves may be politically unstable in the long run. As urban development creeps toward a reserve and the land available for new development grows scarce, the potential commercial value of the reserve increases, and pressure grows to remove the reserve's protections and devote the land to urban use. By diversifying protection strategies, management of the working landscape may provide a useful hedge against such instability. Although farms and ranches will also come under pressure from urban development, the combined commercial and habitat values of working landscapes managed for biodiversity may sometimes prove better at warding off change than single-use conservation reserves. As development pressures mount, moreover, the nation may need to learn how to manage, where possible, for biodiversity in the urban landscape. Placing exclusive reliance on reserves in some cases may be postponing the inevitable and missing an opportunity to shape urban development to address biodiversity needs.

To the degree that the habitat of a species is evolving, a pure reserve strategy also may not be ecologically sustainable in the long run. Reserves attempt to preserve a species on a fixed area of land. If the habitat of the species changes as a result of climate change or other factors, fixed reserves may no longer provide viable habitat. Management of the working landscape may provide needed flexibility and adaptability.

Finally, and again speculatively, a strategy of promoting biodiversity on the working landscape may help promote and sustain a conservation ethic (Doremus 2002). Reserves separate humans from other species and, except where coupled with an on-site educational or recreational program, do not provide the public with the understanding and appreciation of nature necessary for the cultivation of a conservation ethic. A pure reserve strategy, moreover, suggests that humans and other species can and should inhabit separate ecological spheres. Active support of species on working landscapes, by contrast, brings humans and other species together and forces us to think about how we can use the same land compatibly.

Working landscape management will seldom be sufficient by itself to protect listed species. Just as reserves need to be supplemented by landscape management, efforts on the working landscape will also need to be supplemented by reserves. Few imperiled species survive just on working landscapes; most also need areas of native habitat (Brosi et al., forthcoming). The key lesson here, however, is that a strategy relying on reserves to the exclusion of the working landscape is more likely to fail.

The remainder of this chapter examines whether the ESA can be successfully applied to the working landscape and how, if at all, the concept of the working landscape can be better integrated into the ESA. "Section 9 and the Working Landscape" looks at the potential limitations of section 9 of the ESA in addressing threats to listed species on the working landscape. While section 9 has had a major impact on suburban development and timber operations, it has left use of the working countryside relatively untouched. Next, "Habitat Conservation Plans and Privately Owned Lands" examines habitat conservation plans approved under the ESA and finds that they have primarily been used to protect listed species by establishing or funding reserves rather than by regulating working landscapes. Given the structure of the ESA and the problems of managing the working landscape through prescriptive mandate, habitat conservation plans are unlikely to ever play a major role in managing the working landscape.

"Other Options for Privately Owned Lands" examines other efforts under the ESA to promote biodiversity protection on the working landscape, focusing particularly on the growing use of safe harbor and candidate conservation agreements. These efforts suggest that incentives and the active involvement of state and local governments are important to the effective management of the working landscape. Finally, the conclusion briefly considers how the federal government can better integrate the working landscape into its efforts to protect and restore endangered species.

Section 9 and the Working Landscape

It is extremely difficult to estimate the impact of the ESA on those private lands that constitute the nation's working landscape (Thompson 2002b). No public statistics are available on the number and type of governmental enforcement actions and citizen suits under section 9. Even if such data were available, we do not know how often property owners avoid actions that might harm a listed species in order to escape section 9 liability.

Published legal opinions indicate that section 9 has had the greatest impact on active changes in species habitat (e.g., the construction of new subdivisions, timber harvesting, and water diversions) rather than on ongoing commercial uses of the working landscape (e.g., farming and ranching). A review of published opinions involving section 9 over the past ten years reveals no case in which the federal government or a nongovernmental organization (NGO) has sought to prosecute farmers or ranchers for their day-to-day use of the working countryside. The ESA has clearly affected some farming and ranching operations. Property right advocates report that the USFWS has prosecuted at least some farmers for disturbing habitat on their property after being warned of the danger to listed species (Annett 1998). Moreover, where farmers or ranchers have needed federal approval for particular land use practices (such as pesticide use or wetlands modification), section 7 of the ESA has sometimes been used to block the approval of practices that would harm listed species (Riverside County Integrated Project 2003). ESA-driven reductions in water deliveries have also affected farmers and ranchers (Benson 2002a). But published opinions and other official records do not indicate that either the USFWS or environmental NGOs have actively used section 9 to modify or regulate farming and ranching practices on private lands.

The lack of active enforcement actions involving the working countryside may simply indicate that ongoing agricultural and ranching operations seldom threaten currently listed species or that farmers and ranchers have voluntarily modified their practices to eliminate any threat. A variety of legal and practical considerations, however, make it unlikely that section 9 can play a major role in shaping practices in the working countryside. First, the government faces a relatively difficult burden of proof in showing that ongoing uses of the working landscape violate section 9. Only "significant habitat modification and degradation" that "actually kills or injures" listed wildlife violates section 9 (50 CFR sec. 17.3). The USFWS has emphasized that "habitat modification or degradation, standing alone, is not a taking" (USFWS 1981), and courts have repeatedly emphasized that the government must prove "an act which actually kills or injures wildlife" (*Defenders of Wildlife v. Bernal* 2000). In order to regulate the working countryside under section 9, either the government or an NGO must have sufficient evidence to prove that farming or ranching activities will actually kill or injure a listed species.

In one of the few cases that has applied this "taking" standard to working countryside, the USFWS argued that certain ongoing grazing activities "would incidentally take members of one or more protected species." The federal Court of Appeals, however, disagreed since there was no evidence that listed species actually existed on the property. The USFWS "acts beyond its authority" when it attempts to regulate land use "without showing that [a listed] species exists on it." The "mere potential for harm . . . is insufficient." Otherwise, the USFWS could "engage in widespread land regulation even where no Section 9 liability could be imposed" (*Arizona Cattle Growers Association v. U.S. Fish and Wildlife Service* 2001).

The government and NGOs can use section 9, moreover, only to *proscribe* activities that will kill or injure listed species of wildlife and not to *require* activities that may be needed to help a species recover (Thompson 1999). Where normal farming or ranching activities have already driven listed species away from the working countryside, section 9 is immaterial. Section 9 does not require landowners to take affirmative steps, such as controlled burning, needed to reattract species or help them recover.

Second, the USFWS has insufficient funds to police the working countryside effectively (Thompson 1997). Even if particular ranching or farming practices might violate section 9, the USFWS does not have the personnel needed to amass the needed evidence or to monitor individual landowners for compliance. Environmental NGOs are in an even weaker position to put together an effective citizen suit under section 9. Farming and ranching are very different from real estate developments, where local land use planning or environmental impact studies typically trigger section 9 review and where builders are often hesitant to risk investments without the security of an incidental take permit. Activities on the working countryside are usually invisible to outsiders, and farmers and ranchers seldom have an incentive to reveal what they are doing on their land.

Habitat Conservation Plans and Privately Owned Lands

Habitat conservation plans (HCPs) are key to the long-term protection and restoration of listed species. While section 9 enforcement threats can influence landowner behavior, HCPs provide long-term assurances of how land will be used and managed. As of July 31, 2003, the USFWS had approved 429 HCPs covering a planning area of 38 million acres (up from only 20 million acres at the end of 1999 and 30 million acres in February 2001). Historically, however, HCPs have focused on reserves and not, with the exception of forest-based HCPs, on the management of the working landscape. Like enforcement actions under section 9, terrestrial HCPs have focused almost exclusively on building projects, silviculture, and water projects, leaving the working countryside relatively unregulated. As discussed below, moreover, the majority of habitat conservation plans have pursued a reserve approach to mitigating impacts on covered species, with only minor attention to changing practices on the working landscape.

The Origin of Habitat Conservation Plans

The current shape and focus of habitat conservation plans reflect the origin of HCPs. They arose in the early 1980s as a means to resolve the conflict between species protection and new land development. HCPs were not part of the original 1973 ESA, which did not explicitly address private land use. However, after both the USFWS and courts indicated that section 9 prohibits land uses that incidentally injure or kill listed species, developers and landowners confronted a potential obstacle to new land development.

The first private landowners to address the obstacle sought to develop land on San Bruno Mountain, near San Francisco, California, that was the habitat of the endangered mission blue butterfly (*Icaricia icarioides missionensis*). After a two-year biological study found that development would negatively affect the butterfly's habitat, an informal committee of landowners, developers, governmental agencies, and environmentalists developed a plan to simultaneously protect the butterfly and permit development. The resulting plan adopted a reserve approach: landowners would develop only 14 percent of the habitat, with the remainder set aside as open space. Of the open space, 84 percent would remain unused habitat for the butterfly. The landowners also would contribute $60,000 per year to finance conservation efforts on the reserve (Arnold 1991).

In 1982, Congress amended the ESA to permit the USFWS to issue incidental take permits allowing landowners to modify habitat in contravention of section 9 so long as they prepared an acceptable HCP. The San Bruno Mountain agreement served as the model for Congress's new HCP provisions, and the agreement became the first HCP approved by the USFWS under the new provisions (Arnold 1991). Although section 10 of the ESA establishes broad standards for HCPs that express no preference, let alone a mandate, for reserves and leaves the choice of mitigation measures to agreement between landowners and the USFWS, the reserve approach of the San Bruno Mountain HCP has served as the model for the vast majority of subsequent HCPs (Pauli 1999).

Individual Habitat Conservation Plans

As noted, the USFWS had approved 429 HCPs as of July 31, 2003, covering a planning area of almost 40 million acres (or about 3 percent of the total 1.4 billion acres of private land in the United States). The majority of these HCPs address the use or development of single properties, with a small number of regional HCPs involving multiple landowners and sizable planning areas. Individual HCPs, as discussed in this section, seldom include active management of the working countryside, and they mitigate for impacts primarily by creating habitat reserves. Regional HCPs, which are covered in the next section, have more often included some element of landscape management, although reserves are still the principal focus.

California and Texas together have generated over two-thirds of the approved HCPs (fig. 9.1); in Texas, four counties alone account for virtually all of the HCPs in that state. In January 1995, Region 2 of the USFWS (which includes Texas) established an expedited permit program for those individuals or companies in the Balcones Canyonlands near Austin, Texas, who wished to pursue small single-family residential projects in the habitat of the endangered golden-cheeked warbler (*Dendroica chrysoparia*). Although a regional Balcones

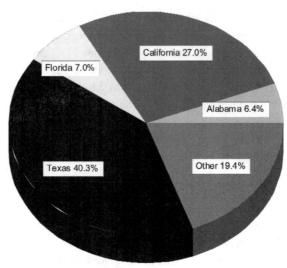

Figure 9.1. Proportions of approved habitat conservation plans by state or region through July 31, 2003. (Data from USFWS 2003j.)

Canyonlands HCP replaced this program in mid-1996, Region 2 has developed a similar program more recently for property owners in Bastrop County seeking to build single-family residences in the habitat of the Houston toad (*Bufo houstonensis*). Because these habitat conservation plans are not representative of HCPs nationally, provisions in Texas residential HCPs must be analyzed separately from the provisions in other, individual HCPs.

INCIDENTAL TAKE PERMITS, 1994 TO 1996

An earlier study of HCPs examined all applications for incidental take permits submitted for approval to the USFWS and reported in the *Federal Register* between June 1, 1994, and June 30, 1996 (Thompson 1997).[1] Texas generated 60 percent of these HCPs. Typical Texas HCPs were prepared by individuals (69 percent) for residential development (95 percent) on a 10-acre or smaller parcel of land (85 percent). None involved farming, ranching, or silviculture. All Texas applications sought to mitigate development impacts by preserving habitat. Under the expedited Balcones Canyonlands program, property owners mitigated the impact of constructing single-family residences by paying $1,500 per house to a conservation fund maintained by the city of Austin, Texas, for the acquisition and preservation of habitat (USFWS 1996b, 1996c, 1996d). The other Texas HCPs proposed onsite habitat reserves, offsite reserves, or both. None of the Texas HCPs sought to minimize or mitigate impacts by regulating the working landscape.

The typical non-Texas HCP submitted during the 1994–96 period also involved relatively small tracts of land, with almost half of the HCPs covering 50 acres or less. Residential projects again generated the most HCPs (40 percent), but most of the residential projects were multiunit subdivisions, and corporations rather than individuals submitted the majority of the applications (70 percent). Timber operations also produced a significant number of non-Texas HCPs (29 percent). None of the submitted HCPs involved farming or ranching.

Outside Texas, the most common mitigation measures proposed in the HCPs were the creation of an onsite reserve (37 percent), direct acquisition and preservation of offsite habitat (18 percent), or a combination of the two measures (9 percent). Only about a quarter of the HCPs proposed land management measures. Virtually all of the HCPs involving significant land management, moreover, dealt with timber operations or the construction or repair of roads or other public infrastructure. Unlike HCPs submitted for the Balcones Canyonlands region of Texas, none of the HCPs sought to mitigate impacts by paying money into a third-party fund to be used to acquire and manage off-site habitat.

INCIDENTAL TAKE PERMITS, 2001 TO 2003

To see whether current HCPs differ significantly from those previously studied, I examined all applications for incidental take permits submitted in the approximately 2$^{1}/_{2}$-year period between January 1, 2001, and July 31, 2003, and reported in the *Federal Register* (see table 9.1). Excluding applications involving the construction of individual single-family homes in Texas, the rate of applications during this period (approximately 3.1 per month) was higher than during the earlier 1994–96 period (approximately 2.3 per month), but still surprisingly small given the ESA's potential reach.[2] The number of applications involving regional HCPs was approximately the same (ten from January 1, 2001, to July 31, 2003, versus eight in the slightly shorter 1994–96 period).

Individuals seeking to build single-family residences or small commercial facilities in Houston toad habitat near Bastrop County, Texas, filed virtually all of the Texas applications. None of these applications involved more than five acres of land. The proposed mitigation in all of the applications was the same— a contribution (at a rate of $4,000 per acre of destroyed habitat) to the Houston Toad Conservation Fund at the National Fish and Wildlife Foundation for the acquisition and management of toad habitat.

Looking at all other terrestrial HCPs, we see that most of the applications again involve relatively small tracts of land, with approximately half of the appli-

TABLE 9.1. Applications for incidental take permits from January 1, 2001, to July 31, 2003

	2001	2002	Jan.–July 2003	Total*
Regional HCPs	3	4	3	10 (8)
Aquatic HCPs	2	4	1	7 (6)
Bastrop County, Texas	20	7	2	29 (23)
Other terrestrial	28	34	19	81 (64)
Total	53	49	25	127

*Numbers in parentheses are percentages of the total.

cations covering 50 acres or less (see table 9.2). As in the earlier study, corporations also constituted the vast majority of applicants (63 percent; see table 9.3).

The types of terrain and activities covered by the permit applications were similar to the those covered by the applications in the earlier survey. The permit applications focused primarily on large-scale developments in suburban regions (see table 9.4). Approximately half of the permit applications involved multiunit residential developments, commercial developments, or combined residential/commercial developments. Another 20 percent of the applications involved other forms of suburban or urban development (single-family residential, industrial, or governmental). Outside the suburban and urban context, a significant percentage of applications covered timber harvesting (silviculture) (12 percent). Only two of the applications sought permits to engage in farming activities, although this was up from zero in the earlier survey. None involved ranching. The one noticeable difference from the earlier survey was the submission of seven applications, or almost 10 percent of the total, for

TABLE 9.2. Permit applications by total acreage covered from January 1, 2001, to July 31, 2003 (excluding regional, aquatic, and Bastrop County, Texas, permits)

	2001	2002	2003	Total*
1–10 acres	6	16	5	27 (37)
11–50 acres	4	4	1	9 (12)
51–100 acres	0	7	2	9 (12)
101–1,000 acres	10	4	4	18 (25)
1,001–10,000 acres	3	1	2	6 (8)
>10,000 acres	1	1	2	4 (5)

*Numbers in parentheses are percentages of the total.

TABLE 9.3. Permit applications by type of applicant from January 1, 2001, to July 31, 2003 (excluding regional, aquatic, and Bastrop County, Texas, permits)

	2001	*2002*	*2003*	*Total**
Business	22	21	8	51 (63)
Individual	2	9	3	14 (17)
Government	4	3	8	15 (19)
Nonprofit	0	1	0	1 (1)

*Numbers in parentheses are percentages of the total.

TABLE 9.4. Permit applications by types of activities authorized from January 1, 2001, to July 31, 2003 (excluding regional, aquatic, and Bastrop County, Texas, permits)

	2001	*2002*	*2003*	*Total**
Single-family residence	4	7	1	12 (15)
Multiunit residential	11	11	5	27 (33)
Combined residential/commercial	0	3	2	5 (6)
Commercial	2	3	1	6 (7)
Industrial	1	0	1	2 (2)
Government buildings	0	2	0	2 (2)
Infrastructure	3	2	4	9 (11)
Silviculture	3	5	2	10 (12)
Agriculture	1	1	0	2 (2)
Mining	0	1	0	1 (1)
Aquaculture	0	0	1	1 (1)
Recreational	4	0	3	7 (9)

Note: Percentages total more than 100 because some applications cover more than one type of land use.
*Numbers in parentheses are percentages of the total.

recreational development (e.g., trail construction or grading in state or county parks).

For minimization and mitigation of species impact, the HCPs again relied more on the creation of reserves than on landscape management (see table 9.5). Based on the summary descriptions provided in the *Federal Register*, almost 75 percent of the HCPs proposed the creation of reserves as the sole form of mitigation. In most of these cases, the applicant proposed to directly

TABLE 9.5. Permit applications by type of proposed minimization/ mitigation from January 1, 2001, to July 31, 2003 (excluding regional, aquatic, and Bastrop County, Texas, permits)

	2001	2002	2003	Total*
On-site reserves	8	15	1	24 (30)
Off-site reserves	9	8	2	19 (23)
On-site and off-site reserves	0	3	1	4 (5)
Landscape management	3	4	6	13 (16)
On-site reserves plus landscape management	2	0	0	2 (2)
Off-site reserves plus landscape management	3	1	2	6 (7)
On-site and off-site reserves plus landscape management	0	1	0	1 (1)
Conservation credits	3	2	7	12 (15)

*Numbers in parentheses are percentages of the total.

set aside habitat for on-site or off-site reserves. In a shift from the earlier survey, however, 15 percent of the applicants proposed instead to purchase credits from conservation banks or to pay into funds for the acquisition of habitat—reflecting an apparent rise in the importance of conservation banking (Fox et al., forthcoming).

Ten percent of the HCPs, including some that involved residential and commercial developments, proposed not only to create reserves but also to manage the landscape of the developed property. In most of these cases, however, the landscape management was relatively minor. One multiunit residential HCP, for example, proposed to educate and encourage homeowners "in the use of xeriscaping" and to prohibit deer and bird feeders that might attract competing species (USFWS 2001d). A multiunit commercial HCP seeking to protect the endangered Bone Cave harvestman (*Texella reyesi*) promised to restrict the use of commercial lots to facilities "that do not have the potential to pollute the underlying karst features" (USFWS 2002c).

Fifteen percent of the HCPs proposed to address potential impacts on listed species entirely through landscape management (down from approximately 25 percent in the earlier survey). A majority of these HCPs involved timber harvesting or recreational development. Three multiunit residential HCPs, however, also relied exclusively on landscape management to mitigate impacts. Two involved snake habitat; the third involved aquatic habitat. The proposed management actions for the residential HCPs included road design and location, speed limits, vegetation planning, habitat construction, footprint minimization, and restrictions on types of land use and on pesticides and other chemical products that can be used on the land (USFWS 2001e, 2002d, 2003e).

COUNTRYSIDE HABITAT CONSERVATION PLANS

As noted, only two of the individual permit applications submitted during the 2001–2003 study period, and none in the earlier 1994–96 period, involved agricultural or ranching operations. Indeed, only four farmers or ranchers have submitted HCPs in the history of the ESA. In one, the applicant sought permission to construct summertime crossings of a local stream that contained listed fish; the core of the HCP was a take avoidance plan (USFWS 1998a). In two of the HCPs, farms sought to mitigate the impact of their operations on listed species by the creation of on-site or off-site reserves (USFWS 2001f, 2002e). In the final HCP, a ranch sought to minimize the impact of its grazing through active land management (USFWS 1998b).

EXPLAINING THE PATTERNS

Individual habitat conservation plans, in summary, have seldom involved the working countryside. Farmers and ranchers have submitted only a handful of the 429 HCPs approved through the end of July 2003, and there is no indication that this level of inactivity is changing. Moreover, the individual HCPs for other types of land use have taken a pro-reserve approach to meeting the statutory requirements, with approximately three-quarters of the HCPs not providing for any significant landscape management.

The extremely low number of countryside HCPs is not surprising in light of the difficulty, discussed earlier, of regulating the working countryside under section 9. Landowners are likely to file for incidental take permits and submit HCPs only when they believe that there is a high probability that their activities otherwise will attract section 9 liability or when the federal government, as a result of a section 7 consultation, tells the landowner that an incidental take permit is needed. HCPs are time consuming and expensive to negotiate and also can be costly to implement (Field Talk 2000). Costs may be even higher for farmers and ranchers, who cannot piggyback the development of HCPs onto other land use planning requirements as developers often can. If HCP negotiations fail, moreover, the landowner who initiated the process will have attracted attention to a potential ESA problem that the USFWS and environmental organizations might otherwise have missed. Finally, most farmers and ranchers are skeptical of the USFWS's willingness and ability to negotiate a workable HCP (Loucks 2003). According to the American Farm Bureau, HCP requirements are insufficiently flexible to deal with the special issues involved in agricultural operations (Pauli 1999). Absent a mandate or a substantial threat, farmers and ranchers thus are unlikely to seek individual HCPs.

Not surprisingly, fear of prosecution for regular agricultural or ranching practices on private lands do not appear to have motivated any of the four countryside HCPs submitted to date. In two of the cases, the applicant was seeking permission to engage in multiple land uses, including residential development and timber harvesting. These latter uses appeared to have motivated the application, with the agricultural uses being incidental. In another case, the need to divert new water supplies, rather than to permit ongoing farming operations, appears to have motivated the application. The applicant also was a large farming corporation that was commercially developing other portions of its property and could afford the HCP process. In the final case, the applicant grazed cattle on both private and public lands and was drawn into the process through a section 7 consultation.

The pro-reserve bias of individual HCPs is also not surprising. All parties with an interest in the HCPs have reasons to favor the use of reserves as the principal or only means of mitigating for impacts on listed species. From the perspective of the landowners, reserves provide the cleanest and least intrusive approach to mitigation. The creation and funding of a reserve typically resolve ESA questions without requiring continuing landowner involvement. In most cases, property owners hand over the reserve to an NGO or governmental agency for long-term management and oversight. Landscape management, by contrast, threatens long-term interactions with and oversight by the government, which may intrude into the landowner's activities (in the case of ongoing land uses) or scare off potential customers (in the case of development projects). Landowners, in short, are likely to favor reserves over landscape management for much the same reason that manufacturers favor end-of-the-pipe pollution controls and emission limits over industrial process changes—the ability to avoid continuing and intrusive governmental oversight.

The USFWS is also likely to favor reserves over landscape management because they are easier to implement and enforce: the government ensures that the land is dedicated as habitat, that an adequate fund is created to maintain the reserve, and, ideally, that the reserve is managed by a governmental agency or NGO with an incentive to maximize the reserve's habitat value. The government can easily monitor these steps, and once the steps have been taken, it need not actively oversee or monitor the reserve in perpetuity.

HCPs that rely on landscape management present far greater difficulties for the government. Assuming that landscape management is costly, the landowner will have an incentive to avoid any management requirements once an incidental take permit has been issued. The exact wording of the HCP, which legally determines what is required of the landowner, becomes extremely important.

As the government seeks to predict likely landowner behavior and to close potential "loopholes" in the HCP, negotiations are likely to become more difficult and costly. The government, moreover, must devote scarce monitoring resources to ensuring that landowners adhere to the requirements of their HCPs in the long term and must spend scarce enforcement resources pursuing landowners who violate the requirements.

Both the USFWS and environmental organizations also are likely to favor reserves over landscape management for scientific reasons. Historically, conservation biology has not focused on how the working landscape can be used to support and restore endangered or threatened species (Rosenzweig 2003a). Conservation biologists, by contrast, have extensively modeled the size and nature of reserves needed to protect various species. Although effective landscape management may be no less certain of protecting and restoring a species than reserves are, government officials and environmental organizations may feel more confident in the existing science underlying reserves. Government officials, moreover, may believe that they are less likely to face criticism if a reserve strategy does not work than if they attempt and fail to protect a species through landscape management.

Regional Habitat Conservation Plans

Regional habitat conservation plans, which affect the land uses of multiple property owners in a broad geographic area, in theory could do a better job than individual HCPs of managing the working landscape. Although farmers and ranchers on private lands seldom have reason to seek an incidental take permit and thus to develop an HCP, the USFWS might insist that a regional HCP with its significant scope encompass all land uses, including farming and ranching, in a covered area. Even if that were not the case, the local governments or sponsors might wish to incorporate the working countryside into its regional HCP in order to avoid all potential ESA problems in the region. In some cases, farmers or ranchers also might believe that a regional HCP will help reduce the risk that public lands in the area will be closed to them because of endangered species concerns (e.g., Hoben 1999). In developing a regional HCP, moreover, the local governments or other sponsors might conclude that by managing the working landscape they can reduce the size or cost of any reserves needed to offset new real estate developments.

In fact, most regional HCPs have focused on the creation of large-scale reserves to enable the development of new residential and commercial projects. A handful of regional HCPs, however, illustrate the opportunity for protecting biodiversity through management of the working landscape. And a number of similar HCPs are currently in development, raising at least the possibility that the working landscape will play a greater role under the ESA in the future (Foster Creek Conservation District 2000).

Of the fifteen regional HCPs with a terrestrial focus approved by mid-2003, all but two rely on large-scale reserves as their principal method of mitigating for the take of protected species. Under the typical regional HCP, developers wishing to build new residential, commercial, or industrial projects pay a fee that is used to help acquire, restore, and manage habitat for the protected species. Local governments or conservation trusts generally hold and manage the reserve lands. As in individual HCPs, reserves in regional HCPs provide both landowners and the USFWS with the simplest and cleanest method of mitigation and offer the USFWS and environmental groups a degree of perceived certainty that the mitigation measures will work.

Virtually all regional HCPs also exclude farming and ranching operations from their coverage. A handful allow farmers or ranchers to participate on a purely voluntary basis. Although local governments typically seek to include the working countryside in their regional HCPs, farmers and ranchers often abandon the HCP negotiations mid-course (Pauli 1999; Hoben 1999; Field Talk 2000), and the USFWS does not require that the resulting HCP encompass the working countryside.

Because farmers and ranchers do not face active threats under section 9, they seldom see any benefit to participating in regional HCPs. Regional HCPs also can be time consuming to negotiate and costly to implement (Pauli 1999). Many farmers and ranchers believe, moreover, that regional HCPs will undermine the local agricultural economy by imposing new restrictions on their operations, promoting more real estate development, and converting working countryside into "unproductive" reserves (Pauli 1999; Hoben 1999; Perkins 2002). They also fear that regional HCPs will shift the burden of mitigating habitat loss from developers to them (Perkins 2002). They are therefore generally unwilling to participate in regional HCP negotiations unless assured that the costs and risks will be minimal. On the other hand, a regional HCP that allows too many concessions to agricultural interests may be vulnerable to legal challenges.

The Natomas Basin Habitat Conservation Plan, which applies to a 53,000-acre area north of Sacramento, California, provides a valuable case study. Rice farming and other forms of agriculture are currently the primary land use in the Natomas Basin, but local governments anticipate extensive residential and commercial development over the next decade (Sacramento and Sutter Counties 2002). A proposed 1997 HCP, approved by the USFWS but never implemented, would have authorized takings of listed species incidental to normal rice farming activities but did not require rice farmers to conform to beneficial farming practices or to take other steps to protect the two principal imperiled species in the area (the giant garter snake [*Thamnophis gigas*], which is listed as threatened under the federal ESA, and the Swainson's hawk [*Buteo swainsoni*], which is listed as threatened under the California ESA). In a judicial challenge brought by several environmental organizations, a federal judge held that this portion of the proposed HCP was invalid because it did not "require even that rice farmers use 'best management practices'" (*National Wildlife Federation v. Babbitt* 2001). Although the government worried that such a requirement might discourage rice farming (which provides generally favorable habitat for the giant garter snake), the court concluded that there was no evidence that a best-management requirement would be "impracticable or would discourage rice farmers from continuing to farm."

In response to the judicial decision, farmers asked to be removed from the regional HCP. Complying with "best management practices" was simply too large a cost to pay for protection from what the farmers believed was a de minimis risk. The HCP that was ultimately submitted and approved would permit farmers to seek a subsequent amendment to the HCP adding them as participants, but it does not apply to or restrict their operations absent such an amendment (Sacramento and Sutter Counties 2002).

Although farmers decided not to seek protection under the HCP, the Natomas Basin HCP also provides an example of how management of the working landscape can be used to reduce the overall cost of an HCP, both to participants and to the local economy, by integrating species protections into economically beneficial land uses. Like other regional HCPs, the Natomas Basin HCP establishes 8,750 acres of reserves as its principal means of meeting the mitigation requirements of section 10. Unlike other regional HCPs, however, the Natomas Basin HCP permits up to 50 percent of the mitigation lands to be used for rice farming—reducing the overall cost of the reserves and helping to preserve the local agricultural economy. A local conservancy will acquire the lands and, in most cases, lease the lands to rice farmers. Another 25 percent of the reserve lands can consist of upland row crops and fallowed agricultural lands.

The Natomas Basin HCP explicitly recognizes that "continued agricultural activities within the Basin are beneficial to the long-term viability" of the giant garter snake and other covered species. Rice farming, for example, can provide both habitat and waterways for the snake's mobility. The regional HCP requires the local conservancy holding the reserve lands to manage the rice farming "to enhance wildlife values and to minimize incidental take of species during farming activities" by "maintaining rice checks, berms, and other water control structures in as natural a state as practicable," taking steps to control species that prey on the garter snake, managing vegetation, fallowing at least 10 percent of the fields each year, and employing "wildlife friendly agricultural practices" such as organic farming (Sacramento and Sutter Counties 2002). Proponents of the HCP believe that these measures will enhance the habitat value. Some environmental groups, however, remain skeptical that "wildlife-friendly agriculture" will "multiply 'habitat values' over present practices," preferring the certainty of a pure reserve approach (Friends of the Swainson's Hawk 2003).

Stakeholders and technical experts involved in drafting other regional HCPs are currently considering similar measures to integrate working landscapes into mitigation reserves. Technical consultants for the proposed East Contra Costa County HCP in northern California, for example, have proposed using reserves not only for habitat but also "to achieve other complementary goals such as recreation, grazing, and crop production, as long as the primary biological goals of the HCP/NCCP are met and not compromised" (East Contra Costa County Habitat Conservation Plan Association 2003). The draft planning document for the HCP proposes acquiring conservation easements on at least 6,250 acres of agricultural land, which would be managed to enhance the land's value to listed species while remaining in active agricultural production.

The Wisconsin Karner Blue Butterfly Habitat Conservation Plan, approved in 1996, provides one of the few examples of an HCP that meets the requirements of section 10 by managing the working landscape (Wisconsin Department of Natural Resources 2002). The HCP's management approach stems in part from the characteristics of the butterfly's needed habitat. The Karner blue butterfly (*Lycaeides melissa samuelis*), which is found in at least twenty-three Wisconsin counties, depends on active land management:

> The Karner blue butterfly is adapted to barrens and other early successional habitats. Because the persistence of these habitats is disturbance-dependent, an important aspect of [the Wisconsin] HCP is to provide for land management regimes that assure a balance between habitat gain from disturbance and habitat loss from vegetational succession. Stopping land management activities which provide desirable disturbance would be detrimental to maintaining this balance. A conventional "do not touch" regulatory approach, therefore, is inappropriate for the particular considerations presented in the conservation of the Karner blue butterfly. Such an approach would discourage, in many cases, the maintenance of habitat and conservation of the species. (Wisconsin Department of Natural Resources 2002)

Under the HCP, twenty-seven private and public "partners," including the state government, industrial forest companies, and utilities, have agreed to actively promote habitat on their lands through various land management activities such as prescribed fires, grazing, and herbicide treatment. The partners also agreed to develop a system of outreach, education, and incentives designed to encourage conservation on other private lands. As the HCP explains, the measures seek to conserve species through "normal land management activities." Studies of the implementation of the HCP report that a broad range of landscape management activities have occurred to date on both partner and nonpartner lands (Moreno and Lentz 2003).

Other Options for Privately Owned Lands

Despite HCPs' reserve bias, the Endangered Species Act has played a role in improving working landscapes. As discussed in this section, both safe harbor agreements and candidate conservation agreements have largely involved the working countryside and efforts to manage the working landscape in manners that provide additional habitat value to listed species.

Safe Harbor Agreements

Rather than encouraging farmers, ranchers, and others to improve the habitat potential of their property, section 9 of the ESA may instead do the opposite. Landowners who enhance, restore, or create habitat on their property risk losing the right to develop their land in the future under the ESA (Thompson 1997; Pauli 1999).

To eliminate this disincentive, in 1995 the USFWS introduced the concept of the *safe harbor agreement*. Under a safe harbor agreement, the USFWS promises that a landowner who takes specified actions to enhance, restore, or create habitat on his or her property may later restore the property to the "baseline" conditions existing prior to the actions without violating section 9 of the ESA. The main purpose of safe harbor agreements is to assure landowners that landscape actions designed to improve the survival and recovery potential of a species do not result in additional regulatory restrictions being imposed (USFWS 2002f).

As of November 1, 2003, the USFWS had approved twenty safe harbor agreements, and six draft agreements were awaiting approval. About half of the agreements involved single landowners, but a growing number were umbrella agreements under which any landowners in the region could use the protections of the agreement (fig. 9.2). Some 120 landowners had enrolled almost 3 million acres of land under one or another of the agreements.

The focus of safe harbor agreements is virtually the opposite of the focus of HCPs. The principal achievement of safe harbor agreements, for example, has been improvement of the working landscape rather than the creation of habitat reserves. Although a small percentage of safe harbor agreements authorize the creation of reserves, the vast majority protect landowners who have chosen

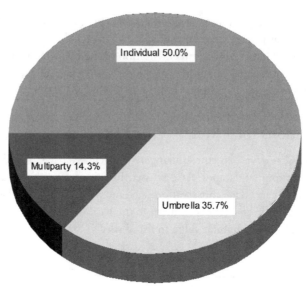

Figure 9.2. Proportions of types of safe harbor agreements. (Data from USFWS 2003j.)

to modify their land use practices in a manner that is beneficial to listed species (fig. 9.3). Farmers and ranchers, moreover, have been active participants in safe harbor agreements. As of late 2003, over 40 percent of the safe harbor agreements involved management of agricultural lands. Timber (silviculture) represented the second-largest category of safe harbor agreements, while only one agreement, involving landscape management on a golf course, touched on suburban development (fig. 9.4).

The Gulf Coast Prairies Safe Harbor Agreement is typical of umbrella agreements. Under the agreement, thirteen landowners owning some 44,000 acres have agreed to take various actions to enhance the potential habitat on their lands for three listed species, including Attwater's greater prairie-chicken (*Tympanuchus cupido attwateri*), in return for protection against new ESA regulation. These actions include management of cattle grazing to maximize vegetation conditions, prescribed burning, and the promotion of native vegetation. Because Attwater's greater prairie-chicken has lost virtually all of its traditional habitat, enhancement of potential habitat on private lands is essential to the future protection and recovery of the species (Thompson 1999).

Although safe harbor agreements are critical in overcoming the perverse incentives of the ESA and have been very effective in improving the status of some species, they are not an affirmative tool for improving the working landscape. Safe harbor agreements do not provide an incentive for property owners

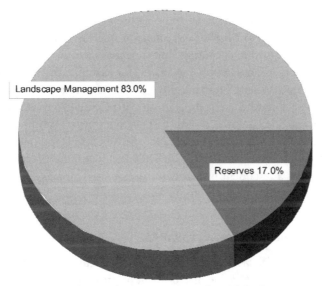

Figure 9.3. Proportions of types of activities authorized in safe harbor agreements. (Data from USFWS 2003j.)

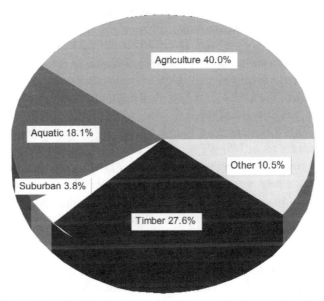

Figure 9.4. Proportions of safe harbor agreements by type of landscape. (Data from USFWS 2003j.)

to manage their lands to benefit listed species but merely remove a disincentive. Not surprisingly, most safe harbor agreements are paired with a variety of financial incentives designed to encourage landscape management. In the case of the Gulf Coast Prairies Safe Harbor Agreement, for example, the USFWS's Partners for Fish and Wildlife Program, the Natural Resources Conservation Service's Wildlife Habitat Incentive Program, and the Coastal Prairie Conservation Initiative all provide landowners with cost-share incentives to improve potential habitat. In past years, the Texas Parks and Wildlife Department also has provided financial incentives to local landowners. Indeed, the safe harbor agreement program is a testament primarily to the potential for and effectiveness of incentives in improving habitat on the working landscape.

Candidate Conservation Agreements

Candidate conservation agreements (CCAs) have even greater potential than safe harbor agreements for changing management practices in the working countryside. In deciding whether to list a species, the USFWS will consider steps that are already being taken by local governmental and private entities to protect and restore the species. In a CCA, local public and private partners agree to take specified actions in aid of a candidate species in the hope of avoiding a formal listing (Phelps 1997; Ortiz 1999). The species benefits from earlier conservation actions, while local entities benefit from the greater flexibility enjoyed when a species has not yet been listed (Ortiz 1999). Taking CCAs one step further, the USFWS has recently begun to issue *candidate conservation agreements with assurances*, which promise signatory landowners that, if the species ultimately is listed, the USFWS will not demand more than the actions to which the landowners have already agreed.

The USFWS had approved over 110 CCAs as of November 1, 2003, covering a broader set of USFWS regions than existing HCPs do (see table 9.6). As in safe harbor agreements (though not in HCPs), the working landscape plays a critical role in CCAs. Ranchers and farmers, for example, are participants in slightly over half of the existing CCAs. About a fifth of the CCAs involve only the working countryside; another third involve multiple forms of land use, including agriculture and ranching (fig. 9.5). Moreover, management of working landscapes, rather than the creation of reserves, is the principal means used in CCAs to protect and restore candidate species.

Given that HCPs and CCAs are similar in function (both are agreements to take actions that will protect a species in return for relaxation of potential regulatory restrictions), the importance of the working landscape under the latter but not the former may seem surprising. A number of factors, however, might help explain the difference. For instance, CCAs may be more attractive to farm-

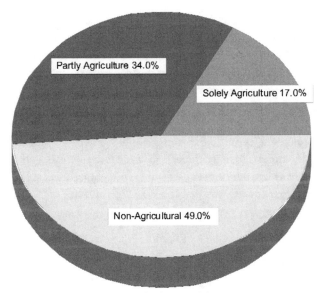

Figure 9.5. Proportions of land uses involved in candidate conservation agreements. (Data from USFWS 2003j.)

Table 9.6. Candidate conservation agreements (as of October 6, 2003)

Region	Total CCAs	Known land type	Agriculture or ranching*	Solely agriculture or ranching*
1	34	11	6 (55)	0 (0)
2	20	16	11 (69)	1 (6)
3	2	0	0 (–)	0 (–)
4	23	12	8 (67)	8 (67)
5	5	1	0 (0)	0 (0)
6	25	5	3 (60)	0 (0)
7	2	1	0 (0)	0 (0)
Total	111	46	28 (61)	9 (20)

*Numbers in parentheses are percentages of the total.

ers and ranchers because they are generally easier to negotiate and less expensive to implement than HCPs, which come into play only after a species has been listed. Indeed, the USFWS explicitly hoped that the greater freedom permitted under CCAs would encourage voluntary participation by farmers, ranchers, and other landowners (Ortiz 1999). Like safe harbor agreements, CCAs are usually tethered to a variety of incentive programs designed to encourage participation in habitat enhancement efforts. And property owners are usually able to negotiate directly with state and local governments in the development of CCAs—an option far more attractive to many rural landowners than working with the USFWS, a federal agency.

Management of the working landscape may also be more feasible under CCAs. As mentioned earlier, the USFWS does not have the resources or presence to effectively police landscape management agreements under HCPs. The signatories to most CCAs, however, include not only property holders but also state and local agencies (e.g., fish and wildlife agencies or soil conservation agencies) with more frequent interaction with farmers, ranchers, and other local property owners. These agencies can help to both encourage and police landscape management in ways that the USFWS cannot.

Conclusion

To date, the Endangered Species Act has only marginally improved the management of working landscapes. Efforts over the past several years to more fully incorporate the working landscape into the ESA, however, point to a number of opportunities for improvement. Regional HCPs, for example, can employ the working landscape more effectively than they have in the past to minimize and mitigate impacts on target species. As the Natomas Basin Habitat Conservation Plan demonstrates, working landscapes can sometimes substitute for or supplement habitat preserves, thereby protecting target species while also preserving and supporting the local economy. The Wisconsin Karner Blue Butterfly Habitat Conservation Plan highlights the opportunity for using working landscape management as the principal means of protecting and restoring those species reliant on successional habitats or habitats consistent with commercial land uses such as farming and ranching.

If HCPs in general are to be effective, the USFWS must also focus more attention on the potential interaction of habitat reserves and neighboring landscapes. As discussed earlier, most HCPs rely on habitat reserves to the virtual exclusion of landscape management. Yet the use of neighboring lands almost inevitably impacts the viability of habitat reserves. Suppression of fires and the importation of nonnative vegetation on the private lands of San Bruno Mountain, for example, may be threatening the long-term effectiveness of the reserve system created as part of the nation's first HCP (Gustaitis 2001). Even where the USFWS determines that reserves are the most viable means of protecting a species, the agency must ensure that the uses of neighboring lands are both consistent with and supportive of the reserves. Inclusion of landscape management provisions in HCPs will increase the long-term costs of HCPs to landowners and will be difficult to monitor, but such provisions are critical to an HCP's long-term success.

Candidate conservation agreements are likely to present the greatest opportunity for successful changes in the ways that the working landscape is managed. As discussed, a majority of CCAs involve the working countryside, and most CCAs also use landscape management as an active tool for protecting and restoring candidate species. The history of CCAs to date, moreover, suggests that farmers and ranchers find CCAs a more acceptable means than HCPs of addressing species' needs on the working landscape.

The first thirty years of the ESA also provides a number of important lessons for both fine-tuning existing tools and designing new tools for managing the working landscape. First, the high costs of negotiation and implementation can easily cause farmers and ranchers to avoid ESA involvement. Therefore, an important step in encouraging greater agricultural involvement in HCPs, safe harbor agreements, and CCAs would be to streamline the approval process. In doing this, the USFWS must abandon unnecessary conservatism. For example, programmatic HCPs and safe harbor agreements, much like general permits under section 404 of the Clean Water Act, could help attract new participants.

Second, because of the problems the USFWS faces in monitoring the working landscape, the agency should make greater efforts to involve governmental agencies at the national, state, and local level that work on a regular basis with farmers, ranchers, and other active land users. Not only can these agencies more carefully observe what is happening on the working landscape but they also better understand the unique needs and objectives of the landowners, and landowners are more receptive to their advice. In some cases, the USFWS may be able to make better use of national, regional, and local land trusts that are connected to a particular working landscape.

Third, conservation biologists must focus more research on how best to manage the working landscape for biodiversity. As discussed earlier, existing research has tended to slight the potential habitat value of the working landscape. Additional research can both help in the design of better HCPs and ease lingering concerns within governmental agencies and environmental organizations over using landscape management as a significant means of protecting target species. Additional research also can help demonstrate where landscape management is not a viable means of biodiversity protection.

Finally, experience with the ESA suggests that, although there is considerable room for improvement, a purely regulatory approach will never be able to maximize the value of the working landscape for biodiversity. Monitoring and enforcement will always be a problem, and efforts to impose uncompensated burdens on ranchers and farmers (not to mention homeowners) are likely to be politically unpopular. The United States therefore must inevitably look toward incentive programs to ensure effective management of the working landscape. A number of programs currently exist, such as the Landowner Incentive Program started by Interior Secretary Gale Norton in 2002. The programs, however, are largely uncoordinated, insufficiently strategic, poorly implemented, and inadequate in size. Moreover, governmental programs to retire land from the working landscape continue to swamp incentives designed to improve the management of the working landscape. In 2000, for example, 85 percent of all federal agricultural conservation payments went to land retirement or restoration, not to working landscape management (National Governors Association 2001). If the working landscape is to provide optimal support of biodiversity, Congress must start by reforming existing incentive programs and adequately funding an appropriate suite of new programs.

IO The Dynamic Urban Landscape

A. Dan Tarlock

The prevention of species loss and, more generally, biodiversity is a major environmental priority. There are two effective ways to conserve at-risk species and enhance biodiversity. First, we can reduce the incentives to kill them by limiting species trade. Second, we can preserve species habitat because habitat loss is the largest cause of species loss. The first approach works only for species with a high commercial value; it remains the focus of the Convention on International Trade in Endangered Species of Wild Fauna and Flora (CITES 1973). The second requires the dedication of large blocks of land for habitat reserves but often frustrates longstanding expectations of land use and exploitation. Nonetheless, habitat conservation through the creation of core reserves—"reserves plus"—and the management of private lands consistent with the objectives of these reserves holds the greatest potential for conserving the full range of species.

The Endangered Species Act (ESA) is not primarily a habitat conservation regime. The need for reserves was less understood in the 1970s because the modern construct of biodiversity had not yet been developed (Takacs 1996). The act, therefore, focused on stopping hunting and other activities that immediately killed species. One important chapter in the history of the ESA is its evolution from an reactive, emergency-room effort to save a species to a proactive effort to sustain species by providing adequate habitat, an evolution that has paralleled our evolving understanding of species conservation. This evolution poses a profound cultural and legal challenge: can humans and wildlife coexist in close proximity to each other? This chapter examines the creation of reserves in urban areas supported by land use controls on related private lands to conserve a wide range of at-risk species.

By the 1980s, two major flaws in the ESA emerged. The first was that the emphasis on at-risk species was the wrong focus; species conservation should be seen as a key element to achieve the larger objective of biodiversity conservation. The second was the initial assumption that the ESA would apply primarily to the activities of the federal government on public lands or to federal licensees and thus that species would be saved by stopping an activity that jeopardized their continued existence.

Serious potential conflicts between real estate development and the ESA emerged during the Clinton administration (1992–2000). To diffuse them, the U.S. Department of the Interior attempted to transform the act administratively, without amending it, into a more general biodiversity conservation program that accommodated both development and species conservation. The primary tool was the *habitat conservation plan* (HCP) (ESA sec. 10(a)). Although Congress had amended the ESA in 1982 to allow HCPs, the option lay dormant. Under the Clinton administration, however, HCPs became the primary tool to adapt the act to long-term biodiversity conservation on the living urban landscape (Thompson, this volume).

Section 9 and Private Lands

The ESA potentially applies to any real estate development in areas where endangered species exist or may exist[1] because section 9 of the act prohibits public and private parties from taking a listed endangered species. "Take" is defined to include, inter alia, "to harass, harm, pursue, wound, or kill" (ESA sec. 3(19)). Although many landowners might be willing to risk the penalties for killing a species in the process of development—since intentional destruction is often hard to prove—"take" is broadly defined by Department of the Interior regulations to include habitat modification that hastens the loss of a species (*Marbled Murrelet v. Babbitt* 1996). This definition gives the U.S. Fish and Wildlife Service and the National Marine Fisheries Service the ability to block any subdivision that threatens to take a listed species by destroying or modifying its habitat. In 1995, the Supreme Court upheld the regulation as a valid exercise of the Interior Department's discretion to interpret the act (*Babbitt v. Sweet Home* 1995), although Justice Sandra Day O'Connor's concurring opinion suggested the need for a proximate cause nexus between the destruction and the species' survival.[2]

The living landscape is a complex mosaic of public and private ownership patterns and political jurisdictions. The rub is that species do not follow political or property boundaries in establishing their ranges. Thus, effective conservation must superimpose a science-based habitat reserve, mapped using conservation biology, over the existing political and legal mosaic. And, like Ginger Rogers who had to dance backward with Fred Astaire, the two federal agencies that administer the ESA, the U.S. Fish and Wildlife Service and the National Marine Fisheries Service, must implement the act with the cooperation of states and local governments. Although the Fish and Wildlife Service administers the

National Wildlife Refuge System, these agencies are not land management agencies and thus have only indirect control over the nonfederal landscape. As a result, federal agencies have had to enter into unprecedented cooperative agreements with states and their local governments.

The law generally structures intergovernmental relationships by vertical principles of authority; higher units can displace the authority of lower ones. However, this traditional hierarchical model does not apply to the negotiation and administration of HCPs. Unlike areas such as the location of religious land uses, telecommunications towers, and transmission lines, the ESA does not preempt state and local land use authority. HCPs are effectively horizontal contracts among the units of local government and the relevant state and federal agencies that specify land use obligations that local governments must undertake to obtain an incidental take permit. There is no displacement of authority; rather the combination of federal, state, and local authority becomes the conservation regime. The threat of a section 9 taking action is the major "stick" that induces cooperation, and the local contributions to the plan must meet section 10 HCP standards, but much of the heavy lifting rests with local governments. For example, the City of San Diego has agreed to establish "[t]he City of San Diego Biology Guidelines for Environmentally Sensitive Land Regulations" to preserve 52,101 acres of private and public lands and to mitigate the impacts of development. In addition, the agreements specify the obligations of the parties for a long period of time and reduce the regulatory capacity of local governments to adapt to changed conditions.[3]

The Evolving Role of Habitat Conservation Plans

States and local governments have two incentives to participate in HCPs. First, they can be liable for failing to take effective steps to protect a species if their failure causes a taking of the species (*Strahan v. Coxe* 1997; *United States v. Town of Plymouth* 1998). Second, few, if any, local governments want to have the ESA become its primary growth management tool. Local governments thus need a variance process to permit development in areas inhabited by endangered species, and HCPs are the primary variance process. The question is how much development is compatible with biodiversity objectives. Section 10 allows the U.S. Fish and Wildlife Service to approve habitat conservation plans that authorize a limited amount of incidental "take" in connection with a development project. Unlike conventional land use variances, they do not simply exempt an activity but rather condition it on a specific land use regulatory regime and reserve creation obligation.

Habitat conservation plans are effectively habitat reserves administered by local governments and financed though a combination of public expenditures and developer exactions. HCPs have progressed through three stages, from single species, to long-term multiple species, to bioregional biodiversity conservation programs (Tarlock 1994; Callahan 1993; Bosselman 1992). Each stage has produced a greater role for state and local governments, which have almost no formal role in the act.

First Stage: Conserving Single Species

First-stage habitat conservation plans involved single-species reserves—the dedication of large blocks of land to maintain single species. San Bruno Mountain, just northwest of the San Francisco International Airport, is the model for the first stage and for the section 10 HCP process. The mountain remained largely undeveloped until 1975 when an 8,500-home project was proposed. After protests by open space advocates, the plan was scaled back and 1,952 acres of the mountain were sold or donated to San Mateo County and the State of California (Bean et al. 1991). Subsequently, three species of butterflies that lived almost exclusively on the San Bruno Mountain were discovered. Ultimately, 90 percent of the mountain was set aside as permanent habitat reserve. In return, the developers received a section 10(a)(1)(B) incidental take permit, which enabled them to consume 14 percent in the mission blue butterfly's (*Icaricia icarioides missionensis*) habitat and 85 percent of the callippe silverspot butterfly's (*Speyeria callippe callippe*).

Second Stage: Conserving Multiple Species

The second stage came in Orange County, California, after the proposed federal listing of a small songbird, the California gnatcatcher (*Polioptila californica*), threatened to stop development in a large portion of the county. At the urging of then governor Pete Wilson, the California legislature passed the Natural Community Conservation Act (1991). This vague framework statute allows voluntary cooperation among local governments and private landowners to prepare *natural community conservation plans* (NCCPs) for the protection of those natural areas that provide habitats for a variety of rare and other species.[4] To test the NCCP program, the California Resources Agency selected as a pilot project the "coastal sage scrub" terrain of Southern California. This still-urbanizing region had already witnessed several troublesome conflicts under the ESA and the hope was that the NCCP process might avoid a federal listing.

Although this objective was not achieved, the Clinton administration embraced the NCCP idea. When the Department of the Interior listed the California gnatcatcher as a threatened species, Secretary Babbitt concurrently proposed a section 4(d) rule that exempted those activities approved as part of the NCCP process from the prohibition of taking the species (USFWS 1993a). In 1996, a 50,000-acre reserve, anchored by a dedication by the Irvine Land Company and part of a national forest, was created to conserve the gnatcatcher as well as several other species.

Third Stage: Conserving Biodiversity

The Orange County reserve was "easy," but few areas have so much public and private land immediately available for a reserve. San Diego took the process a step further by developing an evolving habitat conservation plan. San Diego agreed to participate in the NCCP process because it had more than two hundred listed or candidate species of plants and animals, and it faced the challenge of assembling a reserve over a longer period of time during which development would continue to be permitted. The resulting "multiple species conservation program" substituted a process for the immediate creation of a reserve by committing local governments to an ambitious land-dedication program. Only 17 percent of the land identified as the biological core of the reserve was preserved when the plan was proposed (City of San Diego 2005). The San Diego multiple species conservation program effectively made the reserve design the growth footprint of the area for the foreseeable future.

These HCP initiatives have spawned other local biodiversity conservation initiatives that do not include a federally approved HCP. For example, Pima County, Arizona, faced a similar situation to Orange and San Diego counties when the cactus ferruginous pygmy-owl (*Glancidium brasilianum cactorum*) was listed. The Ninth U.S. Circuit Court of Appeals subsequently remanded the listing because the U.S. Fish and Wildlife Service did not adequately explain the genetic differences between the dwindling Arizona owl population and the more abundant population on northwestern Mexico (*National Association of Home Builders v. Norton* 2003). Although this decision reduces the pressure for a federally approved HCP, two years prior to the decision, the county board of supervisors had adopted the Sonoran Desert Conservation Plan, which identifies the priority biological resources of the county on both public and private lands (Pima County 2001). The county has adopted new limitations on hillside development, native plant protection, and the development of riparian corridors (Behan, this volume).

The Role of Local Governments

Habitat conservation requires that some uses of private property be restricted and that large blocks of public and private land be dedicated to biodiversity conservation. For legal and political reasons, the federal government cannot do this alone. Land use control is vested in the states. Although the federal government can supplant state law to advance a valid constitutional objective, it has seldom chosen to regulate private land use. Furthermore, states have traditionally delegated the authority to regulate land use to subordinate units. States have selectively experimented with regulation but local control remains the norm. Thus, if multiple species reserves are to be effective, state and local governments must coordinate their land use control laws. This means vertical and horizontal power sharing. Local governments must also a bear a large share of the funding to assemble the reserve blocks through subdivision fees.

Zoning

Local governments have the power to control the use of land as well as the timing and location of any permitted development. These powers are subject to legal and political limits. Historically, local governments have used their land use authority primarily to segregate nuisancelike land uses and to finance and coordinate urban services. For the past thirty years, some rapidly growing communities have tried to time the rate of growth and to distribute it in desired areas. More recently, local governments have exercised their authority to prohibit or limit the development of environmentally sensitive lands (Tarlock 1993; *Save the Pine Bush, Inc. v. Planning Board* 2002). Sensitivity is a legitimate factor because development can cause serious external costs. For example, local zoning has long been used to prohibit development in flood plains. Courts have generally accepted environmental protection as a legitimate basis for regulation, but sensitive land use regulation continues to raise questions about the scope of authority (*In re Kisiel* 2001). For example, local governments have created narrow river-corridor vegetation preservation buffers to protect stream quality (*Dail v. York County* 2000). Some states have designated specific areas of critical environmental concern such as the New Jersey pinelands or the Lake Michigan sand dunes (Michigan Compiled Laws Annotated sec. 324.63702).

The Fifth Amendment

The expansion of habitat conservation plans from "simple" reserves to reserves integrated into a landscape of private property rights raises the possibility that courts might find large-scale "integrated" HCPs unconstitutional. The Constitution offers little ground to argue that the state regulation of wildlife is unconstitutional[5] but it does allow landowners to challenge plans that substantially limit the development potential of land or require exactions as a condition to develop land. The application of the Endangered Species Act to private property in the name of natural community protection raises serious Fifth Amendment takings issues and may expose federal, state, and local governments to joint and several liability (*Griggs v. Allegheny County* 1962, Black dissenting). Although the secretary of the interior must approve all section 10 HCPs, these plans will typically be based, in part, on compliance with local land use plans. By adopting the local land use plan as a federal standard, the secretary exposes the United States to liability.[6] The lesson of the HCP experience, however, is that well-crafted plans can avoid takings challenges.

Modern takings law is grounded in the ethical principle that the law should distribute public burdens fairly. The Supreme Court distinguishes between physical and regulatory takings. Physical takings include the actual expropriation of land and the imposition of a servitude on a tract of land. Physical takings require compensation per se (*Nollan v. California Coastal Commission* 1987; *Loretto v. Teleprompter Manhattan CATV Corp.* 1982). HCPs raise regulatory rather than physical taking issues. The court has long held that regulation to achieve a valid government objective is constitutional as long as it does not go "too far." A regulation goes too far when the economic loss is substantial and concentrated on a single or small group of landowners. A complete prohibition on any development of undeveloped land is the most constitutionally suspect form of regulation because it fits neither of the two accepted rationales justifying regulation and also fits the pattern of the strongest justification for compensation: the state is requiring the landowner to confer a benefit of society rather than to remedy a harm caused by the land use.

In 1992, the Court decided a case that has been interpreted by some as holding that much environmental regulation is constitutionally suspect (Sax 1993) because it substituted a more favorable standard for landowners for one that was more favorable to governments. *Lucas v. South Carolina Coastal Council* (1992) invalidated an application of the state's Beachfront Management Act, which established beach setback lines based on historic high-water patterns. The coastal council denied a construction permit for two lots in a tract of five 90-by-160-foot lots on a barrier island near Charleston. Houses already existed on the other three lots. The five-justice majority opinion, written by Justice Antonin Scalia, held that a regulation which "denies all economically beneficial use" justifies categorical treatment just as do physical invasions. Three justifications were offered. First, a total deprivation is the equivalent of a physical invasion from the landowner's point of view as well as the functional equivalent of imposing a nondevelopment servitude on the property. Second, total deprivations do not confer reciprocal burdens and benefits among similarly situated landowners. Third, and most important, regulations that require land to be left in its natural state "carry with them a high risk that private property is being pressed into some form of public service under the guise of mitigating serious public harm."

The Commerce Clause

The fear of section 9 enforcement of the take prohibition drives the HCP process, but it is possible that federal power does not extend to species that live in an intrastate geographical area. The Supreme Court's recent Commerce Clause jurisprudence (Mank 2002; Nagle 1998b) has returned to the pre–New Deal idea that interstate commerce is a significant limitation on federal power. This new jurisprudence makes it possible to challenge the application of the Endangered Species Act to "local" species.

The Constitution permits federal displacement of state land use authority to meet constitutional objectives (*Hodel v. Virginia Surface Mining and Reclamation Association* 1981), but the conservation of species that do not move in interstate commerce could be classified as a noneconomic, local activity that is beyond the reach of the Commerce Power. To date, this argument has been consistently rejected by the courts, although the rationales differ. The reintroduction of the red wolf in North Carolina was upheld on the narrow ground that wolves draw out-of-state tourists and on the broad ground that endangered species conservation is another step in the evolution of the federal government's management of natural resources, which can be traced back to the progressive conservation era (1891–1920) (*Gibbs v. Babbitt* 2001). The protection of the Delhi Sands flower-loving fly (*Rhaphiomidas terminatus abdominalis*), which lives only in Riverside County, California, has been upheld because it involves the use of the channels of interstate commerce and regulates economic activities whose cumulative effects have a substantial relationship to interstate commerce (*National Association of Home Builders v. Babbitt* 1997). The Fifth U.S. Circuit Court of Appeals has upheld the denial of an incidental take permit because intrastate takes may be aggregated with all other takes and thus the ESA is an economic regulatory scheme with a sufficient nexus to interstate commerce (*GDF Realty Investments Ltd v. Department of Interior* 2003). The District of Columbia Circuit Court of Appeals subsequently applied its decisions in the Delhi Sands flower-loving fly case to uphold the denial of a 202-acre housing development in San Diego County (*Rancho Viejo, LLC v. Norton* 2003) and rejected the suggestion that subsequent Supreme Court decisions (*United States v. Morrison* 2002; *Solid Waste Agency of Northern Cook County v. U.S. Army Corps of Engineers* 2001) overruled the 1997 decision.

Rough Proportionality

HCPs are primarily funded by subdivision exactions, either the dedication of land or development fees. All exactions must meet the Supreme Court's nexus and rough proportionality test articulated in the *Nollan-Dolan cases* (*Nollan v. California Coastal Commission* 1987; *Dolan v. City of Tigard* 1994). In brief, the government must demonstrate a nexus between the exaction and the objective of the regulation and that the exaction is roughly proportional to the community externalities caused by the development. As applied to HCPs, local governments bear the burden of demonstrating that they have used available scientific information to construct a ratio between the amount of habitat destroyed by development and the amount that must be dedicated to a permanent reserve through acquisition or restoration.

The potential impact of the *Nollan-Dolan* standard can be seen in a recent case partially invalidating an HCP. The Natomas Basin Conservancy on the edge of Sacramento was premised on the future assembly of several connected blocks of land funded by development fees. All HCPs have to balance front-end development, which is immunized from a section 9 taking suit, with the implementation of a multispecies plan over a long period of time. To do this, the plan has to make crucial assumptions. The Natomas Basin Plan's assumptions were that (1) only about a third of the basin would in fact be developed, and (2) future threats to the species' continued survival as development took place around the reserve system could be minimized through aggressive adaptive management.

National Wildlife Federation v. Babbitt (2001) illustrates the judicial role in policing overly risky HCPs. The National Wildlife Federation challenged the basic theory that the incidental take permits could precede a complete plan based on extensive scientific research; the National Wildlife Federation thus challenged the plan's reliance on adaptive management to correct any errors in the initial scientific assumptions. It argued that the plan must estimate the number of species and the number that will be taken. The court brushed this unrealistic standard aside, holding that the HCP met the minimum statutory requirements. Plaintiffs also challenged the U.S. Fish and Wildlife Service's projection (speculation) that only 17,500 acres of the basin would be developed and the consequent conclusion that a combination of reserve and retention of agricultural land would be sufficient to protect the covered species. These decisions were found to be with the U.S. Fish and Wildlife Service's expertise and were upheld. These were risks "inherent in the market-based mitigation mechanism employed by an HCP" and an inevitable part of the complicated decision making that led to the HCP. The court also refused to invalidate the key risk assumptions behind the plan and the adaptive management strategy on which it was based (Doremus 2001) but zeroed in on the limits placed on the future use of adaptive management (Kostyack 2001). These included the disconnect between the creation of a regional plan and the lack of regional fiscal responsibility; the department had failed to ensure adequate funding (Rodgers 2000).

The court ultimately invalidated the Fish and Wildlife Service's conclusion that the amount of the mitigation fee would be sufficient to acquire the necessary habitat. Judge Levi held that the decision was unsupported by substantial evidence and therefore arbitrary. The court in effect enforced the Supreme Court's *Nollan-Dolan* standard (*National Wildlife Federation v. Babbitt* 2001): in failing to demonstrate compliance with the standard, the Department of the Interior may have over- or underestimated the necessary level of exaction.

Conclusion

The increasing use of habitat conservation plans is a significant step toward making the Endangered Species Act an effective biodiversity conservation statute (Symposium 1997). It is important to recognize, however, that HCPS are an experiment fraught with scientific and legal risks. On the one hand, the reserve design may be inadequate to sustain the species and, on the other, constitutional challenges may prevent the creation of adequate reserves. The success of HCPs relies on the continuous production and application of high-quality conservation biology—and even the best science can only define the risk parameters (Harding et al. 2001). To complicate matters, this science must be applied by local governments who have the least experience and expertise in making science-based regulatory decisions (Nolon 2003). Finally, several units of governments will have to coordinate their efforts to regulate on an ecosystem scale (*Sierra Club v. California Coastal Commission* 2003).

II   Reality Check from Florida

Hilary Swain

Florida is a "hot spot" in the conflict between species and development. In 2003, there were 111 Florida species (54 plants and 57 animals as of November 2003) on the federal endangered species list.[1] These species reflect both biological and political factors: they are biologically unique, possessing a high degree of endemism, especially for plants, and significant rarity among reptiles and mammals, but their listing also reflects the relatively lax protections afforded upland habitats in Florida (Scott, Goble, et al., this volume). This chapter evaluates the effectiveness of the Endangered Species Act (ESA) in protecting threatened and endangered species throughout the United States by examining its application in Florida, where an increase in land use conflicts is putting it to a rigorous test. Florida, in other words, can provide a reality check.

Identifying Species of Concern

The U.S. Fish and Wildlife Service (USFWS) does not systematically track either federally listed species or biodiversity in Florida. Instead, the state relies on the Florida Natural Areas Inventory (FNAI), a comprehensive database of the biological resources of Florida, including rare plants and animals[2] (Florida Natural Areas Inventory 2004). Of 994 species tracked by FNAI in 2003, half were very rare or local throughout range (a ranking of G3) or even rarer (rankings of G1 or G2). Only a quarter of the G1–G3 species were federally listed.

An additional twenty-two species were federally listed but not ranked G1–G3. Thus, in Florida, as elsewhere, the federal list may both under- and overestimate the number of species in need of conservation protection. Furthermore, with only eleven candidate species in the state, the federal list has become increasingly anachronistic.

Identifying and Protecting Working Landscapes

Federal recovery planning is often too general to identify specific locations for species conservation. In Florida, state and local programs have assumed this role, driven by the need to prioritize conservation land acquisition. Federally listed species in Florida may have more protection than the oft-quoted national average that "30% of listed species have no occurrences on federally protected land." Sixty-four percent of all FNAI location records for federally endangered species (and 36 percent of the records for threatened species) occur on publicly managed lands in the state. (This does not mean, however, that these managed lands will maintain viable populations.) In comparison to other—particularly western—states, much of this protection has been achieved as a result of state and local land acquisition. In fact, in 2004 state and local government own or manage 57 percent of the 9,247,646 acres of publicly managed lands in Florida (Florida Natural Areas Inventory 2004). "Florida Forever"—the current phase of a twenty-year, $6 billion state land-acquisition program—has targeted the acquisition of an additional 7 percent of the remaining reported locations for federally listed species. Federal expenditures, on the other hand, are largely planning and public works and are focused on south Florida and the Comprehensive Everglades Restoration Plan (GAO 2000; Congressional Research Service 2003). This leaves the remaining 28 percent of reported locations for endangered species, and 57 percent of known locations for threatened species, outside publicly managed lands and thus reliant on either regulatory protection or private conservation initiatives.

Habitat Conservation for Listed Species

Although the numbers are not quantifiable, the Endangered Species Act does appear to provide indirect protection for listed species. For example, the act sometimes dissuades land use change at sites known to harbor species, generates public support for conservation, and is partially responsible for driving state and local land acquisition. But direct protection of listed species via ESA regulatory permits, at least on private lands, has not been as successful. For example, in Brevard County, Florida scrub jays (*Aphelocoma coerulescens*) have declined over 50 percent in recent years through extensive habitat loss and degradation (e.g., fire suppression), although permitted onsite mitigation and minimization may have reduced losses. ESA-permitted offsite mitigation in this county has purchased only 321 acres of the 37,127-acre designated scrub jay mitigation site at Valkaria, a trivial acreage in comparison to the direct acquisition of 13,367 acres at this site over the same period by state and local governments (Anne Birch, pers. comm.). Similarly, on the Lake Wales Ridge in central Florida offsite mitigation has generated about 200 acres for scrub jay conservation (Archbold Biological Station and the Nature Conservancy, unpublished data) versus over 70,000 acres (not all scrub habitat) purchased directly by local and state agencies. There are several possible reasons for the relatively insignificant amount of ESA mitigation: enforcement actions protect only a small proportion of listed species on private lands (e.g., no plants or invertebrates); reliance on self-reporting; no enforcement on small sites (less than 10 acres) such as in subdivisions where many listed species occur; low or variable requirements for off-site mitigation acres even when cumulative losses are high; allowance for on-site mitigation, even if it has limited recovery value; no enforcement of unoccupied habitat (e.g., long unburned but otherwise suitable land); mitigation needs that are often small with a costly real estate process; and a lack of strategic linkage between permitting and recovery planning.

Conservation through Private Lands Programs

It is neither reasonable nor desirable to protect all Florida lands needed for the conservation of listed species through public acquisition; private lands can and do play a valuable role. Conservation easements are an increasing component of state acquisition programs. There does not yet appear to be much demand for safe harbor agreements or candidate conservation agreements in Florida; the financial incentives seem to be missing (Thompson, this volume; Scott, Goble, et al., this volume). Some private initiatives offer alternative growth management approaches that may benefit listed species.[3] USFWS funding targets private landowners, although these programs offer limited dollars given the need. Significant federal funding, such as that contained in the Farm Bill, could be used to favor listed species protection. Even for an experienced grant applicant, however, these programs represent a byzantine array of options for landowners (e.g., the twenty thousand acres managed by Archbold Biological Station is eligible for eighteen federal, five state, and additional NGO programs). The federal private lands programs are still relatively small, generally reactive, and do not focus on lands with the highest species value so that they are not strategically targeted. A clearinghouse that could assist landowners with access to federal, state, and other funding options for ESA species is badly needed.

One option is to direct funding to private lands that support listed species that have few or no records on public lands. For example, in Florida there are fourteen species, including Florida ziziphus (*Ziziphus celata*), Okeechobee gourd (*Cucurbita okeechobeensis*), Anastasia Island beach mouse (*Peromyscus polionotus phasma*), and American chaffseed (*Schwalbea americana*), with no more than one occurrence record on public lands and ten or fewer records on private lands. Similarly, there are thirty species with five or fewer records on public and ten or fewer on private lands, and forty-two species with ten or fewer records on public and ten or fewer on private lands. Efforts that focus on sites that meet targets for multiple species are also preferable; FNAI and the Florida Fish and Wildlife Conservation Commission have planning processes that could identify such sites.

Conclusion

How have regulatory actions helped to prevent the decline of listed species? What gains have been made from public land acquisition? What are the benefits of federal funding for private lands? The evidence needed to answer these questions is missing. For example, we recently completed a large U.S. Department of Agriculture Wetland Reserve Program on a ranch operated by Archbold in conjunction with the John D. and Catherine T. MacArthur Foundation. As landowners and managers we never received a formal analysis of which federally listed species this project could benefit, nor advice on management to promote these species, nor any requirement to track species responses. Similarly, in reviewing over one hundred recent land management plans for state parks, forests, and wildlife management areas in Florida, only one plan explicitly discusses the site's role in federal recovery planning for listed species. State lands are managed for listed species—they often play a critical role in the conservation of such species—but the planning process is not integrated. To assess the extent to which the ESA works, the cumulative benefits and costs of (a) regulatory actions, (b) private lands initiatives, and (c) federal, state, or local programs must be evaluated to compare relative contributions and to determine the overall effectiveness toward recovery of federally listed species.

Thanks to Florida Natural Areas Inventory, which provided data for this analysis.

12 State Wildlife Diversity Programs

Lawrence Niles and Kimberly Korth

The long-term protection of endangered and threatened species in the United States has always depended on a partnership between federal and state agencies. Many species that are now federally listed were first legally protected under state law. Furthermore, state agencies have substantial human and financial resources. Unfortunately, however, little is known of the collective role of state wildlife diversity protection and even less is known of the combined impact of state actions on the national protection of rare species.

In 1998, the International Association of Fish and Wildlife Agencies (IAFWA) conducted a survey of state agencies to determine the resources dedicated to wildlife diversity conservation. The IAFWA found that states spent a combined total of $134,898,261 in fiscal year 1998—a figure which dwarfed that spent by the U.S. Fish and Wildlife Service (USFWS) under section 6 of the ESA ($29,260,932). In fact, state expenditures were substantially more than the entire federal endangered species budget (Richie and Holmes 1999). The range of state funding varied dramatically, representing real differences in state emphases on wildlife diversity protection. Although states like California, Florida, and Arizona devoted significant resources to the protection of both state and federally listed species, other states spent little compared to the funding allocated to game species. The utility of the IAFWA survey was reduced, however, because it allowed some states to include costs associated with species that were also hunted and fished, while other states restricted their estimates solely to work conducted on rare species. Additionally, the IAFWA survey merely reported survey results and did not analyze how each state used the funds.

Goble et al. (1999) surveyed state ESAs and the protection afforded both state and federally listed species by state governments. They also found significant variation among states and concluded that protection offered by state endangered species regulations was far less than that provided by the federal act. Goble et al. (1999) limited their analysis to state statutes and did not attempt

141

to determine what other resources might be available to state wildlife diversity programs to protect listed species.

Knowing the amount of money each state has available for wildlife diversity protection is only part of the equation. This chapter describes our efforts to survey state wildlife diversity programs to determine human, financial, and regulatory resources used to protect both state and federal endangered, threatened, and rare species. By assessing the time, effort, and money spent by states on both federally listed and state-listed species, we can better determine how resources can be used most effectively.

The Interview Process

We interviewed state program managers to determine the relative focus on state and federal species, the tools they have at their disposal to implement protection measures, and the project that best represents the success of their programs. We attempted to standardize responses to our questions through repeated interviews to allow a reasonable comparison of effort and approach put forth by each state. We consider the survey to be sufficiently comprehensive and uniform to allow comparison between states and to characterize the states' collective national effort to protect wildlife diversity. The data—particularly the budget data—represent the best judgments by the program managers and are not the result of an audit.

In reality, even an audit is unlikely to provide an objective assessment of resources given the often seamless interaction of programs within a state wildlife agency. For example, land management for a rare scrub shrub species in the eastern United States would be similar if not identical to management for game species such as American woodcock (*Scolopax minor*) and ruffed grouse (*Bonasa umbellus*). Unless a rare species or community is being actively managed within the wildlife diversity program, the project could be described as one of game management. Therefore, we relied on state wildlife diversity managers to make this somewhat arbitrary decision since they are most familiar with the intent of their programs. Our goal was to identify activities whose primary intent was to benefit rare species.

To expedite the survey process, we developed a survey and telephoned each state wildlife diversity manager. The survey took an average of twenty-five minutes to complete. In a few cases (less than 10 percent), the survey was e-mailed to the state contact to be completed and returned. Survey responses were tabulated and we developed a revised survey addressing feedback from some managers on the first survey; the revised survey included response verification. This survey was e-mailed to all state contacts; states were given one week to respond. Those that did not respond received a phone call and the survey was conducted over the telephone. Nonresponding states were called at least three times in the interim.

The resulting survey data were compiled and the datasheet was distributed to all state contacts for review. We answered requests for clarification on the spreadsheet and the survey questions through a phone call. Similarly, we initiated a new round of interviews to clear up the discrepancies over Landowner Incentive Program (LIP) funding and other budget questions.

Forty-nine states plus the District of Columbia responded to our surve Because the District of Columbia has not implemented many of the programs we were surveying for, we excluded it from the analysis.

Money and Staff

Due to the extreme ranges of the financial variables, the 2003 state budgets, the 2003/2004 LIP budgets, and the 2003 ESA section 6 budget were not normally distributed datasets. For example, California had the largest 2003 state budget ($110 million); Rhode Island had the smallest ($70,000). The median for state spending on wildlife diversity protection was $1,459,000 in fiscal year 2003 (table 12.1 and appendix 1, www.islandpress.org/esa). A majority of states hav budgets between $1 million and $5 million (fig. 12.1). Thirteen states had budgets of less than $1 million; five had budgets greater than $10 million.

Budgets also varied by region; the median program in the Northeast had a

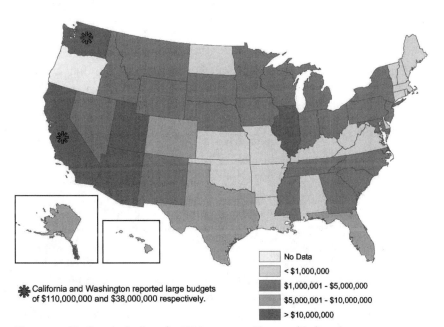

California and Washington reported large budgets of $110,000,000 and $38,000,000 respectively.

No Data
< $1,000,000
$1,000,001 - $5,000,000
$5,000,001 - $10,000,000
> $10,000,000

Figure 12.1. Biodiversity budgets for 2003 as reported by state biodiversity programs. (Data from telephone surveys by the authors.)

TABLE 12.1. Regional comparison of budgets using median of state totals

	2003 state budget ($)	2003–2004 LIP[a] budget ($)	2003 section 6 budget ($)	Percent change in ESA since 1998
Nationwide median total	1,459,000.00	1,054,499.50	90,272.00	191
Northeast[b]	995,000.00	1,054,499.50	32,702.00	9
Southeast[c]	1,400,000.00	975,000.00	256,256.00	592
Midwest[d]	1,466,500.00	535,250.00	41,543.50	22
West[e]	5,176,667.00	1,300,000.00	254,258.00	206

[a]Landowner Incentive Program.
[b]Northeastern states include Conn., Del., Mass., Md., Maine, N.H., N.J., N.Y., Pa., R.I., Vt., and W.Va.
[c]Southeastern states include Ala., Fla., Ga., Ky., La., Miss., N.C., S.C., Tenn., Texas, and Va.
[d]Midwestern states include Ark., Iowa, Ill., Ind., Mich., Minn., Mo., N.Dak., Neb., Ohio, S.Dak., and Wis.
[e]Western states include Alaska, Ariz., Calif., Colo., Hawaii, Idaho, Kans., Mont., N.Mex., Nev., Okla., Ore., Utah, Wash., and Wyo.
Note: Figures are based on state funding for biodiversity programs.

budget of approximately $1 million while those of the Southeast and Midwest had budgets of $1.4 million and $1,466,500 respectively. Western states had a median budget of $5,176,667 (table 12.1; www.islandpress.org/esa). The two states with the largest budgets, California and Washington, devoted a significant portion to a single taxon, salmonids.

The total wildlife diversity budget for the forty-nine responding states was $299,951,740 in 2003. The 1998 IAFWA survey estimated total expenditures devoted to wildlife diversity projects at $134,898,261. Much of the difference between the two surveys can be attributed to California and Washington: California did not report a wildlife diversity budget in the IAFWA survey but reported $110 million in this survey; Washington's budget increased from just over $9 million in 1998 to $38,940,000 in this survey. Excluding these two states, overall wildlife diversity budgets increased only 5.4 percent between 1998 and 2003, less than the rate of inflation. The Southeast and the West accounted for most of the increase in state wildlife diversity budgets (table 12.1; www.islandpress.org/esa).

The actual difference between these years, however, is likely to be higher for two reasons. First, as noted, wildlife diversity projects were more broadly defined in 1998, allowing state agencies to include work that incidentally benefited nongame species but was primarily intended to improve conditions for game species. These projects were largely excluded in our current estimate. Second, new federal funding for wildlife diversity is not devoted entirely to state wildlife diversity programs. State wildlife grants (SWG), administered by the USFWS, were initiated and distributed to states over the last two years. These grants focus on species of conservation concern, including endangered and threatened species and species of special concern. In many states, SWG funds have allowed state fish and wildlife agency biologists to expand their focus from game species only to include species of conservation concern. Because time budgets for regional biologists are not easily separated into game and nongame activities, we did not include them in our estimates. A few biodiversity managers, however, estimated their regional wildlife biologists spent 10 to 50 percent of their time on wildlife diversity projects. This integration of wildlife diversity into the traditional wildlife management network marks a significant change and, as a consequence, SWG funding may not be directly reflected in the resources available to state wildlife diversity programs.

Some federally funded programs such as state wildlife grants are based on the state's population or land area. Others are granted on the basis of the listed species in that state. But a state wildlife diversity budget ultimately cannot be explained by either metric; rather, it is based on the interest of the state's citizenry, the creativity of the wildlife manager, and political will. Wildlife diversity managers from states with large budgets reported being very creative in developing funding sources for their programs; license plate programs, adopt-a-species programs, and grants from nongovernmental organizations (NGOs) are examples. For example, on average, southeastern states spent the least amount per person, $0.33 per person, while western states spent the most, $3.40 per person (www.islandpress.org/esa). Interestingly, California (population of almost 34 million and a land area of 158,674 square miles) and Vermont (population of 608,827 and a land area of 9,615 square miles) spent nearly equal amounts per person, $3.29 and $3.53 respectively. The average regional amount was, however, skewed by a few states within each region (fig. 12.2). For example, in the Northeast, New Jersey, Massachusetts, Pennsylvania, and New York, arguably the richest and most populated states in the Northeast, actually spent the least per citizen, $0.37, $0.27, $0.26, and $0.15 respectively. The western region was the most consistent, with ten of fifteen states spending more than $1 per resident and seven states spending over $3 per resident.

We also contrasted the change in federal section 6 funding over the same time period. To determine the total amount of section 6 funds going to each state, we began with figures provided by the USFWS New Jersey Field Office. We calculated both traditional and nontraditional section 6 funding, the latter including candidate conservation agreements, habitat conservation plans, and safe harbor agreements. We excluded other nontraditional section 6 grants that focused on land acquisition. Based on this information, in 1998, section 6

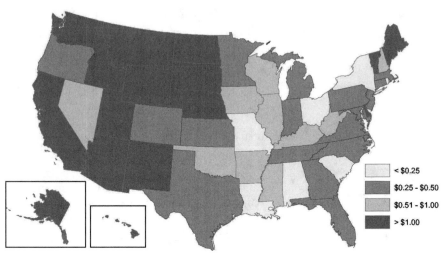

Figure 12.2. Dollars spent per person based on 2003 state budget reports and the 2000 population census. (Data from telephone surveys by the authors.)

funding totaled $5,030,409. By 2003, it had increased to $29,260,932. This increase, however, was not distributed equally among all states. We found that section 6 funding for twenty-six of the fifty states was either unchanged (+/– 5 percent) or had declined. Most of the nationwide increase in federal funding went to nine states (Florida, Georgia, North Carolina, Tennessee, Texas, Alaska,

TABLE 12.2. Regional comparison of state programs

	No. of staff	Percentage of regional biologists on staff (%)	State and LIP funding per square mile ($)
Nationwide average total	25	11	132.46
Northeast[b]	11	23	227.26
Southeast[c]	20	0	42.83
Midwest[d]	13	8	50.74
West[e]	52	8	187.73

All figures are averages.
[a]Landowner Incentive Program.
[b]Northeastern states include Conn., Del., Mass., Md., Maine, N.H., N.J., N.Y., Pa., R.I., Vt., and W.Va.
[c]Southeastern states include Ala., Fla., Ga., Ky., La., Miss., N.C., S.C., Tenn., Texas, and Va.

Arizona, California, and Hawaii). These states accounted for $19.5 million of the $24 million increase. The disparity in federal funding was more obvious from the regional perspective; the Southeast and West received most of the federal funds and the Northeast received the least (table 12.2). This disparity in the distribution of federal funding was not related to land area or to the number of federally listed species (both plants and animals) within the state (fig. 12.3); northeastern states received an average of $3,437 per species while midwestern and southeastern states received an average of $11,259 per species and the western states $19,299 (www.islandpress.org/esa). Based on the total number of federally listed plant and animal species and 2003 section 6 funding, average amounts spent per species ranged from a low of $706 per species in Rhode Island to over $93,000 per species in Alaska (see DeShazo and Freeman, this volume).

Determining the number of people working in each wildlife diversity program was nearly as difficult as determining the amount of money spent on wildlife diversity. A majority of states have utilized a regional biologist approach (fig. 12.4), but approaches varied widely. At one end of the spectrum, in some regions biologists are responsible for oversight of all species, whether game or nongame; at the other end of the spectrum, in other regions, biologists oversee either game or nongame species. Respondents also described a variety of approaches that embrace the use of part-time personnel, contract personnel, and contracts with outside groups. Although the average wildlife diversity program in United States includes 25 people, the range was considerable, from 1

Funding per person ($)	No. of federally listed species	Percent change in ESA funding since 1998 (%)	Sec. 6 funds per federal species ($)
1.53	26	191	6,755.02
0.92	13	9	3,006.70
0.33	46	592	10,680.09
0.90	15	22	3,225.16
3.40	32	206	9,699.17

[d]Midwestern states include Ark., Iowa, Ill., Ind., Mich., Minn., Mo., N.Dak., Neb., Ohio, S.Dak., and Wis.

[e]Western states include Alaska, Ariz., Calif., Colo., Hawaii, Idaho, Kans., Mont., N.Mex., Nev., Okla., Ore., Utah, Wash., and Wyo.

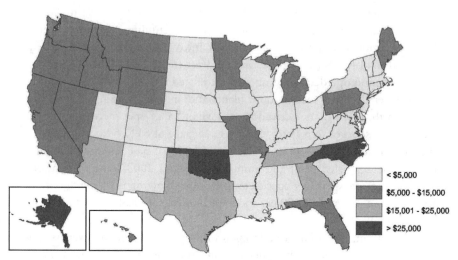

Figure 12.3. Average dollars spent per federally listed species using section 6 funding. (Data from telephone surveys by the authors.)

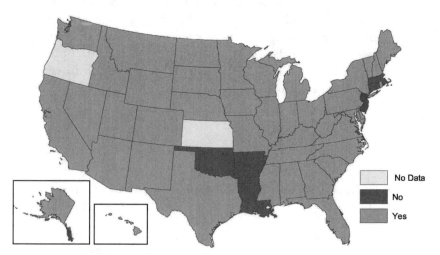

Figure 12.4. States that have implemented a regional biologist approach within their programs. (Data from telephone surveys by the authors.)

in Rhode Island, 2 each in Tennessee and Iowa, to 374 in California. Overall, twenty-two states have 10 or fewer wildlife diversity staff, thirteen have between 11 and 20 staff, and eleven have over 20 staff (www.islandpress.org/ esa). As expected, the western states have the largest programs while the northeastern and midwestern states have the smallest (fig. 12.5).

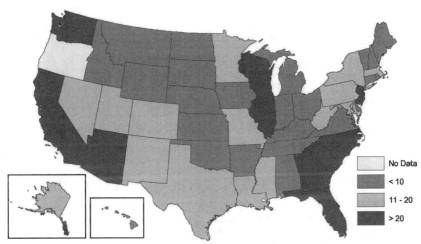

Figure 12.5. Number of biodiversity staff within each state. (Data from telephone surveys by the authors.)

Research, Management, Regulation, and Listing

The role of the state in the management of federally listed species is most apparent in the allocation of responsibility for threatened and endangered species activities. In our survey, we asked each state manager to identify the agency most responsible for listed species (state or federal), the agency with lead responsibility in field projects, and the proportion of time spent by the state agency on federally listed species. Only thirteen states reported that federal agencies are primarily responsible for federally listed species; thirty-six of the forty-nine respondents described either the state or a state-federal partnership as being responsible (fig. 12.6). This relationship was consistent across the country except in the Northeast, where only Maine suggested the federal government was primarily responsible for work on federally listed species in the state. Interestingly, in response to the question on who leads field projects on federal species, only two of forty-nine states characterized the federal government as leading, while thirty-seven states either led or shared the lead with federal agencies. Eight states indicated that the entity assuming the lead depended on the species (fig. 12.7). In our interviews, the distinction between responsibility and leadership clearly emerged as an important issue. In most states, there does not appear to be a mechanism for full cooperation between state and federal biologists.

A potential problem with this component of our survey involves section 7 consultation. The Endangered Species Act requires consultation to be performed by the U.S. Fish and Wildlife Service (USFWS). Most of the managers

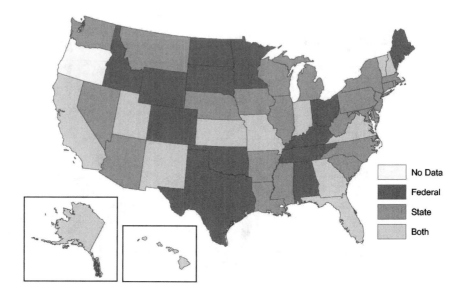

Figure 12.6. Agencies with primary responsibility for federally listed species within each state. (Data from telephone surveys by the authors.)

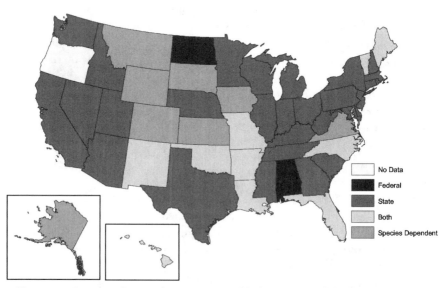

Figure 12.7. Category of agency, by state, responsible for overseeing field projects. (Data from telephone surveys by the authors.)

who raised this question stated clearly that they conducted a majority of the work on federal species when section 7 was not included. Interestingly, several states were unwilling to respond to this question largely because they did not know the actual work the USFWS conducts in their state. Reflecting their leading role in the protection of federally listed species, the average state spent 32 percent of their staff time on federally listed species (www.islandpress.org/esa). The remainder of state biologists' time focused on state-listed threatened and endangered species or other nonlisted rare species.

All but six states had state endangered species lists. Listed species ranged from four in Oklahoma and Montana to over two hundred species in Iowa, Connecticut, and Tennessee. Most states had procedures for maintaining the credibility of their lists. For example, nearly all states had a periodic review process ranging from every year to every ten years. Most states (thirty) reviewed their lists every five years or less, thirteen reviewed their list as needed, and only three reviewed their lists at a frequency of more than five years (fig. 12.8). The review criteria, however, varied substantially. Only nineteen states had explicit criteria for determining the status of species.

Many states are taking advantage of new advances in satellite-based land use–land cover digital mapping to help delineate important habitats for both state and federally listed species. Twenty-five states claimed statewide mapping capabilities, but the detail of most systems was either medium or coarse (equal

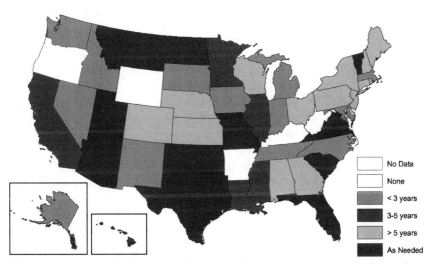

Figure 12.8. Frequency with which each state formally reviews its respective endangered and threatened list.

to Gap Analysis Program [GAP] mapping or Nature Conservancy ecoregional mapping). Six states (Kansas, Minnesota, Missouri, Massachusetts, Maryland, and New Jersey) had fine-grained, statewide maps of endangered and threatened species habitats. Most states with reasonably detailed maps also had some legal authority to protect state-listed species habitat, either through the state ESA or, more commonly, through land use regulation (eighteen of the forty-nine). Land use regulation programs include wetlands (New Hampshire, New Jersey, Rhode Island), caves (West Virginia), colonial waterbirds (North Carolina), pine barrens (New Jersey), Chesapeake Bay shoreline (Maryland), and special conservation districts (Hawaii).

Of the forty-seven states responding to this question, thirty had permanent land acquisition funding available to protect endangered species habitat. Funding ranged from a high of $20 million per year to a low of $500,000 per year. The total for all states that could estimate an acquisition budget was $85 million. But the estimate of acquisition funding for endangered species habitat is hopelessly entangled with other land acquisition justifications. Most program managers described the process for determining land acquisition priority as a complicated process that involves many different factors, including endangered and threatened status, special ecological communities, wetland protection, water conservation, and recreation. For example, the land acquisition budget in New Jersey totals over $200 million per year, and endangered species is an important criterion but is rarely distinguishable from other criteria characterizing the natural value of land. Thus, the money spent by states on endangered and threatened species habitat is likely to be substantially underestimated in this survey.

Exemplary State Projects

As part of our interview with state program leaders, we asked for a description of the project that best characterized their efforts to protect listed species and the single factor that made it successful. Funds and partnerships were the most frequently cited factors, accounting for thirty-nine of forty-nine states. Other reasons given were regulations (four) and information (two). Characterization of these projects can be found at www.islandpress.org/esa.

Conclusion

Our survey identifies a number of interesting aspects of state wildlife diversity programs which demonstrate that states are much more than a "nonfederal partner" to the federal agencies.

First, state wildlife agencies are expanding their role in protecting state and federally listed species. In large part, this is due to an increase in the amount of funding going to the states through two new federally funded programs, state wildlife grants and the Landowner Incentive Program. These funding sources are compelling state fish and wildlife agencies to expand the focus of their existing staff. Some states are becoming a major funding resource for state and local conservation NGOs through new grant programs arising out of SWG and LIP (but see Kareiva et al., this volume). Moreover, with these new funds state agencies are increasing their involvement in county and municipal government projects, indicating a far-reaching effect in managing declining species.

Second, leaving section 7 consultation aside, the state agencies do not believe that the USFWS is the agency with principal responsibility for the protection and management of federally listed species. This finding is contrary to generally accepted opinion. In fact, we found that state agencies are more often than not both responsible for the protection of federally listed species and directing most research and management programs on those species. Interestingly, only a small portion of the activities that states are undertaking for federally listed species is funded through the federal ESA. These results provide a compelling argument that additional funding to states for federally listed species would go far in achieving the federal government's goal in managing and ultimately delisting species. There are two reasons to increase state involvement in managing federally listed species. First, state biologists are more experienced in protecting state and federally listed species because they are commonly responsible for implementing field projects concerning listed species. Second, a state-based approach also allows solutions to be tailored to the unique blend of local factors that often create an intractable problem.

Third, although nearly all state agencies have regularly reviewed lists of state endangered, threatened, and special-concern species and all have SWG lists of Species of Conservation Priority, little is being done to coordinate these lists to promote national conservation priorities. For example, Wells et al. (2004) found only a marginal connection between the continentwide species priority lists developed by Partners in Flight and state lists. This lack of connection is unfortunate because even modest amounts of coordination could lead to operational benefits for many species—especially those not yet proposed but considered for federal listing. A possible model for this type of coordination can be found in the Northeast, where states have produced a regional list based on a combination of their individual state endangered and threatened species lists and national lists developed by groups like Partners in Flight. The lists were gradually finalized with iterative reviews by state wildlife diversity biologists.

The regional list has already been put to several important uses. Currently, the biologists within the USFWS Region 5 Office use it in setting regional priorities for those species not on the federal list. It is also being used by the New England Association of Fish and Wildlife Directors as a regional standard for the SWG Species of Conservation Concern that are used to determine eligibility for SWG funding. We suggest that other fish and wildlife director associations pursue similar regional lists as a first step in developing consistency in both state SWG lists and endangered and threatened species lists. This type of coordination could promote national protection goals for many species that are not likely to receive federal status but are too uncommon or rare to evade conservation concern.

Fourth, many states are pursuing statewide mapping of important wildlife habitats. Lists and mapping provide a solid basis for determining conservation priority and are the first step toward state-level protection of endangered species habitat. National coordination of geographic information systems is an elusive goal because the map resources available within each state vary widely. Differences between neighboring states are likely to be minimal, however, so the coordination of mapping in contiguous states may be feasible. Even the combination of two or three states into one regional map would significantly improve its usefulness for protection of species and would also improve each state's ability to attract funds. Regionalization of species and landcover maps is being pursued by GAP (K. Gergeley, pers. comm.).

Finally, our survey suggests a growing role states are playing in the protection of listed species that is not used to full advantage by federal agencies. The creation of some national standards for surveys of species, management programs, and listing processes would yield enormous benefits without a significant increase in funding. For example, a large portion of bird monitoring projects are conducted or coordinated by state agencies. Most of these survey efforts, however, are not standardized across the country. Thus, these data cannot be combined into a comprehensive national program. In 2003, a new program, Comprehensive Bird Monitoring (Bart 2003), was proposed by U.S. Geological Survey to help states develop consistent monitoring standards for birds that could also create the opportunity for federal agency biologists or academics to combine the data into a national monitoring program. The program was almost immediately endorsed by the U.S. Fish and Wildlife Service, the International Association of Fish and Wildlife Agencies, and many individual state agency directors. Funding similar coordination efforts in survey methods—as well as listing, management, mapping, impact assessment, and other state-based activities—could create a new nationwide wildlife diversity information program coordinated by the Fish and Wildlife Service and the Geological Survey but carried out by state agencies.

The SWG program is a likely avenue for this new coordination. By 2005, all states must complete a statewide comprehensive wildlife plan as a requirement of continued SWG funding. State plans will provide a comprehensive understanding of state actions to protect wildlife diversity. It will also provide a useful tool to coordinate state actions to achieve regional and national goals.

We would like to thank Larissa Smith and Christina Kisiel for their help with the survey. Additionally, Peter Winkler, Patrick Woerner, and Michael Davenport assisted with GIS and mapping.

13   County Conservation Planning

Maeveen Behan

Land development is generally regulated by county and municipal governments through zoning and other land use planning tools. These regulations have traditionally sought to minimize conflicts among uses and preserve public values. Increasingly, conservation of biological resources has become a planning goal. The Sonoran Desert Conservation Plan is a leading example of such conservation planning. The plan was begun in 1998 as a section 10 permit under the Endangered Species Act. It grew into an effort to express the community's conservation ethic in a multispecies conservation plan that also included cultural resource protection, ranch conservation, riparian restoration, and mountain park expansion. The plan thus embodies a range of values including biodiversity, cultural, working landscape, recreational, and aesthetic values. The effort *turned into* a plan that included these aspects, but then integrated them with urban planning through the update of Pima County's comprehensive land use plan. As a result, the community's conservation ethic is fully integrated with urban planning.

The plan has both biological and social goals. Biologically, the plan seeks to ensure the long-term survival of the full spectrum of plants and animals indigenous to Pima County by maintaining and improving habitats necessary for their survival. The plan's social goal is to ensure fiscal sustainability by maintaining the long-term integrity of the tax base and planning for the infrastructure necessary for housing, commercial, and transportation development. This long-range, comprehensive approach allows the conserved and urban environments to not only coexist but also develop in a manner where one enhances the other.

The multispecies conservation plan will lead to issuance of an endangered species section 10, incidental take permit. The conservation plan was drafted to be consistent with the larger local plan and with an extensive economic study performed in advance of drafting the multispecies plan.

Bryan Norton's (forthcoming) insight that "saving biodiversity supports a whole range of values" is exemplified by the Pima County experience. This chapter offers five observations based on this experience and makes three recommendations to those who might attempt future regional planning processes that include an endangered species component.

Integrating information about biological and nonbiological resources at similar spatial and temporal scales can clarify issues of valuation of natural resources.

Mark Lomolino's (forthcoming) insights about the importance of the geography of resources have been applied in Pima County for all aspects of planning. We used a GIS (geographic information system) to map and display data for biological, cultural, ranching, recreation, urban, infrastructure, fiscal, and economic resources. Over a thousand data coverages were assembled—essentially the entire store of community knowledge relevant to our initiative. From this base, over sixteen thousand maps were made and distributed as part of 250 technical studies published during the five-year planning process.

The ability to ask and answer questions and to integrate resource information allowed the community to overcome assumptions that had fueled standoffs between interest groups for decades. Where conflicting interests did exist, we were able to quantify and present pictures of the options as decision support tools for the public. The GIS system and its coverages were made available to the community and this system is currently used by the public at a rate in excess of a half a million map-based requests for information per month.

The multispecies protection approach offered by section 10 of the Endangered Species Act should promote protection of a group of species that reflects the natural system.

Section 10 permits generally have been issued within the paradigm of single-species protection, which may underestimate the complexity of interactions and establish management prescriptions that are ineffective, insufficient, or shortsighted (but see Tarlock, this volume; Thompson, this volume). Multispecies planning efforts, on the other hand, create opportunities to give meaningful scale to conservation efforts and adaptive management planning and to begin to identify natural resource conservation approaches that accommodate complexity and temporal scale. As this occurs, an understanding grows that section 10 plans are, in one sense, experiments.

This understanding can inform our transition from the single-species paradigm to one that includes a truer picture of the complexity of natural systems. Such a transition might also allow a movement away from the "command and control" administration of natural resources described by Shahid Naeem and Claire Jouseau (forthcoming) and away from exclusive reliance on litigation to resolve conflicts. A multispecies plan should protect a suite of species that (1) reflects the natural system, and (2) includes as a subset the federally listed species for purposes of resolving and monitoring compliance issues. This approach offers an incremental transition from the current management and compliance paradigm to a paradigm of protection at the system level.

The current federal approach to species protection under sections 4, 7, and 9 of the Endangered Species Act is insufficient to protect endangered species in certain areas.

In addition to single-species and system-level considerations, the Endangered Species Act should include consideration of the importance of biogeographic crossroads in particular areas. Pima County is vast, covering almost 6 million acres and including two bioregions, the Sonoran Desert and the Sky Islands. Just as the importance of biogeographic crossroads is being understood at an international level, it is sometimes discounted under ESA analysis. Lomolino's discussion (forthcoming) and his prior work make available the knowledge that periphery populations are potentially among the most important to conserve because range collapse often occurs from the center, and evolution often happens at the edge. If considerations such as the importance of edge populations are not included in conservation planning efforts, the single-species approach to protection of biogeographic crossroads will too often take the course of the debate of the cactus ferruginous pygmy-owl (*Glaucidium brasilianum cactorum*) listing, leaving us with a logic that justifies writing off many species.

The ecosystem approach to conservation improves opportunities for collective learning within communities and can enhance community participation in governance, as James Wilson and other policy scholars have articulated. But the constraints on local planning require input from federal agencies charged with resource protection.

The Sonoran Desert Conservation Plan Steering Committee had more than eighty members appointed by the elected board of supervisors. When the planning process began in 1998, an open invitation to participate was issued and more than eighty individuals responded. The committee was made up of 38 percent neighborhood and environmental interests, 33 percent real estate and development interests, and 29 percent ranchers and private property interests. Five years later, after a two-year education process involving monthly meetings and after years of facilitated deliberations, the membership of the group remained largely unchanged. Along the way, each participant received copies of the 250 studies along with lessons on map making and full access to the meetings of the expert teams. This open approach filtered out conflicts and created opportunities for experts to explain or adjust their terminology and for members of the public to master the technical information. The public related to the local government but relied on the experience and knowledge of the federal agencies and the experts, and they respected the federal rules regarding endangered species protection. The local and federal roles are both important to conservation planning. It is the partnership that creates the opportunity for a successful outcome. Between 1998 and 2003, the Tohono O'odham Nation and every stakeholding federal and local government entity (with one exception at the state level) had signed cooperative agreements with Pima County.

Local solutions under section 10 are arrived at in a creative and ad hoc manner, but successful large-scale processes require (a) science that is verifiable, consensus based, and peer reviewed, and (b) solutions that include a range of values important to participants.

Over four hundred experts participated in the planning process through four technical teams: the Cultural Resource Team, the Ranch Team, the Recreation Team, and the Science Team. An interdisciplinary team was formed after several years, including the chair and lead expert from each technical team, along with representatives from the Tohono O'odham Nation. These experts donated their time for five years to explain the complex underlying data of the plan to thousands of community members, including over ten thousand youth participants. Although conflicts occurred, throughout the process the scholarly community developed expertise and in turn educated the public and provided elected officials with consensus-based policy recommendations. In describing the process of developing a conservation plan for protecting species at the county level, we've shown that the Endangered Species Act is most successful when community members, experts, and government stakeholders fully participate in the process. Three lessons have emerged from the years of evaluating theory, data, politics, constituent issues, and legal issues pertaining to the Sonoran Desert Conservation Plan:

- Adopt a problem-solving approach.
- Cast a wide, multidisciplinary net.
- Keep the technical, public, and intergovernmental processes open and inclusive.

14 Indian Tribes

William H. Rodgers Jr.

The role of Indian tribes in the biology of North America is a work in progress. The tribes are at the center of ambitious restoration efforts ranging from the salmon of the Pacific Northwest (Northwest Indian Fisheries Commission 2005) to keystone species in the Everglades (Miccosukee Indian Tribe 2003). This chapter explores tribal roles in the politics of recovery (Nez Perce and wolves), in ecosystem management (Intertribal Bison Cooperative), in science policy (low flows on the Klamath), and in protection of critical habitat (White Mountain Apache).

Tribes as States: Nez Perce and Wolf Reintroduction

> The association with, and imitation of, the wolf among American Indians was absolutely pervasive.
>
> —*Barry Lopez*

Opportunism rules in politics, and it moves in sudden, sweeping, and unpredictable bursts. Opportunism gave the Nez Perce tribe a central role on the matter of wolf reintroduction when Idaho refused to participate in the reintroduction of gray wolves (*Canis lupus*) (*Idaho Code*, sec. 36-715(4); Wilson 1999; Zuccotti 1995). The tribe was an obvious candidate. Wolf behavior is admired in Nez Perce mythology (Lavender 1992) and often scorned outside of it (McNamee 1997; Steinhart 1995). It was the tribe, not the state, that embraced the idea that wolves had a future in the West and that government had a duty to shape this future.

This example of tribes daring to go where states fear to tread is no aberration on environmental questions. It reappears in issues as diverse as the stringency of standards, disposition to enforce, and attitudes toward future outcomes (Rodgers 2001). States as the "laboratories" of experimentation in the federal system often backpedal and drift in the harsh light of contemporary politics; controversy is not their lubricant of change but their glue of stalemate and caution. Tribes have their own politics, of course, but they are a different politics—and far more self-assured when they speak of the natural world.

In 1978, the gray wolf was listed as endangered in the forty-eight states (except for the small population in Minnesota that was listed as threatened) (National Wildlife Federation 1998a; Goble 1992). Recovery planning drifted along for several years but took shape in 1987 with proposals to bring back three populations of wolves: one each in northwestern Montana, central Idaho, and Yellowstone National Park (National Wildlife Federation 1998a; Goble 2002). Slowed by legal and political conflict, action was delayed until 1994 when Interior Secretary Bruce Babbitt signed off on a plan to bring gray wolves from Canada into central Idaho and Yellowstone (Bangs and Fritts 1996, 1998).

Despite attempts to stop it in court (*Wyoming Farm Bureau Federation v. Babbitt* 2000; see Bean 2001), the first release of individual wolves occurred in January 1995 (Fischer 1995). The releases took place within Nez Perce traditional grounds in central Idaho and in places where the tribe retains fishing, hunting, and gathering rights. The Nez Perce people were present at the inception. Elder Horace Axtell, of the Seven Drum religion, recalls the welcoming ceremony: "I sang one of our religious songs to welcome them back. Then I looked into the cage and spoke to one of the wolves in Nez Perce; he kind of tilted his head, like he was listening. . . . That felt so good. It was like meeting an old friend" (National Wildlife Federation 1998a).

From the earliest moments, the Nez Perce were attentive to the public education, management, and scientific nuances of wolf reintroduction. Initially, the tribe made a wise decision to welcome a Wolf Education and Research Center, a nongovernmental organization (NGO) established to promote the return of wolves to the northern Rocky Mountains. The Center was opposed by the livestock industry and stymied by the U.S. Forest Service when it sought to set up shop on Forest Service lands. But it found a willing ally in the Nez Perce:

> In 1994 the tribe and the center agreed to build a facility on tribal land near Winchester, Idaho. The facility opened in June 1997 and offers interpretive exhibits and an opportunity for the public to view a wolf pack. It also provides an opportunity to experience Nez Perce history and tribal culture. Further, staff and Nez Perce tribal representatives draw on the center's resources to provide a variety of educational activities for schools and community organizations throughout the region. (Wilson 1999, 555)

The Nez Perce also have gone out of their way to quiet the wolf-livestock conflict that has threatened to derail reintroduction more than once. They have done this from impulses of "good neighborliness" and without rancor, resentment, or acute recall of a settlement history that had its extraordinarily bitter moments (Woods 2001). They figure the tribe is here to stay in central Idaho, along with the wolf and other folks living there. They are giving reciprocity its full due.

The science part of restoration has fallen mostly on the shoulders of Curt Mack, wildlife biologist, nontribal member, a creative, accommodating, and flexible man. Mack oversees "a team of seasonal employees that tracks the wolves through about 13 million acres of national forest in central Idaho. The biologists trap wolves and place radio collars around the animals' necks so they can follow the wolves' movements through the forest, warn ranchers if the wolves are approaching livestock, learn if the wolves are reproducing and try to get up-to-date population counts" (National Wildlife Federation 1998a; *Lewiston Morning Tribune* 1999).

The wolves took hold of their new home with gusto. By the spring of 1997, a total of thirty-two pups had been born to six pairs of wolves. "Biologically speaking," said Mack, "the wolves are recovering very well" (National Wildlife Federation 1998a; Mack and Holyan 2003). At least one wolf has dispersed to Oregon where another Indian tribe (the Umatillas) are anxious to repeat the Nez Perce experiment in facilitation and management (Odell 2002).

Events are moving rapidly. On April 1, 2003, the U.S. Fish and Wildlife Service (USFWS) took action to reclassify wolves north of Interstate 90 (now the Western District Population Segment) from "endangered" to "threatened" (USFWS 2003f, 2003g, 2004e; but see *Defenders of Wildlife v. Secretary* 2005). Delisting is in the wings. Idaho has been born again as a competent and sympathetic wolf manager and it is back in the good graces of the USFWS. But the "legislative intent" leaves nothing to the imagination:

> It is the public policy of the state of Idaho to use every option to assert state sovereignty and mitigate the impact of gray wolves on residents of the state of Idaho and to seek the delisting and management of gray wolves at recovery levels that will ensure viable self-sustaining populations pursuant to the Idaho Wolf Conservation and Management Plan. The state of Idaho arrived at this policy in 2002 . . . after objecting to the reintroduction of wolves and after adopting a memorial seeking the removal of wolves from the state. (Idaho House Bill 294 2003)

Law is often angry and divisive. It does not have to be that way. The state of Idaho is no more destined for termination than the Nez Perce tribe. Leaders within the state—such as Jim Caswell from the Office of Species Conservation in the governor's office—are well positioned to redirect and put another tone on Idaho's future with wolves. He could do worse than follow the example of the Nez Perce tribe. A tribal progress report (Mack and Holyan 2003) on wolf reintroduction applauds the work of more than twenty organizations and forty-five individuals who contributed to the success of this recovery effort. It is grand and charitable and inspirational. It claims no credit but speaks movingly of collaboration by example.

Ecosystems Not Species: Intertribal Bison Cooperative

> I see the rebirth of the buffalo and the rebirth of the Indian people taking place together.
>
> —Louis LaRose, Winnebago

The destruction of the buffalo (*Bison bison*) on the North American continent was sudden and transformative. In a few short years (the spasm of destruction was concentrated in the 1870s), numbers of these massive grazers went from many millions to "near extinction" (White 1991; Hornaday 1889). Today, return of bison to the Great Plains has gone from idea (the "buffalo commons") to movement to halting reality (Callenbach 1996; Mathews 1992). The Yellowstone herd (that almost blinked out at a low of thirteen animals) now numbers 3,800–4,000. Total bison population in the United States is perhaps 150,000, found mostly in commercial enterprises on private lands (Chadwick 1998).

The return of the bison is a useful template to consider two recurring criticisms of the ESA—that it arrives too late and aspires too little. The act comes into play too late because species listed as "endangered" or even "threatened" are already in deep trouble, past the point of "ecological extinction." The ESA aspires too little because the remedy it prescribes is responsive to the listing alliteration of a "species in trouble." The remedy for a "species in trouble" is a single-species recovery plan making incremental moves to quiet the "trouble."

To be sure, a variety of innovations challenge these ESA limitations of too late and too little. There are "watch lists" and "candidates" and "species of concern" and "distinct population segments" that can roll back the eleventh-hour aspects of ESA listings. There are multispecies and habitat-wide and ecosystem-defined responses (Bean and Rowland 1997). There are bold and timid baselines against which to measure recovery. Still, the ESA was written for the species in crisis. It is satisfied if it quiets the crisis. It comes too late and gives too little.

These limitations are being challenged in Indian country. In 1990, the Intertribal Bison Cooperative (2003) was formed to bring back the bison to Indian lands. The bison is ecologically extinct in the United States and below the radar screen of the ESA. But it has never been "delisted" in Indian country. Memories of it run deep. Restoration stirs hope.

A comeback of the bison is a story of sustainability, according to Ernest Callenbach:

> The ecological virtues of bison are exceptional. They digest grasses and other plants more efficiently than do livestock, and "harvesting" of bison, if such a term can be used, would utilize that basic, renewable, solar-driven process with maximum efficiency. They do less ecological damage to the land than livestock do, especially in waterside areas. Their presence on the Plains would be sustainable for as long as we can see ahead. (Callenbach 1996, 6)

The fifty-one tribes within Intertribal Bison Cooperative are united in a common goal: "Restoring the American Bison to its rightful range" (Intertribal Bison Cooperative 2003). Ambitious. Provocative. Implicit within this goal is a "baseline"—mid-nineteenth-century numbers and conditions. Unrealistic perhaps. Yet easily imagined. Ecosystem repair on a grand scale, according to Douglas Chadwick:

> With more than 13 million acres under tribal ownership nationwide, the potential is enormous—not only for the bison but for fritillary butterflies, prairie fringed orchids, vanishing swift foxes and other species that rely on the same kinds of habitat. This is what Indians really mean when they speak of the Buffalo Nation: the whole, wonderfully diverse array of flora and fauna that revolves around grazing, trampling, wallowing, dustbathing and constantly moving herds. (Chadwick 1998, 3)

There is joy and satisfaction in resurrecting smaller pieces of this larger vision. The Cheyenne River Sioux reservation, more than half of it in trust status, encompasses more than 2.8 million acres in north-central South Dakota. It is a mixed-grass prairie, with rolling hills and attractive bottomlands—ideally suited for broad-based restoration efforts. Bison country, to be sure (Cheyenne River Sioux Tribe and National Wildlife Federation 2001). And the tribe is making it happen. "Right now," scattered across the reservation, the tribe insists, it "is conserving or restoring virtually every component of a native prairie." Absent the wolf and grizzly bear (*Ursus arctos*), the tribe "has the capacity to restore all the missing pieces of the grasslands, while possessing the foresight and courage to conserve what remains." The tribal vision is to establish a Cheyenne River Sioux Tribal Park, "a large prairie reserve" (Cheyenne River Sioux Tribe and National Wildlife Federation 2001).

This prairie restoration effort features bison. In 1991, the tribe established Pte Hea Ka Inc. (the Buffalo Program), which aims to establish a herd of five thousand on tribal lands. The bison restoration is complemented by a black-footed ferret (*Mustela nigripes*) restoration effort—sixty-nine ferrets were released on reservation in October 2000 (see Miller et al. 1996). The ferrets, of course, depend upon thriving colonies of black-tailed prairie dogs (*Cynomys ludovicianus*), whose decline is marked by their candidate status under the Endangered Species Act (Nagle and Ruhl 2002). The Cheyenne River Sioux Tribe now manages approximately 7 percent of the remaining prairie dog habitat in the United States (Cheyenne River Sioux Tribe and National Wildlife Federation 2001).

Another member of the Intertribal Bison Cooperative is the Fort Belknap Reservation of the Assiniboine and Gros Ventre tribes in north-central Montana. Fort Belknap was the first reservation selected for reintroduction of the black-footed ferret. It has the obligate prairie dogs. It has the mountain plovers that nest in habitat created by the colonies. It has burrowing owls (*Athene cunicularia*) that rear their young in the prairie dogs' holes.

The Fort Belknap bison program is guided by a vision bolder than its present 10,000 acres. "I hope we can add at least another 40,000 acres," says Mike Fox, tribal biologist, "most of it from a tribal ranch now being used for cattle. Beyond that, well, we've got 400,000 acres here." The reservation abuts U.S. Bureau of Land Management property that leads into the Charles M. Russell Wildlife Refuge along the Missouri River. "Who knows?" adds Fox. "We might have a real, migratory bison range going one day" (Chadwick 1998, 3). Bison restoration is also under way at the Three Affiliated Tribes of the Fort Berthold Reservation (*Minot Daily News* 2003) and the Confederated Salish and Kootenai Tribes (in Montana) (*Missoulian* 2003; see also *Billings Gazette* 2003).

Whatever the "rightful" range of the bison, times are tough within the species' existing range. The Yellowstone herd has rebuilt itself. Bison migration out of the park now occurs on contested grounds. Conflicts at the boundaries have spilled into the courts for more than a decade. An interagency bison management plan has been in place since the year 2000 (NPS et al. 2000a, 2000b). Its strategies of hazing, capture, and slaughter have not brought peace to the terrain.

Strongest objections to bison expansion at Yellowstone come from the domestic livestock industry, represented at Yellowstone by the Montana Department of Livestock. Since 1996 the department has killed 2,064 wild bison (Buffalo Field Campaign 2003) on the grounds that migrating bison may infect domestic livestock with brucellosis. There is, however, no known case of free-ranging bison passing the microbe to cattle, and reasons to believe it will not happen.[1] Nonetheless, litigation seeking to halt the killing has been largely unsuccessful (*Fund for Animals v. Lujan* 1991; *Cold Mountain v. Garber* 2004; *Fund for Animals v. Clark* 1998).

Stymied at Yellowstone, ecosystem management is on the march elsewhere in Indian country. With bison as the keystone, the goal is to protect the full array of ecological processes. For the long term. Sustainability without fictions. An enthusiastic prospect.

Tribes and Science: Klamath Fisheries

> Support for the best available science is often based on the belief or hope that science will support previously held opinions.
>
> —*Dr. Gordon Orians, Chair, Board on Environmental Studies and Toxicology, National Research Council*

As far back as the administration of Abraham Lincoln, long before today's "best available science" jousts, technical advice has been given to the federal agencies by the National Research Council (NRC), the research arm of the National Academy of Sciences. Annually, the NRC prepares dozens of reports on all aspects of environmental policy. Its august reputation and frequent voice mean that its work product and processes are under constant scrutiny (Boffey 1975)—and so it is on the Klamath.

In 2001–2002, the academy's scientific apparatus met the Indian tribes in a memorable study on the Klamath River of northern California and southern Oregon. The experience was sobering for both and perhaps instructive.

The NRC could not escape being drawn into this conflict. All agencies of government woo the academy when they come up against hard-to-handle scientific issues. Water on the Klamath is exceedingly hard to handle. Three threatened or endangered fish are found in the Klamath Basin drainage—the Lost River sucker (*Deltistes luxatus*), the shortnose sucker (*Chasmistes brevirostris*), both listed as endangered in 1988, and the Klamath River Basin coho salmon (*Oncorhynchus kisutch*), listed as threatened in 1997. Three federal agencies jockey for position on fish—the Bureau of Reclamation, which serves the need of irrigators for water developed under the federal Klamath Basin Project, and the "biological" agencies, the Fish and Wildlife Service and the National Marine Fisheries Service, which seek to protect the suckers and coho, respectively. The drainage is home to what the NRC's Klamath Committee describes as any number of other "interested parties," including "farmers, commercial fishing interests, Native Americans, environmental interests, hunters, and hydropower production interests" (National Research Council 2002, xvi; see also Doremus and Tarlock 2003; Benson 2002b; McHenry 2003).

Four of these interested parties are Indian tribes. In the lower basin are the Karuk, Yurok and Hoopa Valley reservations (Doremus and Tarlock 2003), with rich histories and powerful off-reservation fishing rights. In the upper basin are the Klamath Indians composed of descendants of Klamaths, Modocs, and Yahooskin Paiutes, who were the aboriginal owners of over 20 million acres in present-day Oregon and California.

The academy was immediately put into a tight spot in bargaining with the Department of the Interior over the issues to be addressed. The government wanted a short answer to the question of whether the "biological opinions" developed in connection with Bureau of Reclamation operations of the Klamath Project were "consistent with the available scientific information" (National Research Council 2002, 32). The academy is wary of giving short answers to questions being contested in the courts; such answers are vulnerable to misuse and put the NRC in an adversarial posture. It prefers bigger questions, longer time frames, and contexts not so constraining. In the end, the charter for the Klamath Committee was a compromise—the department would get its short answer and the academy would get its long answer. There would be an interim report *and* a final report.

The academy was soon reminded why it usually avoids short answers. Its answer was short, unmistakable, and a total delight to farmers in the Klamath basin and critics of the ESA:

> There is no substantial scientific foundation at this time for changing the operation of the Klamath Project to maintain higher water levels in Upper Klamath Lake for the endangered sucker populations or higher minimum flows in the Klamath River main stem for the threatened coho population. (National Research Council 2002, 4).

This happy bit of news was quickly taken up by the Bureau of Reclamation, extolled in its 2002 biological assessment, and expressed on the ground as it protected agricultural diversions while stubbornly ramping down flows "just as the (unlisted) Chinook salmon began returning to the river" (Doremus and Tarlock 2003, 66). This part of the story culminated in September 2002 in a massive fish kill (at least thirty-three thousand adults, mostly unlisted chinook [*Oncorhynchus tshawytscha*] but with some ESA-protected coho) in the lower river (California Department of Fish and Game 2003).

The tribes were critical of the interim report. Most telling was a letter from John E. Echohawk, executive director of the Native American Rights Fund, to Dr. Bruce Alberts, president, National Academy of Sciences. The Echohawk letter made two useful points.

First is the question of "the baseline," a concept popularized by writers such as Jeremy Jackson of the Scripps Institution of Oceanography (Jackson et al.

2001). This is a fundamental issue in any environmental protection policy. Any aspiration to remediate or to restore or to save or to protect embraces an implicit understanding of some "baseline" of normalcy. Echohawk accused the NRC interim report of accepting the status quo as the baseline; he is correct in the charge. The committee found no science for "changing the operation" and thus clung to what is (National Research Council 2002, 4).

Echohawk's second point must have been especially galling to academy insiders because it is so frequently true. He charged the Klamath Committee with ignoring a policy pronouncement—notably, the precautionary principle—extolled in an earlier NRC study on the ESA (National Research Council 1995). This kind of omission happens frequently with NRC studies. Assembled for the particular issue and self-contained, committees often show no allegiance to what came before.

The academy had an answer to both objections. The "baseline" and "precautionary principle" ideas are in the agency policy domain that it does not like to touch. The committee would have another go at the "baseline" in its final report. And the "precautionary principle" would not help in any event. The conclusion of the interim report was that it would not assist the fish to send more hot water from the lake down the river. The committee was firm in its conclusion, steadfast in defense, and unshaken by criticism. It never wavered and needed no "precautionary principle" to guide it.

In the long run, however, the tribes are likely to become strong supporters of the academy work on the Klamath. The final Klamath report is out (National Research Council 2003), and it has been ignored just as the interim report was hailed and denounced. It is an impressive document that pulls no punches in its descriptions of current and historical conditions. It explains why the interim report addressed a question that was far too narrow ("so many things have been altered that lake level alone doesn't provide a strong signal") (Orians 2003). It gives useful environmental histories of the major tributaries, including those below Iron Gate Dam—the Shasta, Scott, Salmon, and Trinity rivers. It tells the story of the Lost River (it is now "so degraded that restoration of conditions suitable for sucker spawning seems unlikely unless land-use or water-management practices change") (National Research Council 2003, 124, 205). It has a chapter on adaptive management ("working examples of adaptive management in the upper Klamath basin are virtually absent") (National Research Council 2003, 290). It recommends expansion of the scope of ESA analysis. It underscores that the suckers are in trouble ("Because the suckers currently are not showing evidence of recovery, new types of actions intended to promote recovery are essential"), and recommends serious reparative action ("Removal of Chiloquin Dam to increase the extent of spawning habitat in the upper Sprague River and expand the range of and conditions under which larvae enter Upper Klamath Lake") (National Research Council 2003, 294). It says that "hydrologic manipulation" of the main stem at Iron Gate Dam is an "excessively narrow basis for recovery actions" for a species (coho salmon) "strongly oriented" toward tributaries for most life stages (National Research Council 2003, 296). It includes among the "remediation measures" that can be "justified from current knowledge" the following:

> Removal or provision for effective passage at all small dams and diversions throughout the distribution of the coho salmon, to be completed within [3 years.] In addition, serious evaluation should be made of the benefits to coho salmon from elimination of Dwinnell Dam and Iron Gate Dam on grounds that these structures block substantial amounts of coho habitat and, in the case of Dwinnell Dam, degrade downstream habitat as well. (National Research Council 2003, 297)

The tribes, true to their own traditions, will not be among those who forget these recommendations. They will be urging implementation and will be praised for their longer memories and deeper understandings of "best available science."

"Critical Habitat": White Mountain Apache Tribe

> In our Apache tradition, we do not manage our lands for the benefit of a particular species. We strive to protect the land and all the life forms it supports. Our homeland is too vast to manage for just one species. Our reservation traverses five life zones from Upper Sonoran to Sub-Alpine Forests.
>
> —*Ronnie Lupe, Chairman, White Mountain Apache Tribe*

Environmentalists relish the prospect of "critical habitat" (see Suckling and Taylor, this volume). Tucked into section 7 of the ESA, "critical habitat" is the highest promontory in the boldest section of the strongest environmental law in the world. What makes it so attractive to would-be protectors of wildlife is that section 7 is written to assure that federal actions do not "jeopardize" the species *or* "result in the destruction or modification" of critical habitat. The "destruction or modification" language stretches legal protection across designated landscape. Backing the tractor over a single salmon redd is an actionable deed of "destruction" or "modification" if the necessary paperwork is done.

The aspirations that drive "critical habitat" are duplicated in other corners of the law where owners' prerogatives are constrained by protective obligations. The classical "conservation easement" extends protective "clouds" across the titles of landowners (National Research Council 1993, 158). Similarly, owners give up fractional proprietorship of their lands to others who may manage for "critical" habitat. Implicit in the idea of "critical habitat" is the expectation of better management. The metaphor of the conservation easement is useful. For the dominant owner it signifies loss of title and management authority. Both prerogatives go to a newly designated owner of the easement.

Tribes have their own functional versions of "critical habitat" that work to enhance tribal authority to manage wildlife. The best known, but by no means only, example is the off-reservation treaty fishing right reserved in the Stevens treaties of the Pacific Northwest (*Washington v. Washington State Commercial Passenger Fishing Vessel Association* 1979). These reserve the "right of taking fish" across vast landscapes in four states that once served as aboriginal fishing grounds. The treaties have the feel of a conservation easement. The fishing right is place based, which means it is dependent upon protecting the geography. It is expressed as a property interest, which means it is disposable if at all only by choice of the owner. It is owned by native people for whom sale is an anathema.

It has been put to use to protect habitat that is critical to the survival of salmon. In a key ruling in 1980 Judge William Orrick held that "implicitly incorporated in the treaties' fishing clause is the right to have the fishery habitat protected from man-made despoliation" (*United States v. Washington* 1980, 203, 204, 207; Freyfogle 1993). Judge Orrick reasoned that "the most fundamental prerequisite" to exercising the right to take fish "is the existence of fish to be taken." He said that the conditions for successful reproduction in nature were well known—among them good water quality, suitable gravel, acceptable shelter. The treaties thus became the path to better habitat.

Since 1980, the northwest tribes have used their treaties to protect important habitat outside the interstices of the ESA (Blumm and Swift 1998; Belsky 1996; Sanders 1996; Meyers 1988; Monson 1982; Henderson 1982; Hornstein 1982; Katzen 2000; Goodman 2000; Anderson 1999). A striking example is the still unresolved "culvert case" that was initiated in January 2001 when the tribes filed a motion in an ongoing case alleging that "the blocking of fish passage at human made barriers such as road culverts is one of the most recurrent and correctable obstacles to healthy salmonid stocks in Washington" (*United States v. Washington* 2001). The tribes claimed that state agencies (the Department of Transportation and the Department of Fisheries and Wildlife) had determined that inadequately maintained culverts blocked or obstructed adult salmonid access "to at least 249 linear stream miles, at least 407,464 square meters of productive salmon spawning habitat, and at least 1,619,831 square meters of productive salmonid rearing habitat in the State of Washington" (*United States v. Washington* 2001). It was estimated that removal of these blockages would result in the production of two hundred thousand adult salmonids—many of them available for harvest by the tribes (*United States v. Washington* 2001). The formal claim was that the treaty "right of taking fish" imposes a duty on the State of Washington "to refrain from diminishing, through the construction or maintenance of culverts under state owned roads and highways" the fish runs to the detriment of the tribes' ability to maintain a moderate living (*United States v. Washington* 2001). The tribes sought an injunction requiring the state to identify and fix all culverts blocking fish runs.

The "culvert case" is a bold initiative to move management prerogatives to the "better" managers—in this instance the tribes. But what happens when tribal lands are swept into ESA designations of "critical habitat"? This issue arises repeatedly in Indian country (Zellmer 1998; see *Center for Biological Diversity v. Norton* 2003). Without exception, tribes resist these designations. They believe they are the "better" managers of endangered species. Their legal positions are consistent with this belief. There is ample discretion in the process that allows tribal escape from "critical habitat" designations when federal authorities concur in the capacities of tribal management.

The interesting case is when federal officials insist upon "critical habitat" designations that touch Indian lands over tribal objection. One striking showdown arose on the Fort Apache Indian Reservation of the White Mountain Apache Tribe along the Mogollan Rim in the high mountain country and forested region of northeastern Arizona.[2] The reservation covers 1.7 million acres of land. Tribal resource and environmental laws are longstanding. Tribal efforts to promote recovery of the endangered Apache trout, for example, predate the modern ESA (Fjetland 1999).

In the early 1990s, tribal disputes with the USFWS over ESA authority on the reservation intensified. Consultation was virtually nonexistent. Unilateral assertions of federal authority were commonplace—and naturally resented. Under the ESA, conflicts broke out over a tribal drinking water facility and a proposed tribal ski resort. The latter had come into conflict with the plant *Salix arizonica* (the Arizona willow) and it was rescued fortuitously by discovery of a wider distribution than expected for the plant (USFWS 1995b).

At White Mountain Apache, the designation of "critical habitat" was unwelcome. The doctrine offered no discernible legal advantage that could not be better achieved under traditional tribal jurisdiction and trust doctrines. In 1994, the tribe was moved to say all this and more:

> Whereas, the importation by Europeans of foreign trees, plants, birds, fish and animals into what is now known as the United States of America displaced native animals, birds, trees, plants and fish and changed the ecology thereof forever; and

Whereas, the State of Arizona's ecology has been and continues to be irretrievably and irreversibly damaged and altered by non-Indian "civilization"; and

Whereas, the Department of Interior has been responsible for the destruction of thousands of cottonwoods and other riparian vegetation along tribal streams which are tributaries of the Salt River, in order to increase the flow of tribal reserved waters to the Phoenix Valley and the Salt River Project; and

Whereas, Indian reservations, because they have *not* been extensively populated or developed by non-Indians, frequently remain the last refuge of plant and animal species which have been exterminated or virtually eliminated by non-Indians outside reservations for the sake of non-Indian economic or recreational development. (White Mountain Apache Tribe 1994)

"Critical habitat" received similar treatment in the same document, on grounds both of management competence ("tribal members, tribal biologists, botanists, foresters, soil scientists and hydrologists employed or under contract by the White Mountain Apache Tribe possess knowledge of the Tribe's Reservation far superior to that of federal and state agencies or environmental organizations and are best able to manage the lands, fauna, flora and waters of the Tribe's Reservation to ensure ecological maintenance and stability for all such species"); and overreaching application ("well-intentioned environmental groups whose members often reside in areas where native animals, plant species, forest and prairies have been virtually eliminated, or from which American Indians have been removed, have initiated aggressive efforts, including litigation, and have acted in concert with the Ecological Services Branch of the United States Fish and Wildlife Service to assert non-Indian jurisdiction and management over Indian lands, by declaring 'Critical Habitat' thereon without tribal consent in violation of American Indian tribal rights, tribal Sovereignty and Federal Indian law principles").

Consequently, the Tribal Council moved to evict most federal employees from the reservation, especially those of the USFWS. This move marked a dramatic phase change in the slowly deteriorating relationships between tribal and USFWS employees. The White Mountain Apache Tribe received considerable national publicity and the immediate attention of Mollie Beattie, director of the USFWS (White Mountain Tribe 1994; R. Lupe, statement of relationship, signing ceremony, Dec. 6, 1994). The crisis yielded hasty negotiation of a highly creative document entitled "Statement of the Relationship between the White Mountain Apache Tribe and the U.S. Fish and Wildlife Service" (*Apache Scout*

1994). It was worked out personally by Director Beattie and Chairman Lupe—with attorneys excluded from the room. The goal was to avoid intrusive on-reservation listings and "critical habitat" designations while skirting delicate questions of jurisdiction. In four pages, the document covers purpose, guiding precepts, tribal management, communication, and coordination. It has a detailed "matrix for communications" spelling out who talks to whom about what kind of issues. It is an example of good legal work outside the smoke and fire of litigation.

Among the "guiding precepts" is a declaration that the tribe and the USFWS "have a common interest in promoting healthy ecosystems." The USFWS "recognizes the tribe's aboriginal rights, sovereign authority, and insti-tutional capacity to self-manage the lands and resources within the Fort Apache Indian Reservation as the self-sustaining homeland of the White Mountain Apache people." The tribe is committed to preparing an ecosystem manage-ment plan that "addresses sensitive species, based on existing knowledge, active conservation practices, and current management plans. The plan will be con-tinuously enhanced with new information obtained from ongoing surveys, habitat assessments, and other planning processes." The USFWS and the tribe "will cooperatively develop and propose management practices based upon threats to sensitive species and their habitats for incorporation into the Tribal Management Plan (TMP), which consists of the portions of the Ecosystem Management Plan and integrated resource management plans which address sensitive species." Adoption and implementation of the tribal management plan "will normally mean no additional special management considerations or protection for sensitive species will be needed."

The White Mountain experience figured conspicuously in development of Secretarial Order 3206 (U.S. Department of the Interior and U.S. Department of Commerce 1997), which spells out tribal-agency expectations in implemen-tation of the ESA (Cates 1998; Wilkinson 1997).

Where does this leave "critical habitat"? It will not enter Indian country except as a last resort and upon a showing of dire need. Indian lands are "crit-ical habitat" for Indian people and it is their choice to afford protections to other living things. The federal agencies long have insisted that "critical habi-tat" adds little to the protections afforded by the ESA. Many doubt this, but the last place for an empirical study is on Indian lands—where we are least likely to observe additive legal effects.

Conclusion

The Indian relationship to the natural world is so subtle, complex, and inspir-ing as to defy summary restatement. The tribes' conspicuous influence on the

Endangered Species Act is a useful reminder that these "third sovereignties" can become the creative laboratories long promised by the state/federal duopoly. A source to look to is the Native American Fish and Wildlife Society (see http://www.nafws.org/). Here gather the tribal biologists, managers, elders, and doers who bring energy to the tasks of protecting the natural world. The society has a "Chief Sealth" award (for work and dedication on behalf of tribal natural resources) and a "Biologist of the Year" for creative contributions in management. Its many agendas mirror the work across Indian country that is striving to sustain the natural world.

I5   Nongovernmental Organizations

Peter Kareiva, Timothy H. Tear, Stacey Solie, Michelle L. Brown,
Leonardo Sotomayor, and Christopher Yuan-Farrell

Several national and international nongovernmental organizations (NGOs), including over 1,200 land trusts, cite the protection of biodiversity as part of their mission (see Land Trust Alliance 2005). But given the Endangered Species Act's mandate to prevent extinction, is there a need for NGOs and land trusts? Conversely, given land trusts and conservation NGOs, is there a need for the Endangered Species Act (ESA)? One response would be that over 60 percent of federally listed species in the United States occur on privately owned land (Groves 2003), where NGOs and land trusts can perhaps be more effective than the federal government. A more nuanced distinction between conservation NGOs and the ESA involves differences in how the simple phrase "protecting biodiversity" is interpreted. Whereas the ESA is dedicated to preventing extinction and recovering at-risk species, most major conservation NGOs embrace loftier missions (see box 15.1). For example, most conservation NGOs seek to protect natural communities and ecosystems, as well as species (e.g., Defenders of Wildlife, World Wildlife Fund, Ocean Conservancy, Audubon Society, Sierra Club, and the Nature Conservancy). Many of these prominent NGOs also mention wildlands and responsible use of the earth's resources as a mission component, suggesting that many conservation NGOs seek to protect natural processes as much as they do species. Indeed, the missions of major conservation NGOs are remarkably close to the theoretical view of what it means to preserve nature and natural processes (Naeem et al., forthcoming). Of course this does not mean that NGOs leave species protection by the wayside. Rather, NGOs explicitly embrace both species protection and ecosystem or wildlife protection.

There is also a subtle difference in how the ESA treats human concerns versus how some NGOs address these concerns. Although the ESA mentions humans, the act is implemented as though species have a fundamental right not to be terminated by human activities. In other words, the ESA is an ethical law.

BOX 15.1. Mission Statements of Major Conservation NGOs Active in the United States

Audubon
www.audubon.org/nas/
Audubon's mission is to conserve and restore natural ecosystems, focusing on birds, wildlife, and their habitats for the benefit of humanity and the earth's biological diversity.

Defenders of Wildlife
www.defenders.org/about/
Defenders of Wildlife is dedicated to the protection of all native wild animals and plants in their natural communities. . . . Our programs encourage protection of entire ecosystems and interconnected habitats.

Sierra Club
www.sierraclub.org/inside/

1. Explore, enjoy and protect the wild places of the earth.
2. Practice and promote the responsible use of the earth's ecosystems and resources.
3. Educate and enlist humanity to protect and restore the quality of the natural and human environment.
4. Use all lawful means to carry out these objectives.

The Nature Conservancy
www.nature.org/aboutus/howwework/
The Nature Conservancy's mission is to preserve the plants, animals and natural communities that represent the diversity of life on Earth by protecting the lands and waters they need to survive.

Wildlife Conservation Society
www.wcs.org/home/about
The Wildlife Conservation Society saves wildlife and wildlands. . . . Together these activities change individual attitudes toward nature and help people imagine wildlife and humans living in sustainable interaction on both a local and global scale.

World Wildlife Fund
www.worldwildlife.org/
World Wildlife Fund's mission is the conservation of nature. . . . We work to preserve the diversity and abundance of life on Earth and the health of ecological systems. . . . We are committed to reversing the degradation of our planet's natural environment and to building a future in which human needs are met in harmony with nature. We recognize the critical relevance of human numbers, poverty, and consumption patterns to meeting these goals.

In fact, the U.S. Fish and Wildlife Service (USFWS) officially states that the listing of species as endangered or threatened should be based solely on biology and should not reflect the perceived value of the species to humans or the economic cost of that species protection. This has led many critics of the ESA to complain that the federal government is egregiously insensitive to the needs of people when applying the ESA (Mann and Plummer 1995). Many NGOs deflect this perceived conflict by emphasizing the benefits to society such as ecosystem services derived from conservation efforts (e.g., cleaner water and air, medicinal drugs, etc.). The explicit recognition of these practical social values highlights the connection between human society and other species and may encourage support for conservation beyond the abstract principle of species rights.

In this chapter we examine how NGOs in the private sector can complement the work of the federal agencies implementing the Endangered Species Act. We focus specifically on the Nature Conservancy (TNC) for two reasons: (1) it has a large national membership and budget; and (2) as TNC staff, we are familiar with its policies and have access to relevant internal data.

Selecting Targets for Conservation Action

Although Congress has stated that species should be protected on the basis of their risk of extinction without regard to taxonomic classification (U.S. Congress 1982c), there is strong evidence that certain types of species are favored over others in the ESA listing process. For example, although vertebrates comprise only 2 percent of U.S. biodiversity (fig. 15.1a), they represent almost 30 percent of federally listed species. Invertebrates, on the one hand, make up 84 percent of the species composition of overall U.S. biodiversity but are only 14 percent of the listed species. Early criticisms of the ESA also lamented strong biases toward listing charismatic animals over plants (e.g., Tear et al. 1995; Schultz and Gerber 2002). This situation has improved. In comparing listed species in 1982 to 2002, it is clear that the listing frequency of plants is catching up to that of animals (Scott, Goble, et al., this volume; Wilcove and McMillan, this volume; fig. 15.2). Species listings can be misleading, however, because charismatic species such as birds are still favored, with better-funded recovery plans (Miller et al. 2002; Restani and Marzluff 2002) and greater numbers of recommended recovery actions (Schultz and Gerber 2002).

These biases predictably mimic broad public opinion (Czech et al. 1998) so that more attention is paid to highly visible species than to inconspicuous or rarely seen species. The strength of these biases as societal values is further demonstrated by noting that in the United States there are fifty-seven NGOs devoted exclusively to birds but only four devoted to invertebrates (Czech et al.

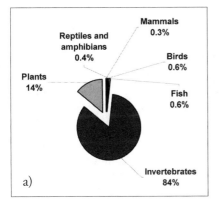

a)

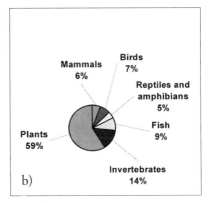

b)

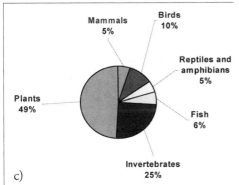

c)

Figure 15.1. Distribution of species among major taxa for (a) total biodiversity in the United States (b) federally listed species and (c) species targets within Nature Conservancy ecoregional plans.

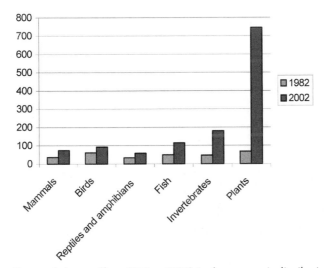

Figure 15.2. Temporal changes (from 1982 to 2002) in the taxonomic distribution of federally listed species.

1998). Is the disproportionate attention given birds over more diverse and abundant species groups justified? Certainly, if ecosystem services are to be valued, there is no reason to neglect invertebrates, no matter how inconspicuous. Consider, for example, that the biomass of earthworms in the United States is twenty-seven times that of all vertebrate species combined (Pimentel et al. 1992) and that the functions performed by invertebrates like pollination or decomposition are absolutely essential to our well-being (Buchman and Nabhan 1996). Moreover, it appears that invertebrates are as likely to be at risk of extinction as vertebrates. It is estimated that 10–34 percent of all invertebrate species are rare, endangered, or threatened (Black et al. 2001).

Given the bias evident in ESA listings, does TNC do any better? TNC uses a structured process called "ecoregional planning" to guide its conservation efforts (Groves et al. 2002; Groves 2003). Ecoregions are relatively large areas characterized by similar floral and faunal composition and predictable large-scale ecological processes. Typically, they are classified based on their underlying soils, geology, vegetation, and climate (Groves et al. 2002). Ecoregions are widely used by conservation organizations (e.g., World Wildlife Fund, Conservation International, TNC) throughout the world to prioritize and stratify their activities (Redford et al. 2003). As a first step in its ecoregional conservation planning process, TNC identifies species and community targets for each ecoregion (see Groves 2003). Although target species are often rare or endemic, they are not necessarily federally threatened or endangered. Thus, where the ESA selects species targets based on risk of extinction, TNC selects targets based on proactive protection of a region's total biodiversity, with the target being a mix of threatened and nonthreatened species, as well as distinctive plant communities. We examined a sample of twenty-five ecoregional plans from TNC, spanning all of North America; our sample entailed all plans that we could obtain electronically by writing directors of science in various TNC state programs. We found that roughly half of all the conservation targets are species. Examining species targets, we calculated the percentage of species represented by each of the major taxonomic groups for each plan, and averaged over all plans (fig. 15.1c). Notably, both TNC species targets and federally listed species include a preponderance of plants (49 percent and 59 percent, respectively). A major difference between TNC and federally listed species arises with the treatment of invertebrates. TNC includes a larger proportion of invertebrate targets than the ESA list of threatened and endangered species (compare figs. 15.1c and 15.1b). As is the case with ESA-listed species, TNC is heavily biased toward identifying vertebrates as its conservation targets—far out of proportion to the diversity of vertebrates in the United States (compare figs. 15.1c and 15.1a).

There are two obvious ways in which conservation targets for TNC complement the ESA. First, TNC does not need to wait until a species is at risk of extinction to make a species a focus of conservation planning. Ideally, if TNC (and other NGOs) was tremendously successful at its mission, then fewer and fewer new species would need to be added to the endangered species list. At this time, however, we know of only one case where action by a private or conservation NGO has successfully averted a listing decision (the slickspot peppergrass [*Lepidium papilliferum*]; see USFWS 2004f, 2004g). The second obvious way that TNC can complement the ESA is through its different taxonomic emphases. TNC's attention to invertebrates may help compensate for the ESA's comparatively reduced enthusiasm for invertebrate protection. Finally, TNC's emphasis on nonspecies targets is effectively a habitat-based approach, and hence nicely complements the ESA's species-based focus.

Designating Habitat

One of the fundamental criticisms of the ESA is that species are listed much faster than they are delisted, resulting in a backlog. This view of ever-increasing numbers of imperiled species has been coined "the extinction curve" and reflects the fact that the number of listed species has increased more than sevenfold from 1976 to 2000 (Scott, Goble, et al., this volume; Shaffer et al. 2002a). Given that the ESA alone cannot reverse the extinction curve, what else is needed?

The existing system of protected areas includes less than 6 percent of the coterminous United States in nature reserves; the majority of these are at higher elevations and on less productive soils (Scott et al. 2001b). On the other hand, the habitat needed for numerous imperiled species is primarily privately owned. Scott et al. (2001b) conclude that any effort to protect biodiversity adequately must fully engage the private sector.

The authors of the ESA knew the value of habitat and therefore included the act's provisions on critical habitat. By 2000, however, only 10 percent of listed species have designated critical habitat (Hoekstra et al. 2002b). Even after the USFWS diverted all available funds in 2001 to address this backlog, Hoekstra et al. (2002b) concluded that critical habitat designation had little positive influence on the recovery planning process (but see Suckling and Taylor, this volume). By the end of 2004, 36 percent of all species had critical habitat designated (Suckling and Taylor, this volume).

Recognizing the need for a more proactive, habitat-based approach to conserving the full range of biodiversity, TNC has consciously shifted its conservation planning to focus on the best available representative examples of *all* habitat types, independent of rarity or degree of imperilment. TNC identifies "portfolios" of sites that it feels are needed to capture a region's biodiversity. It is interesting to note the mix of private versus public lands. In a sample of sixteen ecoregions that reported this information, the amount of the conservation portfolio in public lands (54 percent) was roughly equivalent to the amount in private lands (46 percent). In short, TNC's conservation plans rely as much on private land as on public land to achieve their goals.

This leaves open the question of how much land is enough. Shaffer et al. (2002a) suggest that between 20 and 30 percent of the land in any state is an appropriate initial goal for a habitat-based reserve system. Since TNC identifies habitat for protection and establishes goals for those habitats, it would be interesting to know how much habitat TNC thinks is needed. If we accept the 20–30 percent range as a reasonable first approximation, our analysis shows that TNC portfolio designs called for a wide spectrum of habitat protection (ranging from 3 to 42 percent) with an average of 24 percent (SD ± 0.11, $n = 24$).

Evaluating TNC's Goals for Species Recovery

A second step in TNC's ecoregional planning process is the establishment of quantitative goals. Similarly, a crucial step in protecting ESA-listed species is the establishment of recovery criteria. A recurrent criticism of ESA recovery criteria is that they are set too low or seem to be insensitive to the species' biology (Schemske et al. 1994; Tear et al. 1993, 1995). Do TNC's goals suffer similar weaknesses, or are they more demanding than recovery plans?

TNC faces an even more daunting task than the federal government. Each ecoregional plan identifies several hundred conservation targets (mean = 301, SD = 178.70, $n = 24$), presenting an organizational goal-setting demand over all ecoregions that totals as many as fifty thousand targets. Consequently, TNC has evolved a more generic approach to goal setting that is largely devoid of place- and species-specific data. TNC's rapid and detail-free process thus is virtually the opposite of the standard federal recovery process, which has typically required several years to develop explicit recovery criteria for each species.

Federal agencies are also moving away from species-by-species recovery planning. The USFWS currently prefers multispecies recovery plans (Jewell 2000) both as a way of overcoming the slow pace of the species-by-species approach and as a strategy to ensure that recommendations for one species do not run counter to recommendations for other species. Unfortunately, recent analyses suggest that federal multispecies plans are not as well conceived as single-species recovery plans (Boersma et al. 2001; Clark and Harvey 2002).

For example, the South Florida multispecies recovery plan includes sixty-eight federally listed species and most of the species in that plan lack quantitative goals.

It is also revealing to compare TNC and federal recovery objectives in those cases where both have set quantitative goals. We relied on the Society for Conservation Biology's recovery plan database as the most comprehensive list of species with recovery plans (Hoekstra et al. 2002b). We surveyed seventeen ecoregional plans and compared the ecoregional species target lists with the recovery plan database. Direct comparison of quantitative goals was only possible for a few species, primarily for plants rather than birds and mammals. Nonetheless, analysis revealed what is likely to be a common trend for most listed species with explicit recovery goals (table 15.1). The quantitative goals set by TNC are either the same as or more demanding than those stated in recovery plans. Even for species for which analyses are not yet complete (e.g., red-cockaded woodpecker [*Picoides borealis*]), TNC's quantitative goals are substantially higher than those in the recovery plan. Apparently, TNC's rapid goal-setting process has resulted in recovery criteria that err on the cautious side of recovery and are less inhibited by concern about what is feasible (see Scott et al. 1995). For example, while the TNC ecoregional plans identified fifteen populations as the goal for the Florida panther (*Puma concolor coryi*), the federal recovery plan identified only three populations.

A final, intriguing way of looking at conservation goals is to examine how closely an ecoregional conservation plan is to meeting its set goal for species population levels at the time it is written. Since threatened and endangered species are at risk of extinction, one might expect their population levels to be substantially below conservation goals established in the plan—otherwise, why would the species be labeled critically at risk? It turns out that this commonsense expectation is incorrect. In many ecoregional plans, a large proportion of federally listed species have enough viable populations to meet TNC's goals (see fig. 15.3, especially plans for the northern Gulf of Mexico and the Arizona–New Mexico Mountains). Of course, meeting these goals by recruiting a sufficient number of populations does not mean the populations are adequately protected in perpetuity. Nonetheless, the implication is that these federally listed species require protection rather than restoration. Even more puzzling is that in many ecoregions, federally listed species do not fare more poorly (as measured by the percentage that meet TNC's conservation goals) than other species (fig. 15.3). Because most species are chosen as targets in ecoregional plans based on their rarity (most are classified as G1–G3), it could be that many of TNC's unlisted targets are in fact seriously at risk (see Scott, Goble, et al., this volume) and perhaps should be federally listed.

TABLE 15.1. Comparison of quantitative recovery criteria for delisting federally listed species and the quantitative goals stated in the Nature Conservancy's ecoregional plans

Federally listed species	Federal recovery plan criteria for delisting (no. of viable populations)	Cumulative no. of viable populations sought by TNC	No. of TNC ecoregional plans reviewed to tally necessary no. of populations
Dwarf wedgemussel *Alasmidonta heterodon*	10	29–43	Complete (five plans)
Florida panther *Puma concolor coryi*	3	15	Complete (one plan)
Karner blue butterfly *Lycaeides melissa samuelis*	29	23–28	Complete (three plans)
Lakeside daisy *Hymenoxys herbacea*	4	17	Complete (two plans)
Lower Keys marsh rabbit *Sylvilagus palustris hefneri*	8	15	Complete (one plan)
Northern wild monkshood *Aconitum noveboracense*	20	20–24	Complete (four plans)
Tennessee purple coneflower *Echinacea tennesseensis*	5	10	Complete (one plan)
American burying beetle *Nicrophorus americanus*	12	4	Not yet determined (one plan)
Bayou darter *Etheostoma rubrum*	4	33	Not yet determined (one plan)
Blowout penstemon *Penstemon haydenii*	10	2	Not yet determined (one plan)
Bog turtle *Clemmys muhlenbergii*	185	5	Not yet determined (one plan)
Clubshell *Pleurobema clava*	20	3	Not yet determined (one plan)
Cooley's meadowrue *Thalictrum cooleyi*	16	2	Not yet determined (one plan)
Decurrent false aster *Boltonia decurrens*	12	10	Not yet determined (one plan)
Eastern prairie fringed orchid *Platanthera leucophaea*	22	4	Not yet determined (one plan)
Fanshell *Cyprogenia stegaria*	12	3	Not yet determined (one plan)
Fat pocketbook *Potamilus capax*	3	4	Not yet determined (one plan)
Gray wolf *Canus lupus*	2	1	Not yet determined (one plan)

Table 15.1. *Continued*

Federally listed species	Federal recovery plan criteria for delisting (no. of viable populations)	Cumulative no. of viable populations sought by TNC	No. of TNC ecoregional plans reviewed to tally necessary no. of populations
Higgins eye (pearlymussel) *Lampsilis higginsii*	5	6	Not yet determined (one plan)
Leafy prairie-clover *Dalea foliosa*	15	1	Not yet determined (one plan)
Mead's milkweed *Asclepias meadii*	21	4	Not yet determined (one plan)
Northeastern bulrush *Scirpus ancistrochaetus*	20	5	Not yet determined (one plan)
Northern riffleshell *Epioblasma torulosa rangiana*	20	7	Not yet determined (one plan)
Pallid sturgeon *Scaphirhynchus albus*	3	7	Not yet determined (three plans)
Red-cockaded woodpecker *Picoides borealis*	25	40	Not yet determined (four plans)
Tar River spinymussel *Elliptio steinstansana*	5	12	Not yet determined (one plan)

Complete analysis of all ecoregional plans contained within the global range of the species was determined for only seven species at the time of writing. TNC plans that identified "all viable occurrences" as a goal were excluded from the analysis unless this goal was quantified.

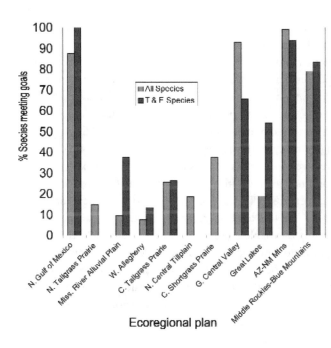

Figure 15.3. The percentage of species-level targets that met quantitative goals. Goals are most often stated as the degree of redundancy required to be secure, such as the number of populations needed to be considered conserved. The Y-axis represents the number of species in an ecoregional plan selected as a conservation target that fully met goals. For example, if a species was given a goal of ten viable populations, it would not meet its goal until ten populations deemed viable were included within the ecoregional portfolio.

TNC has established quantitative goals for many listed species for which there is no recovery plan (e.g., Topeka shiner [*Notropis topeka*], slackwater darter [*Etheostoma boschungi*], Florida golden aster [*Chrysopsis floridana*], northern spotted owl [*Strix occidentalis caurina*], and Chinook salmon [*Oncorhynchus tshawytscha*]). Such goal-setting efforts by NGOs could help fill a void created by an overtaxed federal system. If TNC could catalyze monitoring efforts coincident with its conservation goals, it would provide federal agencies with ready-made scientific justification for many difficult decisions.

Comparing the Distribution of Money and Biodiversity

A strength of TNC and many conservation NGOs is support from within communities for local conservation efforts. On the other hand, a possible limitation of local action is the potentially poor match between resources and conservation needs. For example, wealthy communities that face minor biodiversity threats may keep their money at home, while poorer communities at risk of significant biodiversity losses may go begging for meager funds. Put more simply, the money may not be where the need is greatest. To quantify the match of money and need, we examined the distribution of biodiversity and at-risk species by state versus the annual budget of each TNC state chapter. In particular, we obtained the dollars spent on all conservation activities per state for fiscal year 2003 (July 2002 through June 2003). For each state, we also determined the number of endemic species, the total diversity, and the number of at-risk species (see http://www.natureserve.org/). Using the number of endemics, the number of at-risk species, and total species richness as measures of need, we asked whether money tracked conservation need. This is complicated, however, by the fact that the cost of land varies enormously from state to state. For species protection that is achieved by conservation easements or land acquisition, housing and land costs will determine conservation costs. Therefore, we added the median house value for each state as an additional possible explanatory variable along with the biological metrics mentioned above. We then asked how well we could predict each state's conservation expenditure. Although all regression analyses indicate that conservation funding generally increased with the number of species, at-risk species, and endemics, the relationship was remarkably weak (see table 15.2). In fact, if California is removed from the analysis, any single variable explains at most 17 percent of the variation in state expenditures and a multiple regression model with all four predictor variables explains only 46 percent of the variation in expenditures. In the absence of California, state expenditures do not track endemism or the number of species at risk (fig. 15.4). Similar results have been reported for expenditures by state governments (Niles and Korth, this volume).

TABLE 15.2. Regression analysis examining Nature Conservancy state expenditures in dollars for fiscal year 2002 as a function of number of endemic species (ENDEMICS), number of species at risk (ATRISK), number of species (TOTSPECIES), and median house value (HOUSE$)

Independent variable(s)	% variation explained	No. of states included (N)
CALIFORNIA INCLUDED		
ENDEMICS	53	50
ATRISK	56	50
TOTSPECIES	37	50
HOUSE$	21	49
ALL OF ABOVE	71	49
CALIFORNIA EXCLUDED		
ENDEMICS	13	50
ATRISK	16	50
TOTSPECIES	17	50
HOUSE$	10	49
ALL OF ABOVE	46	49

Analyses were carried out with and without the state of California, because for all regression analyses, California is a statistical outlier. Dollars are the dependent variable in all regressions. All variables are significant at the p *** .05 level. Data were missing for a few states, so the sample size (N) varies slightly. *Source*: Species data obtained from NatureServe; house values obtained from Census Bureau (2000).

Regression analyses that seek to predict variation among states in conservation investments may not be the right way to look at the question. A better way of exploring inequities in conservation investment might be to think of schoolchildren and investment in school districts. It is routine when discussing our nation's public school system to report on the dollars spent on each schoolchild per year. Similarly, we can use our data to ask how many dollars are spent on each at-risk species per year. A graph of dollars per at-risk species for all fifty states reveals pronounced geographic and among-state inequities (fig. 15.5). In fiscal year 2002, New York invested $4.8 million per species at risk, whereas Alabama invested only $138,320. That forty-fold discrepancy dwarfs any metric of per capita inequities in human or educational

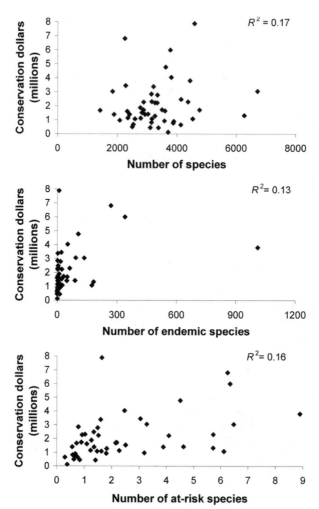

Figure 15.4. The relationship between statewide spending on conservation by the Nature Conservancy and several metrics of conservation need. Each point represents a different state, and the scatter of the points reflects how well TNC funds per state correlate with each state's needs. *Source*: TNC's financial management system for fiscal year 2002.

investment among different states. Even when expenditures are rescaled by dividing by median house value, the inequities are extreme (with New York still at the top, thirty-fold higher than the lowest-ranking Nevada). This does not mean that New York is spending too much money on conservation, since many habitats and species remain imperiled in New York despite the comparatively large investment. It does mean that special effort should be made to

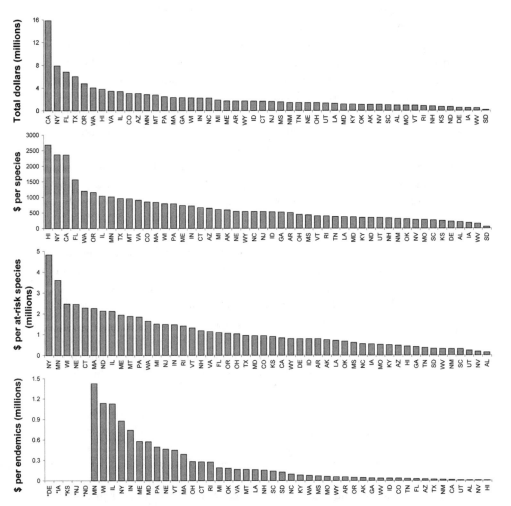

Figure 15.5. Funding inequities among states as measured by dollars per "unit need," where that need is expressed either as endemic species or species at risk. The top graph represents the dollars per state, without reference to any metric of conservation need; note that it gives a very different impression of the distribution of funding than the lower figures, which are expressed in terms of dollars per "need." *Source:* TNC's financial management system for fiscal year 2002.

elevate the funds available in states such as Alabama and Nevada that are poor, yet have many at-risk species.

The lesson is that although TNC clearly seeks to protect biodiversity, its investment in that endeavor is constrained by the fact that generated funds do not necessarily bear a relationship to the at-risk biodiversity. To redress this imbalance, TNC encourages its local state chapters to share funds with poorer states and countries whose needs are great and opportunities are available. One advantage of federal funding is that recovery funds are distributed from a centralized source. In theory, the federal government can be more responsive to local needs, directly targeting species that might suffer because the local community lacks wealth. Unfortunately, the distribution of state and federal funds for endangered species recovery is woefully low and bizarrely distributed (see DeShazo and Freeman, this volume). Using USFWS reports (1995c) on expenditures, we found that a mere 6 species received 50 percent of the recovery funds, leaving most of the remaining 950 or more threatened and endangered species with tiny budgets. In fact 400 species had to share $4 million in 1995, while 4 salmon species (all in the same genus) received over $100 million in 1995. The top 6 species that accounted for over half of the federal and state funding in 1995 have species ranges that are all clustered west of the Rocky Mountains, and thus in no way can act as a conservation umbrella for widespread biodiversity. Clearly both TNC and the federal government have a difficult time distributing conservation funds according to biodiversity needs.

Assessing TNC Conservation Priorities

There is no question that the Nature Conservancy—and probably all conservation NGOs—complements the work of the federal agencies charged with implementing the Endangered Species Act. Where general biases in conservation exist, TNC appropriately prioritizes federally overlooked species and taxonomies, with greater attention to invertebrates. TNC's emphasis on both species and community-level targets allows the capture of systems that might be threatened but do not as yet include any endangered species. TNC's focus on community types and habitats also allows efficient capture of several listed species all at once. Clearly, TNC and the federal government emphasize different targets, different strategies, and different goals for conservation. Just as clearly, TNC and the federal agencies share common values and missions.

Given the commonalties and differences, we believe that a more formalized, coordinated public-private partnership could improve the effectiveness with which both NGOs and the ESA achieve their conservation missions. One opportunity entails the protection of critical biodiversity habitat (TNC's approach) in support of the ESA. A second opportunity might involve taking advantage of TNC's rapid and precautionary goal-setting process, especially if it were supplemented with monitoring. The last great opportunity for synergy lies with the federal government's greater ability to redistribute wealth among states. Contemporary political pressures have reduced federal activism. If this trend continues, it is essential that federal and NGO conservation sectors better coordinate to ensure that they collectively make up for each other's deficiencies.

We would like to thank all of the recovery planning teams and ecoregional planning teams. We would also like to acknowledge the help of Laura Landon and Zoe Kant of the Nature Conservancy for the use of their unpublished analysis of ecoregional plans.

Part III Prospects

Parts 1 and 2 are primarily retrospective, focusing on what we have learned from three decades of implementing the Endangered Species Act. This final part is primarily prospective: how can the efficiency of the act be improved? The chapters are in broad agreement on two points: (1) the act has been successful at preventing extinctions, but (2) there is room for improvement. Many of the authors are also hopeful that new conservation institutions and relationships are emerging that transcend the polarization that has characterized much of the act's history. The encouraging tone of these chapters suggests that we may be creating a new land ethic that redefines the balance between the responsibilities and the rights of private property owners.

16 Lessons Learned

Holly Doremus

Thirty years ago, the United States launched a bold experiment: through regulation of a broad sweep of both governmental and private actions, it undertook to protect against extinction the broad range of other creatures that share our planet. With enactment of the Endangered Species Act of 1973, the nation for the first time moved beyond a strategy narrowly focused on protection of favored species through management of federal reserve lands and trade restrictions to a comprehensive approach applicable to virtually all species[1] wherever they might occur. The law was, and remains, a landmark, the strongest mandate for protection of the biota on the globe.

From a human perspective, thirty years is a long time. It represents the sweep of a professional career, or in personal terms the length of a generation. From today's vantage point, notwithstanding the recent return of some of the absurd fashions of those times, 1973 seems a world away. Six different presidents have occupied the Oval Office since Richard Nixon signed the Endangered Species Act (ESA). At that time, slide rules were still in common use, calculators were a newfangled, high-tech, expensive invention, and computers were room-filling machines that had to be programmed with stacks of punch cards. More directly to the conservation point, in 1973 the population of the United States stood at roughly 212 million (Census Bureau 2000). Since then, it has increased nearly 40 percent, to almost 293 million today (Census Bureau 2004a). Many related pressures on resources have also progressively increased. For example, urbanized land area increased 34 percent between 1982 and 1997 alone (U.S. Department of Agriculture 2004).

By contrast, thirty years is merely a moment in evolutionary time, and most of the species on the list have been protected nowhere near that long (USFWS 2004h; Scott, Goble, et al., this volume). Some species have been protected for many of their generations, but others have spent less than one full generation on the list. From a biological perspective, therefore, it is far too soon to judge the act's success.

Less recognized is that it may also be premature from a human legal and institutional perspective to make conclusive judgments about the act. Law moves at a slower pace than technology, population, or fashion. By the crusty standards of the common law or the constitution, and even by comparison to a good number of familiar statutes, the ESA is still very young. Furthermore, it marked a remarkable departure from past practice, and it has not been static since 1973. Its first fifteen years were punctuated by frequent amendment, and since then it has seen remarkable administrative development. The ESA as it exists today, in other words, is barely in its adolescence. Perhaps some gawkiness should be tolerated at this stage. Ideally, we might want to let its identity settle more firmly before doing a full-scale review.

But we do not have the luxury of waiting another generation. For one thing, if we are currently on the wrong conservation road, we need to discover that and reverse course as soon as possible lest we set in motion extinctions and other irreversible consequences. For another, the political situation demands evaluation now. Given the continuing controversy and escalating potential for conflict, not to mention the current legislative paralysis, it is time to appraise what we have learned from this first generation of the ESA experiment and to make decisions about whether and to what extent we should adopt different strategies for the next generation.

I draw five key lessons from the experience of the past thirty years.

Lesson 1: There Is Much to Celebrate

If the act were currently pleasing all observers, there would be little need for this book. Not surprisingly, there is a broad consensus that the ESA does not provide the perfect answer to our conservation challenges. There are of course critics from the fringes who completely reject the ESA and, no doubt, its conservation goals. But most of the serious criticism is strikingly muted, focused on the details of implementation rather than aiming at the law's heart. That focus reflects a continuing general consensus that the act's goals are important ones and that the act has helped us move, if only haltingly, toward those goals.

It is not disputed that the ESA has done far more to protect America's biota than any other law. That is not to say, of course, that it has done enough or that changes could not increase its effectiveness. But we should take care that we do not, in our desire to achieve perfection, undermine a law that has in fact made remarkable strides toward accomplishing its goals.

Conservation Effectiveness

Especially in light of its breathtaking ambition and departure from past practices, the ESA has been surprisingly successful in achieving its conservation goals. Anyone who is seriously committed to conservation must recognize that fewer species have been lost in the United States over the last thirty years than would have disappeared had the pre-1973 legal regime continued. Using admittedly very rough but conservative assumptions about the likelihood of stochastic extinction, Mark Schwartz has estimated that listed species could be expected to go extinct at more than twenty-seven times the rate actually observed (Schwartz 1999, 86–87), suggesting that in fact the law acts as a powerful guard against extinction.

Over the past several years, there has been substantial discussion of whether the number and rate of delistings is an appropriate measure of the ESA's success. I remain firmly convinced, as I have previously argued (Doremus and Pagel 2001; Doremus 2000a) that the rate of delisting is not a useful metric. That is true in part for biological reasons. Most species do not reach the ESA's protected list until their populations are very small or dwindling rapidly (Wilcove et al. 1993). It takes time to turn around those declines. But even without that biological lag, it is simply unrealistic to expect rapid delisting. Species cannot be removed from the protected list until threats to their survival are adequately controlled for the foreseeable future. That is a difficult process, in many cases requiring major changes to state law, at least for species threatened by habitat degradation (Doremus and Pagel 2001). While the ESA has not fulfilled rosy expectations that it would function as a conservation "emergency room," providing intensive but relatively short-term care until "recovered" species were ready to make it on their own, that failure is properly attributed to unrealistically optimistic expectations rather than to fundamental flaws in the act.

In fact there is considerable empirical evidence that species do benefit from listing under the ESA. The U.S. Fish and Wildlife Service (USFWS) is required to deliver to Congress periodic reports on the status of all listed species. Although the agency routinely misses the statutory reporting deadlines (as is so typical of ESA implementation), it has now prepared reports covering up to 2002 (USFWS 2004c). The reports categorize every listed species under the jurisdiction of the USFWS as improving, stable, declining, or unknown. Assignments are made by field personnel on the basis of their knowledge of population trends and the degree to which threats are controlled.

Based on examination of earlier reports, Rachlinski noted in 1997 that time on the protected list correlated with improving status (Rachlinski 1997). The latest reports, evaluated by Suckling and Taylor (this volume) and Taylor et al. (2005) show the same pattern. At least for species listed less than fifteen years, the longer they have been on the list the more likely they are to be improving and the less likely they are to be declining.

It is more difficult to sort out precisely what might be responsible for the benefits of listing. The role of critical habitat designation, in particular, is hotly disputed. The USFWS has long believed that designation is an expensive, politically difficult process that provides little conservation benefit (U.S. Congress 2003; USFWS 1999d) and therefore continues to resist. Some environmental groups, however, view critical habitat as a valuable conservation tool. They have brought and won numerous lawsuits requiring that the USFWS designate critical habitat (Patlis 2001). Taylor et al. (2005) conclude that species with designated critical habitat are more likely to be improving than those without. Of course, this is only a correlation, and one necessarily drawn from a very small sample, since only a small number of species have had designated critical habitat for more than a few years. Other observers are more skeptical about the benefits of critical habitat designation. A recent analysis of recovery plans, for example, concluded that critical habitat designation had little impact on the recovery planning process (Hoekstra et al. 2002b). While these studies have yet to provide a clear answer about the usefulness of critical habitat designation, the attempt to bring data to bear on the subject represents a positive step in a world where political debate too often takes the form of unverifiable anecdotes and "tribal" posturing (Kysar and Salzman 2003).

Political Stability

The ESA has also proven remarkably robust politically, despite the level of controversy it has engendered. It has been amended a number of times, and some of the changes have been significant (Goble, forthcoming). The two most important amendments introduced some measure of pragmatism into what began as a perhaps unrealistically starry-eyed law. In 1978, an exemption procedure was introduced to allow the federal government to make the choice to extinguish a species if a project was sufficiently important, and in 1982 a permit procedure was added to allow private parties to take listed species provided their actions would not cause jeopardy. But the core assumptions underlying the ESA have remained the same since 1973: all species have great value; none should be extinguished by human action without the utmost consideration and strong justification.

Even as the reach of the law has become progressively more apparent, the ESA has been impervious to fundamental revision and remains relatively untouched by legislative exemptions and stealth amendments. In the aftermath of *Tennessee Valley Authority v. Hill* (1978), Congress did exempt the Tellico Dam from compliance with the ESA, but there have been few other project-specific exemptions.[2] Frontal assaults on the law have been notably unsuccessful. In the mid-1990s, when the Republican party gained control of Congress, one of their announced goals was to revamp and significantly weaken the ESA.

The combination of a strong coalition of environmental and religious groups and aggressive executive-branch efforts to minimize irreconcilable conflicts between conservation and development successfully beat back that challenge (Barry 1998; Nagle 1998a; Doremus 2000b; Leshy 2001). ESA opponents did, however, manage to get a temporary moratorium on listing (Act of April 10, 1995; Ortiz 1999, 432–33). The lesson of this history is that the ESA's general goals enjoy sufficient public support to survive open attack, but the law remains potentially vulnerable to backdoor encroachments.

Creative Flexibility

An important element of the ESA's political stability has been its inherent, but long unrecognized, flexibility. Although the key legislative changes in the act were complete by 1982, they were not fully explored by the Reagan or George H. W. Bush administrations. Not until the Clinton administration came into power in 1993 with the promise that it would prevent ESA "train wrecks" was the flexibility of the act fully tested. By 1995, the Department of the Interior under Bruce Babbitt had implemented a series of administrative reforms designed to strike a balance that would provide for conservation while allowing economic activity to the extent consistent with conservation. Key elements of the reform package included emphasizing ecosystem protection to the extent feasible; promoting habitat conservation planning by streamlining the incidental take permit process and aggressively providing landowners with "no surprises" assurances against escalation of mitigation requirements; encouraging early intervention and affirmative conservation measures by developing candidate conservation agreements and safe harbor agreements with similar regulatory assurances; calling for provision of better information in listing rules about activities that would be likely to violate the take prohibition; and adopting a policy of implementing recovery plans in ways that would minimize social and economic costs (Ruhl 1998).

The jury is still out on the conservation effect of many of these changes, which are relatively recent and have not all been enthusiastically carried forward by the current administration. The legality of the keystone reform, no-surprises assurances in incidental take permits remains open to question. In late 2003, a federal district court remanded the no-surprises rule because of procedural failings in the adoption of a related rule limiting grounds for permit revocation (*Spirit of the Sage Council v. Norton* 2003). The USFWS can cure the procedural failing by going through a notice and comment rulemaking, but at the end of that process it seems likely that substantive challenges to the no-surprises rule will be renewed. Should the rule fall, landowner interest in incidental take permits, particularly large regional permits, is likely to plummet dramatically. How that would affect the politics of the ESA is unclear.

A Catalyst for Positive Change

The effects of the ESA go well beyond its direct impacts on specific activities. Throughout its history, the ESA has been an inspiration and catalyst for substantive and procedural changes. By 1973, several states already had laws in place protecting certain wildlife species designated as endangered or threatened (Goble et al. 1999). These laws, though, emphasized regulation of commerce to protect species. Following passage of the ESA, and encouraged in part by the opportunity for federal funding, many more states enacted endangered species legislation. By 1999, only five states lacked explicit endangered species laws. Although most state laws still fall short of the full scope of federal protection, a large number are closely modeled on the federal ESA in many respects. The ESA has also served as an inspiration for strong conservation efforts in other countries and internationally.[3]

Additionally, the ESA has subtle effects that are difficult to identify or quantify. The threat of the ESA's prohibitions, or simply of federal interference in state matters, has catalyzed changes in entrenched state law. Litigation under the ESA, for example, inspired the Texas legislature to move away from the state's historic reliance on the rule of capture to authorize regulation of groundwater withdrawals for the first time (MacNaughton and Folk-Williams 2003; Opiela 2002). Threats of ESA enforcement have brought diverse interests to the bargaining table in the Colorado River basin (Getches 1997, 2001), sparked cooperative efforts involving upstream and downstream states in the Platte River basin (Sax 2000), produced a new state-federal cooperative management structure in the San Francisco Bay-Delta (Getches 2001; Rieke 1996), and helped to catalyze the recent interest in linking land use approvals to water supplies in the arid West. States wishing to avoid the regulatory burdens of the ESA have agreed to conservation efforts they surely otherwise would not have undertaken. For example, Idaho, which once staunchly opposed gray wolf (*Canis lupus*) reintroduction, has developed a wolf management plan calling for the state to support at least fifteen wolf packs (Idaho Legislative Wolf Oversight Committee 2002).[4]

None of these changes is a magic bullet. They do not instantly or automatically resolve difficult conservation problems, and not surprisingly they have inspired doubts as well as praise (Echeverria 2001). At a minimum, however, they represent increased conservation awareness, and in many cases they have spawned new institutions, cutting across institutional and jurisdictional boundaries, that are necessary if not sufficient for long-term conservation success. The ESA, in other words, may be quietly promoting development of the tools needed for successful conservation over the next generation.

Yaffee (this volume) reinforces this lesson. Yaffee explains that the ESA has produced important general changes in the process of natural resource decision making (Yaffee, this volume). Although section 7 consultation rarely halts federal projects (Houck 1993), backed by the strong interpretation of the Supreme Court (*Tennessee Valley Authority v. Hill* 1978) it frequently leads to modifications that reduce or mitigate project impacts. Section 9, coupled with the incidental take permit process, has a similar effect. It encourages both developers and local governments to factor endangered species impacts into the early stages of project planning and to avoid endangered species habitat where it is feasible to do so.

Despite these positives, the ESA remains the target of high-profile criticism by both conservation advocates and development interests. The following two lessons reflect the fact that each of these very different criticisms has a strong grounding.

Lesson 2: ESA Implementation Often Falls Short of Expectations

This lesson is not a new one. It has been repeatedly documented over the last thirty years that the seemingly clear pronouncements of Congress do not always translate into the actions for which they seem to call. That is true of listing (Yaffee 1982; Metrick and Weitzman 1996; Ando 1999), of designation of critical habitat (Patlis 2001), of recovery efforts (DeShazo and Freeman 2003; Miller et al. 2002; Metrick and Weitzman 1996),[5] and of consultation (Houck 1993). Both listing and funding decisions are biased toward "charismatic megafauna" (Yaffee 1982; Metrick and Weitzman 1996; Ando 1999). Committed advocates willing to pursue citizen suits are often essential to the listing of controversial species (Greenwald et al., this volume). Both listing and recovery funding decisions also depend upon the power of legislators whose districts overlap the species' range (DeShazo and Freeman, this volume).

Recognizing these problems, of course, is not the same as solving them. If the gap between the act's bold words and its more limited implementation were easy to bridge, it would have been done long ago. Implementation problems are bigger than the ESA; they have proven stubborn in a variety of environmental policy contexts. Familiar examples include the mere handful of criteria pollutants that have been regulated under the Clean Air Act (Act of July 14, 1955), the federal reluctance to require permits under the Clean Water Act (Act of June 30, 1948) for point sources other than factory outfalls,[6] and the virtual paralysis with respect to regulation of hazardous air pollutants until Congress in 1990 stepped in with a specific list of chemicals that must be regulated (Goldstein and Carruth 2003).

One way to address this "slippage" (Farber 1999) would be through tighter delegations to the implementing agencies. Congress could, for example, define the degree of risk required for listing. That might not be a desirable solution, however, given the variation between species and the possibility that such tight delegation might stand as a barrier to conservation in the face of thin information. Alternatively, clearer administrative guidelines (or, even better, formal regulations issued after notice and comment) could constrain agency action. It is clear from the last thirty years, however, that wildlife agencies lack any incentive to constrain flexibility through such generalized pronouncements. Congress could force the agencies to regulate, but it has little incentive to clear up the confusion. Courts might play a role in breaking this stalemate by refusing to defer to inconsistent or ill-explained agency decisions. That could provide the implementing agencies with a strong incentive to move away from the current ad hoc approach.

Funding decisions are even harder to control. The USFWS has long had policies for prioritizing both listing and recovery actions, but these are widely ignored. Congress has complicated the problem by specifically earmarking appropriated funds for uses inconsistent with agency priorities. Funding could be rationalized by the creation of a targeted fund that does not require annual appropriation but includes mandated priorities on expenditures. That, however, is unlikely. Congress does not readily give up its politically advantageous control of the appropriation reins.[7] Unless extraordinary political pressure can be brought to bear, creation of a fund that would be automatically appropriated without further action to endangered species conservation is unlikely. The lack of an obvious, politically appealing funding source makes such a fund even less likely. It therefore seems nearly certain that annual (or at least regular) appropriations fights and chronic underfunding of the ESA will continue for the foreseeable future. Learning how best to deal with that difficult funding situation ought to be a high priority for conservation advocates.

Lesson 3: Conservation Costs Will Continue, and Therefore So Will Controversies

The most fundamental complaints about the Endangered Species Act, not surprisingly often raised by economists, relate to costs. But even then, the suggestions for improvement are remarkably tame: speed up permit processing and concentrate efforts to the extent possible on lands with the lowest economic values. Most mainstream economists do not question the ESA's rejection of efficiency or cost justification as a metric.

That is both consistent with the current political situation and eminently sensible. A cost-benefit test for species protection would not serve our goals well. As Jason Shogren points out, the costs of protective measures are always much easier to monetize and measure than the benefits of saving species

(Shogren, forthcoming). More fundamentally, struggling to monetize the benefits of conservation is misguided. Mark Sagoff has noted that as a society we simply do not believe that all choices are properly reduced to dollar values. Most of us would say that species have a dignity, rather than a price (Sagoff 1982). Many of our environmental laws have a utilitarian feel, but the ESA is different. It expresses a strong view about what is right. The idea that we have a duty not to casually cause the extinction of other species continues to resonate strongly with American voters and, indeed, is not openly disputed by ardent development advocates.

But conflicts between conservation and economic development are only going to become more common and more pointed as both the number of listed species and the human population continue to increase. So far, the ESA has primarily deflected development from one location to another, or encouraged minor project modifications. At some point, though, if it is to serve its purposes, it must draw hard lines, imposing limits on, say, the urbanization of Southern California or the diversion of water from the Rio Grande. The need for effective, ongoing control of threats means that even delisting, rare as that is likely to be, will not end conservation efforts or costs (Doremus and Pagel 2001). In most places we have not yet faced up to the idea of permanent limits on our ecological footprint. It remains to be seen whether we will accept them, although the Sonoran Desert Conservation Plan described by Maeveen Behan (this volume) is a hopeful sign.

A different kind of cost issue will become increasingly important in future years: cost-effectiveness. While the ESA clearly rejects a cost-benefit test for species protection, it endorses cost-effectiveness, at least in the context of critical habitat designation (ESA sec. 4(b)(2) [areas may be excluded from critical habitat if the economic or other costs of designation outweigh the conservation benefits]). Similarly, the USFWS has long applied a policy of choosing recovery steps that minimize social and economic costs (USFWS and NOAA 1994b). Sizeable amounts of money, both public and private, are being devoted to measures intended to benefit species. Between 1982 and 2001, for example, federal agencies spent well over $3 billion on recovery efforts for Columbia River salmon runs (GAO 2002). Those paying that money understandably want to know that it is providing concrete, demonstrable, benefits. Unfortunately, data demonstrating, and especially data quantifying, those benefits are frequently difficult to obtain. That brings us to the next lesson.

Lesson 4: We Have Not Learned Enough

Despite thirty years of experience, what we don't know about dwindling species and their protection could still fill volumes. The many gaps in our knowledge and understanding limit both our ability to implement the Endangered Species Act and our ability to evaluate it.

We lack a solid nationwide, or even species-specific, estimate of conservation costs. By and large, we don't even know how to make these estimates. We can and do track direct expenditures (USFWS 2001g) but opportunity costs are more difficult. Estimates vary wildly (Sunding, forthcoming; Meyer 1998) and, obviously, are highly dependent upon the availability of alternative development outlets and the costs assigned to development delays. On the other side of the cost-benefit equation, it is extraordinarily difficult to produce persuasive economic estimates of the value of conservation or to generate alternative quantitative metrics.

Moreover, we have little systematic understanding of the extent to which conservation measures from the very general, such as the designation of critical habitat, to the very specific, such as precise instream flow levels in a given river, benefit protected species. What evaluation we have undertaken, which has not been much, has relied almost entirely on simplistic counts of actions taken rather than measures of their effectiveness. Even for simple bean counting we lack well-organized, accessible databases. The dearth of information makes it extraordinarily difficult to undertake quantitative studies of ESA implementation. Too often, anecdotes are the only information available. It would be well worth it to pay the relatively low costs of creating, keeping, and updating national databases, which would allow researchers access to full habitat conservation plans, annual reports, biological opinions, enforcement data, and the like. The federal government would not have to bear the costs of data synthesis and evaluation; if the data were made freely available, it is likely that others would undertake the cost and effort to analyze it. Independent, even competing, analyses would be highly desirable, providing over time credible estimates of effectiveness.

The biggest gaps in our knowledge, of course, concern the biology of the species we are trying to protect. Mary Ruckelshaus and Donna Darm (forthcoming) point out, for example, that the task of identifying critical habitat—those areas and only those areas essential to the conservation of the species—is at best daunting. To have confidence in the decisions we must make, including listing decisions, jeopardy or no jeopardy determinations, recovery goals, and critical habitat designations, often requires years of data collection, modeling, and analysis. Even with good information about the past, we will find it difficult to predict the future impacts of global climate change on individual species.

Frequently, little or no research or data collection effort is expended on a species until after it is listed. Especially in the early years, therefore, both the wildlife agencies and the regulated community are working almost in the dark.

That is especially challenging in today's political climate, where the scientific underpinnings of decisions are routinely questioned in litigation[8] and ever more frequently become the subject of high-profile oversight by the National Research Council committee (National Research Council 2004a–d).

As I see it, there are three distinct aspects to solving the problem of limited biological information. The first is that the agencies implementing the Endangered Species Act need to make better use of the act's information-generating power. If the agencies do not take the initiative to do so (as they have not for most of the act's first thirty years), the courts can and should force them in that direction. As an example, section 7 requires that agencies "insure" that their actions are not likely to jeopardize a listed species or adversely modify or destroy formally designated critical habitat. If the information base is not sufficient to allow the wildlife agencies to evaluate the effect of the action on the species, the action cannot meet this test.[9] Applied more forcefully, that interpretation would provide action agencies and applicants with a powerful incentive to collect and disclose reasonably obtainable information. Much the same could be said of the section 10 incidental take permit process (Doremus 2001).

But gathering information at one point in time is not enough. We have every reason to expect that our knowledge base should increase with time. We need to find funding for the monitoring, research, data organization, and data synthesis efforts needed to support robust learning.[10] We also need institutional arrangements that will ensure new knowledge feeds into future decisions so that biological opinions, critical habitat designations, and recovery plans improve over time. It is easy to fall into the trap of thinking we have identified problems and solutions early on, then to rest on that understanding, simply imposing the same regulatory requirements or taking the same recovery steps without carefully evaluating their effectiveness. Because our knowledge base is often so thin at the outset, following the pattern will lead to many listed species failing to improve.

Even with strong data collection and evaluation efforts and good feedback loops to bring new information into our decision-making processes, though, we will never have anything approaching perfect data. We must therefore learn to live with data gaps. For this purpose, I am an advocate of transparency, even though it can be understandably intimidating for the implementing agencies. Articulating clear, principled guidelines for decision making in the face of uncertainty can make it safer for agencies to admit their ignorance. For example, the National Marine Fisheries Service has long said that it gives the benefit of the doubt to species in the section 7 process when there is uncertainty (as indeed I believe section 7 requires), but it has not explained what that means in practice. While differences between species and contexts may make it impractical to draft one-size-fits-all regulations detailing the meaning of precaution, the wildlife agencies could surely articulate some principles to be applied in individual cases. Making such principles public and clearly committing themselves to increasing their knowledge base over time could help the agencies defuse opposition to regulation based on limited data.

Lesson 5: Balancing Flexibility and Discretion Is a Continuing Challenge

Finally, with respect to implementation, there is an inevitable tension between affording agencies the flexibility to respond to unique circumstances and new insights, and providing oversight mechanisms to cabin discretion we fear may be exercised for the wrong reasons or in ways that take us away from rather than toward our goals.

Bureaucratic rigidity produces real problems. Measures we are confident would help a listed species simply may not happen if regulators cling to standard operating procedures or established ways of doing things. Recognizing the need for quick action and creative thinking, both call for greater decentralization of certain decisions.

But happy results from the exercise of flexibility depend upon the actor wanting (or, if you prefer to cast it in economic terms, having appropriate incentives) to do the right thing. The history of the ESA provides reason to doubt whether that will always, or even often, be the case. Formal agency guidance on listing determinations, defining critical habitat (and the exclusions therefrom), and acceptable risk levels in section 7 consultations would reduce agency discretion, provide coherence to agency decisions, and, by articulating principles, reassure those affected by regulation that decisions are not arbitrary or based on improper factors.

Each of these conflicting visions has considerable foundation. Striking the balance between flexibility and accountability will be the key implementation challenge for the next generation of the ESA. There is no inherent conflict between freeing an agency (or state or tribe) to do creative work on some fronts and carefully cabining its behavior on others. But one wonders where we will find the trust needed to make us comfortable with discretion on one front if we distrust the agency on other fronts. It also seems unlikely that a tightly constrained agency could develop the entrepreneurial skills and truly creative thinking we would like to see in some contexts. This is a point on which we could benefit from more discussion between scientists, policy makers, and interest groups or stakeholders, addressing such issues as where flexibility is needed, what are the risks of offering it, and how best can we address that tension. Could clearer legislative sideboards provide more room for flexibility (which in turn could provide the incentive for legislative change)? Does putting the agency in a more marketlike situation encourage it to find and undertake more effective conservation measures? On this point I am pessimistic, based on my experience with the CALFED Bay-Delta Program's Environmental Water Account. That experiment has encouraged state and federal water management agencies to become flexible, light-on-their-feet resource managers, but the regulatory agencies have not notably increased their flexibility. We need to know if this lack of response is typical, and if so we need a clearer understanding of the impediments to regulatory flexibility.

Conclusion

On the whole, the first thirty years of the Endangered Species Act have been remarkably successful. The law has directly aided many listed species and has indirectly encouraged federal, state, and private decision makers to give greater thought to the needs of imperiled species in designing projects. Fundamental change is not needed. It is unrealistic to expect the ESA (or any other policy) to operate in a frictionless, perfect manner. That simply is not the way the world works. We should not, therefore, allow our desire for a perfect conservation law to get in the way of making the best possible use of the ESA.

Nonetheless, there is room for improvement. The act has not fulfilled the expectations of the environmental community, and at the same time it has been far more controversial than expected. This is an appropriate time to be thinking about what sorts of tinkering around its edges could make the ESA more effective (and more cost effective). In my own view, the most helpful (and at the same time the most realistically possible) changes would be increased funding for information collection, organization, synthesis and analysis, and stronger use of the ESA as an information-generating tool. In the longer term, learning to better balance flexibility and discretion will help the Endangered Species Act mature beyond the gawky adolescent stage to stable, productive adulthood.

17 Collaborative Decision Making

Steven L. Yaffee

Although there is debate on whether the Endangered Species Act (ESA) has been effective at protecting biological diversity, it is clear that the act has fundamentally changed natural resource decision making in the United States. The act's power was demonstrated when a lawsuit almost stopped the Tennessee Valley Authority's efforts to impound the Little Tennessee River. It was nothing short of astounding that the snail darter (*Percina tanasi*) was the short-lived winner of a Supreme Court decision despite an incredibly powerful political coalition and a highly successful public agency (Yaffee 1982).

Numerous decisions since then reflect the influence of the ESA: major changes in the way federal lands are managed in the Pacific Northwest followed the listing of the northern spotted owl (*Strix occidentalis caurina*) (Yaffee 1994); shifts in the U.S. Bureau of Reclamation's management of dams on the Colorado River due to the humpback chub (*Gila cypha*) and other endangered fish (*Arizona Republic* 2002); alterations in the Army Corps of Engineers–regulated flow regime of the Missouri River to respond to the needs of the endangered pallid sturgeon (*Scaphirhynchus albus*) and the interior least tern (*Sterna antillarum athalassos*) (USFWS 2003i); and changes in operations on Defense Department lands due to the needs of the red-cockaded woodpecker (*Picoides borealis*), the California least tern (*Sterna antillarum browni*), and the West Indian manatee (*Trichechus manatus*) (Boice 1996). The ESA may or may not be the most effective way to protect endangered species, but as a force promoting greater sensitivity to environmental concerns, it has been unparalleled.

Although valuable, these changes have placed significant burdens on the ESA and the federal agencies charged with its implementation. To ease these burdens, it is critical to enlist the efforts of individuals and organizations often outside the ESA process and to encourage their support by fostering the development of integrative, multiparty collaborative processes (see Clark and Wallace, this volume; Burnham et al., this volume). This chapter explores the underlying reasons that endangered species decision making has changed. It draws on several examples of collaboration in endangered species management and the evolving literature on collaborative processes to identify factors that promote successful processes. I present fifteen specific recommendations for policy and organizational change that follow from these success factors and that can foster better endangered species decision making. I conclude with a commentary about the meaning of the recent rush to "collaboration" by people from both sides of the political spectrum.

The Endangered Species Act and Decision Making

The Endangered Species Act has changed resource management in at least three ways. First, it has created new decision-making processes. Second, it has altered the functioning of previously existing decision-making systems. Third, it has altered the negotiation dynamics within decision-making processes.

New Decision-Making Processes

New decision-making processes include the listing provisions, the recovery planning process, and habitat conservation planning. Although habitat conservation plans are often plagued by limitations and inadequacies, that Riverside and San Diego counties in California, Pima County in Arizona, and Clark County in Nevada created land use plans in response to rats, tortoises, and birds is remarkable. Also remarkable are the many landscape-scale restoration and planning processes motivated by the ESA. Ecosystem restoration projects in the San Francisco Bay-Delta, for example, were prompted by the fear of restrictions on water transport to Southern California due to the needs of the delta smelt (*Hypomesus transpacificus*) (CALFED Bay-Delta Program 2003). Although these processes can be viewed as endangered species protection, they can also be viewed as attempts by development interests to assure planning certainty for their own activities (see Sunding, forthcoming; T. Scott, Fernandez, et al., forthcoming).

These projects have had significant positive effects. Many endangered species hot spots, such as Las Vegas, the San Francisco Bay Area, the Everglades, and the Colorado River, are fully appropriated natural resource systems sorely in need of planning that considers the integrity of underlying environmental systems. The incentives created by the ESA have moved these places through the back door into land use planning, growth management, and ecosystem-scale decision making—changes unlikely to have happened otherwise.

Changed Decision-Making Processes

Just as important as the ESA-created decision-making processes has been the act's impact on other governmental rule making, planning, and permitting processes. The power of the ESA lies in its absolute mandates not the least of which is the interagency consultation process. It was this provision that enabled the U.S. Fish and Wildlife Service to stick its nose into the Tennessee Valley Authority's tightly controlled decision-making process. The consultation requirements also played a significant role in changing insular U.S. Forest Service decision-making procedures in the Pacific Northwest and the Southeast. The same is true with the National Marine Fisheries Service and decision making on salmon by numerous federal, state, and local agencies in the Puget Sound. These impacts on agency decision making may not be as absolute as some would like; nevertheless, through endangered-species proxies, ecosystem integrity has a place at the decision-making table. It may sit on a small stool and be acknowledged only grudgingly, but it has a point of access that did not exist prior to 1973.

Changed Negotiation Dynamics

The third change produced by the Endangered Species Act has been an alteration of the negotiation dynamics within existing decision-making processes. Most natural resource management decisions are the result of negotiations among agencies and interested parties. This includes decisions affecting endangered species (Tobin 1990; Yaffee 1982). Negotiations affect listings; actions required to recover them or to protect critical habitat; mitigation necessary to allow other agencies to proceed; and conservation actions needed to allow individuals, agencies, and firms to proceed despite incidentally taking listed species.

The framing of the ESA has significantly affected the framing of these negotiations in several ways: endangered species advocates gained access to administrative and private-sector decision making. By challenging these decisions, they slowed decision making and could build political support, mobilize media and public interest, and develop science parallel to that held by agencies.

In addition, the ESA has also changed negotiating dynamics by creating a need for new information. These changes drove the need for a science bureaucracy in state and federal agencies (see Ruckelshaus and Darm, forthcoming), which has in turn shifted intra-agency politics. Just as important, it provides advocates of species protection with the incentive to conduct their own scientific studies, which in turn has in many cases changed agency decision making.

By providing advocates the ability to delay and alter projects, the ESA has shifted the balance of incentives facing the development community. Agencies fear the potential loss of control associated with ESA litigation. Developers fear the financial costs associated with an uncertain investment environment. As a result, regulatory uncertainty creates significant incentives for agencies and developers to negotiate. In many cases, it is this uncertainty, rather than the fear of significant restrictions, that motivates changed behavior. That development interests simultaneously cite uncertainty and lack of flexibility as its fundamental flaws would seem to confirm the power of the ESA.

The Burden

Although the Endangered Species Act has changed natural resource decision making, it was never intended to resolve the broad set of issues we face today. As a result, a large burden has been placed on the act, its implementing agencies, and its political supporters. This burden includes a huge demand for information, calls for certainty by the regulated community (Sunding, forthcoming), and agency involvement in many venues.

When the act was framed as a symbolic statement of support for charismatic animals, no one understood the magnitude of the biodiversity problem. Scientific knowledge of conservation biology has exploded since 1973 with the realization that diversity is far more complex than species-level diversity. Science has also developed on the fundamental complexity of ecosystems and their processes, expanding our understanding of critical habitat requirements and highlighting the need to protect private as well as public lands. For example, although many ecologists viewed old-growth forests as biological deserts in the 1970s, we now know they provide critical habitat for thousands of species (USFWS 1992b; Yaffee 1994).

Changes in political organization, the availability of information, public values, and the magnitude of the human footprint on natural systems have also increased the challenges associated with implementing the ESA. In the 1970s, environmental advocates used litigation and political lobbying in only limited ways. Since then, there has been a tremendous diffusion of legal and political power, which has enabled groups as small as the Center for Biological Diversity to fight agencies and corporate interests to a standstill. In 1973, agency and university scientists largely controlled information about species; access for outsiders was limited. Today, there has been a tremendous democratization of science and information fostered by technological changes such as the Internet as well as the development of parallel expertise in a host of interest groups. In 1973, a broadened set of public values was evident in the passage of landmark environmental legislation, but these values were not yet translated into significant claims on public resources. Today, the Federal Energy Regulatory Commission and the U.S. Bureau of Reclamation must consider serious arguments for dam decommissioning, and the U.S. Forest Service has dramatically reduced timber harvest on the national forests to accommodate other values. And in the same thirty years, demands for water and land to support unsustainable development patterns have substantially increased the size of the human footprint on natural systems.

These changes have magnified the burden of implementing the ESA. In 1973, no one anticipated the behavioral changes in public agencies and private landowners engendered by endangered species policy. Ironically, framing the ESA as a command-and-control statute has diminished its ability to accomplish these changes creatively, even as it provides the raw power to foster implementation of necessary changes. Amendments and administrative changes—habitat conservation planning, safe harbor agreements, candidate conservation agreements, experimental populations, and the like—have sought to adapt the act to this changing knowledge base and context. But those implementing the changes have struggled with the magnitude of required actions and consistently impoverished budgets. The political coalition that supports the act struggles to protect it rather than to promote positive changes. Parties spend countless hours in court, but litigation rarely provides enduring solutions (Suckling and Taylor, this volume; Greenwald et al., this volume). The agencies have shifted limited funding to species in crisis rather than to those that most need assistance. In short, although the ESA is an enormously powerful law, it has proved a blunt instrument for promoting needed change.

Easing the Burden

These are not easy problems to solve without undercutting the source of the act's power: its powerful incentives for agencies, individuals, and firms to take into account the long term when faced with short-term choices. *Yet, critical to solving biodiversity problems is the need to enlist the resources and power of people and legal structures that are often outside the ESA process.* If biodiversity protection is confined to the ESA, the best-case outcome will be maintenance of an "emergency room" strategy. If endangered species protection is limited to the use of traditional regulatory strategies, we can expect only grudging compliance with legal mandates and limited gains for biodiversity protection. To go beyond, it is necessary to enlist the powers of other laws. It is also necessary to include strategies that promote problem solving, encompass larger scales, embrace multiple sectors and multiple issues in ESA decision-making processes, and promote a shared sense of ownership of problems and the strategies to solve them.

A Broader Set of Policy Strategies

A more effective conservation strategy would employ a broader set of federal, state, and local policy instruments to manage the impacts of development on ecosystems. They would include federal public lands, agriculture, water quality, wetlands conversion and transportation policy, as well as state agriculture, wildlife and public lands policies, and local land use policy. They would also include incentive-based instruments such as the Conservation Reserve Program, and incorporate the use of tax policy to promote stewardship, including tax breaks for maintenance of important conservation values on private lands. It also calls for expanding local zoning and growth management to moderate the impact of sprawl. Ultimately, enlisting this suite of policy instruments requires changing existing policies that promote extraction at unsustainable, subsidized rates. Together, these policy instruments have tremendous power to influence the character of the human footprint on the environment and hence on endangered species. To achieve these changes, it is necessary to broaden the political coalition supporting endangered species protection by making clear the connections between biodiversity conservation and the economic and social health and quality of human life.

Collaborative Problem-Solving Processes

A perhaps less sweeping but equally important set of strategies involves expanding the use of collaborative processes in the implementation of the ESA (see Clark and Wallace, this volume; Burnham et al., this volume). These processes promote involvement by a full range of interested groups, encourage decision making that is proactive and problem resolving, and foster a sense of ownership and responsibility for problems and their solutions (Brush et al. 2000). Collaborative processes have the ability to encourage individuals and agencies to move beyond reluctant compliance with regulatory mandates. If they function well, they can overcome the impasses that have characterized endangered species decision making, leading to action on the ground rather than in the courtroom.

In the past two decades, literally hundreds of collaborative processes have developed in the United States for addressing community-based and regional ecosystem concerns (Community-Based Collaboratives Research Consortium 2004; Yaffee et al. 1996). These include urban collaboratives such as Chicago Wilderness, a consortium of more than 170 agencies and organizations working to protect the biodiversity of the Chicago Metropolitan Area (Chicago Wilderness 2004), as well as rural collaboratives, such as the Northeastern Nevada Stewardship Group (Northeastern Nevada Stewardship Group 2004).

Some of these processes, like the Darby Partners, have arisen organically in response to an evolving sense of place in a region and a belief that more could be accomplished through cooperation than by going it alone (Wondolleck and Yaffee 2000; Nature Conservancy 2004). In most cases, groups work toward a mix of social, process, and ecological goals, which often include ecosystem health and biodiversity protection.

Other collaborative efforts have focused more specifically on endangered species. For example, the Clark County Nevada Habitat Conservation Plan process was developed in response to specific opportunities and incentives created by the ESA as a result of the listing of the desert tortoise (Coughlin et al. 1999; Aengst et al. 1998). Finally, other collaborative processes have developed as means for implementing specific provisions of the ESA, particularly recovery planning. For example, the Upper Colorado River Endangered Fish Recovery Program was created in 1988 to recover endangered fish species in the Colorado River basin while simultaneously providing for future development of agricultural, hydroelectric, and water-supply uses (USFWS 2004i).

Making Collaboration Work

Although the Darby Partnership, Clark County Habitat Conservation Plan, and Upper Colorado recovery program each have created momentum toward endangered species protection, it has not been easy. How do we determine what makes these processes work so that we can promote effective processes in the endangered species realm? An evolving literature on collaboration has isolated a number of factors that can promote effective and accountable collaboration (Gray 1989; Yaffee et al. 1997). For our purposes, four broad themes are important: (1) motivation, (2) organization and process management, (3) resources and energy, and (4) legitimacy. Below we identify a set of specific recommendations that apply these themes to ESA decision making.

Motivation

Collaboration does not just happen. People face incentives established by a range of external conditions that compel them to work together. Often, motivation is provided by a sense of urgency created by a perceived crisis, for instance, when development is blocked by endangered species listings, or, conversely, when environmental quality is threatened by development. In other situations, an evolving sense of place, such as a shared concern for the future social and ecological health of a watershed, has encouraged different groups to come together to work toward common goals, particularly when they realize that achieving these goals requires the interdependent efforts of all. Sometimes the potential to mobilize new resources, such as the opportunity to secure congressional funding for activities involved in a restoration program, motivates joint action. And for many collaboratives, the incentives created by the alternative to collaboration—what will happen if they do not work together—compels them. Successful ESA-related collaborative processes would do the following:

Maintain existing ESA incentives that motivate effective action. These incentives include the absolute mandates contained in the ESA's section 7 and the strong take prohibitions in section 10. They also require a likelihood that these prohibitions will be enforced, which means maintaining opportunities for judicial review and administrative appeals. Indeed, one could argue that expanding these absolute requirements to protect other ecosystem processes and characteristics could have a salutary effect on biodiversity protection by further motivating proactive, landscape-scale action.

It may seem ironic that a regulatory hammer is needed to motivate voluntarism, and some may view this as coercive collaboration. But collaboration occurs because organizations decide that it is a preferable means of achieving their individual goals (Fisher et al. 1991). American history suggests that goals that are rational in the long term (such as biodiversity protection) but hard to justify in the short term (because a specific development will affect only a small amount of habitat) will not be sought by public or private players (Yaffee et al. 1997). Fear of the hammer is necessary to cause all players to consider the possibilities of joint action.

Expand the positive incentives provided to landowners and governments through grants and opportunities to participate in decision making. As others in this book have argued, it is necessary to go beyond the negative incentives created by the regulatory structures of the ESA and incorporate positive incentives (Parkhurst and Shogren, this volume). Incentives include matching grants and technical assistance to motivate stewardship activities. Incentives may also include assurance of more certainty for investment decisions so long as investments do not undercut recovery and restoration goals. Positive incentives are also created through collaborative processes that provide opportunities for significant involvement in identifying and implementing solutions.

Incorporate a variety of educational strategies to inform landowners of the value of biodiversity protection as well as their obligations under the ESA. Motivation also comes from understanding the problems and ways that individuals, agencies, or firms can effectively address them. Landowner education is needed to explain the value of biodiversity protection and to suggest actions, both large and small, that landowners can undertake to promote recovery and restoration. Educational strategies should be put in terms that landowners care about, such as emphasizing the value of conservation behavior to their own health and economic prospects and to the quality of life of their grandchildren. Highlighting success stories involving similar individuals and issues can also be motivating. By influencing knowledge and values—and potentially offsetting the need to change behavior through lengthy and costly regulatory processes—education may be one of the cheapest long-term strategies for biodiversity protection.

Streamline ESA administrative processes where possible to motivate involvement. One barrier to participation in both regulatory and collaborative processes is the perception that they are burdensome. To the extent possible, streamlining these activities and making them transparent to participants so that efforts can be focused more on problem solving and less on procedure would help motivate individuals to stay involved.

Organization and Process Management

Motivation may get people to the table, but it is effective organization and process management that keeps them there. An extensive literature highlights a number of themes related to effective process management (Carpenter and Kennedy 1988; Moore 1996; Susskind et al. 1999). We can apply these themes to endangered species recovery in two ways:

By supporting ecosystem-scale structures and/or creating new structures that foster collaborative decision making. The literature on ecosystem-based management suggests the value of working at the landscape, ecoregional, or watershed scale; this matches the orientation of the ESA toward recovery planning bounded by the range and habitat needs of endangered species (Grumbine 1994; Kohm and Franklin 1997). Creating and supporting new ecosystem teams organized at the watershed or ecoregional level can be an effective and efficient way to move toward broader biodiversity protection. Collaborative multiparty and interagency teams can pool information and resources to produce better assessments and restoration strategies. They can also help build the trust needed to support the kinds of long-term adaptive management strategies necessary for ecosystem restoration (Gunderson et al. 1994; Holling 1978; Walters 1986).

Incorporate concepts of effective collaborative decision making into existing ESA processes. Many provisions of the ESA can promote collaborative decision making. Recovery planning, habitat conservation plans, candidate conservation agreements, and safe harbor agreements are examples. Ensuring that they conform to current knowledge about effective collaborative process (Carpenter and Kennedy 1988; Moore 1996; Susskind et al. 1999; Clifford 1995; Wondolleck and Yaffee 2000) can yield incremental improvements.

Resources and Energy

While collaborative processes are voluntary, they are not free. As with all planning and management efforts, they require human power, expertise, time, and money. Indeed, since they are explicitly designed to bridge organizational and interest boundaries, such processes often cut across budgetary lines that tightly match traditional organizational and policy boundaries. For volunteers and representatives of nongovernmental organizations (NGOs), the time and funding needed to effectively participate may be particularly problematic. Agency staff time is also needed. As state and federal resource management agencies have been downsized, their ability to engage in these collaborative processes has diminished. The irony is that ultimately these processes can leverage the unique resources of disparate organizations and agencies to synergistically create an effort more effective than any single element. But such an integrative process still requires core funding. Support could include the following:

Funding for the U.S. Fish and Wildlife Service and the National Marine Fisheries Service to implement ESA decision-making processes. Impoverished programs lead to impoverished decision making (Sucking and Taylor, this volume; Scott, Goble, et al., this volume; Miller et al. 2002) and result in frustrating delays. Increasing appropriations for all ESA duties would help build the capacity of the U.S. Fish and Wildlife Service and the National Marine Fisheries Service to participate in negotiated decision-making processes. Having agency personnel decline to participate in collaborative efforts undercuts their effectiveness and shortchanges their ability to craft legitimate and effective decisions. Although those who oppose endangered species protection have used underfunding as a control strategy, ironically, it has contributed to landowner and corporate frustration by causing delays and prohibiting interest-based problem solving that may allow development objectives to be met.

Assistance to state and local governments and private landowners that enables them to participate in biodiversity protection decision making. Biodiversity protection is both a public and private good, and hence it is appropriate for the government to partially support the collaborative efforts of individuals, groups, and agencies. Low-level investments that facilitate better planning and management will pay off severalfold. Investments include planning grants for conservation action and travel funds to enable those who represent key interests to participate in collaborative efforts.

Training for agency personnel and others involved in collaborative decision-making processes. While our grandmothers may have encouraged us to be cooperative and collaborative, our society is in fact manifestly competitive. Providing training in negotiation and collaboration to agency staff and nongovernmental individuals can promote the effectiveness of collaborative decision making. Process facilitation is also critical, and agencies need to set aside funds for hiring independent facilitators or train their personnel in facilitation and mediation strategies.

Funding for ecosystem restoration programs. The best endangered species policy is to restore ecosystem processes, and funding ecosystem restoration will be cost effective in the long term (Daily 1997). Because they cut across land-ownership and interest-based boundaries, restoration efforts are necessarily collaborative. In addition, funding from government and philanthropic foundations often elevates restoration on regional and local agendas. Whether these efforts are seen as updated pork-barrel politics or proactive recovery strategies, they have the ability to motivate and enable action that will benefit biodiversity in numerous ways.

Recognition of and rewards for efforts of individuals involved in collaborative processes. To motivate individuals to participate in sometimes difficult, often lengthy collaborative processes, it is important to recognize their efforts. This can be done by creating government performance review processes that reward outreach and collaborative behaviors; by publicly recognizing examples of effective partnerships and collaboration; and by acknowledging the efforts of nongovernmental personnel through awards and thank-you letters. Mobilizing political leaders to champion the processes can help, particularly when such leadership is bipartisan.

Legitimacy

An often-voiced criticism of collaborative processes is that they lack the legitimacy of formal governance process such as congressional and courtroom decision making (McCloskey 1996). Therefore, it is clearly necessary to develop collaborations in a way that ensures their accountability to law, science, and public values. This can be done in several ways (Wondolleck and Yaffee 2000):

Ensuring that clear scientific and legal sideboards buttress collaborative processes. Collaborative decision making needs to be well informed by science and law, which in essence define the boundaries of the decision space in which groups can work. As applied to endangered species, these processes should pay particular attention to the need to engage in joint fact finding and data negotiation, which may require solicitation of independent scientific judgment through peer review and other mechanisms. One important role that agency representatives bring to collaborative processes is the ability to identify scientific parameters, legal sideboards, and regulatory floors that are needed to bound discussions.

Providing clear understanding of agency roles and what is expected of agency staff. The need for agency personnel to play a variety of roles in these collaborations is confusing and difficult for many (Wondolleck and Ryan 1999). Agencies are often the conveners, facilitators, and leaders of these processes. They are scientific experts and stakeholders with organizational interests as well. And, ultimately, they are the final decision makers for many of the items on the negotiating table. Agencies need to help their staff understand the implications of these multiple roles and ways to manage them in the process, such as having different individuals play different roles in a process or using nonagency personnel to provide facilitation to avoid real or perceived conflicts of interest.

Following through on obligations and commitments. While agency decision makers cannot bind themselves to the outcome of a collaborative process, they can commit to supporting it with information and staffing and by taking its products seriously. Where collaboratives find effective and credible solutions, follow-through is important to motivate people to be involved. Ultimately, the likelihood of implementation assures the legitimacy of the processes by raising the stakes for all parties.

Maintaining opportunities for comment and review on products of collaborative processes. A final mechanism for ensuring the legitimacy of a collaborative process is to allow for post-process administrative or judicial review of decisions. Some will find this recommendation strange because it potentially undercuts the incentive to take the process seriously. Care must be taken, but I believe that if a process is effective, credible, representative, and open to a variety of concerns, and if it produces scientifically well-informed choices, then it will survive scientific, administrative, and judicial reviews, and participants will support it. Providing participants the opportunity to review decisions at the conclusion of a collaborative process ultimately assures accountability and ties in the results of such efforts to traditional governance mechanisms.

The Unseemly Rush to Collaboration

It is confusing to many, and concerning to some, that individuals of disparate ideological stripes all embrace collaboration. Individuals on both sides of the political spectrum use the same terms. To some on the right, these processes are about pushing power downward to reduce the effect of government on private property rights. For others on this end of the political spectrum, it is about locating decision making at a level where development interests have a greater chance of dominating (Coggins 1998; McCloskey 1996). When high-level Bush administration officials embrace collaborative conservation, it is partly because of ideology and partly a strategy to shift power from the national level to the local level where environmental groups are less organized. For those on the political left, these processes are about empowering individuals to be involved in societal choices, expanding the possibility of broader environmental protections, and supporting the ability of government to promote social progress. Both sides embrace the goal of building a stronger sense of ownership and responsibility on the part of public and private parties, which should encourage greater levels of stewardship.

One should view statements of support for collaboration with a careful eye. The goal of these processes should be improvements in the ecological and social qualities of the landscape. This is not to diminish the very real procedural improvements that can come from collaboration, which include increased understanding, reduced conflict, and greater levels of trust in communities. But in the endangered species realm, we should be bottom-line collaborationists. That is, if there are better ways to achieve these improvements than a lengthy collaborative process, we should pursue them. I am convinced, however, from studying thirty years of ESA history (Yaffee 1982) that effective collaboration can often result in net benefits for species and the people that interact with them. The challenge lies in creating effective, accountable collaboration (Clark and Wallace, this volume) and in creating structures that promote ownership and stewardship responsibility while maintaining the incentives and processes that ensure their scientific credibility and legal validity.

Is collaboration a panacea or a Pandora's box? It is clearly neither. But in many places, it can be a route to a more effective, more proactive, recovery-oriented future, particularly when contrasted with the real alternative: the likelihood of full regulatory action under the provisions of the Endangered Species Act. The U.S. Fish and Wildlife Service and the National Marine Fisheries Service will never have the staffing or political will to force endangered species protection by the many decision makers across a diverse public and private landscape. And as one moves from protection of endangered species to ecosystems, and diminishment of jeopardy to recovery as core biodiversity protection goals, the job becomes many orders of magnitude more difficult. Recovery and restoration require not only grudging compliance but also concurrence, engagement, and active support. In many situations, collaboration can help.

18   Keys to Effective Conservation

Tim W. Clark and Richard L. Wallace

The history of the Endangered Species Act (ESA) features both high-profile successes (such as recovery of the peregrine falcon [*Falco peregrinus*], whooping crane [*Grus americana*], and gray whale [*Eschrichtius robustus*]) and pervasive problems. Evaluating the act is difficult. Scientists, managers, policy makers, and the public often differ in their expectations about how the act should work and on what basis it should be appraised. This lack of consensus complicates evaluation because it produces disagreement on assessment criteria and ultimately contributes to suspect conclusions.

In this chapter, we present criteria by which the ESA can be appraised and describe how practitioners can both learn from experience and apply lessons to ongoing implementation efforts. We evaluate systematic, avoidable weaknesses in implementation and diagnose them in a way that sheds light on these sometimes "invisible" problems. Although we offer strong criticism, our goal is to introduce new methods for increasing the act's effectiveness. Our focus is on identifying lessons from past experience and applying them to current and future planning.

Problem Definition

Clearly, work remains in order to achieve the act's goals (Scott, Goble, et al., this volume). Indeed, implementing the ESA is a process of such complexity that the challenges likely will never diminish. Viewing recovery as a process, however, suggests that comprehensive appraisals of the act ought to occur simultaneously with its implementation. Furthermore, such assessment must be based on clear evaluative criteria and be designed to produce information that can be usefully fed back into the implementation of the act (Clark 1993, 1997, 2002; Wallace 2003). Discourse in which the act is praised or vilified without a clear basis for evaluation is not helpful in promoting either public understanding or improved implementation.

Specifically, three highly interactive problems are apparent. The first problem is one of *translating* a broad federal law across a large, diverse nation. Implementation must occur in many different contexts, often without consensus among the participants. Contexts for protecting and recovering endangered species vary in critical ways—biologically, organizationally, and politically— each of which requires that the ESA be adapted to local circumstances. This can be difficult when, for example, local politics are hostile to endangered species protection or national authority is not employed in ways that support the act's goals.

The second problem, related to the first, is *rigidity*. It is a challenge to administer the ESA flexibly when bureaucratic arrangements (such as relationships among agencies or between different offices within the same agency) are rigid. Agencies are often wedded to standard operating procedures that impede innovation when innovation may be exactly what is needed to address biologically, organizationally, and politically complex scenarios. In addition, federal or state agencies charged with conserving natural resources may be statutorily or administratively committed to goals that compete with the ESA. The long-standing conflicts within the National Marine Fisheries Service between that agency's mandates to manage commercial fisheries and protect marine resources are an example of this (Brailovskaya 1998; Wallace 2000; Zabel et al. 2003).

The third problem arises from the *skill sets* of the individuals involved, that is, the professional skills that practitioners bring to a program. Typically, professionals use conventional disciplinary approaches to the issues they face. By "conventional," we mean the approaches commonly taught in graduate programs and promoted in natural resource agencies, for example, the application of technical biological or ecological knowledge to complex policy problems. These conventional approaches are often employed to the exclusion of other kinds of knowledge. As a result, professional skills can trigger a "disconnect and imbalance in knowledge and skills concerning natural science research (on the one hand) and social, organizational, and values-related concerns (on the other). This leads directly to many complex and sometimes glaring problems in recovery efforts" (Wallace et al. 2002a, 70). These difficulties underscore the need for varied professional skills to address multifaceted problems.

Problem Elaboration: Three Cases

We explore ways to improve performance under the ESA through three cases, concluding with general recommendations. These cases elaborate the three problems introduced above and suggest opportunities to improve implementation of the act. Many recovery efforts are problematic because of both biological and social challenges (Abbitt and Scott 2001). Often, it is the human system that is more problematic.

The Black-Footed Ferret Case

The black-footed ferret (*Mustela nigripes*) originally ranged across more than 100 million acres of the western Great Plains and intermountain basins from southern Canada to northern Mexico. The species began to decline in the late 1800s with the introduction of extensive prairie dog (*Cynomys* spp.) eradication. Prairie dogs provide habitat and prey for ferrets. As late as the 1920s, ferrets were still widespread, with a population of perhaps a million or more individuals (Clark 1997). In 1915 the federal government began a coordinated national effort to eradicate prairie dogs and other species considered to be agricultural pests. Poisoning eliminated more than 98 percent of the prairie dogs. Ferrets were also eliminated, both directly and indirectly. By the 1980s the ferret was considered "unrecoverable" or already extinct by the U.S. Fish and Wildlife Service (USFWS) (Clark 1997).

In 1981 the serendipitous discovery of a remnant ferret population near Meeteetse, Wyoming, created a test case for the conventional ESA formula for species recovery. The formula failed in the ferret case because it did not organize the coalition of interests concerned with ferret restoration into a functioning team. This is a "translation" problem in which statutory and administrative guidelines for recovery were undermined by local and regional participants whose conception of the common interest defied the ESA recovery mandates. Early on, operational control of the ferret program was transferred by the USFWS to the Wyoming Game and Fish Department (WGF), with the USFWS retaining overall authority. This decision was made despite evidence that Wyoming had a weak commitment to the ESA and limited organizational capability to lead a complex recovery program (Lester 1990). This transfer of responsibility fragmented management authority and control arrangements, and it precipitated a process that proved to be highly corrosive to the recovery program. The ferret recovery program turned into a power contest between Wyoming, with its states' rights ideology, and the USFWS, with its federal mandate. The program illustrates the complexity of translating the ESA into effective action at the state level when participants (in this case, the lead federal and state agencies) and their perspectives conflict. WGF institutionalized a set of organizational relationships that were then mismanaged in the context of the recovery challenge. These conflicts introduced many weaknesses into the program that unwittingly led to near catastrophic failures. WGF became entrenched and defensive. This in turn led to poor decision making and subsequent actions that undermined the restoration goals for the ferret population.

Productive working relationships could not be established. Coordination of efforts was weak at best. Intelligence failures and delays in management decisions occurred. Failure to appreciate the vulnerability of the wild population by agency officials, even after catastrophic diseases were found in the wild and captive populations, almost led to the ferret's extinction. After more than twenty years and millions of dollars, ferrets are still at high risk from plague, canine distemper, and other small population threats (Biggins et al. 1997).

WGF's program design led to "goal inversion," where control of information and decision making became more important than saving ferrets. Participants clashed and, because there were competing goals (e.g., species recovery versus bureaucratic control), conflict was rampant. Crass power came to be used to manage conflict, integrate personnel, and carry out the work. Using power for these ends is a dangerous outcome of the translation problem and underscores the failure of participants to apply the ESA successfully in this context. Successful conflict management tools were ignored or rejected, as were more appropriate program designs and operations. WGF sought to legitimize itself in the face of the conflicts and in so doing further bureaucratized the program by creating advisory teams, coordinator positions, and field teams, all for the purpose of appearing to be in control of decision making. The state also sought exclusive contact with the media to control its public image, promote itself as the "savior" of ferrets, and charge other participants with causing the problems. In short, the ferret program's core ideology, arrangements, and dynamics made it impossible to correct shortcomings in order to better approximate the goals of the ESA. As a consequence, ferret recovery became a model of states' rights trumping federal resource conservation mandates.

The analytic error in this case was that both state and federal officials reduced ferret restoration to a narrowly bounded set of decision and management processes. The formula used was conventional, top down, power oriented, and bureaucratic. Given the conflict-ridden history of state versus federal relations in Wyoming, the ferret case turned into just one more battle in a very long war. The program fell victim to the "translation" problem, the failure to prepare for implementing the ESA in a specific, highly conflict-prone environment. The resulting discord in turn exacerbated inadequacies in technical research and husbandry methods and organizational behavior in the lead agencies. Acting synergistically, these problems nearly caused the ferret's extinction. Many of these problems could have been predicted and ameliorated had participants made efforts to match the ESA's mandate to the dominant paradigm in Wyoming prior to transferring authority for ferret recovery to WGF. The failure to do so illustrates the challenges of "translating" the ESA into applied conservation, despite the act's unambiguous mandate.

The Black-Tailed Prairie Dog Case

Prairie dogs are two-pound, colonial rodents that socially aggregate in large populations. The black-tailed prairie dog (*Cynomys ludovicianus*) is the most widespread and gregarious of the five species of prairie dogs. The species ranges over the short- and midgrass prairies of western North America, eating grasses, forbs, and shrubs along with roots and insects.

The prairie dog historically occupied parts of eleven western states (Hoogland 1995), two Canadian provinces, and one Mexican state. It is a "keystone" species in the American grasslands. Prairie dog colonies and associated species together make up the "prairie dog ecosystem" (Clark et al. 1989). Their abundance has dropped dramatically by about 98 percent over the last century. The species faces ongoing threats from uncontrolled recreational shooting, introduced diseases (especially sylvatic plague), continued poisoning, inadequate regulatory mechanisms, and lack of adaptive management (Predator Conservation Alliance 2001). Despite its population decline, the species made it onto the ESA agenda only when conservationists petitioned the USFWS to list it and the USFWS designated the prairie dog as a candidate for listing in 1999 (National Wildlife Federation 1998b).

Conflicts concerning species and habitat restoration are among the most contentious in the United States (Reading et al. 2002). The complexity and conflict comes from opposing perspectives of participants and the way they interact. The prairie dog situation is a classic example of these problems.

Several groups have organized around deeply felt, often contradictory views of the species. Each has a unique vantage point that defines the problem in narrow, incomplete, and self-interested ways. Thus, each viewpoint calls for a different solution. Ranchers and the agricultural industry want to eliminate prairie dogs or maintain them at very low numbers. Conservationists want the species recovered and their ecological function protected. Animal rights activists want abundant prairie dogs and protection of individuals. Recreational hunters want prairie dogs to be sufficiently abundant to continue hunting. Native Americans have diverse views but are generally supportive of prairie dog recovery. Although most citizens are unaware of the issue, the public also generally supports conservation. Most agencies seek to keep the species off the endangered species list. Some agencies are allied with ranchers and other land use interests. Agency personnel also hold personal and professional views that vary.

Presently, there is no adequate means to integrate these diverse and often conflicting interests into an overall program for prairie dog conservation. The response from all levels of government is best described as "defensive policy." The USFWS belatedly took the most risk-aversive path when it designated the species as "warranted" for listing as threatened, but "precluded" from listing because other, higher priority species needed attention (USFWS 1999e). The designation sent shock waves through the western cattle and real estate industries, which oppose any formal recognition under the ESA. The prairie dog's new status focused the controversy and fueled activity by agricultural interests, wildlife and land management agencies, and nongovernmental conservation groups.

Since the USFWS did not list the species, the agency had no formal regulatory power. The warranted-but-precluded status, however, did send a strong message to the states that doing nothing was no longer an option. Western states formed a coalition to oppose listing, a manifestation of the strong states' rights ideology of most western states (e.g., Cawley 1993; Wilkinson 1998). The states prepared an interstate management plan, the main goal of which was to prevent listing prairie dogs. It was adopted by western states. More recently, the states have sought to achieve as much management authority as possible. To the states, maintaining authority and control over prairie dog conservation efforts arguably has taken precedence over substantive conservation efforts, a classic case of "goal substitution" driven by competition for power (Daft 2003). Recovery is never discussed as such in the interstate plan. Instead, the plan calls for preventing federal listing (Luce 2003). The long-term goal is to increase the prairie dog population, but in less than 1 percent of the species' former range, a goal that is only marginally better than the species' present conditions, if that. The plan primarily focuses on more research and monitoring, economic incentives for ranchers to participate, and more government oversight of poisoning and shooting. Annual reviews by the USFWS indicate that the agency's judgment is that the states have been making adequate progress. Indeed, some progress has been made, but it has been minimal and slow. The steps taken to date are necessary for recovery, but far from sufficient.

The interstate plan raises several questions. First, it is not clear why an interstate program is necessary to conserve prairie dogs within each state since each state already has the necessary authority to conserve its own wildlife. To date, the states have not used their existing legislative and administrative authority to aid prairie dog conservation. The new arrangement only adds more "red tape" to an already complex problem. Second, most western states have limited institutional capabilities (Lester 1990). Eight of the eleven states that contain prairie dogs have been classed as "low capability" in a twenty-three-variable study. Finally, although the interstate plan cites a number of causes for prairie dog declines, it does not indicate how it will remedy these, especially those factors that fall under "human dimensions." Overall, the interstate plan fails to demonstrate that a state-led effort will be successful.

The analytic error in this case is that officials reduced a complex challenge to a traditional, standardized program led by agencies that have historically shown little interest in prairie dog conservation. The program is therefore highly vulnerable. First, the states have dominated planning with little input from other stakeholders. Second, the plan replays old ideas and promotes interactions that have, in fact, contributed to the decline of prairie dogs and their habitat. Third, the plan promotes traditional decision making and generally serves local, primarily agricultural, interests. And fourth, the follow-on state plans fail to provide mechanisms for addressing the human factors affecting prairie dogs, especially the widespread negative attitudes and economic and agricultural practices that harm the species. One measure of the plan is that ranchers are already resisting voluntary measures, including financial incentives that reward them for protecting prairie dogs on their lands. Recovery is unlikely. In fact, the species was removed from the candidate list in 2004.

The Southern Sea Otter Case

The southern sea otter (*Enhydra lutris nereis*) was believed to be extinct, largely a result of trapping for the fur trade, by the early 1900s. A small population, however, was rediscovered along the central California coast in 1938. Following enactment of the ESA in 1973, the USFWS took little action to investigate the species' status. To fill the void, the federal Marine Mammal Commission in 1975 sponsored research on the otter population and its habitat and found both to be at risk from possible oil spills along the coast. Risks were also mounting as fisheries, especially for abalone and other shellfish, grew, increasing both direct competition for prey species and the threat of otters becoming entangled in fishing nets. In response, the USFWS listed the sea otter as threatened under the ESA in 1977. A recovery plan was published in 1982 and revised in 2003 (USFWS 2003h).

Otters are the source of both biological and socioeconomic conflicts. Although they are opportunistic predators, otters prey actively on abalone wherever the two coexist. This creates competition between the otters and the abalone fishing industry, triggering the related dynamics between the state and federal agencies, fishers, and nongovernmental organizations involved in otter conservation. The lead state agency, the California Department of Fish and Game (CDFG), has often sided with the fishing industry in conflicts between marine mammals and fisheries; although its relationships with other participants in the otter case have often been contentious, they have remained professional. CDFG has been a willing partner in efforts to develop strategies to conserve otters while mitigating otter-fisheries conflicts. Other participants, such as the Marine Mammal Commission and the nongovernmental Friends of the Sea Otter, exert conservation-oriented pressure on the USFWS. The USFWS, for its part, was willing to follow rather than lead, often taking the actions it was pressured to take.

In 1981 the Marine Mammal Commission suggested to the USFWS a recovery strategy described as "zonal management," similar to a strategy considered, but not ultimately pursued, by CDFG in the mid-1970s. As eventually adopted, zonal management was intended to mitigate the ongoing conflicts between shellfisheries and otter recovery by creating an "otter-free" management zone in which shellfish stocks would be unaffected by otter population expansion. Zonal management consisted of establishing a translocated, ESA-designated, experimental population at San Nicolas Island in the Channel Islands and authorizing the removal of otters from the entirety of the Southern California Bight south of Point Conception except for the area around San Nicolas (the otter management zone) (USFWS 1987a).

According to the USFWS, the goals for establishing the new colony were to eliminate the possibility that a single natural or human-caused disaster (such as an oil spill) could wipe out the entire population and "to obtain data for assessing translocation and containment techniques, population status, and the influence of sea otters on the structure and dynamics of the nearshore community in order to better understand the characteristics and impacts of a sea otter population at its optimum sustainable level" (USFWS 1987b, 22). Implied in the second goal is the study and assessment of the community ecology of sea otters, including interactions between otters and shellfish. The role and influence of otters on shellfisheries in California, especially as compared to overharvesting, has been a point of contention between the fishing industry and CDFG on the one hand, and federal managers and researchers, Friends of the Sea Otter, and other otter recovery advocates on the other (e.g., Estes and VanBlaricom 1985; Hardy and Wendell 1982). Participants were hopeful that with zonal management, the conflicts would subside.

The translocation began in the summer of 1987 and lasted three years. During that time, 139 otters were moved to San Nicolas Island (fewer than the 250 that the USFWS had planned to establish the new colony). Soon after the first series of releases in 1987, it became apparent that the otters were not establishing a colony as had been hoped (USFWS 1991b, 1991c). The translocation of otters ended in 1990 when the permit authorizing the project was suspended. The resident population has remained stable at about 15 to 17 animals since 1989; the reasons for the lack of population growth at the island are unknown (USFWS 1996e). No otters have been removed from the management zone since February 1993, when two otters died following their capture and release, calling into question the federal permit requirement that otter control measures be nonlethal (USFWS 1993b, 1996e). Since that time, neither the USFWS nor CDFG has allocated funds or staff to capture otters in the management zone.

In the aftermath of the zonal management experiment, several events occurred that had profound effects on the otter program. First, in March 1989 the *Exxon Valdez* ran aground, spilling 11 million gallons of crude oil into Alaska's Prince William Sound. The spill's magnitude undercut the principal assumption of the sea otter recovery program: that expanding the otter population to San Nicolas Island would reduce or remove the threat of a single oil spill devastating the entire population. Since prevailing ocean currents off the California coast move in a southerly direction, a spill north of the otters' range could affect the entire population (USFWS 1996e). Second, following the suspension of the translocation, both the USFWS and CDFG began systematically disassembling their long-standing otter programs. The USFWS discontinued its otter recovery coordinator position, deleted its budget line for otter recovery, and reassigned its otter staff to other duties. Third, following a long and apparently inexorable decline, all five species of abalone were declared commercially extinct throughout California by CDFG in 1998 (Rogers-Bennett et al. 2002). This effectively ended the California abalone industry and forced CDFG and the fishers to develop abalone conservation plans in the absence of any fishing effort, but with the existence of otters in abalone habitat. Fourth, the otter population unexpectedly expanded its range into the otter management zone. In the spring of 1998, 101 otters were observed south of Point Conception, the northern limit of the "otter-free zone" delineated by the zonal management plan (Estes and Hatfield 1998; USFWS 1999f, 1999g). Although the otters retreated to the north and out of the management zone during the summer, they returned in the winter, and by January 1999, 152 otters occupied the waters of Cojo Anchorage, south of Point Conception. These animals are not part of the translocation effort and so represent a natural expansion of the population southward along the California coast (USFWS 1999g). Needless to say, the abalone industry and other fishing interests became alarmed and immediately called for the otters to be removed from the management zone (in accordance with zonal management policy) while Friends of the Sea Otter and other otter recovery advocates called for the immediate full protection and study of the population. These events occurred when the state and federal agencies had no dedicated otter staff or funding.

There are two analytical errors in this case, and the removal of either one would have substantially reduced the problems encountered by program participants. The first involves the failure to collect adequate data on the capture and relocation of otters. Because no prototype research program was conducted before the translocation effort was begun, the agencies were unprepared for the failure of the translocation effort and had no workable alternatives other than to end the program at great emotional and resource expense. Had agency managers better prepared for a full spectrum of possible biological outcomes, a range of alternatives could have been discussed and contingency plans developed to address them. Instead, the agencies placed all of their proverbial eggs in one basket, and when the effort failed they were unable to face the logistical, budgetary, and emotional cost of starting over.

Their abandonment of what they had accomplished, and the learning opportunities it afforded, is the second analytical error. The otter program suffered from bureaucratic rigidity and an inability to adapt to unexpected programmatic change. The natural expansion of the otter population into the management zone was an eventuality that the USFWS and CDFG could have projected and one for which they should have been prepared. Instead, no contingency plan was in place, and following the events of 1998–99 the agencies were left scrambling to reinitiate their management programs while simultaneously operating in a conflict-prone crisis arena, far from ideal circumstances in which to implement the ESA. In this case, the USFWS has been able to build on its past experience. In the wake of the otter expansion, the agency opened the decision-making process to former program participants (notably abalone fishers, Friends of the Sea Otter, Marine Mammal Commission, and the public), initiated processes to formally end the zonal management program (which had been codified by Congress), and clarified its intent to apply the ESA fully to the newly expanded population. In conjunction with its renewed efforts on behalf of the otter, the USFWS reconvened the otter recovery team to complete the revised recovery plan, which the agency subsequently adopted.

Net Assessment

Other reviews of the implementation of the ESA suggest the analytic errors evident in our three cases may be common. Based on reviews of endangered species programs, we found three aspects of current recovery operations (i.e., decision-making process) that need explicit, systematic attention (Clark 1996, 2001; Wallace 1994, 2003). First, managers need to spend more time clarifying the conservation goal, defining the problem(s) contextually with respect to goal attainment, and examining alternative ways of achieving the goal again given the context. Second, it is essential to establish a thorough, ongoing appraisal mechanism in order to learn systematically from past conservation experience and to make practical improvements. Third, it is essential to recast the challenge of species recovery in terms of upgrading the decision-making process and learning at individual, organizational, and policy levels—in other words, focusing attention on the adaptive management of endangered species programs.

By looking at recovery as a set of interactive activities (i.e., a decision-making process), we can systematically determine how well each activity functions case by case. One model of decision making useful in evaluating recovery programs is to illustrate the "life cycle" of a policy or program as including the following activities: planning, open debate of alternatives, deciding among alternatives, implementation, resolving disputes that flow from implementation, monitoring and evaluation, and termination or modification as indicated by the evaluation (Clark and Brunner 1996). This sequence of activities is called a "decision process" (Lasswell and McDougal 1992). By knowing how a decision process works, or does not work, people in endangered species conservation can maintain good practices or correct poorly functioning ones.

Based on reviews of nearly a hundred cases, we see recurring but preventable weaknesses. Guidelines to avoiding twenty-two common problems were offered by Clark (1997) and Clark et al. (2000, 2001) and are outlined below. A recent appraisal by Pagel et al. (forthcoming) also discovered implementation problems in many programs.

In conclusion, it appears to us and other analysts that implementation of the ESA reveals too many preventable errors. If this is true, then remedial steps could increase overall performance as well as case-by-case performance. Weaknesses in recovery programs occur when, in an effort to translate national ESA policy to specific cases, we simplify complex challenges and use only fragments of contextual knowledge potentially available on which to formulate and implement programs (i.e., the "translation" problem). Furthermore, agencies often apply standard agency operating procedures in case after case. This can impede innovation and lead to mismatches between chosen and necessary methods (i.e., the "rigidity" problem). Finally, application of traditional biological skills may predispose individuals to overlook or misconstrue important aspects of the social and organizational as well as biological context. Traditional approaches may only compound problems (i.e., the professional or skill problem).

Recommendations for Improving Performance

What can we do about these problems? Strategies, tools, and models exist to improve our individual and collective response to recovery. Together they call for a more active, systematic, and integrated approach than currently exists. They also call for more innovation and increased learning on a case-by-case basis, across programs, and about the ESA overall. These strategies, tools, and models can be used in various ways to address the problems illustrated above.

Use a Practice-Based Approach to Find Best Conservation Practices

One solution to "translation" problems is to adopt a practice-based approach to recovery. This strategy focuses on cases and best practices to improve performance. ESA policy is a complex system, the totality of which is beyond comprehension for most practitioners. Therefore, the key to improving recovery is to focus attention and resources on selected parts of the system. Much of the debate about improving the ESA focuses on top-down changes to policy. Although such changes can marginally improve the act's operation, significant improvement can take place at the "bottom" or operational level. Recovery problems stem from a multitude of private and public decisions, many of which predate the ESA and many of which take place far from Washington, D.C. Recovery depends on many local, small-scale, private, and public decisions. It is these decisions that are the appropriate focus for improving recovery efforts.

We recommend a three-part, practice-based strategy: (1) find and describe successful recovery efforts, (2) adapt and diffuse them widely, and (3) create new opportunities to build further recovery program successes (Wallace 2003). Actual programs should be identified, described, and reviewed critically to determine the reasons for their success or failure. Identifying and describing successful practices is best done through independent and continuous appraisal (Lasswell 1971). Cases are real efforts rather than theoretical constructs. Case studies can be one source of information for participants in other cases who can then adapt the prototypes to their specific situation (Clark et al. 1995). This adaptation should be iterative and designed to avoid rigidity and maximize learning. Federal and state agencies could provide leadership by supporting successful prototypes. At present, unfortunately, the ESA policy arena has few mechanisms for appraisal, prototyping, and dissemination.

A key task is creating processes that encourage improved communication. These can be formal, such as intergovernmental task forces, or less formal, such as electronic networks. Combining economic strategies for private and business interests should be considered. Because endangered species recovery varies geographically as well as ecologically, politically, and economically, it should be decentralized at the operational level. The use of case-specific strategies can help avoid a top-down approach and bureaucratic hierarchies by emphasizing the importance of individual policy contexts (and thus recognizing the dangers of taking a "one size fits all" approach to endangered species policy). To accomplish this, there is a need to shift to more progressive action plans.

Use Appropriate Tools to Address Substantive, Process, and Structural Problems

The disconnect between a broad top-down mandate and varied local context can be dealt with, at least in part, by using workshops, group problem solving, and special "decision seminars." Workshops and group-based problem solving are sometimes used in endangered species conservation, but not to their fullest potential (Clark et al. 2001).

Effective, group-based problem solving involves "ways and means for blending wisdom and science, for balancing free association and intellectual discipline, for expanding and refining information, and for building a problem solving culture that balances 'permanent' with 'transient' membership, thereby remaining open to new participants and to fresh ideas while retaining the capacity for cumulative learning that refines, clarifies, and simplifies" (Burgess and Slonaker 1978, 1). Workshops are a means that groups can use for problem solving, capacity building, and consensus development. In a consensus workshop, the group articulates the common interest. Consensus is a shared understanding that enables a group to move forward in problem solving; it does not mean that everyone agrees (Stanfield 2002). Guides to the design of workshops are readily available (e.g., Stanfield 2002).

To address planning and implementation successfully, recovery personnel need a comprehensive understanding of their own organizations and institutions relative to the recovery problem and its context. One means to achieve this outcome is through a "decision seminar" (Wallace and Clark 2002; Burgess and Slonaker 1978). This tool was first proposed by Harold Lasswell (1971). It is a tool for group problem solving that increases the likelihood of realistic, timely, and comprehensive solutions (Muth and Bolland 1983).

A decision seminar differs in many ways from traditional, short-term, focused workshops. First, it may not be responsible for making immediate decisions. Typically, it does not come under pressures of operational decision making. Second, it is unique because of its more thorough analysis conforming to the five tasks of problem solving described by Lasswell (1971). These tasks are (1) clarifying the goals of the program, agency, or policy; (2) describing the social, organizational, biological, and other relevant trends that pertain to the issues at hand; (3) analyzing the factors that have caused or influenced the trends; (4) projecting likely outcomes from the current state of the program or policy; and (5) inventing, evaluating, and selecting alternatives or options to solve the problem(s). These five tasks allow "the context to emerge as the focus of individual or group attention" (Lasswell 1971, 39; Cunningham 1981, 26).

Use an Integrated Framework and
Civic Professionalism to Improve Recovery

Using a proven, integrative framework for problem solving combined with a civic model of professionalism can reduce the limitations of the conventional fragmented and positivistic model of professionalism. Regardless of how much knowledge or experience a professional has, each new recovery problem is unique. This requires creative application of strategies for posing, solving, and resolving the problem. A framework for problem solving and an appropriate model of professionalism are essential, but frequently absent, requirements. Wallace et al. (2002b) introduce a framework and model of professionalism that can aid recovery efforts.

Problem solving is just an effort by an individual or group to think of a way out of a difficult situation. The first requirement for improved recovery decision making is an integrated problem-solving framework that can accommodate both conceptually and practically diverse data, epistemologies, and disciplines (Clark et al. 2001). Categories are essential parts of the recovery process because they permit systematic, explicit thinking. The categories in an integrated framework can serve as a "checklist" of variables to address in any recovery problem. Furthermore, they allow us to deal intellectually, efficiently, and effectively with complex concepts and a large volume of data. Such a framework is a tool for thinking and giving direction to thought and action. It encourages professionals to ask: Why are we doing this? What should we think about? What will result from our thoughts and actions? This permits users to construct a realistic map of the conservation process, its context, and to define and solve problems.

Conventional problem solving draws on ordinary, everyday images, notions, and vocabulary about people, problems, and the process of making decisions. In the black-tailed prairie dog case, this style of problem solving is inadequate. Nevertheless, the record shows that it is used regardless of whether it is effective or not. As a result, decision makers muddle through problems and crises without fully understanding their nature, solving them, or gaining insight into why the process is not as effective as hoped. This traditional approach is inadequate to resolve the real complexity and conflict inherent in many recovery efforts.

The framework we recommend and that has served us well through many years of professional practice was developed by Lasswell (1971) and Lasswell and McDougal (1992); it was cast in terms of species and ecosystem conservation by Clark et al. (2001) and Wallace et al. (2002a, 2002b). It captures what is typically described as the facets of effective problem solving: orienting to the problem, being contextual (including mapping the social and decision processes), and applying multiple methods to the problem at hand. It requires users to explore a problem fully through an analysis of goals, trends, conditions, projections, and alternatives. It requires users to ensure an adequate conservation decision process by mapping the activities or functions that make up that decision process and then reflecting upon and learning from them. It requires users to understand the context, that is, the human environment, that is central to understanding the biological problems and finding a solution to the recovery problem. The framework also welcomes any and all methods from the natural and social sciences and humanities, and it recognizes that information and expertise from each of these areas can help users to understand and resolve problems. Finally, the framework allows users to array categories of analysis (and data within them) in ways that reveal connections and insights not otherwise apparent. The framework encourages systematic thinking directed at the achievement of recovery goals (Brewer and Clark 1994).

The second requirement for improved decision making is that the professional understands his or her standpoint relative to society and behaves accordingly (Schön 1983; Clark and Wallace 2002). Recovery practitioners are specialized in their training, operate following some standards of practice, and show some commitment to society. The training, standards, and commitment vary dramatically. Too often problems afflict professionalism: these may include myopic overspecialization, loss of integrity, weak civic ethic, self-interested behavior, and blindness to the role of specialists in a democratic society. Professionalism requires the knowledge and skill to blend technical matters, civic responsibility, leadership, and learning into a mode of operation that contributes to communal standards of problem solving in a responsible way (Clark and Reading 1994).

Civic professionalism stresses use of an integrated approach (via a framework, as above) and commitment to public service. It requires practitioners to be self-reflective about their work and interactions with others (Schön 1983). This model requires an orientation of professional life that brings it into accord with a profession's deepest aims and goals. It requires a greater awareness of self and the social context of problem solving than does conventional professionalism. It requires new habits of thinking, leadership, and participation for some professionals. It also often requires changes in professional education and on-the-job working arrangements.

Conclusion

Conservation of a nation's biological heritage is a long-standing goal that is now widely recognized throughout the world. The Endangered Species Act is among the high points in our nation's commitment to sustain biodiversity as an element in our national security. Despite this noble goal, however, ESA implementation is problematic and successes have been too few and too slow for some analysts. Problems stem from analytic errors on the part of implementers. These are remedial. We recommend three ways to improve matters using a practice-based strategy, workshops (especially decision seminars), and new, integrative, problem-solving skills. Our recommendations are designed to shift the conventional formula for endangered species conservation to a more practical, integrated, and continual-learning approach. This approach shifts science from a reductionistic, predictive, positivistic mode to one that addresses multiple independent sources of information, consequences of practical experience, and qualitative, context-sensitive methods. It shifts problem solving from a reliance on normative models of rationality, confidence in positivistic science, and technical fixes to problem solving that relies on integrated behavior sciences that address context and complexity, and contextualized, procedural solutions. It shifts decision making from discrete decisions, experts, and authorities that are bureaucratized and "top down" to decision making that is continuous and interconnected, involves a broad spectrum of participants including nonexperts and nonofficials, and is relatively informal and "bottom-up." These needed shifts can capture and institutionalize our collective wisdom for improving programs and policies. Examining these matters openly, comprehensively, and empirically, as this volume and the conference on which it is based have done, can help us ensure a healthy future for humans and nature, not only in our country, but worldwide.

We want to thank many colleagues, organizations, and funders who have aided our work over the years. They are too numerous to mention by name here but are included by name in our publications. Denise Casey offered critical advice on the manuscript.

19 Hands-on Restoration

William Burnham, Tom J. Cade, Alan Lieberman,
J. Peter Jenny, and William R. Heinrich

The Peregrine Fund is one of the most experienced nongovernmental organizations (NGO) in hands-on restoration of endangered vertebrate species in the United States. The organization began working toward restoration of the American peregrine falcon (*Falco peregrinus anatum*) several years before the Endangered Species Act of 1973 was enacted (Cade et al. 1971; Burnham and Cade 2003; Cade 2003) and has since played an important role in the recovery of the endangered northern aplomado falcon (*Falco femoralis septentrionalis*) (Jenny 2003; Jenny et al. 2004; Montoya et al. 1997), California condor (*Gymnogyps californianus*) (Cade et al. 2004), many endemic avian Hawaiian species (Kuehler et al. 1995, 1996, 2000, 2001), and several nonnative species listed as endangered under the Endangered Species Act (ESA), in particular the Mauritius kestrel (*Falco punctatus*) and harpy eagle (*Harpia harpyja*). Most people agree abstractly with the importance of saving species from extinction. Problems arise, however, in defining what that means and how to achieve that objective. This is particularly true when legal requirements for preserving species conflict with human desires for resources.

Lessons for Species Recovery

The Peregrine Fund collaborates with state and federal agencies and other NGOs to prevent species extinction and to restore viable wild populations (Burnham 1997). Our work under the ESA serves as the basis for several lessons about what is and is not successful.

Species Restoration and the Endangered Species Act

Species cannot be successfully restored unless the reasons for the species decline are successfully mitigated. In our experience, conservation actions under the ESA have seldom significantly ameliorated the causes of population declines. For example, the Endangered Species Act had little impact on habitat improvement for recovery of the peregrine because the insecticide DDT had been banned prior to passage of the act in 1973, and the peregrine was already protected by state and federal laws. Similarly, the California condor was protected against human persecution by the State of California and the federal Migratory Bird Treaty Act before passage of the ESA, and no actions have been taken to reduce the presence of lead, a major cause of mortality in this species (Kiff et al. 1979; Pattee et al. 1990; Cade et al. 2004). Changes in ranching and land management practices that allowed aplomado falcon restoration in Texas occurred before the falcon was listed under the ESA. And the act has yet to produce any measurable effects on the causes for declines and extinctions of endemic Hawaiian species. These examples suggest that the additional direct and indirect (habitat) protection provided under the ESA does not enhance recovery. In the case of endemic species in Hawaii, however, the act may yet have a positive effect if the right corrective actions are taken to improve habitats at biologically significant scales (removal of exotic herbivores and predators).

Most endangered species depend significantly on habitats found on private lands; some occur only on such lands (Bean and Wilcove 1997). Hawaii (225 listed species) and Texas (70 listed species) have only 16 percent and 1 percent, respectively, of federal land (Wilcove et al. 1996). The use of safe harbor agreements and nonessential experimental population status can reduce the concerns of private landowners and users of federal lands thus making it easier to work with ESA-listed species. Creating incentives for private landowners is critical in many cases to the recovery of endangered species (Brook et al. 2003).

Benefits of Species Listing

Just the threat of listing can provide benefits but also cause problems for a species. For example, peregrine falcons were taken from the wild shortly before the passage of the ESA in 1973 by individuals who knew that peregrines would be listed as endangered under the new act and thus their legal taking for any purpose would become impossible; later, these birds became the foundation for the captive population and restoration program of peregrine falcons (Burnham 2003).

Listing focuses attention on a species and can increase support for conservation actions on its behalf, as was the case with the peregrine falcon. The threat of listing has caused state wildlife departments and federal land management agencies to develop plans to address concerns and benefit species such as the greater sage-grouse (*Centrocercus urophasianus*). Even without the ESA and listing, however, there was significant support for the conservation of the peregrine and California condor.

On the other hand, it is commonly acknowledged that the petition for listing the black-tailed prairie dog (*Cynomys ludovicianus*) resulted in large-scale poisoning of prairie dog colonies by landowners who feared intrusion on their property by the U.S. Fish and Wildlife Service (USFWS). Other examples of negative responses to listing include the Preble's meadow jumping mouse (*Zapus hudsonius preblei*) and red-cockaded woodpecker (*Picoides borealis*) (Brook et al. 2003; Pickrell 2004). Brook et al. (2003) found that listing did not enhance the prospect of survival for listed species on private property.

Once a species is listed as threatened or endangered, delisting is difficult, even when the species no longer meets listing criteria. Delisting the Arctic peregrine from threatened status, for instance, took about three and a half years from the publication of the delisting proposal to the final *Federal Register* notice. Likewise, the American peregrine falcon delisting process required four years and three months (Burnham and Cade 2003). Opposition to delisting is often motivated by a desire to continue habitat protective measures mandated by the listing of a species.

The Role of Recovery Teams

Following enactment of the Endangered Species Act, four regional recovery teams were established for the peregrine falcon. The teams were assigned the task of writing (and updating) recovery plans as well as advising the USFWS. Although there were multiple recovery teams for the peregrine, each was a manageable size and largely composed of peregrine experts. The teams advised on strategic programmatic issues as requested by the USFWS. In large part, they did the jobs requested of them, and their contributions facilitated restoration.

Another success story is the working group to recover the aplomado falcon. Although a recovery plan was written for the aplomado falcon (USFWS 1990c), a recovery team was not established. Instead, effective coordination was accomplished through regular communication among municipal, state, federal, and private cooperators, and most aplomado falcon experts are actively involved in recovery actions.

Other efforts have been less effective. For example, in California, the condor recovery team gradually evolved from a small group of experts focusing on strategic issues to a large group of stakeholders attempting to micromanage restoration actions. As a result, the effectiveness of the restoration program was diminished for a time; the situation has subsequently improved. In Hawaii, where conservation issues are nearly overwhelming and in need of quick action, recovery teams took over ten years to update and draft two recovery plan revisions (`alala, the Hawaiian crow (*Corvus hawaiiensis*), and Hawaiian forest birds) that are only now being reviewed by the public.

Organizational structures called *working groups* were formed in many states to coordinate peregrine recovery actions (Burnham and Cade 2003). Participants were drawn from state wildlife departments, NGOs such as the Peregrine Fund, federal land agencies, and affected private landowners. Working groups are often brought together by state wildlife agencies to plan and fund recovery actions. Meetings tend to be informal, congenial gatherings, with participants frequently adjourning afterward to local bars to share a few beers.

The Players in Species Restoration Programs

For any given species restoration program, there can be many stakeholders, at several levels. Although national, and even international, cooperation is sometimes needed to implement restoration programs, successful programs generally require the input of nearby local communities, including landowners and other interested individuals. Species restoration programs require trust to succeed. Often, people do not trust governments but do trust other people. Such trust cannot be legislated; rather, it develops gradually, over time and through interactions among concerned parties.

The help of state wildlife agencies in facilitating and supporting species recovery has been key to the success of many programs, including peregrine recovery programs (Oakleaf and Craig 2003). This holds true for current efforts with the aplomado falcon in Texas, the California condor in Arizona and California, and the forest birds in Hawaii.

Successful restoration programs also require extensive participation by the private sector, along with support of local communities. In the case of the peregrine falcon, private organizations spearheaded recovery efforts, but they also collaborated closely with state wildlife and federal land management agencies where jurisdiction overlapped. Recovery programs for the aplomado falcon in Texas and the California condor in Arizona similarly involved significant participation by private organizations. In Hawaii, leaders in restoration programs within the private sector include the Zoological Society of San Diego, the Nature Conservancy, Kamehameha Schools, the Silversword Foundation, and public-private partnerships such as the Olaa-Kilauea Partnership.

The Science behind Recovery

Knowledge of an at-risk species' biology and ecology, the reasons behind its decline in population, and its primary limiting factors (e.g., winter habitat, food during breeding) are crucial (Scott, Goble, et al., this volume; Lomolino, forthcoming). Considerable knowledge about the peregrine falcon, based on research and centuries of the species use in falconry, existed at the time of its listing. Further research documented population trends and causes of decline (Newton 2003). This information ultimately facilitated its recovery. There was also substantial additional research (often funded by federal land managing agencies) that was rarely used by the biologists actually engaged in recovery actions. Much of this work consisted of due-diligence studies that agencies believed were necessary to comply with requirements of the ESA and the National Environmental Policy Act (Act of January 1, 1970). A similar situation has developed with aplomado falcon restoration in New Mexico. Prioritizing expenditure of the limited ESA funds for information gathering is an important but often neglected task.

Programs often tout their use of "best available science" to guide species recovery, but scientists, lawyers, and other professionals are fallible and can find it difficult to separate personal opinion, bias, and agendas from pure science (Burnham and Cade 1995). Nevertheless, the need to keep science free from political alliances is critical (Brussard et al. 1994; Scott et al. 1995).

Funding and Species Recovery

Hands-on restoration programs are expensive; therefore, every effort should be made to prevent species from declining to a level requiring such action. Recovery costs increase dramatically when moving from managing a species in a functional ecosystem to conducting highly focused, hands-on species restoration (Conway 1986).

Hands-on restoration can also require long-term action. Restoration of the peregrine took about three decades, restoration of the aplomado falcon will likely require two decades, that of the California condor may extend a half century or more, and restoration of Hawaiian bird species may continue indefinitely. Obtaining sufficiently long-term funding for such projects is difficult because the private sector and the government eventually tire in their support.

Annual appropriations for threatened and endangered species conservation have never approached the limits authorized by Congress. Such funding must compete with other budgetary demands. Furthermore, increases do not necessarily mean more dollars for actual recovery actions because developing and maintaining the bureaucracy to implement the complex regulations associated with the ESA are expensive. Although public funds are critical, we believe that species recovery programs in which individuals and organizations assist financially are more likely to succeed than those that are supported only by government funding. Dollars contributed for restoration actions reflect the acceptance and commitment of the public.

Permitting and Species Recovery

ESA regulations are complex, especially in regard to permitting (Burnham and Cade 1995). Permits and the permitting process have discouraged species conservation action and hindered research and recovery action. Although the USFWS is trying to simplify the permitting process, existing regulations and other statutory protections, such as the Migratory Bird Treaty Act (Act of July 3, 1918) and the Wild Bird Conservation Act (Act of October 23, 1992), limit what can be accomplished without additional legislative changes.

Recommendations for Species Recovery

We recommend that the Endangered Species Act be restructured to emphasize incentives rather than regulations. Below, we offer specific recommendations on listing and delisting species, recovery planning and implementation, research, regulations and permitting, revisions to the Endangered Species Act, and biome conservation.

Listing and Delisting Species

The U.S. Fish and Wildlife Service has emphasized listing as a primary means of protecting imperiled species. Although we understand the importance of listing at-risk species, petitions for listing should only be accepted from established experts on the species under consideration. Delisting should also be a priority if for no other reason than to showcase proof of success. In reality, delistings are often held up for a variety of reasons. The bald eagle (*Haliaeetus leucocephalus*), for example, was originally proposed for delisting ten years ago, but action has been held up owing to concern about the adequacy of habitat protection after delisting—a misapplied application of the "precautionary principle." It would be better to transfer ESA decision making about species status, listing, and delisting to an independent panel of experts on each species, appointed by the National Research Council of the National Academy of Sciences (see Cade 1998; Greenwald et al., this volume).

Recovery Planning and Implementation

Recovery planning and implementation should be substantially restructured to clarify the roles of the various parties.

First, recovery teams should be composed of small groups of biologists (seven to nine individuals) selected on the basis of their scientific knowledge of the species in question and the threats it faces. When individuals are included in a representative capacity, all organizations (particularly governmental organizations) will seek representation; the result will be a team that is inefficient, expensive, and difficult to manage. USFWS staff should be precluded from serving on teams, although exceptions may be made for species experts; USFWS interaction with recovery teams should be limited to facilitation of team activities and recommendations for recovery.

Second, the recovery plan should be brief, requiring only a few pages to outline the problem and make general recommendations on the recovery goals for downlisting and delisting the species. Detailed documents requiring years to write result in plans that are outdated before they are finished and thus are of limited value (Burnham and Cade 2003). Short plans also simplify revision and updating as new information becomes available.

Third, the sole task of the team should be to write the recovery plan. Recovery teams should recommend, not implement, species recovery. By allowing the recovery team to focus on planning for species recovery, they can avoid entanglement in the desires and political interests of stakeholders and thus produce a better plan.

Fourth, after the recovery plan is developed, stakeholders should meet to discuss its implementation. It is at this point that input, needs, recommendations, and involvement of stakeholders should occur. From these discussions, an implementation agreement can be developed between the USFWS, local communities, and other interested parties; recovery plans should be implemented much as habitat conservation plans are. Although complete agreement among all involved may not be possible, if stakeholders know where they stand and what is to happen, the potential for collaboration is increased. For both the California condor releases in Arizona and aplomado falcon restoration in Texas, agreements were developed for implementation of recovery actions as part of the 10(j) and safe harbor agreements.

Fifth, a working group is a useful organization to facilitate recovery if participants are limited to entities that actively contribute to the restoration effort. It functions best when led by the organizations or individuals engaged in the recovery action in cooperation with appropriate governmental agencies. Implementation should be accomplished by those best qualified in the private sector and in state and federal wildlife agencies. To the extent possible, private landowners should be included and compensated for their participation in recovery efforts.

Sixth, the role of USFWS should be limited to oversight and facilitation rather than implementation of restoration projects and programs. USFWS administrators continue the transition from ESA enforcers to recovery facilitators. Land management agencies should take the lead in recovery implementation. Finally, state governments and wildlife agencies should be given increased responsibility for implementing recovery. In the long term, much of what the USFWS is attempting to accomplish should be transferred to qualified state agencies. Conservation of endangered species needs to become a local desire and focus.

Research and Recovery

Having the best possible information is important to guide recovery actions for species (Ruckelshaus and Darm, forthcoming), but research should not be perceived as recovery action. The primary value of research is to (1) define the reason(s) for the species' decline, (2) determine the factors limiting populations, and (3) help support and guide restoration. Recovery should include monitoring to evaluate the success or failure of restoration actions. Federal land management agencies should carefully evaluate use of ESA funding and support recovery actions first and research second.

Regulations and Permitting

Regulations related to the ESA are complex and often overlap with those of other laws and treaties (Burnham and Cade 1995); they should be reduced and simplified. A comprehensive permit (inclusive of all applicable laws) should be developed, eliminating the need for multiple permits and reports. Every effort should be made to increase the flexibility, efficiency, and effectiveness of the ESA.

Revisions to the Endangered Species Act

The ESA should be amended to provide objective definitions for "threatened" and "endangered" that incorporate specific criteria (Mace and Lande 1991) and emphasize the degree of jeopardy and urgency (Cade 1998). The "threatened" category in particular is too vague as presently defined.

The overlapping meanings and functions of "harm" and "critical habitat" need to be reexamined. The designation of critical habitat may be most useful when it is applied to special localized habitats critical to species survival, such as nest sites that limit the number of breeders (e.g., peregrine falcons) or springs that serve as the entire distribution area for a species (e.g., Bruneau Hot springsnail [*Pyrgulopsis bruneauensis*]). When it is applied to major habitat units on a wide scale encompassing millions of acres (e.g., old-growth forest for the northern spotted owl [*Strix occidentalis caurina*] or the proposed designation of major reaches of the Chihuahuan Desert in southern New Mexico for the largely nonexistent aplomado falcon), then its use becomes questionable, even though protection of such large areas may be justified in a broader, more inclusive environmental context. Critical habitat provides little additional protection to a listed species. Moreover, designation of critical habitat lasts only as long as the species requiring it remains listed (Doremus and Pagel 2001); therefore, it is not a permanent solution to habitat protection and, in fact, can become a disincentive for species recovery. Considering the high costs involved in designating and defending critical habitat against lawsuits, the benefits appear to be problematic, even unjustified.

We recommend that the definition of "critical habitat" established by the 1978 congressional amendment be rescinded and that the definition of "take" and "harm" be suitably modified to encompass all requirements for protection of essential habitat of listed species. Where essential habitat is needed for protection on private lands, owners should be compensated through a system of purchases, leases, easements, or other economic incentives.

The act should be amended specifically to authorize safe harbor agreements. Section 10(j) should be clarified by including the "open-minded" safe harbor concept for application in a mixed land status of federal, state, tribal, and private properties.

The ESA should also include conservation and research organizations, universities, and private landowners as cooperators. Ultimately, conservation will not be accomplished by government alone. Private sector cooperation and leadership will determine the fate of many endangered species (Burnham and Cade 2003). Section 6 of the ESA should be amended to recognize this fact by authorizing funding for NGO participation.

Biome Conservation

Unless the ESA is modified or until the nation has a law focused on habitat and biome conservation, endangered species will continue to suffer from lack of private sector and landowner support. This will continue to produce conflicts over designation of "critical habitat," "take," and other punitive measures; and litigation will continue to consume dollars critically needed for recovery actions. Congress should consider passage of a new law dealing with habitat and biome conservation. A first step would be to inventory all public lands, nonprofit conservation holdings, and private land with conservation easements to determine the potential to conserve the various ecoregions and associated species. Key to this inventory would be use of gap analysis where habitats and the known and potential distribution of species are mapped (Scott et al. 1988).

Conclusion

Our experiences confirm that hands-on restoration efforts are expensive and that recovery is unlikely without a highly focused effort that has the support of the states and private sector. In those successful efforts in which we have been involved (aplomado falcon, peregrine falcon, Mauritius kestrel), the limiting biological factors were substantially reduced or eliminated over landscape scales. The ESA provided a platform for cooperation, particularly among government agencies, and added a new source of funding. Section 6 funding to states was particularly important. The section 10(j) experimental population provisions of the act have also assisted in recovery efforts both by allowing greater flexibility and by helping to build trust and support among private and state groups. Safe harbor agreements were critical to the success of aplomado recovery in Texas (Jenny 2003); we found greater support when NGO, rather than agency, personnel negotiated the agreements. Bureaucratic red tape (particularly in the wpermitting process) can be an obstacle to recovery (Burnham and Cade 2003).

We thank Frank Bond and Lloyd Kiff for review and comments and Michael Bean, Pat Burnham, and others for other assistance provided. A special thanks to Ellen Paul for researching litigation related to the Endangered Species Act.

20 Incentive Mechanisms

Gregory M. Parkhurst and Jason F. Shogren

Aldo Leopold long ago argued that conservation policy "ultimately boil[s] down to reward[ing] the private landowner who conserves the public interest" (see Bean 1998; but see Freyfogle 2004). This chapter examines six rewards designed to help protect endangered species on private land: impact fees, subsidies, tradable development rights with zoning, conservation banking, fee simple acquisition, and conservation easements in the form of either purchased development rights or donations for tax relief. See Parkhurst and Shogren (2004) for a more complete discussion.

Impact Fees

An impact fee is a cash or in-kind payment by a developer to a government as a precondition to a development permit. These fees have become popular in the last two decades. Governments frequently require developers to expend resources to finance public parks, streets, or other public goods as a precondition to receiving the necessary permits for development. The goal is to offset the negative consequences of development on the surrounding environment and existing infrastructure. Impact fees are usually paid when the developer obtains his permit, which allows the new public goods to be created before completion of the development project. Impact fees have the additional attribute that those creating the new demand for public goods pay for that demand, allowing existing residents to maintain a level of public good provision by requiring development to "pay its own way."

Subsidies

Subsidies are financial assistance offered to landowners by regulators. Subsidies encourage landowners to maintain their land in an undeveloped state or to mitigate the environmental impact of development by helping the landowner meet maintenance and restoration costs of environmentally sensitive areas. Subsidies usually take the form of grants, loans, cash payments, or tax allowances that are offered by federal, state, or nonprofit organizations (Hanley et al. 1997). Subsidy programs are funded by numerous methods, including tax revenue, lottery funds, and special permits (California Resources Agency 2000).

Tradable Development Rights with Zoning

Tradable development rights (TDR) programs specify a predetermined maximum level of development within a specified region and then distribute development rights equal to the permissible total amount of development to landowners within the region. Landowners who remain within their allotted level can sell their surplus development rights to other landowners or use them to offset development on other properties. To ensure that development rights serve their purpose as an incentive to change development control to desired social levels, total development levels within a given region are limited so that the development rights are seen as a scarce resource valuable to developers (Hanley et al. 1997). TDR programs ensure that development occurs on the properties with the highest development values, but they do not guarantee that the most environmentally sensitive land is left undeveloped (Boyd et al. 1999). This can reduce the net benefits to society when land has a greater habitat value than development value. If this land is still developed under the TDRs, the mechanism has performed poorly. The most common approach to overcome this inefficiency is to combine TDRs with zoning (Miller 1999).

Government agencies responsible for land use planning determine which properties within a specified region should be protected for their environmental qualities. Development is restricted on these properties and landowners are provided with TDRs to compensate them for the loss of economic use. These rights can then be sold to developers in the less restricted properties within the region. Properties that are restricted are called *sending zones*; development properties are called *receiving zones*. Once sending and receiving zones are determined, the regulator decides on a formula for transferring the development rights from one zone to the other. To ensure that developers purchase TDRs from sending zones, the density of development in receiving zones, prior to acquisition of TDRs, is restricted to less than the demanded density (Miller 1999). The price of a TDR is determined through the open market. To facilitate trading and minimize transaction costs, regulators can establish a *TDR bank* or *exchange*, which brings together willing buyers and sellers (Tripp and Dudek 1989). TDRs have been used by various states for close to three decades to protect historical buildings and landmarks, agricultural and ranch lands, open spaces and view corridors, and to protect riparian areas, forests, and other ecologically sensitive lands (Miller 1999; Levinson 1996).

Conservation Banking

Developers undertaking a new project are frequently required to mitigate adverse effects. Mitigation can be onsite or the developer may purchase development credits (Heal, forthcoming). These credits can be purchased as needed or banked to fulfill future requirements. Developers purchase these credits from private or publicly owned *conservation banks* or *mitigation banks* (Fox et al., forthcoming), which determine the prices of the credits based on demand and supply. The developer purchases credits if and only if the cost of mitigation through credit purchase is less than the costs of alternative approaches to mitigation, such as onsite mitigation. If bank owners make a profit, other conservation bank owners will be attracted into the market and the resulting competition will lower the price of the credits (see e.g., California Resources Agency 1999).

The amount of credits that a conservation bank sells depends on the quality and type of habitat, and the number of a specific endangered species supported on a specific parcel of land. Bank owners increase credits by managing land to increase either the quality or the quantity of the land to protect endangered species or both. Conservation banking has proven a useful tool in the conservation of red-cockaded woodpeckers (*Picoides borealis*) and California condors (*Gymnogyps californianus*) (Environmental Defense 1999).

Fee Simple Acquisition

Fee simple acquisition is the purchase of land, with all of its inherent property rights. Landowners voluntarily enter into an agreement to sell their land. Local governments often purchase land for public goods such as playgrounds, nature trails, and other park lands (Boyd et al. 1999; Utah Critical Lands Conservation Committee 1997). Land trusts and other nonprofit organizations often purchase land and then sell or transfer it to government agencies (Land Trust Alliance 1998; Utah Critical Lands Conservation Committee 1997; California Coastal Conservancy 2000a, 2000b).

Land trusts and other nonprofit organizations protect land in ecologically sensitive regions through fee simple acquisition, donation of land with all property rights intact, purchased development rights, and donated easements (Nijhuis 2000). Acquiring the land in fee simple gives the trust more control over land uses. The price of this control is the cost to manage the land, which often requires significant staff and resources. Trusts try to reduce management costs by serving as a middleman between the landowner and a larger trust or government agency. Land trusts also avoid management costs by acquiring a conservation easement or purchased development rights, which allows the landowner to remain on the land and maintain it according to the terms of the acquisition document. The trust is responsible for monitoring and enforcing the terms of the easement.

Conservation Easement

An easement is a legal instrument that separates specific rights in land and transfers them from the landowner to another entity (Wiebe et al. 1996). Easements are typically *affirmative* and *appurtenant*. *Affirmative* means the easement holder is given the right to conduct specified activities on the land, such as a right-of-way. *Appurtenant* means the benefits provided by the easement are attached to another piece of land (Wiebe et al. 1996). A conservation easement prohibits the landowner from specified uses on his or her land to protect species or habitat (Wiebe et al. 1996). In contrast to conventional easements, conservation easements often are *negative* and *in gross*. *Negative* means that, rather than allowing the holder of the easement to engage in affirmative activities on the land, the holder of the easement can restrict the landowner from engaging in specified activities; *in gross* means that the easement holder can be someone other than an adjacent landowner.

In general, conservation easements are classified into two broad categories: *purchased development rights* (PDR) easements and *donated* easements. The type of sellers, the type of buyers, the mode of compensation, and the duration of the easement characterize the difference between the two easements. A PDR easement is typically entered into by profit-maximizing landowners who require full compensation for their forgone opportunity, the land's development value. The purchaser of a PDR easement is often a government agency, which generally has a larger coffer than most nonprofit organizations and is better able to finance the purchase of the easement. The payment for a PDR easement is typically a one-time, lump sum payment. PDR easements can be purchased for limited time periods or in perpetuity.

The donated easement is based on a tax incentive, which typically appeals to landowners who value the preservation of land and are willing to be compensated at less than fair market value for the easement. Federal tax law requires that land must be donated to a nonprofit conservation organization and donated in perpetuity to qualify for tax incentives (Small 1998; Wiebe et al. 1996, 12). Tax incentives can take a variety of forms (Small 2000).

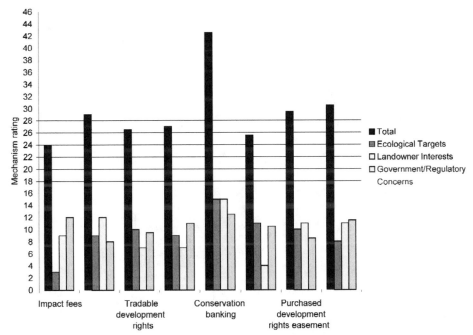

Figure 20.1. Total impact of each incentive mechanism on three criteria: ecological targets, landowner interests, and governmental and regulatory concerns. Numerical values were given to the qualitative evaluations of the authors. The chart implies equal weighting of all criteria; alternative weighting schemes can be used.

Evaluating Incentive Mechanisms

We briefly evaluate each incentive mechanism against three criteria: (1) ecological targets, (2) landowner interests, and (3) governmental concerns (fig. 20.1).

Ecological Targets

Each incentive offers a range of advantages and disadvantages when evaluated against the three primary concerns. The first is the question of whether the incentive can guarantee that the land will remain in conservation in perpetuity (fig. 20.2).

Ability to Conserve in Perpetuity

The incentive mechanism best able to guarantee that land stays in conservation in perpetuity is conservation banking. To obtain regulatory approval,

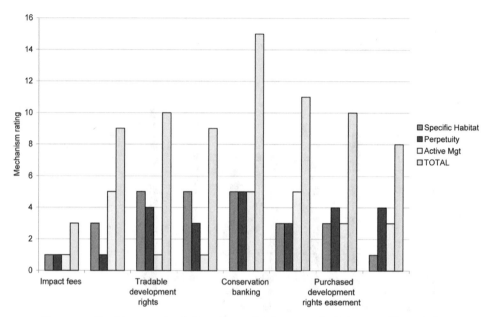

Figure 20.2. Total impact of each incentive mechanism on ecological targets. Numerical values were given to the qualitative evaluations of the authors; the chart implies equal weighting of all criteria.

conservation banks are required to establish a conservator and to fund the management of the bank in perpetuity. Although PDR easements and donated easements are designed to conserve land in perpetuity, they are risky. Easements require monitoring and are susceptible to attempts by subsequent landowners to undercut conservation and increase personal returns from the land. Fee simple acquisition and zoning are even less likely to conserve land permanently. These mechanisms depend on the goals of the government remaining constant through time; goals are likely to change when political power changes. The least effective at preserving land in perpetuity is subsidies (because they require annual expenditures) and impact fees (because they only keep land from being developed).

Ability to Protect Specific Habitat Characteristics

Zoning, TDRs, and conservation banks have a very high potential for targeting species-specific habitat needs and consolidating parcels into larger habitat reserves. With zoning and TDRs, the regulator can prevent the land desired for conservation from being used for any other purpose. Conservation banking can achieve the same result because the bank owner has the incentive to create the most effective conservation reserve (County of San Diego 2000; Environmental Defense 1999). Subsidies, fee simple acquisition, and PDR easements are voluntary; this limits the regulator's ability to target specific land for conservation to willing sellers. The regulator has the least control over impact fees because the land that remains undeveloped (or conserved) is the land with a development value less than the impact fee; it is unlikely that the conserved land is the land with the highest-quality habitat.

Ability to Implement Active Habitat Management

Active habitat management techniques are incorporated in an incentive mechanism best when participation is voluntary, each contractual agreement can be negotiated independently, contracts are of short duration, and assurances are included in the agreement. The mechanisms that have a very high potential for implementing active habitat management are subsidies, conservation banking, and fee simple acquisition. Although easements are voluntary, they do not have built-in assurances to offset the negative effects of their lengthy terms. TDRs, zoning, and impact fees each have a very low ability to require landowners to undertake active habitat management because they force landowners to conserve land involuntarily.

Landowner Concerns

The second evaluative metric for incentives is how successfully they meet the concerns of landowners. Landowner concerns include voluntariness, privacy (will people be permitted to freely enter the property?), and public recognition (fig. 20.3).

Voluntary Participation

Zoning and TDR policies predetermine which land is to be conserved and then force those landowners into conserving their land (Epstein 1996; Boyd et al. 1999). Fee simple acquisition can either be involuntary (eminent domain) or voluntary. When an impact fee is used, landowners have the choice to not pay the impact fee, but that entails an opportunity cost of forgoing development of the land. Subsidies, PDRs, and donated easements are voluntary.

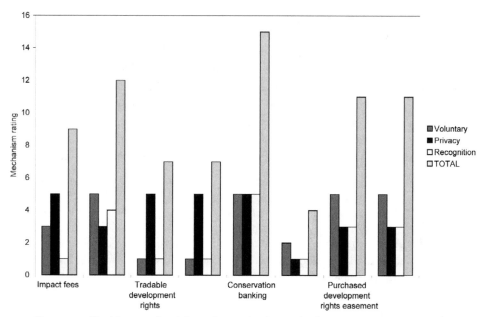

Figure 20.3. Total impact of each incentive mechanism on landowner concerns. Numerical values were given to the qualitative evaluations of the authors; the chart implies equal weighting of all criteria.

Privacy Maintained

Policies that do not alter or split the property rights to the land are more effective at maintaining privacy. When the property rights remain intact, confusion over who has what rights is avoided. Impact fees and zoning maintain the rights to privacy because the landowner retains all rights to the land and can restrict access to it. Conservation banking and TDRs are also highly effective at maintaining the landowner's privacy. Although they allow the regulator access to the land to monitor and enforce the agreement, access is typically specific. For subsidies, PDRs, and donated easements, the ability to maintain privacy is dependent on the negotiated contracts or the rules of the program. Fee simple acquisition transfers title to the purchaser.

Stewardship Recognized

Conservation banking rewards bank owners for good stewardship by increasing the number of credits that the bank owner can sell when the owner enhances the property, increasing the quality of the habitat or the number of listed species. Subsidies also reward stewardship, but only to the extent that it is built into the program. The subsidy policy can require that the landowner restore or

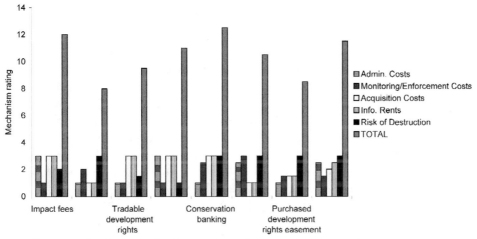

Figure 20.4. Total impact of each incentive mechanism on governmental concerns. Numerical values were given to the qualitative evaluations of the authors; the chart implies equal weighting of all criteria. In this evaluation, high ratings were given to the mechanisms with the greatest benefit to the participants and administrators. For example, high administrative costs would result in a low numerical rating.

create habitat, or it might only be a mechanism to keep the land from being developed. PDRs and donated easement contracts may or may not specify the landowner undertake habitat management techniques. Impact fees, zoning, and TDR policies do not provide landowners with any incentive to enhance and maintain the habitat on their land. In fact, these instruments may be a disincentive since the landowner may choose to destroy the habitat to avoid being forced to conserve (Innes et al. 1998; Boyd et al. 1999).

Governmental Concerns

The third evaluation criterion is the degree to which governmental concerns are satisfied by the individual incentive. Governmental concerns focus primarily on costs—administrative, monitoring and enforcement acquisition, information, and habitat destruction (fig. 20.4).

Administrative Costs

Administrative costs are expenditures necessary to establish conservation plans, process applications, establish markets to facilitate trades of tradable development rights and bankable credits, process and maintain records for property right transfers and land use restrictions, and staff and fund programs that maintain government-owned conservation lands. Flexible programs usually increase the administration costs to the local government and subject the developer to more governmental control due to the project-by-project review process (Miller 1999; Utah Critical Lands Conservation Committee 1997). These costs are lowest for the status quo zoning and impact fees because necessary infrastructure is already in place. Fee simple acquisitions have low to medium administrative costs, reflecting the need to manage the land once it has been acquired. Government agencies responsible for managing these lands are largely intact, and only a minimal increase in staff may be necessary. Donated easements also have low to medium administrative costs because the necessary infrastructure (e.g., the Internal Revenue Service) is already in place.

In contrast, conservation banks, PDRs, subsidies, and TDRs have high administrative costs. Conservation banks require the regulator to staff the oversight of an extensive application process as well as to establish a market for and track the transfer of bankable credits. For PDRs, negotiations constitute the bulk of the administrative costs. Subsidies typically require applications and a review process; as the process becomes more extensive, it is also more costly (Innes 2000). For TDRs, administration costs center on the need to establish a market to facilitate trades and to record transfer of TDRs.

Monitoring and Enforcement Costs

Monitoring costs accrue to the regulator to ensure that land use restrictions and conservation agreements are being upheld. Fee simple acquisition has low monitoring and enforcement costs since title passes. Conservation banking has low to medium monitoring and enforcement costs because the agreement stipulates reporting and monitoring criteria, establishes a bank manager, and specifies remedies for violations of the agreement. Incentive mechanisms that allow the landowner to retain complete or partial property rights have higher costs; the magnitude of costs are related to many factors including the timing of payments to the landowner, the length of the agreement, and the landowner's permissible range of uses. Longer contracts that compensate landowners with a one-time lump sum payment (easements) have larger costs, particularly when owners remain on the land and have an incentive to invest in rent-seeking activities (National Research Council 1993). Subsidies generally have periodic payments and lower monitoring and enforcement costs. Involuntary incentive mechanisms—zoning, TDRs with zoning, and impact fees—have high monitoring and enforcement costs.

Acquisition Costs

Acquisition costs are the cash outlays required to purchase species protection. Subsidies and fee simple acquisition have very high costs; fee simple acquisition because acquiring all rights requires the greatest financial resources initially; in the long run, however, the sum of payments is likely to exceed the costs of purchasing the land. Although PDRs require payment of acquisition costs, these are less than those for fee access acquisition because the regulator is only purchasing partial interest in the land (Boyd et al. 1999). Donated easements are funded through federal tax deductions, decreasing the federal government's annual budget. Zoning, TDRs with zoning, conservation banking, and impact fees all have relatively low acquisition costs because those costs are largely shifted to developers.

Information Rents

Information rents occur when landowners are paid more than their opportunity cost of the lost land simply because the landowners know more about themselves than the regulator. Information rents are highest when the regulator must conserve specific parcels through voluntary incentives because landowners can act strategically to extract payment that exceeds their opportunity cost. Donated easements have the smallest potential for information rents. Information rents are low to nonexistent for zoning, impact fees, conservation banking, and TDRs either because there is no compensation (zoning and impact fees) or because the compensation is determined by the market (conservation banking and TDRs with zoning). Subsidies and fee simple acquisition have high to very high potential for information rents, and PDR easements have a medium to high potential for information rents because they have the most potential for strategic action since they are individually negotiated (Smith and Shogren 2001, 2002).

Risk of Habitat Destruction

When involuntary incentive mechanisms are used, government regulations impose uncompensated out-of-pocket expenses on landowners. To avoid incurring these regulatory costs, landowners have an incentive to destroy the habitat on their land prior to regulation (Burnham et al., this volume). This can occur as a result of either premature development of the land or explicit habitat destruction.

Conclusion

No single incentive mechanism is preferable in all situations; each has its strengths and weaknesses depending on the species and land under consideration. Factors such as development pressure, funding, the range of land quality, quantity of suitable habitat, the range of land values, and types of landowners are all relevant to determining which mechanism or combination of mechanisms meets the regulatory objectives most efficiently. Expending resources to understand these factors for different cases will be costly, but worth it—it is better to address questions of incentives without delay than to waste even more resources later in unnecessary conflicts.

Our thanks to Katie L. Frerker and Defenders of Wildlife for assistance with the graphs.

21   Beyond Set-Asides

Michael L. Rosenzweig

Almost by definition, endangered species have small, even tiny, geographical ranges. So, in practice, the Endangered Species Act often translates into a set-aside strategy: "This reserve exists to protect the Chiricahua leopard frog. Look, perhaps, but don't touch!"

Can a set-aside strategy work? Endangered species are alive and dynamic, not static museum displays in carefully sealed chambers. They must live in nature, not in a glass case. Can a strategy that relies on hermetically sealing them off work for long in the face of nature's dynamism?

I suspect that human nature, all by itself, will prevent set-asides from doing their job for very long. The very word *set-asides* suggests the problem: We have not forgotten about them; it is just that, for now, we don't need to use them for ourselves. It is not hard to see what will happen when we do. Set-asides are foredoomed to last only so long as people do not perceive a need for them. Surely this matter is crucial. However, I'll leave it to those who understand human nature better than I do. I'll take refuge in science.

Can a set-aside strategy work? Science gives us a clear, unqualified answer. Unfortunately it is "no." Set-asides can slow our loss of species but cannot stop it and cannot much affect how many species we lose in the long run.

With excellent justification, conservationists agree that loss of habitat is diversity's worst problem. That loss creates both of the principal reasons for the "no." One is well known, the other less so but just as important. The first is global warming (and other pervasive anthropogenic alterations of the world's air and water). The second has to do with issues of extent—that is, the area available to species. As it turns out, scale matters. This chapter examines the impact of global warming and the loss of area as it affects species and their habitat requirements. It also introduces the concept of reconciliation ecology and how it can be used to increase the effectiveness of the Endangered Species Act.

Global Warming

Fundamentally, species have habitat needs and those needs have changed very little in the past few centuries. For most species, those needs do not include a football field, let alone the grounds of a steel foundry. As a matter of fact, they do not even include most city parks or gardens or "modern" farms or tree plantations.

Germans have a good word, *kulturmeider*, to describe species that cannot use anthropogenic habitats. To fulfill their habitat needs, *kulturmeider* depend on the environmental relics of millennia past. Set-asides are nothing other than those environmental relics.

The places where these relics hang on have become especially small and fragmented in the past century. However, as we change the climate of the globe, those relictual habitats change, too. A degree or two of global warming and, behold, what was a habitat that could support its residents becomes one they can no longer use (Peters and Darling 1985). In times past (say, when glaciers were retreating at the end of the last ice age), many species just drifted poleward or upslope (Coope 1987; Davis 1983). Today, that tactic may take them into a Wal-Mart parking lot, where they will die because they cannot digest asphalt. The point is simple, but deserves two brief illustrations.

One comes from South Africa, whose healthy fynbos ecosystems gave birth to nearly nine thousand species of plants (Cowling et al. 1989; Cowling and Richardson 1995). A few of these have been domesticated (such as *Pelargonium*) and grace our homes. But most are at the mercy of man's need for land. Several set-asides contain much of this plant diversity. One of the most important is the national park at the Cape of Good Hope. Many of its plant species grow only in the park or nearby, quite likely because the climate is not appropriate much farther north. With a degree or two of global warming, their climate will have been driven into the Southern Ocean. To survive, they must learn how to take root in sea water.

A second example, also from the southern hemisphere, comes from the limited highland habitats of tropical Queensland (Williams et al. 2003). Sixty-five species of montane rainforest vertebrates are endemic to these highlands. There are herbivorous possums (Strahan 1983) and a number of species of tiny frogs and birds and lizards. Most of these species inhabit a restricted band of elevations—a mountain in tropical Queensland's far north is a layer cake of diversity. What will happen to the species in the top layer when global warming sends the temperatures of their habitats up into the heavens? Will the frogs grow wings? Highland habitats around the world, especially tropical ones, often contain endemics. These Queensland natives typify the peril to them all.

Loss of Area

Even without global climate change, set-asides are too small to help for very long. Set-asides try to preserve ecosystems, but area turns out to be one of the intrinsic properties of ecosystems, especially with respect to the generation and maintenance of diversity. A preserved, shrunken ecosystem is thus a contradiction in terms. A preserved, shrunken ecosystem works little better than a preserved, shrunken head. I shall explain.

Species-Area Relationships

Science has been aware for two centuries that more area supports more species. During that time, many have participated in gathering data to quantify the relationship of species diversity to area. Many others have worked on analyzing them and modeling them (Rosenzweig 1995; Rosenzweig and Sandlin 1997).

There are several species-area relationships (Rosenzweig 1999a, 1999b). Which one governs a set of places depends on the time scale of the most important process that contributes species to a place.

- If different areas each have their own endemic species, then those areas are known as *biogeographical provinces*. (Note: one or more may be geographical islands; e.g., the state of Hawaii, no doubt a set of geographical islands, is a biogeographical province for its birds and plants.) Evolutionary processes (speciation) rule in biogeographical provinces, and the species-area relationship among different provinces has a slope near unity (in logarithmic coordinates). This means that for each increment of area, diversity grows linearly (Rosenzweig 2001).
- If different areas share a pool of species produced by the same set of evolutionary events, and all species can almost always replace their populations generation by generation, then those areas are *biogeographical islands*. (Note: they may not be *geographical* islands; for example, a set of mountaintops is often a biological archipelago; Vuilleumier 1970). Immigration processes rule because they happen faster than speciation. The species-area relationship among islands is characterized by a law of diminishing returns: with each successive increment of area, diversity grows less and less. In logarithmic coordinates, the slope of a species-area relationship among islands is generally close to 0.25 (MacArthur and Wilson 1963; Preston 1960).
- In some cases, different areas share a pool of species produced by the same set of evolutionary events, but some populations in each place cannot manage to reload on their own. To persist, they depend on generation-by-generation dispersal from more fortunate populations. Dispersal processes rule because they

happen so much faster than the others. A set of such places also exhibits a law of diminishing returns. But it is even more pronounced than that of islands: as area increases, diversity grows very quickly at first, but practically levels off once a rather modest amount of area is censused. In logarithmic coordinates, the slope of a species-area relationship among such places is generally close to 0.15 (MacArthur and Wilson 1967).

Applying Species-Area Relationships: Scale Matters

The first application of species-area thinking to the conservation of species came from island biogeography (Wilson and Willis 1975). Set-asides were viewed as islands in a sea of artificial, sterile habitats. The theory was used to ask questions about how money should be allocated for optimal design of reserves. The most famous: SLOSS, single large or several small?

A century ago perhaps, one could justify approaching set-asides as islands. Many relictual or quasi-relictual habitats could still be found across the land. But this is no longer true. Today's set-asides are not islands because they are usually all that remains for so much of life's diversity. Islands, remember, get most of their species as immigrants from a mainland source pool. If our set-asides were to lose a species, they would have no source pool from which to replenish their stock. No, in most cases, if today's system of set-asides were to lose a species, it would be gone forever. Species can get added to a place, but only by speciation. That means today's system of set-asides is more like a set of provinces than anything else.

But that is a crucial distinction. Because of the strong law of diminishing returns that characterizes the species-area relationships of archipelagos, islands do not have to be very large to contain a high percentage of a source pool's species. For example, a single island with only 1 percent of the area of a source pool can rather reliably harbor about 32 percent of its species. Given the power of small islands, one can easily imagine that a set of island reserves could conserve most of the species of the pool. However, this is not at all the case if reserves are actually provinces (Rosenzweig 2003b). A province reduced to 1 percent of its former area can maintain only 1 percent of the old diversity; one reduced to 5 percent can maintain only 5 percent of the old diversity, and so forth. With provinces, you get what you pay for; there are no bargains.

Because people wisely and carefully target what they set aside by focusing on assembling a wide variety of scarce species and scarce habitats in our reserve system, they are managing to slow extinction rates (Rosenzweig 2003a). Targeting species in obvious trouble has helped a few of them (e.g., Denton et al. 1997). Targeting the ecosystems that have suffered the most has helped some of the threatened and endangered species that live in them (National Research Council 1995). But these gains will be temporary unless we find ways to expand the habitats that species can use. Eventually nature will establish a new, much lower diversity in our reserve system, a diversity that reflects its proportion of the continent. And global climate change will hurry the approach to this new and depauperate state.

Reconciliation Ecology

Guarding species from extinction requires thinking outside the set-aside box. People are doing that all over the world. They are reconciling human and non-human use of habitats by inventing, establishing, and maintaining new habitats where people live and work and play (Rosenzweig 2003a). The goal? To conserve species diversity by allowing wild species to use our spaces. I call this kind of science *reconciliation ecology*.

Efforts to save longleaf pine (*Pinus palustris*) forests involve two good examples of reconciliation ecology, one directly related to the Endangered Species Act (ESA). Found only in the southeastern United States, longleaf pine forests support dozens of plant and animal species. Three hundred years ago, they covered some 36 million hectares (90 million acres). By 1990, only 2,000 hectares (5,000 acres) remained—and they were disappearing fast. Enter four well-known organizations: the Nature Conservancy, the U.S. Department of Defense, Environmental Defense, and the U.S. Fish and Wildlife Service (USFWS).

Environmental Defense and the USFWS were wrestling with the problem that many rare and endangered species have populations on private property, and private landowners feel threatened by the ESA (Wilcove et al. 1996), seeing it as depriving them of their property rights. Many landowners will not even allow survey work to be done on their land for fear that the government will find "one of those species" and shut down use of their own land. A perverse way to avoid that from happening is to destroy good habitat that might support a rare species, and this has apparently taken place.

So Environmental Defense and the USFWS cooperated to produce safe harbor, a purely voluntary set of programs keyed to the Endangered Species Act. Each program is conducted in the name of one or more endangered species. Safe harbor began in the sandhills of North Carolina in 1995, where the hook was the red-cockaded woodpecker (*Picoides borealis*)—listed since 1973 when the ESA was born. Red-cockaded woodpeckers virtually depend on longleaf pine trees for their nesting sites (for an economic analysis of safe harbor agreements for red-cockaded woodpecker see Heal, forthcoming).

Land to be enrolled in a safe harbor agreement might already support woodpeckers and be subject to restrictions under the ESA; these baseline restrictions continue. Whether or not a baseline population exists, each landowner agrees to improve the enrolled land for the woodpeckers over a fixed period of years. "Improve" can mean many things. Perhaps one owner will undertake controlled burns to rid the understory of oak species that can choke out longleaf pine seedlings. Perhaps another will agree to drill holes in the pines for woodpecker nests. (The woodpeckers take years to do one; drilling crews take an hour.)

In return for improving the habitat, only the baseline restrictions apply. Should the improved habitat attract new woodpeckers or other threatened species, a safe harbor agreement shields the landowner from any further ESA restrictions. This shield lasts for the term of the agreement. At its conclusion, the landowner is free to withdraw the land or renew the agreement.

By the spring of 2003, 169 landowners in six states had enrolled almost 200,000 hectares (500,000 acres) on behalf of red-cockaded woodpeckers— much of it longleaf pine. The pine forest is coming back. And the woodpeckers are breeding in places long abandoned. These and a growing number of other safe harbor programs in a total of fourteen states are now protecting a diverse set of habitats in the names of various species of threatened or endangered birds, mammals, frogs, mussels, and fish (Environmental Defense 2004).

The Nature Conservancy, which cooperates with USFWS by administering Virginia's safe harbor program, is actually the veteran private organization when it comes to producing reconciled longleaf pine forest. In 1990, the Nature Conservancy and the Department of Defense began work on Eglin Air Force Base near Pensacola, Florida. Over the years, they have chopped and planted, burned and drilled, until they created a new longleaf pine forest of nearly 100,000 hectares (250,000 acres). They have not restored the original longleaf pine ecosystem. Nothing can do that. But they did fashion, and do manage, a new one, fully used by the military and by campers, loggers, fishermen, and hunters. Just before the Iraq war started, the United States demonstrated the 21,000-pound MOAB ("mother of all bombs") by dropping one on a bombing range in Florida. Eglin Air Force Base was that range; it is no nature reserve.

Meanwhile, the pocket parks of Mayor Richard Daley's Chicago convert abandoned gas stations into islands of nature for inner city residents (Shore and Packard 2000). Prairie Dunes Country Club's golf course in Hutchinson, Kansas, hosts some thirty-five thousand rounds of golf per year but also manages its roughs to support a large number of wild species (Terman 1997). Florida Power and Light's Turkey Point nuclear- and coal-powered electricity-generating station near Miami has 80 miles of cooling canals that it has made into crucial managed habitat for the rare American crocodile (*Crocodylus acu-*

tus) and many other species (Gaby et al. 1985). Over thirty thousand home owners cooperate with the National Wildlife Federation to build and manage "Backyard Wildlife Habitat" sites on their own property (National Wildlife Federation 2004; Tufts and Loewer 1995). There are many more examples (Rosenzweig 2003c). Reconciliation ecology is already freeing many wild species from their set-aside ghettos. It works.

Reconciliation Ecology and the Endangered Species Act

Reconciliation ecology can help the Endangered Species Act do its job effectively. By the same token, reconciliation ecology won't be effective without the ESA or something very like it. These interrelationships involve

- changing the way people think about saving species
- expanding species ranges
- stimulating research on species' habitat requirements
- easing some of the pressure on set-asides

I explain each of these points below.

Changing Conservation Attitudes

Reconciliation ecology impinges on the attitudes that pervade conservation. It does this by first heeding the significant new science which shows that set-asides cannot work for long. Reconciliation ecology admits that area is an intrinsic property of ecosystems and that global climate change menaces the set-aside strategy even in the relatively near future. Thus, reconciliation ecology, although it is applied ecology, uses basic ecology to the hilt and encourages all branches of conservation ecology to follow suit.

Reconciliation ecology also contributes to environmental peace by encouraging continued use of the land by people and their enterprises. Its strategy involves using land better, instead of setting land aside. (But it also supports the limited use of other strategies that do set land aside.) It is neither ascetic nor Luddite. It does not advocate depriving human beings of comfort or profit; rather it seeks to find ways to allow those profits to continue and those comforts to increase. These attitudes, it seems to me, ought to foster a milieu of détente—perhaps even cooperation—between ecological and economic interests. How much time, energy, and money do we now spend battling each other over the issue of endangered species? How much more effective could we become if we could reduce the inefficiencies of our friction?

To be effective, efforts to conserve diversity, such as the ESA, require popular support. Reconciliation ecology will increase that support dramatically, not by preaching but by surrounding people with diversity.

Pauly (1995) points out that we evaluate our environments in relationship to what we have known. If something seems familiar, we tend to endorse it. If, on the other hand, it seems a deterioration of our previous environment, we tend to oppose it. Because each generation experiences a new set of environments, each starts with a new baseline of expectations. Pauly calls this set of realities the "shifting baseline syndrome."

Since diversity has declined in man-made habitats, so has the baseline of human expectations. People are happy seeing fewer species and find it impossible to imagine a world teeming with diversity—as impossible as meeting a living dinosaur. In such a world, the goals of the ESA become hard to take seriously. People wonder what diversity might be good for. If they were to experience diversity as commonplace, the way their forebears did, they would not wonder.

Enter reconciliation ecology. Because it increases diversity in places used intensively by people, it raises the shifting baseline. That should redound to the benefit of all efforts to conserve species diversity, including those of the ESA.

The reciprocal effects seem clear and straightforward. Among other things, the Endangered Species Act serves as our formal recognition that many species need help. It is society's call to arms. Reconciliation is one response; it would have no meaning without the call.

For now, the ESA also provides a bulwark that allows one to imagine reconciliation ecology. By delaying the tide of so many extinctions, it gives a face to the species we might welcome into our habitats. It also helps us take heart, to believe that we have some time and can do some good. In my view, that hope is not misleading.

Expanding Species Ranges

Reconciliation ecology results in the expansion of species ranges into newly designed habitats, often within unprotected private property. What if these species are endangered or threatened? Will the ESA and reconciliation ecology conflict?

Because the overriding concern here is saving species, we must ensure that the two do not conflict. Perhaps this will not be difficult: all conservationists worry about species with small geographical ranges. A species newly limited to a very small geographical range is an ominous sign indeed. If reconciliation ecology can reverse that, if it can expand species ranges, it may allow us to remove some threatened species from the red list.

But there are devils in the details. Reconciliation ecology may advocate the establishment of populations away from the protective wing of reserve managers. It may wish to break down the genetic differences between demes in a metapopulation—not merely for the sake of doing so, but because establishing a new deme may require translocations of a few individuals each from several old demes. Will conservation allow the removal of individuals from established populations of threatened and endangered species to locations where they may once have lived? Under the ESA such translocations can be difficult (but see ESA sec. 10(j)).

Some safe harbor agreements tacitly admit such problems by solving them. For example, by the summer of 2002, the Georgia Department of Natural Resources, under the auspices of its safe harbor agreements, had already moved seven groups of red-cockaded woodpeckers to enrolled sites. If the safe harbor program, which is an extension of the ESA, can allow translocation of such a charismatic endangered species, reconciliation projects should face nothing more onerous than a bit of extra paperwork.

Arizona provides another example. In April 2004, two topminnows and two pupfish—listed species that are potentially useful for mosquito control (USFWS 2004j)—were granted safe harbor status. This means that they can be released (within their natural range) to waters—even artificial bodies of water—where they do not now live.

Genetic purity is also an important issue. Biodiversity includes the concept of genetic diversity, which the ESA strongly protects. Evolutionary biologists recognize the strong possibility of local genetic differentiation among the demes of a species, and it is considered a well-documented phenomenon. Won't expansions of endangered species into new habitats blur or erase such differentiation?

By definition, the "original" subspecies, clone, or race of every species inhabiting a new habitat is "none." But we cannot expect to avoid genetic change in translocated individuals. New habitats always bring new adaptive challenges.

Suppose, then, that we succeed in designing and deploying a new habitat for (say) Heermann's kangaroo rat (*Dipodomys heermanni*). Suddenly, they are hopping around in Santa Monica backyards and many other places that may seem improbable now. If we can satisfy their habitat needs, most individuals of the species can coexist with humans. And that will force them to change, perhaps rather quickly (Ashley et al. 2003). California will retain a species of *Dipodomys*, but it may not look or act quite the same as it does today. Will we have saved Heermann's kangaroo rat? Or hastened its extirpation?

What a philosophical gold mine! Nevertheless, those who care about diversity should refuse to exploit it. Pointless scholarly debates, obfuscating learned symposia, and the large grants awarded to support such activities do little but siphon money and public respect away from practical conservation. How many genes will fit on the head of a pin?

Reconciliation ecology ignores such questions. It admits that life evolves and genomes change naturally. It seeks to supply an immense theater in which such change can happen. The alternative is total species loss. If, under the current ESA, we cannot save a species in its current genetic state, must we then ignore it? If that is so, then the act should be revised.

Stimulation of Habitat Research

Proponents of both the Endangered Species Act and reconciliation ecology share a profound interest in understanding the habitat requirements of the species they wish to protect. But they share only the goal. Attaining it could involve serious disagreements about methods and interpretations.

Consider the fact that the usual strategy to determine the habitat requirements of a species is to combine spatiotemporal censuses with measurements of the habitat variables likely to affect it. For instance, suppose a grassland species reaches peak populations in places with annual summer precipitation of 150 millimeters (38 inches) and is not seen in areas with annual summer precipitations below 75 millimeters (19 inches) or above 200 millimeters (51 inches). From this, one might hypothesize that the species requires both grassland and such levels of rainfall.

Actually, most of us do not hypothesize; we conclude. And therein lies the rub. The habitats used by a species in nature may not accurately reflect that species' real needs or preferences (Rosenzweig 1981). How can that statement be true?

In the simplest case, a species may not have the opportunity to live in a better place simply because such a place may not actually exist in nature. For example, the city of Tucson, Arizona, teems with several desert bird species living at population densities more than twice those found anywhere in nature. This has created previously unknown high densities of food for some previously scarce raptors, especially Cooper's hawk (*Accipiter cooperii*). Cooper's hawk has responded with high densities of its own (Boal and Mannan 1999; Mannan and Boal 2000). I have seen the latter hunting mourning doves 3 meters (10 feet) above the tarmac of a city gas station. Nothing I ever saw in Arizona's canyons, where Cooper's hawk is a scarce native, prepared me for that sight. Some species will astonish us with their ability to exploit the new habitats we create.

A more complex case stems from population interactions among species. For instance, competition may force a species that can tolerate a wide variety of habitats to live solely in marginal habitats (Rosenzweig 1991). Meanwhile, its competitors cannot tolerate the marginal habitats and must have the best ones in which to live and reproduce. We often misinterpret such a competitive relationship. We observe the intolerant species in one type of habitat and the tolerant species in another. Then we erroneously conclude that each species is living in its best habitat.

It takes field experiments to ferret out the truth of tolerance-intolerance competition. Experiments may involve manipulating population sizes in field enclosures (e.g., Abramsky et al. 1990), temporarily removing individuals from nature (e.g., Pimm et al. 1985). They may also involve manipulating the habitat (e.g., Rosenzweig 1973).

Manipulative experiments make the guardians of endangered species and the managers of set-asides bristle with disapproval. During our twenty-year study in a sand dune reserve in Israel, Zvika Abramsky and I experienced this attitude firsthand. Despite our being the managers' allies in species preservation, we faced their repeated interference with our experimental plans. "Look, don't touch," they often insisted. We attribute this interference to misguided devotion to duty on their part, but interference it was.

A similar dispute involved experiments planned to discover the habitat requirements of the northern spotted owl (*Strix occidentalis occidentalis*) in northern California. After years of cooperative planning involving the Forest Service, a commercial timber company, community representatives, and an academic (me), we called a public meeting to announce a plan whose goal was sustainability for both the forest and the owls. Our plan did not involve setasides and the owl was not listed as threatened or endangered. Yet, the very next day, the plan was challenged in court and stopped.

Species enter modern times with much evolutionary history behind them. Natural selection has molded them to succeed with a certain body having certain behaviors in certain habitats. They cannot adapt instantly to the new demands we place on them. Reconciliation ecology calls for natural history research so that we can learn the limits of their current state. What do they need? What do they have that they can do without? We're not likely to succeed if society will not encourage us to conduct our research in the natural areas that best reflect the opportunities and constraints that shaped these species in the first place. Yes, such experimentation may occasionally turn out badly. Heart surgery has risks, too. But the alternative is more frightening. Lacking the fruit of aggressive experimental field research, we cannot build the new habitats, the new natural communities, and the new ecosystems that most wild species need in order to survive for long. We will lose them.

Easing the Pressure on Set-Asides

Even if we succeed in deploying a large variety of reconciled habitats all over the earth, our set-asides will retain great importance. For one thing, some species, such as those that are fierce, annoying, or disease-carrying, will be unwelcome near our homes and may be best restricted to reserves. A recent public brouhaha in Arizona about the fate of a puma (*Puma concolor*) roaming close to the outskirts of Tucson may not be unusual. "Kill 'im," said some. But Arizona's governor, Janet Napolitano, intervened and had the animal moved to another locale. A short while later (May 16, 2004), a less-lucky lioness was gunned down by an Arizona Game and Fish officer for "stalking" people near a recreation site in a national forest close to the city.

Occasionally, people do consent to be in harm's way. In Nepal, for example, the World Wildlife Fund has an extensive project that works on behalf of tigers, rhinoceros, and many other threatened but less-dangerous vertebrates, all of which live intermingled with people and their enterprises despite the risk to local inhabitants (Dinerstein 2002). But in truth, the Nepalese people tolerate the dangerous wildlife because it helps them earn their livings in ecotourism and community forestry projects. The overarching rule remains: most of us will choose to be safe even though, regrettably, that might mean losing some truly magnificent species (Dinerstein 1998).

Yet some large reconciled places will be able to support fierce species without endangering people, such as the crocodiles in the cooling canals of the Turkey Point Power Plant, discussed earlier. We may bridle at the prospect of crocodiles in our gardens, but we do not mind them in cooling canals. Reconciliation ecology may indeed help us to coexist safely with the fierce, the annoying, and the pestilential.

Not all species will find homes in reconciled habitats, however. Reserves will provide the only habitat for inveterate, unreconcilable *kulturmeider*, the species that cannot survive without set-asides. *Kulturmeider* are probably the truest endangered species. Perhaps we need to expand the definition of endangered species to include any that are *kulturmeider*—even those whose populations now appear to be thriving. Certainly, we have long been aware that population size alone is inadequate to assess a species' status. Populations can change quickly and dramatically, often over an order of magnitude. Witness the passenger pigeon (*Ectopistes migratorius*), which declined from a population of around 5 billion to zero within a century (Schorger 1955). And the abundant eelgrass limpet, *Lottia alveus*, which utterly depended on a narrow band of salinity values and vanished in less than a decade when a disease destroyed eelgrass habitats with those salinities (Carlton et al. 1991).

Reconciliation ecology eyes *kulturmeider* with a view to converting them into *kulturfolger*—the species that do live with us. (*Kulturfolger* is roughly equivalent to "culture follower" in English.)

Species conversion has happened, sometimes on purpose. Most cases involved the negative direction: *kulturfolger* to *kulturmeider*. But the reverse has also occurred. For instance, people supplying nest boxes to eastern bluebirds (*Sialia sialis*) have converted no-bluebird-gardens into bluebird Edens (Davis and Roca 1995; North American Bluebird Society 2004).

Reconciliation ecology seeks to multiply the helpful conversion rate by several orders of magnitude. It would prefer that many of the new *kulturfolger* species be formerly threatened or endangered. But even if that does not happen and the new *kulturfolger* emerge from the ranks of unthreatened *kulturmeider*, at-risk species will benefit in two ways. Managers of reserves will be able to (1) focus on the habitat requirements of threatened species, and (2) reduce competitive and predatory pressures on threatened species.

More intense focus will come because reserve management involves trade-offs: Improving habitat for one species often means degrading it for another. Relieved of the responsibility of satisfying the new *kulturfolger*, the manager will be free to maximize improvement for a *kulturmeider* species in trouble.

Reducing competitive and predatory pressure will result if society allows managers to reduce or even eliminate key *kulturfolger* in reserves. Competitive pressure on threatened species often comes from close relatives that are common and widespread. I believe many of these more common species are habitat-tolerant partners to their habitat-intolerant cousins. Hence, if we wish to help a threatened, habitat-intolerant species to the fullest extent possible, we may need to restrict the abundance of—or even eliminate—the common species in some reserves. It sounds controversial and it is: reduce diversity at a small-scale in order to increase it at a larger one. But in a world of reconciliation, it may also be good science and good public policy.

One can easily appreciate cases of excessive predation on *kulturmeider* in reserves. For example, in the autumn of 2002, I visited a spectacular reserve in New Zealand, a reserve that utterly depends upon the exclusion of predatory *kulturfolger*. Tiritiri Matangi is a 230-hectare (568-acre) island sanctuary in the Hauraki Gulf only 4 kilometers (2.5 miles) from the New Zealand mainland. Yet Tiritiri overflows with bird and plant species rarely seen today anywhere on the mainland. Some bird species (like the stitchbird, *Notiomystis cincta*, and the saddleback, *Creadion carunculatus*) are extinct on the mainland. One, a large, flightless gallinule called takahe (*Porphyrio mantelli*), parades in numbers around the island's picnic spot, although from about 1900 to 1950 it was thought globally extinct. Bellbirds, North Island robins, whitefaces, brown teal, red-crowned parakeets, little spotted kiwi, fantail, tui, fernbird, spotless crake—they are all there. A visit to this reserve is a trip in a time machine back to the New Zealand of 150 years ago.

Tiritiri had been an ecological disaster. By 1983, 94 percent of its native woody vegetation had been cleared (Olliver 2002). In the following decade, volunteers planted more than 250,000 trees. Then the New Zealand Department of Conservation began to get rid of many of Tiritiri's common species, especially its introduced plants and mammals. The only mammal native to New Zealand is an extinct bat. All others—such as rats, mice, cats, possums, and weasels—form part of a long list of deliberately introduced exotic plants, birds, and even insects (two wasps), many of which have wreaked havoc on the native bird species.

Once rid of its mammals, Tiritiri became a haven into which many native bird species were successfully introduced. But one species, kokako (*Callaeas cinerea*), the scarce, blue-feathered and melodious "New Zealand crow," which happens to be one of only two surviving members of an endemic New Zealand family, is having a problem with a native raptor, the Australasian harrier (*Circus approximans*).

Should people eliminate this harrier, this successful and widespread *kulturfolger*, from the island to ensure the future of the kokako? Simon Fordham (2001) thought so. But several letters to the editor in *Dawn Chorus*, the official newsletter of the Supporters of Tiritiri Matangi, reflected a deep difference of opinion that is likely to characterize debates of this sort (*Dawn Chorus* 2001). The harrier's supporters won the debate and the kokako may be disappearing. It was one thing to get rid of exotics, but quite another to remove a local population of a charismatic, native species. Let nature take its course, said the winning side. And she will.

Meanwhile, in the United States, another listed species was having trouble with a predator (Roemer and Donlan 2004). The island fox (*Urocyon littoralis*) lived only on six of the Channel Islands off the California coast. A century ago, so did at least twenty-four breeding pairs of bald eagles (*Haliaeetus leucocephalus*) (Kiff 1980). By 1950, the bald eagles were gone, probably from eating fish contaminated by pesticides.

The bald eagles, primarily fish eaters, were replaced by the mammal-eating golden eagle (*Aquila chrysaetos*), protected by Congress in 1962. Golden eagles support themselves mostly by eating the feral pigs on Santa Cruz and Santa Rosa Islands. But by 1994 they were taking foxes, too. On Santa Cruz Island and nearby San Miguel Island, the fox population declined from 1,312 and 350 (respectively) in 1993 to 133 and 15 adults in 1998; the population on Santa Rosa Island was also low (Roemer et al. 2001). By summer 2002, 75 survived on Santa Cruz but foxes on both San Miguel and Santa Rosa had become extinct in the wild (Nature Conservancy 2005).

Channel Islands National Park is a nature reserve, like all U.S. national parks. Santa Cruz Island does have some private property but it belongs to the Nature Conservancy, which is also devoted to the preservation of wildlife. The managers faced a dilemma. Either stand by and watch a listed, endemic fox disappear or actively remove a protected, majestic eagle. Based on the recommendations of scientists and laypersons, they chose to remove the eagles.

So far, managers have removed thirty-one golden eagles from Santa Cruz Island to northeastern California (Coonan 2001; Coonan and Rutz 2003; Nature Conservancy 2003c). To defend the islands against stray golden eagles that might wander across the channel from the mainland, they are also reintroducing bald eagles to Santa Cruz Island (Nature Conservancy 2003a). Meanwhile, as many as ten trap-wary golden eagles still reside on the islands and hinder fox recovery (Roemer and Donlan 2004). Ensuring the survival of the fox might mean shooting the eagles. As Roemer and Donlan put it, "Lethal removal of an emblematic bird like the golden eagle is . . . emotionally charged, politically unsavory and legally challenging" (Roemer and Donlan 2004, 27). Indeed, the very idea of tampering with eagle populations on a nature reserve in order to protect diversity is revolutionary. But it is just the kind of new thinking we need to save the earth's species.

Recommendation

The ESA of tomorrow will be much more effective if it embraces reconciliation ecology. But in no case should it oppose reconciliation either overtly or indirectly. To do so would condemn the Endangered Species Act to eventual failure.

22 Second-Generation Approaches

Michael J. Bean

Interest in "second-generation" approaches to the conservation of endangered species is warranted for a simple reason: the first generation has achieved only modest and insufficient success. It is obvious that at the present pace recovery under the Endangered Species Act (ESA) is likely to remain a distant and elusive goal for most of the species that it seeks to protect. To make recovery more likely and more rapid, new ideas are needed, particularly those that enlist the cooperation of landowners and others. Since the mid-1990s, a number of such new approaches have been tested. They include safe harbor agreements, candidate conservation agreements with assurances, conservation banking, and new financial assistance programs targeted at landowners (Fox et al., forthcoming; Heal, forthcoming). Collectively these and other new approaches can be thought of as a "second generation" of Endangered Species Act approaches.

It is almost certainly too soon to draw definitive conclusions about the success or failure of these approaches. Nevertheless, initial results are promising for at least some. Safe harbor agreements have been used to encourage private landowners to undertake—or to allow—beneficial management activities that are not required by law. Landowners with nearly 3 million acres of land are participating in safe harbor agreements. They include timber companies, small woodlot owners, ranchers, major agricultural growers such as California's Paramount Farming Company and the Robert Mondavi Winery, horse farms, golf course resorts, quail plantations, residential property owners, and even a Trappist monastery. Those with completed or pending agreements run the ideological spectrum from CNN founder Ted Turner to Bob Long, a self-described "gun-toting redneck right-wing Republican preacher." More important, safe harbor agreements are accomplishing positive biological results. For example, they have played an important role in the ongoing recovery in Texas of the northern aplomado falcon (*Falco femoralis septentrionalis*), North America's rarest falcon. A decade ago, there were none in the wild in the United States. Today there are at least thirty-seven nesting pairs, more than half the number needed to trigger a reclassification from endangered to threatened. Safe harbor agreements have also made possible the return of the nene (Hawaiian goose) (*Branta sandvicensis*), state bird of Hawaii, to the island of Molokai, from which it was absent, possibly since before the visit of Captain Cook in the late eighteenth century. Conservation banking for endangered species, which began in California in 1995, is beginning to catch on elsewhere as well. The U.S. Fish and Wildlife Service's recent formal guidance on the topic—the first national written guidance it has offered—should encourage the growth of this tool still more. Finally, the Private Stewardship Grants Program of the U.S. Fish and Wildlife Service, launched in 2003, attracted many more applications for funding than it had funds to support.

Despite these impressive initial indications, it is hard to avoid the conclusion that the record of accomplishment for these new conservation tools may be no more inspiring than the record for older tools unless a number of self-imposed obstacles to success are removed. Those obstacles, many of which are described below, are self-imposed because they do not inhere in the law itself but are instead the product of an unimaginative, process-preoccupied, and ultimately self-defeating implementation that discourages and deters opportunities for tangible, on-the-ground improvement. These debilitating constraints have no partisan or ideological provenance; they have stifled effective conservation efforts for endangered species in both Democratic and Republican administrations and will continue to do so until they are overcome.

The discussion that follows describes some of these self-imposed obstacles and illustrates them with real-world examples of lost or diluted conservation opportunities. The aim of this exercise, however, is not simply to bemoan these obstacles to conservation but to suggest solutions that can remove or reduce them. An imaginative, results-oriented administrator of the Endangered Species Act, regardless of political party, can do better—much better—than has been done in the past. Moreover, both conservation interests and regulated interests will benefit from doing better. For conservation interests, the stakes are straightforward: removing obstacles to recovery helps the species with which they are concerned. For the regulated community, the connection is no less direct. Every conservation opportunity missed as a result of the government's self-imposed obstacles constitutes a conservation deficit that can only be offset, if at all, by other—and generally regulatory—measures.

Illustrating the Problem

The self-imposed obstacles discussed here encompass a broad range of issues. They include obstacles to voluntary recovery efforts by private parties; obstacles to recovery efforts by state and federal agencies; failures to capitalize on opportunities provided by conservation programs for nonendangered species; and still others. To begin, however, the examples below typify the problems.

In May 2003, Paramount Farming Company in California got the sort of favorable press attention that is the envy of most businesses. The *Los Angeles Times*, *Sacramento Bee*, and *Fresno Bee* all ran stories lavishing praise on the company's novel safe harbor agreement for the endangered San Joaquin kit fox (*Vulpes macrotis mutica*). So did an Associated Press wire story that was carried around the nation. The agreement was newsworthy because it was the first in the country to involve an agricultural grower and only the second with any California landowner. The essence of the agreement was simple: Paramount would install a series of artificial dens across its intensively farmed agricultural fields so that kit foxes traversing those fields would have an opportunity to avoid being killed by coyotes (*Canis latrans*) (the most significant known source of mortality to kit foxes). The U.S. Fish and Wildlife Service (USFWS), in return, would assure Paramount that if its farming operations accidentally killed a kit fox in the area where the dens were to be installed, no action would be taken against it.

The press accounts of the agreement showered effusive praise on Paramount Farming Company and the USFWS. Only weeks later, however, Paramount's chief executive told an audience at a continuing legal education conference in San Diego that, despite all the favorable publicity, he was not sure he would do it again. The experience had been too time consuming, expensive, and frustrating, in his view. Because of Paramount's prominence in the California agricultural community, it could have been an effective salesperson for safe harbor agreements to other landowners. Instead, Paramount's experience may only discourage other landowners from getting involved in similar conservation efforts. The experience negotiating a safe harbor agreement for the reintroduction of the Hawaiian goose onto Molokai, on the Puu O Hoku Ranch, had a similar effect. Well after that agreement had been completed, a representative of the ranch owner told me that the experience had been both exasperating and expensive. Instead of glowing about the success of the effort, he was glowering about its frustrations.

Another more recent safe harbor agreement in California is with an even better known company, the fabled Robert Mondavi Winery, a prominent leader in the California wine industry. That agreement entailed restoration of riparian habitat along an intermittent stream on vineyard property in San Luis Obispo County. The species expected to benefit include the California red-legged frog (*Rana aurora draytonii*) and two riparian-associated birds. In this example, at least, the Robert Mondavi company seems altogether happy with the outcome. However, the long time that it took to complete the agreement was not lost on other observers who followed its progress. For example, another nearby winery contemplated establishing a multiple ponding system using created wetlands for wastewater disposal, wetlands that might have provided habitat for the California red-legged frog. When it became apparent from the Mondavi experience, however, that a safe harbor agreement was not likely to be processed quickly enough to meet that landowner's business timetable, he opted instead for an irrigation disposal system with no potential to create habitat useful to the red-legged frog.

Still a third example from California concerns a private land trust, part of a burgeoning local land conservation initiative that is working with extraordinary effectiveness around the country. This particular land trust is one of the most professional and successful, the Peninsula Open Space Trust, which has helped save over 40,000 acres of land on the San Francisco Peninsula. One of the properties the trust owns is the 4,733-acre Cloverdale Coastal Ranch, with stunning views of the Pacific Ocean and great restoration opportunities for coastal terrace prairie grasslands, a natural community both rich in rare species and highly imperiled. The trust was ready and willing to carry out an ambitious restoration effort utilizing prescribed burning to return overgrazed land to native coastal prairie grassland. When it sought the USFWS's views as to whether prescribed burning would be desirable, the response was both reassuring and alarming. It was reassuring because the USFWS agreed that prescribed burning was needed and would create better conditions for two endangered species, the San Francisco garter snake (*Thamnophis sirtalis tetrataenia*) and the California red-legged frog. It was alarming because the needed burning might incidentally kill some of these species still occupying the degraded grasslands, and in order to do that USFWS authorization would be required. How to get such authorization was the next question. The agency initially suggested a habitat conservation plan, but the trust was wary of the associated expense and delay. Moreover, habitat conservation plans require mitigation for actions that cause incidental taking of listed species. What the trust proposed to do was habitat restoration, and it made no sense to require mitigation for that.

Ultimately, the trust proposed a better solution, requesting a permit under the provision of the ESA authorizing permits to "enhance the propagation or survival" of listed species. Such permits are most often used for captive breeding efforts, but to the trust it appeared that they could just as sensibly be used to authorize actions that enhanced the survival of a species by restoring its habitat. The trust requested a programmatic permit that would allow it to carry out a series of burns and other restoration activities over several years and to incidentally take listed species in the course of doing so. The trust was pleased to receive a permit in the mail but dismayed upon reading it to learn that it bore scant resemblance to the one requested. Instead of a permit authorizing the unintentional killing of a frog or snake in a prescribed burn, the trust got a permit authorizing it only to "harass by survey, capture, handle, transfer, and release individuals in conjunction with habitat enhancement activities." If, despite best efforts to avoid killing anything, an individual frog or snake turned up dead, the permit did not cover it. Moreover, instead of the programmatic approach sought by the trust, involving a single review of an annual restoration work plan, the permit required prior USFWS review and approval of every individual project before it could commence. The net result was that the trust got a permit that was not the permit it requested, did not meet its needs, and would not be used. It eventually got the USFWS to change the terms of the permit to reflect what it initially wanted and is optimistic of eventual success. In the meantime, however, the restoration effort was held up for two years, to the ultimate detriment of the species it was intended to benefit.

The tendency to tie oneself in knots is even more pronounced when two governmental agencies are involved in a recovery effort. Shortly after the bull trout (*Salvelinus confluentus*) was listed as a threatened species in 1998, the U.S. Forest Service proposed a number of habitat restoration and enhancement activities to aid the fish. Though the net impact of these activities was intended to be positive, there was the potential that some individual bull trout would be incidentally taken. The situation is similar to that of the land trust discussed above. Where it differs, however, is in the added complexity stemming from the fact that because the Forest Service is a federal agency, its planned restoration and enhancement activities trigger interagency consultation obligations under section 7 of the ESA. In a nutshell, the USFWS concluded that although the net effect of the proposed restoration activities would be beneficial, the fact that some individual fish could be harmed meant that the activities were "likely to adversely affect" the species. That improbable determination in turn triggered a Forest Service determination that it would have to do significantly more paperwork to comply with the National Environmental Policy Act (NEPA) (Act of January 1, 1970) than it had originally contemplated. At that point, the Forest Service signaled that it would be easier just to abandon the planned restoration effort. The USFWS avoided that by proposing to issue permits to the Forest Service for those same projects rather than address them through an interagency section 7 consultation. Under this scheme, the issuance by the USFWS would be the federal action triggering section 7; instead of an interagency consultation between the two, the USFWS entered into an intra-agency consultation (i.e., it consulted with itself), and issued to itself a written biological opinion covering issuance of the proposed permits. Through this contrivance, the Forest Service avoided any determination that its restoration actions were "likely to adversely affect" a listed species and thus avoided the deal-killing additional NEPA burdens. In short, the agencies ultimately found a solution, but it was a solution to a self-created problem.

Not so auspicious is the apparent outcome of a similar conundrum involving one of Interior Secretary Gale Norton's signature initiatives, the "Landowner Incentive Program." LIP is a state-administered program involving financial support for conservation activities on private land to benefit so-called "at-risk" species. Secretary Norton announced the new program as part of the Bush administration's fiscal year 2002 budget request. Congress appropriated the full $40 million requested, but the Department of the Interior was unable to spend a cent of that initial appropriation in fiscal year 2002. As a result Congress rescinded the 2002 appropriation but appropriated another $40 million for fiscal year 2003. In the spring of 2003, Interior announced the awarding of competitive LIP grants to most states. However, though the grants were announced, the states still had to do both NEPA and ESA paperwork before they actually received any money. By midsummer of 2003, most states had still not seen the first cent. Moreover, as the case of New Jersey illustrates, LIP's potential to further the recovery of endangered species may not be realized.

New Jersey sought and received what is known as "Tier 1" funding, meaning funding to establish the basic infrastructure of a program and to carry out a few demonstration projects. The demonstration projects were to feature habitat restoration for the endangered bog turtle (*Clemmys muhlenbergii*). However, when the state's LIP administrator conferred with the USFWS regarding needed documentation, she concluded it would be simpler if the demonstration projects involved other, nonendangered species. Whether this conclusion was premised on a misunderstanding of the complexity of those requirements is unclear. What is clear, however, is that New Jersey not only abandoned the bog turtle demonstration projects in favor of projects for other, nonendangered, species but also decided to take bog turtles out of the "Tier 2" application it was preparing for the following year. The bottom line: a missed opportunity to put a promising new landowner assistance program into use for the benefit of an endangered species.

A final example concerns yet another and older landowner assistance program that the USFWS itself administers, the Partners for Fish and Wildlife Program. The Partners program provides financial assistance to landowners for habitat restoration and enhancement benefiting federal "trust species," in other words, migratory birds and endangered species, primarily. Most of the investment of the Partners program has been for the benefit of migratory birds, though significant investments have been made for endangered species as well. These latter, however, are often with conservation landowners (e.g., the Nature

Conservancy, land trusts, and other conservation organizations). Rather more unusual are endangered species projects with farmers, ranchers, forest landowners, and others for whom conservation is not already the principal purpose of their land ownership. One of the reasons is that these landowners face the dilemma that the voluntary restoration of habitat that is subsequently used by an endangered species potentially encumbers the future use of that land. Safe harbor agreements are intended to address this dilemma, but when the USFWS published its safe harbor policy in 1999, it indicated that in lieu of pursuing individual safe harbor agreements for Partners program participants, it was "developing an appropriate process to provide assurances on a programmatic basis to the landowners" who participate in the program. That was June 17, 1999. Today, more than six years later, the promised programmatic approach is still awaited.

When this failure was brought to the attention of USFWS director Steve Williams in mid-2002, he made clear what the promised programmatic response would be. According to Williams, "in order to develop a streamlined, effective, and efficient mechanism to provide the necessary incidental take authority to willing participants, formal programmatic section 7 consultations are recommended" for the Partners program at an appropriate subnational level, such as a state or ecosystem level. That was August 14, 2002, roughly three years before the time of this writing. In the past three years, how many of those recommended programmatic consultations have been undertaken? Not one. The only one even considered, to this author's knowledge, originated in the Annapolis field office of the USFWS, only to be rejected by the regional office as an inappropriate approach. Bottom line: no resolution to the issue of providing future assurances regarding land use to landowners who participate in the Partners program and thus a continued missed opportunity to use that program more expansively to aid endangered species.

Remedying the Problem

In all of the above examples, and in numerous others like them, conservation opportunities have been lost or diminished because of delays, inconsistencies, and other problems that were unnecessary and avoidable. Without a focused effort to understand and eliminate those problems, however, they will be repeated again and again, causing still other conservation opportunities to be lost in the future. What follows are four suggestions aimed at remedying these problems and at making conservation results the foremost concern:

- Keep voluntary landowner agreements short and simple
- Eliminate successive layers of review in voluntary landowner agreements

- Eliminate the biological opinion requirement in most voluntary landowner agreements
- Develop a simple way to achieve compliance with the National Historic Preservation Act (Act of October 15, 1966)

Writing Short and Simple Agreements

Voluntary landowner agreements, such as safe harbor agreements and candidate conservation agreements, are aiding the recovery of many rare species in many different places, including the red-cockaded woodpecker (*Picoides borealis*) in the Southeast, the northern aplomado falcon and black-capped vireo in Texas (*Vireo atricapilla*), and the nene in Hawaii. Despite these promising beginnings, it is likely that only a small fraction of the potential benefits of this new conservation tool will ever be realized unless the USFWS takes action to reduce the cost and delay associated with reviewing and approving agreements. Based on our experience with many of these agreements, we believe there are several actions the agency can and should take to eliminate unnecessary delay and cost for landowners.

If the USFWS genuinely wants private landowners to enter into voluntary conservation agreements, those agreements must be as short as possible, readily understood, and expeditiously processed. The reasons for this ought to be fairly clear. The longer and more complex an agreement, the more intimidating it is to the average landowner and the less likely he or she is to sign it. The essential elements of any agreement are a clear statement of what one party (the landowner) agrees to do and an equally clear statement of what the other party (the USFWS) agrees to do. That is fundamentally all that is important in a safe harbor agreement. It is not necessary—indeed, it is counterproductive—to include in an agreement lengthy background information about the biology and status of the species, causes of its decline, threats to it, and so forth. Yet, it is quite common for safe harbor agreements to include such information. At a minimum, such information makes agreements longer and therefore more daunting for the landowner who is asked to sign. Beyond that, by signing, a landowner is "agreeing" with statements on matters that are usually not within his knowledge. If the USFWS needs to compile this information for purposes of its own decision making, fine. But that is not a reason to put it into the agreement.

There has been less experience to date with candidate conservation agreements with assurances than with safe harbor agreements, but early experience suggests that the USFWS is headed in the same, wrong, direction. Candidate conservation agreements with assurances are agreements in which landowners make conservation commitments on behalf of a species not yet on the threatened or endangered species list. In return, the landowners receive an assurance that, if the species is later listed, their only obligation will be to fulfill those commitments. The USFWS's draft *Candidate Conservation Agreement with Assurances Handbook*, recently issued for public comment, requires the inclusion—in the agreement itself—of extensive information not required by the USFWS's policy or regulations, and certain to make agreements lengthier and more off-putting to landowners than they need to be.

Eliminating Successive Layers of Review

Successful conservation efforts between landowners and the government are built on a foundation of trust. That foundation is eroded by the all-too-frequent practice, after the terms of a safe harbor or candidate conservation agreement are worked out between a landowner and the USFWS field office, of asking the landowner to agree to changes recommended by the regional office or by the recovery coordinator for the species covered by the agreement. Such changes have been recommended both before an agreement is put out for public comment, and afterward. Multiple and successive layers of agency review may be appropriate in other contexts, but they are poison in the context of voluntary undertakings by landowners to implement beneficial management actions for rare species. It is hard for a landowner to avoid the conclusion that the USFWS is less interested in getting something useful done on the ground than in getting a second and third bite at the apple in its dealings with the landowner.

Remedying this problem is entirely within the ability of the USFWS. The field office biologist negotiating a safe harbor agreement ought to have the responsibility to solicit the views of the regional office and of the recovery coordinator *before* concluding a draft agreement with a landowner. Public comments received thereafter might identify other desirable changes, but they should not be regarded by the USFWS as a license to reopen the entire agreement. Lodging final authority to issue a permit in conjunction with a safe harbor agreement in the field office rather than the regional office would both expedite a final decision and spare the appearance of whipsawing the landowner. Current agency policy is for all permit decisions to be made at the regional level. However, section 5.4B of part 032 of the USFWS manual allows regional directors to delegate the authority to issue endangered species permits. The regional directors should delegate to the field offices the authority to approve permits issued in conjunction with safe harbor agreements. Such delegation would expedite the approval of such agreements.

Eliminating Most Biological Opinions

No safe harbor agreement may be approved unless the USFWS first determines that it is expected to have a "net conservation benefit" to the species covered by the agreement. Given that determination, one might expect that the USFWS would dispense with the preparation of a biological opinion to determine whether the agreement is likely to jeopardize the continued existence of that same species. After all, by definition an action that produces a net conservation benefit for a particular species cannot also jeopardize its continued existence. Nevertheless, the USFWS routinely prepares biological opinions for safe harbor agreements, needlessly wasting time, staff resources, and the patience of the landowner to prepare a document, the principal conclusion of which is foreordained. Except in the unusual case where the activities to be undertaken for the benefit of one listed species have the potential to affect adversely another listed species, the preparation of formal biological opinions for safe harbor agreements ought to be scrapped.

Scrapping this requirement will require revising or overriding the USFWS's *Consultation Handbook* (USFWS and NMFS 1998), which was promulgated in 1998, a year before the USFWS issued its safe harbor policy. Part 3.5 of the handbook requires that formal consultation be done whenever any federal agency action is likely to adversely affect a listed species. However, in making the determination whether an action is likely to adversely affect a listed species, the handbook does not allow the USFWS to look at the net effect of the action but forces it instead to ask only if there are *any* negative effects, even if they are clearly outweighed by beneficial effects. Any action that results in the taking of a listed species is automatically considered to be an action that is likely to adversely affect a species. Since safe harbor agreements always entail the possibility of incidental taking in the course of returning to baseline conditions, the result is that the USFWS must consult with itself and issue a formal biological opinion for every safe harbor agreement. The principal conclusion of that opinion is never in doubt, however, since no safe harbor agreement can be approved unless the USFWS concludes that it is expected to result in a net conservation benefit for the species. Thus, biological opinions are routinely prepared, not because they contribute anything to the analysis or review of the proposed agreement, but because the handbook says they have to be prepared.

The obvious solution to this problem is to revise the handbook to clarify that agreements that meet the "net conservation benefit" standard of the safe harbor policy do not have to be the subject of formal consultation, notwithstanding that incidental take may occur in the course of returning to baseline conditions under such agreements. To recommend revising the handbook, however, is to recommend an action that is more likely to consume years than weeks. Pending a revision of the handbook, the policy change can be accomplished with a stroke of the pen through a "Director's Order," the mechanism by which the USFWS can set temporary policy pending revision of the appropriate handbooks or manuals.

Complying with the National Historic Preservation Act

Unless simplified, the requirements of the National Historic Preservation Act have the potential to derail voluntary landowner agreements that require ESA permits, such as candidate conservation agreements with assurances and safe harbor agreements. Consider the case of a landowner contemplating entering into a safe harbor agreement. Through that agreement, he seeks the certainty that if he voluntarily creates habitat that an endangered species later uses, the presence of that endangered species will not restrict his future use of the site where he created the habitat. The premise of this arrangement is that the landowner today is able to use the site in any manner he wishes, without restriction under the ESA. He is willing, however, to create conditions beneficial to a listed species there, and to maintain those conditions for an agreed-upon period, provided that thereafter he is again free to use it in the manner he wishes.

Now enter the National Historic Preservation Act. Issuance of the ESA permit that authorizes the future incidental take of listed species that occupy the created habitat constitutes a federal undertaking subject to the requirements of the National Historic Preservation Act. What the practical consequences of that are have not been consistently articulated by the USFWS. Should the focus of the inquiry be on the conservation actions to be undertaken by the landowner (the creation of the habitat), which do not require a permit? Should the focus instead be on the narrow activity actually authorized by the permit (the incidental taking of the listed species)? Or should it be broadly on the activity that results in the incidental taking (e.g., shopping center construction, timber harvest, etc.)? The latter is made difficult by the fact that the permit does not authorize any particular activity; it simply authorizes future taking incidental to any use of the landowner's choosing. The various field offices and regions have struggled with the question of what the National Historic Preservation Act requires in such circumstances. Some have suggested that the landowner ought to pay for an archaeological survey prior to securing a permit. If that is to be required, it will likely end landowner interest in safe harbor agreements, which, it is important to remember, are voluntary undertakings. Others have suggested that a landowner might have to do such a survey in the future, if he or she decides to use the permit to take the species incidental to a surface-disturbing activity. That requirement would likely have a similar effect, since it introduces considerable uncertainty with respect to the landowner's future rights—uncertainty that it was the purpose of the safe harbor agreement to eliminate.

Conclusion

At present, there is neither a consistent nor a well-thought-out agency position on this set of issues. One is urgently needed, because of its potential ramifications for voluntary conservation initiatives by landowners under the ESA. Experience to date strongly suggests that the more and the higher the obstacles put in front of such initiatives, the fewer of them there will be. The ultimate losers are the very species the ESA aims to protect.

23   Proactive Habitat Conservation

Mark L. Shaffer, Laura Hood Watchman, Sara Vickerman,
Frank Casey, Robert Dewey, William J. Snape III, Michael Senatore,
and Robert M. Ferris

The Endangered Species Act of 1973 has proved to be a landmark in conservation efforts. It has led to a new respect for the diversity of life and has been the foundation of remarkable conservation successes (Yaffee, this volume). But the list of threatened and endangered species has grown steadily over the past three decades, from 178 in 1976 to 1,263 in 2004 (USFWS 2004c). Another 5,000–6,000 species may eventually need to be listed (Master et al. 2000). Clearly, we are not doing enough to adequately address the underlying causes of species endangerment. Eighty-five percent of currently listed species and those likely to require listing in the future are at risk, at least in part, because of the continuing loss of habitat (Wilcove et al. 2000). A proactive, state-based, incentive-driven policy for the conservation of key habitats, broadly outlined in this chapter, could complement the existing Endangered Species Act (ESA) and help develop a nationwide system of habitat conservation areas that could maintain our native biodiversity and reduce the need for federal regulatory intervention in the future.

Lessons Learned

Thirty years of implementing the ESA have provided valuable lessons that should be reflected in a new habitat-focused policy initiative to conserve biodiversity. The principal lessons are scientific, political, and economic.

Science has taught us that the underlying threat to U.S. biodiversity is the loss of habitat (Wilcove et al. 2000). Science has also taught us that waiting to take conservation action until a species is listed minimizes the chances of long-term viability (Shaffer et al. 2002b). Because options are limited when a species' habitat is greatly reduced, continuing habitat loss also tends to maximize the costs of conservation. Moreover, habitat loss may worsen the impacts of climate change on biodiversity, even as climate change accelerates extinction risk by reducing the amount of suitable habitat (Thomas et al. 2004). Given these lessons from science, it is clear that maintaining the full array of plant and animal species and natural communities is going to require the protection of a large amount of habitat (Shaffer and Stein 2000). Much of that habitat is on privately owned land (Groves et al. 2000).

The politics of the ESA have taught us that a strictly regulatory approach is politically controversial. It is also unlikely to be completely successful in the current political climate. The controversy over critical habitat designation is one case in point: opponents to these regulatory designations believe that they are redundant with other habitat protections and incite conflict rather than collaboration, while proponents state that regulatory habitat protection is essential to species recovery, citing evidence of its success (Bean 2004; Suckling and Taylor, this volume). It should be noted, however, that a variety of ESA regulations, including critical habitat designations, tend to be better supported when they are tied to specific habitat goals and when the process is clearly transparent (Snape et al. 2001).

Although the ESA provides some regulatory flexibility through habitat conservation plans and "second-generation" tools such as safe harbor agreements, candidate conservation agreements, and related instruments (Bean, this volume), these tools are both inherently regulatory and not aimed at comprehensive habitat conservation. As a result, they are applied in an uneven fashion taxonomically as well as geographically (Scott, Goble, et al., this volume). Habitat conservation plans also often authorize substantial habitat loss. Moreover, they have had limited and uneven success in promoting systematic, large-scale habitat conservation for multiple species (Hood 1998).

We have also learned that a strong law can be seriously weakened by its annual appropriation. Congress has consistently failed to provide the program with funding sufficient to attain the act's goal of species recovery (Miller et al. 2002).

Politics has also taught us that, in contrast to regulatory programs that are controversial with a large part of the American public, conservation funding programs are enormously popular with voters. From 1998 to 2003, voters approved 79 percent of conservation-related ballot measures, resulting in $24 billion in funding (Trust for Public Land 2003). In addition, over the last thirty years, Congress has significantly expanded incentive-based agricultural conservation programs, in contrast to its stalemate over the ESA. For example, in fiscal year 2001, total expenditures for the U.S. Department of Agriculture's resource conservation programs (including cost-share agreements, easements, technical assistance, research, and other programs) amounted to over $3.66 billion. While these examples are only partially aimed toward habitat conservation, they illustrate the political appeal of nonregulatory conservation programs.

Economics has taught us that nonregulatory, incentive-based programs that do not involve fee simple acquisition can successfully promote the use of land for conservation purposes (Fischer and Hudson 1993; Vickerman 1998a; Casey et al. 1999; Shogren et al. 1999; Brown 1999). Examples include land retirement or cost sharing of stewardship practices through federal programs such as the Department of Agriculture's Forestland Enhancement Program, Wetlands Reserve Program, Wildlife Habitat Incentives Program, and various state-based incentive programs (Libby 1998; Boyd et al. 1999; Defenders of Wildlife 2002). Economics has also taught us that there are substantial economic benefits associated with habitat and species protection, indicating that taxpayer investment in landowner incentive programs may yield high returns (Fausold and Lilieholm 1999; Hagen et al. 1992; Loomis and White 1996).

To date, instead of learning from these lessons, groups have pitted losing strategies against each other. If species need more habitat protection than current regulation is producing, then some believe the regulations should be strengthened. Because regulation is unpopular with some constituencies, and land acquisition is expensive, others want to believe we can get by with less habitat conservation effort. And, because the endangered species list continues to grow despite the money spent on conservation programs, some believe we can't afford a solution.

Greater progress in achieving the effective conservation of our nation's biodiversity requires that society accept these lessons and formulate a habitat conservation policy that reconciles the legitimacy of each. Saving biodiversity at all its levels (genes, species, communities, ecosystems) will involve protecting a significant portion of the American landscape from intensive development, but it will not require protecting the whole landscape. Achieving the necessary scale of habitat protection through regulation alone is not the only option. The economic costs of large-scale habitat protection are large when viewed through the lens of immediate acquisition, but not every parcel must be bought, and not all at once (Shaffer et al. 2002a). In fact, many lands currently managed primarily for purposes other than conservation—especially low-intensity agriculture, forestry, and recreation—provide important conservation values that could be maintained or even improved with application of the right management techniques (Rosenzweig, this volume; Thompson, this volume).

Principles for a New Policy Initiative

National biodiversity conservation policy should complement the regulatory protections of the ESA with a new program for habitat conservation based on the lessons learned to date. Such a new habitat program should be proactive, state based, and incentive driven.

Proactive Policies

Biodiversity conservation efforts are likely to be more successful and less expensive if we design and protect adequate habitat conservation areas *before* species become threatened or endangered. If we do so on a biologically comprehensive basis (all natural community types and all at-risk species), and in accord with principles for the long-term viability of such systems (Shaffer and Stein 2000; Groves 2003), then we should be able to prevent the future endangerment of thousands of species. Designing and implementing such systems of habitat conservation areas would also provide opportunities for better addressing the habitat needs of currently listed species and providing a common framework for recovery efforts on their behalf.

An important corollary for a proactive approach is integration. Integrated conservation strategies that address both terrestrial and aquatic ecosystems simultaneously will be more successful in the long run because both are impacted by human activities across the landscape. And, if habitat needs are addressed within a broader context along with water quality, flood control, transportation systems, growth management, and outdoor recreation, then biodiversity is more likely to receive adequate attention (Beatley, forthcoming).

State-Based Policies

A prevailing trend in American politics is placing more authority and discretion for the achievement of social goals with the states. This pattern is evident, for example, in the implementation of federal air- and water-quality statutes. While maintaining a strong federal Endangered Species Act is essential as a fail-safe mechanism, there are sensible ways to empower the states to play a greater leadership role in biodiversity conservation that, over time, could reduce the need for federal regulatory intervention. Moreover, as Wilkinson (1999) points out, the traditional role of states with regard to wildlife and other public trust resources, and their role in the land use decision-making process, makes the states essential players in habitat conservation efforts.

Although state government can still seem far removed from local communities, it is a step closer than the federal government. Furthermore, states could, where appropriate, empower local governments to formulate coordinated local habitat conservation strategies that could, collectively, produce a comprehensive statewide effort (Cohn and Lerner 2003). States can also facilitate and support regional efforts to develop and implement integrated conservation strategies like those currently under way for the Chesapeake Bay, the San Francisco Bay-Delta in California, the Sonoran Desert in Arizona, and the Willamette Basin in Oregon.

Incentive-Driven Policies

Under our form of government, wildlife is a public trust resource not subject to private ownership. At the same time, most wildlife habitats—other than wetlands and waters protected by the Clean Water Act (Act of June 30, 1948)—do not have an equivalent public trust status. The result is that the public trust often critically depends on habitats found on private land. Land is a commodity traded in the free market, and government prohibitions of certain land uses to protect habitat may diminish the financial value of that land to the owner. On the other hand, one individual's decision to alter habitat could extinguish a species and irreversibly diminish the rights of other citizens and future generations to the full benefits of the public trust. An incentive-driven habitat conservation policy would apply public funds to conserve or manage public trust resources on private lands, thus attempting to reconcile these competing interests. It would also complement the ESA's largely regulatory approach.

Essential Elements of a National Habitat Conservation Policy

Translating these principles into concrete policy initiatives is easier to envision than to achieve. But the nation could have a habitat conservation policy that embodies these principles through the expansion and coordination of existing programs. Three elements are essential: a plan or strategy, a menu of incentives, and the coordination of these efforts with future highway development.

Comprehensive State Wildlife Conservation Strategies

Congress and the Clinton administration took a giant step toward enabling an improved habitat conservation policy in the fall of 2000. The fiscal year 2001 Interior and Commerce Appropriations legislation established a state wildlife grant program that, among other things, requires states to complete comprehensive wildlife conservation strategies by October 2005. These strategies will be developed by state fish and wildlife agencies, along with other state resource agencies, and private and federal partners. The strategies are to be reviewed every ten years. They are expected to identify those land and water areas essential to the conservation of the state's at-risk plant and animal species, and natural communities.

Ideally, state wildlife conservation strategies should not only identify but also map priority habitat areas and address the full array of species and ecological communities. Prior to 2001, some states had already recognized the need for a comprehensive habitat plan: early examples of excellent state habitat conservation strategies are from Florida (Cox et al. 1994), Oregon (Defenders of Wildlife 1998), and Massachusetts (Massachusetts Division of Fisheries and Wildlife 2001), and these efforts can serve as models for other states.

The methodology for creating such strategies has been developed and tested over the years by government agencies and conservation organizations (Groves 2003; Groves et al. 2002; Margules and Pressey 2000). This methodology generally includes identifying new conservation targets and goals, assessing the adequacy of existing conservation areas, and identifying priority conservation areas. Based on the experience of Defenders of Wildlife and its partners in Oregon, the state wildlife conservation strategy will be easier to implement if it is developed with input from multiple sectors (public and private), multiple agencies (including wildlife, forests, agriculture, transportation), and multiple jurisdictions (local, state, and federal).

Habitat Conservation Incentives

Public lands—especially federal and state lands—are the logical starting points for providing the habitat necessary to support the public trust of biodiversity. Enhanced multiagency coordination and planning can assure that the public gets the most biodiversity value from the very significant investment it has already made in our public lands. Nevertheless, the distribution of existing public nature reserves is biased toward protecting high-elevation habitats that are relatively poor in biodiversity, and many habitat types are not adequately protected by public nature reserves (Scott et al. 2001a, 2001b). In fact, nearly 40 percent of at-risk species are not known to occur on federal lands that constitute the vast majority of public lands. For the other at-risk species, the habitat that existing federal lands provide is often not enough to assure their viability because 67 percent of populations of threatened and endangered species exist on nonfederal lands (Groves et al. 2000). Consequently, many important habitat conservation areas will be, in whole or in part, on private lands.

There is thus a need for new incentives to promote habitat protection on private lands, either permanently or as an interim step until acquisition is feasible. A national habitat conservation policy should address this need in three ways: first, by improving the targeting of current incentive programs; second, by enhancing and streamlining the provision of information; and third, by creating new incentives for the voluntary conservation of priority habitat areas identified by the states in their comprehensive wildlife conservation strategies.

Targeting Incentive Programs

Although there are several private and public incentive programs that target specific species, these programs are not oriented toward the conservation of key habitats that are important for multiple species. By improving the connection between existing conservation incentive programs and state comprehensive wildlife conservation strategies, these conservation programs will be more biologically effective and economically efficient.

Making Information Available

Currently, there are substantial incentive programs for habitat and wildlife conservation at both the federal and state levels. Many of these programs, however, are poorly known or awkward to use. The federal government could improve the effectiveness of existing programs by funding state "private land conservation clearinghouses." These offices would provide information to existing local conservation districts and extension agents who already provide assistance to landowners but who may not be aware of the state wildlife conservation strategies or incentive programs focused on habitat conservation and restoration. The office could also provide one-stop shopping directly to landowners wishing to take advantage of federal, state, and local incentive programs that might be used to conserve habitat. The offices could help facilitate strategic investments in accordance with state comprehensive wildlife conservation strategies by focusing on priority ecoregions, communities, and important landscapes. Over time, such offices could also provide feedback to federal, state, and local policy makers on how existing incentive programs for natural resource management are working and how they could be improved to more effectively conserve habitat.

Creating New Incentives for Voluntary Conservation

Although existing incentive programs have resulted in some significant benefits, they are often criticized for being too narrowly focused, too administratively complex, and underfunded, particularly relative to commodity programs. They also tend to be applied opportunistically rather than strategically. A more effective national habitat conservation policy would need to provide a menu of flexible incentives to private landowners whose lands lie within the priority habitat areas identified in their state's wildlife conservation plan. Incentive options must be structured to acknowledge that not all landowners respond to the same social and economic factors in making conservation decisions. There is no one-size-fits-all approach to conserving habitat.

There are a variety of possible incentives to accomplish habitat protection activities for lands identified as priority habitat areas in state wildlife conservation stategies. Conservation easements and conservation rental agreements can be used to maintain lands in their current natural or near-natural condition.

Federal cost-share programs can encourage habitat management activities such as the control of exotic species. Supported management activities can also include the return of ecosystem processes, such as fire, that are essential to maintaining or restoring priority habitat areas.

Funding for direct habitat conservation payments could be accomplished either through amendment of one of the existing incentives programs under the conservation titles of the farm bill (e.g., the Wildlife Habitat Incentive Program) or creation of a new habitat protection program. The goal should be to make it easy for landowners to receive assistance in implementing management strategies consistent with the state's wildlife conservation strategy.

Other possible incentives involve preferential federal tax treatments to provide incentives to landowners either not involved in agriculture or whose participation in habitat conservation is more likely the result of tax considerations than the availability of funds. Such incentives might include a tax credit for habitat management expenses or, for land that is kept in natural habitat, either a credit in the amount of local property taxes or an exemption from estate taxes.

To qualify for these incentives, the landowner would enter into a written stewardship agreement with a state-designated habitat conservation authority affirming that the landowner will keep the lands in a use compatible with their identification as priority habitat areas, and, where applicable, undertake habitat management activities deemed necessary under the state's wildlife conservation plan. To encourage participation, the minimum term for such agreements could be five or ten years, with the option of a permanent agreement. Each state would need to establish a system for enrollment and monitoring to ensure that the habitat has been conserved and management activities undertaken.

Such a menu of incentives might begin to change the underlying dynamic of land conservation for biodiversity. Whether these incentives would prove equal to the task is an empirical question. Congress could include the authority and funding to assess the efficacy of the incentives at some suitable point (five or ten years) in the future. Many of these incentives have been identified as potentially useful instruments in previous studies (Fischer and Hudson 1993; Keystone Center 1995; Vickerman 1998a) and several have been considered by Congress.

Habitat and Transportation Coordination

Because a more comprehensive national habitat conservation policy would provide major federal resources for voluntary, state-based habitat conservation efforts, it is important that such a national policy also address coordination of other federal expenditures that could impact the prospects for the success of the states' efforts. Various federal policies and subsidies encourage habitat conversion, including subsidies for agricultural conversion, federal land management policies, and water resources development policy. However, transportation is the most important federal program in this category, because roads have an array of impacts on ecological systems, including habitat destruction, habitat fragmentation, and introduction of invasive species (Forman et al. 2003). In addition, because roads are often on the leading edge of urban development (Cervero 2003), transportation is the federal program most related to urbanization. Urbanization is second only to agriculture as a leading cause of the destruction and alteration of habitat for imperiled species (Wilcove et al. 2000).

As part of a sound national habitat conservation policy, the impacts of road development on biodiversity can be substantially reduced through two crucial mechanisms. First, earlier coordination between state transportation planning and state wildlife conservation strategies could reduce the impacts of roads on state habitat conservation areas. Second, states could develop mitigation banks that would conserve state habitat conservation areas in advance of transportation impacts at sites of less ecological importance.

Enhanced coordination could be accomplished through the use of state wildlife conservation strategies at the initial stages of the transportation planning process. Utilization of this habitat mapping data can serve effectively as an early warning system to identify projects with major wildlife impacts. Some states are already beginning to recognize the advantages of more closely coordinating highway construction plans with natural resource mapping data. For example, the Florida Department of Transportation's Efficient Transportation Decision-Making system overlays early transportation plans with priority habitat areas (among other data layers) in an effort to flag, change, or eliminate transportation projects that would have impacts on priority lands.

Comparing proposed highway plans with the state's wildlife conservation plan should reduce delays for transportation projects and yield greater natural resource protection. It would also help identify many of the most controversial projects—ones likely to have the longest average approval times—at a time when the number of options for addressing environmental concerns is the greatest.

By setting up transportation mitigation banks that conserve state habitat conservation areas, states can harness considerable transportation funding sources for land conservation and active management, and transportation agencies can use their mitigation funds more effectively and efficiently than through piecemeal, project-by-project mitigation. Various state transportation agencies have undertaken habitat mitigation banks, although these banks have not yet been linked with state wildlife conservation strategies.

Biodiversity is our "green" infrastructure, providing important public services not unlike the "gray" infrastructure of roads, bridges, and water systems (see Beatley, forthcoming). The public gains little if its investments in one type of infrastructure negate its investments in the other. Roads and conservation have often been in conflict in the past and will often be in conflict in the future. The first step toward minimizing such conflict is to recognize the importance of both types of infrastructure and to coordinate planning for the adequate provision of each. But for these state wildlife conservation strategies to lead to the systems of habitat necessary to maintain our green infrastructure, they must be supported by a transportation and overall infrastructure policy that recognizes their value to society.

Conclusion

By the midpoint of the twenty-first century the human population of the United States is expected to increase by at least 50 percent. If that increase takes place in the absence of more focused, effective, and proactive means of identifying and protecting a comprehensive system of habitats, our native biodiversity is likely to be severely and irreversibly diminished. Upward of five thousand additional species may have to be listed as threatened or endangered, and a good many may become extinct, if not in our lifetimes, then in our children's. This need not be the case. We are still sufficiently wealthy in natural resources that conservation and development are not alternative choices we must make but widely shared values we can blend and balance. Wisdom can still make a difference. We are also sufficiently experienced in our practice of conservation to have a general sense of what works best in our society. Adding a proactive, state-based, incentive-driven policy for habitat conservation will allow us to apply our collective wisdom to meet the need we still face—securing the place of nature's diversity in the American landscape.

24 Renewing the Conservation Commitment

Frank W. Davis, Dale G. Goble, and J. Michael Scott

As we write this in early 2005 there are several ESA-related pieces of legislation pending before Congress. Most of the proposed legislation is championed by Republican leaders from western states, who promise to strengthen the use of science or ensure fairer treatment of private landowners. It has become a perennial drama on the American political stage: "conservatives" rally to rein in a law that they believe has reached too far and "conservationists" mobilize to defend the law that they believe offers the best hope for protecting biodiversity from relentless economic exploitation. There is much posturing, finger pointing, and, ultimately, political stalemate (Barry 1991).

With the current political balance in the nation's capital, ESA reform is suddenly a real possibility. Idaho senator Mike Crapo, Rhode Island senator Lincoln Chafee, California representative Richard Pombo, and others have announced their intent to forge a bipartisan congressional coalition to achieve ESA improvement by moving critical habitat designation into recovery planning, strengthening the role of the states, and expanding incentives for habitat conservation on private land. Given these developments, it seems especially timely and important to synthesize and reiterate ideas and recommendations from the three-year Endangered Species Act at Thirty project. The authors in this volume and its companion, *The Endangered Species Act at Thirty: Conserving Biodiversity in Human-Dominated Landscapes*, have many specific constructive recommendations that fit within three recurrent themes: the role of the federal government in species conservation, the emergence of new actors and institutional relationships, and the limits of the ESA as a tool for conserving biodiversity.

Theme 1. Implementation of the Endangered Species Act Falls Short of the Statute's Intent

All participants agreed that steady federal leadership, funding, and technical expertise are required to implement coherent species protection and recovery strategies. They highlighted numerous examples of federal-state-private partnerships that were making a difference on the ground. They also agreed that inconsistent federal policies have hindered recovery actions and diminished private-sector interest in conservation partnerships (Bean, this volume; Swain, this volume). While the act has prevented the extinction of hundreds of species that would have disappeared without intervention, and while protection under the act has improved species' chances for recovery, there are obvious flaws in the federal government's implementation of the law:

- The entire program is chronically and grossly underfunded (Miller et al. 2002). One result is that the implementing agencies are operating with a shortage of trained staff.
- Implementation is too vulnerable to the political whims of the congressional and administrative branches of government (DeShazo and Freeman, this volume).
- The listing process is too late (Wilcove et al. 1993) and too lengthy (Greenwald et al., this volume) such that the agencies are letting population size and habitat decline too far before listing species, leaving species' chances of recovery low even with extremely lengthy and costly recovery measures.
- Recovery programs have perpetuated biologically unrealistic expectations of rapid species recovery.
- Conservation opportunities are being lost to unnecessary bureaucratic delays, costs, and rigid adherence to doctrine (Swain, this volume; Doremus, this volume).

The Listing Process Is Broken

Effective species conservation under the ESA depends fundamentally on a timely, scientifically credible, and unbiased listing process. All agree that the current process—which averages eleven years between initial consideration and final listing, is driven by litigation, and increasingly condemns species to warranted-but-precluded status—is far from ideal. The federal list represents a diminishing percentage of actual at-risk species, perhaps 15–20 percent at present, and an increasing fraction of species are listed as endangered versus threatened (Scott, Goble, et al., this volume). In short, the agencies are falling farther and farther behind the actual conservation need (Master et al. 2000; Scott, Goble, et al., this volume).

A number of administrative and legislative reforms to the listing process have been proposed that would variously increase funding for listing, create more explicit biological guidelines, expand the role of state agencies, limit administrative listing moratoria, and limit litigation. Greenwald et al. (this volume) go so far as to recommend mass listing of at-risk species by an independent scientific body such as the National Academy of Sciences; Burnham et al. (this volume) also recommend having listing and delisting decisions made by the academy.

Absent significant funding increases, the agencies may need to better prioritize species for listing. Currently, agency priorities are driven by litigation and crisis management. Instead of this "worst-first" mode of operating, conservation efficiencies might be achieved by focusing on species in hotspots of rarity and endangerment, on keystone species, or perhaps on umbrella species whose listing could benefit a large number of other species (J. Cochrane, pers. comm.).

Critical habitat designation can cause extensive and expensive delays. Although the agencies maintain that critical habitat designation adds little protection (Clark 1999; Bruce Babbitt remarks, November 13, 2003; Craig Manson remarks, November 13, 2003), empirical analyses contradict these assertions (Greenwald et al., this volume). The benefits of critical habitat designations on species recovery continue to be debated and no consensus emerges from the analyses and discussions in this project. Similarly, there was no consensus on whether it would be advantageous to designate critical habitat at the time the recovery plan is drafted. At a minimum, implementation of critical habitat will require increased funding. The process would also benefit from closer cooperation with state agencies in compiling and analyzing available information and from increased analytical rigor and consistency in critical habitat delineation (Ruckelshaus and Darm, forthcoming; Reed et al., forthcoming; Scott, Goble, et al., this volume). These steps are unlikely to reduce the conflicts over critical habitat designation but would at least increase the credibility of the final products. To reduce conflicts with private landowners, the federal government should consider expanding financial incentives such as tax reductions or habitat conservation and improvement funds (Shaffer et al., this volume; Parkhurst and Shogren, this volume).

Recovery Does Not Happen Overnight

The recovery program is also underfunded by a factor of two to five (Miller et al. 2002), and the limited funds available are distributed inequitably due to political and social pressure as well as agency priorities (DeShazo and Free-man, this volume; Kareiva et al., this volume; Suckling and Taylor, this volume). Currently less than 0.5 percent of listed species account for over 50 percent of state and federal recovery expenditures (Kareiva et al., this volume). A systematic analysis of all currently listed species in order to identify and invest in species that could be recovered at relatively low cost could improve recovery statistics (M. Bean, pers. comm.). Ideally, such prioritized investments would come from a new "special opportunities" recovery fund to avoid diverting existing funds in a way that would amount to triage for the species at greatest risk.

There are biological limits to the rate at which species with small populations and limited habitat can be recovered. It is therefore reasonable to expect the number of recovered species to be a small fraction of those listed. Citing the small number of delisted species as evidence of a failed policy is disingenuous absent full funding and reference to the relevant biological time frames (Doremus, this volume). The public must be better informed with realistic cost estimates and reasonable expected time scales for recovery.

Even when recovery goals are met, the risk factors that led to a species' decline are often not adequately mitigated (Burnham et al., this volume) and agencies are thus understandably reticent to delist the species. Downlisting and delisting might be expedited through the creation of "recovery management agreements" between the federal agencies and local conservation management entities that have the regulatory authority to ensure that risk factors are meaningfully addressed and that the species continues to be managed for recovery (J. M. Scott et al., forthcoming). Such agreements would acknowledge that few listed species can be delisted without assurances of continuing conservation management.

For a significant subset of listed species, irreversible habitat degradation, exotic species, and climate change make it unlikely that they can ever be fully recovered and delisted. Instead their continued existence will require ongoing, active conservation management. Policy makers and the public must be made aware of this reality, perhaps by creating a new ESA status to recognize species that may never achieve full recovery. These "conservation reliant species" would include wild populations that are self-sustaining as long as ongoing management actions (e.g., exotic species control, scheduled water releases from dams, controlled burning) are taken on their behalf (J. M. Scott et al., forthcoming).

Based on experience to date, successful recovery often requires new institutional models in order to procure long-term, cross-agency and cross-jurisdictional management and funding. Currently, recovery planning is not well coordinated with other ongoing habitat conservation and management efforts, even in obvious cases such as integrating the national wildlife refuge system into the design of recovery plans (Davison et al., this volume). Better interagency coordination could also leverage additional federal funds for species recovery. For example, federal habitat restoration programs authorized by the Farm Bill and the Partners for Fish and Wildlife Program could be deployed to improve the chances for more rapid and lasting species recovery. Interagency coordination is easier said than done, but there are some highly successful recovery programs (e.g., the Willamette Valley/Puget Trough Cross-Program Recovery Effort) that could serve as role models for others to emulate (Clark and Wallace, this volume; Environmental Defense 2004).

Conservation Opportunities Are Being Lost

Almost every discussion of ESA reform begins with the verb "streamline," whether addressing conservation incentives, listing, recovery planning, permitting, or delisting. Federal streamlining is not always feasible or desirable (Doremus, this volume), but virtually all stakeholders and legal analysts in this project agreed that bureaucratic complexity is undermining opportunities for effective conservation. Ironically, a number of the ESA reform bills currently before Congress actually increase the process rather than streamline it.

Opportunities for administrative streamlining include reduction of ambiguity and redundancy between the administering agencies (NOAA and USFWS), elimination of unnecessary multiple layers of administrative review, and better coordination among federal and state conservation programs in terms of priority setting and funding (Bean, this volume; Swain, this volume; Burnham et al., this volume). Unfortunately, federal programs often operate at cross-purposes in the same locations because of conflicting policies and priorities for subsidizing habitat conservation versus subsidizing habitat conversion through agriculture, water, and transportation programs. Reconciling these deeply embedded policy conflicts will take more than coordination and instead would require a hard look at social priorities, program costs, and comparative benefits.

As emphasized by Goble (forthcoming), Yaffee (this volume), and Clark and Wallace (this volume), the administration of the ESA has shifted from a top-down, prohibitive regulatory approach to a de facto permitting system where resolution is increasingly achieved by negotiation, conflict resolution, and compromise. This requires the federal agencies to be more flexible, opportunistic, and responsive to other actors both in public and private sectors. It also requires involving state and local governments and the public early and throughout the ESA decision-making process (Behan, this volume).

Decision Making Can Be Improved with Better Information

The Endangered Species Act at Thirty project did not focus on the role that science plays in the implementation of the act since the topic has been the subject of several previous studies (National Research Council 1995, 2003, 2004a; Hoekstra et al. 2002a; Boersma et al. 2001). Science plays a central role in determining the status of species for listing, reclassification, and delisting decisions (ESA sec. 4(b)(1)(A)), in designating critical habitat (ESA sec. 4(b)(2)), and in making jeopardy determinations during consultation (ESA secs. 7(a)(2), (c)(1)). Each of these decisions is to be made "on the basis of the best scientific and commercial information available." Science also plays a key role in recovery planning.

Despite the fact that there is little in the record of the act's implementation to support claims of unsound science, the use of science in ESA decision making has recently come under intense criticism. Several bills pending in Congress call for changes in the act to promote "sound science." Such calls date back at least to 1978 and some commenters interpret these proposals as an attempt to impose additional scientific hurdles to regulatory action (Doremus 2004; Wagner 2003). There is, of course, always room for improvement (Doremus, this volume; Ruckelshaus and Darm, forthcoming; Waples, forthcoming; Reed et al., forthcoming; Hoekstra et al. 2002b; Boersma et al. 2001). During this project, the most frequently voiced concerns focused on the need for better data on species status and trends (Scott, Goble, et al., this volume: Reed et al., forthcoming; Waples, forthcoming), the need for more scientific transparency in reporting the methods and assumptions underlying listing decisions, determinations of critical habitat, establishing recovery goals, and the design of habitat conservation plans (Ruckelshaus and Darm, forthcoming), and the need for greater interaction between scientists and managers in identifying key uncertainties and information needs. There were several calls for increased rigor and clarity in defining recovery, jeopardy, harm, adverse modification, and other terms that are in the everyday lexicon of the act's implementation. In addition, it is also true that we are making decisions based on woefully incomplete information. Biodiversity on private lands in the United States is not systematically surveyed or monitored, and information is especially weak for rare and endangered species because they are difficult to survey and often little studied. Obviously, investing in better biological surveys can improve the reliability of listing decisions.

These problems, however, generally reflect the substantial uncertainties both as to facts (e.g., the population size of an at-risk species) and as to the underlying science (e.g., what is the taxonomic status of a species) (National

Research Council 1995). While both types of uncertainties could be reduced with enough time and money, the ESA reflects a different fundamental policy choice: decisions are to be based on the best data available. Congress chose not to study species into extinction.

Theme 2. Successful Conservation Institutions and Relationships Are Emerging

The Endangered Species Act is a powerful young law with broad impacts on both the implementing agencies and the regulated community, and the social and legal impacts of the act are still evolving. The act has precipitated a wave of legal and administrative reforms at all levels of government, including the enactment of state endangered species acts (Doremus, this volume), incorporation of natural resource planning into local land use decision processes (J. M. Scott et al., forthcoming; Tarlock, this volume), and new kinds of conservation partnerships and management systems (Yaffee, this volume; Rodgers, this volume). Meaningful public involvement has proven critical in example after example (e.g., Behan, this volume; Yaffee, this volume; Clark and Wallace, this volume). These changes in the administration of the act and in related governance structures are being sorted out in conservation "experiments" ongoing in many parts of the country. Based on results to date, several authors in this volume conclude that successful conservation and recovery programs only emerge through local engagement, creative conflict resolution, and problem solving. They suggest that attempts to fix the act via significant top-down ESA reform are ill-advised and premature at best (Clark and Wallace, this volume; Yaffee, this volume; Burnham et al., this volume; Niles and Korth, this volume).

Many ESA-induced institutional changes have been in response to the large spatial scales required for species conservation and recovery. Although localized restoration and recovery efforts continue to play an important role in endangered species conservation, most single-species and multispecies habitat conservation and recovery programs must operate over large areas—thousands to millions of acres—invariably spanning public and private lands and multiple jurisdictional boundaries. Today's showcase habitat conservation programs (e.g., Southern California's Natural Communities Conservation Planning Program, Pima County's Sonoran Desert Conservation Plan, Wisconsin's Karner Blue Butterfly Habitat Conservation Plan) have involved creating and maintaining new institutional relationships in order to integrate traditionally segregated local public land and water planning, private land management systems, and state and federal natural resource management. These innovative programs require a willingness on the part of federal and state agencies to take risks, to be more forthcoming with data and information, and to relinquish some authority and funding to other entities. How far the federal government can and should go in this direction is not clear. As noted by Doremus (this volume), "Striking the balance between flexibility and accountability will be the key implementation challenge for the next generation of the ESA."

An Expanded Role for the States

It was telling that in their keynote remarks in Santa Barbara, Idaho governor Dirk Kempthorne, former secretary of the interior Bruce Babbitt, and assistant secretary of the interior Craig Manson all called for more use of cooperative agreements with the states. Since 1973, the role of states has expanded continuously but still falls short of state roles under similar cooperative federalism provisions in the Clean Water Act (Act of June 30, 1948). To date, however, the states have been reticent to establish regulatory programs that are as protective as the ESA (Goble et al. 1999), a basic requirement of cooperative federalism.

There are strong arguments in favor of an expanded state role (Niles and Korth, this volume). States have the governmental structures and expertise in land use planning necessary to conserve habitat. For nonfederal lands, state personnel are usually more familiar with the landowners, the affected species, and the field conditions and thus are better able to design successful conservation strategies. State funding for endangered species already exceeds that of the federal government and is expanding further through federally funded state wildlife grants and landowner incentive programs. Most states now have endangered species programs (Goble et al. 1999; Niles and Korth, this volume) and all maintain heritage databases on species of special concern. Many states are developing wildlife conservation plans as a requirement for continued state wildlife grants, and these plans present an important opportunity to identify, prioritize, and conserve vulnerable species and their habitats before they become endangered (Shaffer et al., this volume). If fully implemented, state conservation plans provide an opportunity to get ahead of the extinction curve.

There are also reasons to be cautious in transferring authority to the states, notably potential conflicts of interest in devolving ESA authority to the same jurisdictions whose land- and water-use decisions often create the problem (Clark and Wallace, this volume). Furthermore, states have shown little propensity for interstate coordination of conservation efforts, whether it be in jointly maintaining lists of species and communities of concern, setting regional conservation priorities, or implementing status and trends monitoring. Perhaps a good starting point for state-led management and recovery programs would be the sizeable set of narrowly distributed species whose distributions are largely or wholly confined to one or two states.

Although the appropriate balance of federal and state authority is a matter of continuing debate, most commenters agree that states should be consulted earlier in the ESA process and should play a greater role in recovery planning and implementation. Expertise, data, and information should be freely shared among state and federal agencies. An expanded role for the states will certainly require increasing federal money to the states, perhaps by a significant increase in the section 6 Cooperative Endangered Species Conservation Fund.

Private Landowners Carry Much of the Conservation Burden

With 50 percent of listed species having 80 percent or more of their known occurrences on private lands, it is obvious that the act must also be responsive to the capabilities and competencies of private landowners.

Most observers agree that habitat conservation plans are an important tool of the ESA but that as currently administered they are too costly and complex for small individual property owners. A number of participants called for regional and state conservation plans to prioritize areas for conservation and offsite mitigation banking, thereby reducing piecemeal and often ineffective onsite mitigation on small landholdings (Shaffer et al., this volume; Thompson his volume; Fox et al., forthcoming). The Southern California Natural Communities Conservation Planning Program serves as an early model of this kind of approach.

There was also consensus that incentive-based approaches promoted by former interior secretary Bruce Babbitt, such as safe harbor agreements, candidate conservation agreements with assurances, conservation banking, and new financial assistance programs that provided funds to states and private property owners, were steps in the right direction. Such programs, however, need to be made more accessible and less costly to participating landowners (Bean, this volume; Parkhurst and Shogren, this volume). Large corporate landowners can afford inhouse legal and biological experts to help navigate the labyrinth of ESA-related processes and programs. Individual ranchers, farmers, small developers, and other private landowners who lack this capacity are understandably threatened by and frustrated with the time and costs of ESA compliance, are wary of any federal ESA-related programs, and are unlikely to be attracted by cumbersome incentive programs (Swain, this volume; Thompson, this volume).

Private landowners are also confronted with a myriad of non-ESA conservation programs operated by state and federal agencies and nongovernmental organizations (Swain, this volume). Information about these programs should be organized and presented in a way that is easier for individual owners to access and understand. Creation of "one-stop shopping" Web sites and offices where landowners could obtain information on the habitat and species conservation programs available from all agencies would help to relieve landowner frustration.

There is a profound lack of data and information on the cost of the ESA to the nation's private lands, whether it be the cost of agency enforcement, landowner compliance, or incentive systems (Parkhurst and Shogren, this volume; Sunding, forthcoming). The examples provided to this project suggest that there are multiple direct and indirect costs and benefits of the ESA that need to be better quantified, documented, and analyzed in order to design cost-effective incentive programs for private landowners.

Theme 3: The ESA Should Be the Last Rather Than the First Conservation Bulkhead

Critics of the Endangered Species Act often cite the long and growing list of endangered species and the small number of recovered species as indicators of a failed policy, but these trends are symptomatic of a more fundamental problem: we are not making choices at the local, state, and federal levels that could prevent species from becoming endangered in the first place. Tinkering with the ESA will not solve this problem.

This is not to say that we cannot operate the ESA more proactively. Candidate conservation agreements with assurances are a move in that direction but thus far have seen limited use (Thompson, this volume). Adding an "at-risk" category to the ESA that would precede listing a species as threatened or endangered might serve as an earlier-warning system to help guide proactive conservation (Paul Weiland, pers. comm.). Increased funding for measurement and monitoring could help to better ascertain the status of at-risk species so that we might intervene earlier. Systematic statewide and regional conservation planning can prioritize areas for species protection and recovery (Shaffer et al., this volume; Behan, this volume; Swain, this volume) and help design conservation mitigation banks and other incentives for more robust, market-driven conservation solutions (Fox et al., forthcoming; Heal, forthcoming).

In practice, however, waiting until species are at risk before acting to conserve them is an end game that leaves few options; all too frequently, the final moves are limited to setting aside the few remaining bits of habitat to be managed as biological reserves (Rosenzweig, this volume). This approach has become politically and economically untenable as the United States continues to expand; a projected 60 million new housing starts by 2030 promises additional large increases in the number and distribution of at-risk species (Scott, Goble, et al., this volume). Although we can gain efficiencies using multispecies reserves, eventually rapid climate change and the large area requirements of most species make biodiversity in all but the largest reserves dependent on sur-rounding nonreserved areas (Rosenzweig, this volume; Root et al. 2003).

Ultimately, the Endangered Species Act and its derivative reserve-based con-servation may slow but cannot prevent the accelerating, pervasive erosion of native species and ecosystems from the American landscape. If we want to restore and maintain the biota of the United States and the benefits that biodi-versity provides, we must look beyond reserves and find ways to accommodate more native species in the areas where we live, work, and recreate. A new land ethic is needed in which the responsibilities of private property are acknowl-edged (Freyfogle 2004; Leopold 1949).

There are encouraging examples in this volume and elsewhere showing that working farms, ranches, residential, and even urban areas can be part of the conservation solution (Thompson, this volume; Rosenzweig, this volume; Beatley, forthcoming). Similarly, freshwater and marine ecosystems can be restored and managed for sustainable exploitation without jeopardizing non-market species (Armsworth et al., forthcoming). To be sure, most programs and projects are still experimental and many have been motivated by the threat of listings under the ESA (Yaffee, this volume; Doremus, this volume), but eco-nomic reasoning and aesthetic and conservation values have also been signifi-cant forces for change (Brosi et al., forthcoming; Heal, forthcoming; Norton, forthcoming; Callicott, forthcoming).

Reconciling the needs of humans and other species is a daunting challenge requiring scientific research to better understand species requirements, reedu-cation of an American population conditioned to lifestyles that leave little room for other species, new market incentives, political will, and leadership. But based on the chapters presented here, such changes are imaginable. In another thirty years, perhaps the ESA will have assumed its proper role as the final conservation option, and practicing sustainability will be the first bulk-head of biodiversity conservation in America.

Notes

Complete references for the works cited in short form are given in the References section.

Preface

1. Virginia Albrecht (board member, National Center for Housing and the Environment), Maeveen Behan (assistant to county administrator, Pima County, Ariz.), Troy Bredenkamp (director, Congressional Relations, American Farm Bureau Federation), Jeff Eisenberg (director, Environmental Issues, National Cattlemen's Beef Association), John Kostyack (senior counsel and manager of wildlife conservation programs, National Wildlife Federation), James Kraft (senior vice president, general counsel, and secretary, Plum Creek Timber Company), Michael Mittelholzer (director, Air, Waste, and Wildlife Regulatory Affairs, National Association of Homebuilders), Dennis Murphy (University of Nevada-Reno, Biology Department), Kieran F. Suckling (president, Center for Biological Diversity), Mark L. Shaffer (senior vice president for programs, Defenders of Wildlife), and Hilary Swain (director, Archbold Biological Station).

2. Paul R. Armsworth (Stanford University, Department of Biological Sciences), Timothy Beatley (University of Virginia, Department of Urban and Environmental Planning), J. Baird Callicott (University of North Texas, Department of Philosophy and Religion Studies), Chris Costello (University of California, Santa Barbara, Donald Bren School of Environmental Science and Management), Ray Dacey (University of Idaho, Department of Business), Gretchen Daily (Stanford University, Department of Biological Sciences), Andy Dobson (Princeton University, Department of Ecology and Evolutionary Biology), Holly Doremus (University of California, Davis, School of Law), Peter Kareiva (The Nature Conservancy), Mark V. Lomolino (State University of New York, College of Environmental Science and Forestry), Craig Moritz (University of California, Berkeley, Department of Integrative Biology), Shahid Naeem (Columbia University), Bryan G. Norton

(Georgia Institute of Technology, School of Public Policy), Stuart Pimm (Duke University, Nicholas School of the Environment and Earth Science), Steve Polasky (University of Minnesota, Department of Applied Economics), William H. Rodgers Jr. (University of Washington School of Law), Michael L. Rosenzweig (University of Arizona, Department of Biological Sciences), Mary Ruckelshaus (National Marine Fisheries Service, Northwest Fisheries Science Center), Jason F. Shogren (University of Wyoming, Department of Economics and Finance), A. Dan Tarlock (Illinois Institute of Technology, Chicago-Kent College of Law), Barton H. Thompson Jr. (Stanford University School of Law), Robin Waples (National Marine Fisheries Service, Northwest Fisheries Science Center), and Steven L. Yaffee (University of Michigan, School of Natural Resources and Environment).

Chapter 4.　The Class of '67

1. The actual percentage of Hawaiian species on the endangered list is somewhat higher than 25 percent. The Department of the Interior lists all Hawaiian tree snails in the genus *Achatinella* as endangered but counts the genus as one "species" in its tally. In fact, the genus consists of 41 separate species. Thus, the total number of species on the U.S. list is actually 1,305, rather than 1,265, of which 352, or 27 percent, are from Hawaii. We thank Tim Male for alerting us to this discrepancy.

2. Since publication of McMillan and Wilcove (1994), we have added the Kauai `o`o (honeyeater) to the list of species that are probably extinct. Because several hundred `o`os may have been alive at the time the Endangered Species Act became law, we consider it a potentially salvageable species (see Scott et al. 1986).

Chapter 5.　The Listing Record

1. Dale Goble (forthcoming) also divides the Endangered Species Act into four historical periods. Our division, based only on the listing program, is largely, but not entirely, consistent with his, which is based on the entirety of ESA policy.

2. This chasm between legal theory and empirical history should stand as a warning to excessively theoretical interpretations of the Endangered Species Act. The tendency to interpret the history, successes, and failures of the act through the narrow lens of the "law," without taking adequate stock of the empirical record, has led to many misinterpretations of how the act actually works and to many naive and overly legalistic reform suggestions.

3. The emphasis by nongovernmental organizations on critical habitat protection can be traced to several factors: the virtual shutdown of the listing program, the publication of a 1997 study demonstrating that critical habitat improved the status of the species (Rachlinski 1997; see Suckling and Taylor this volume; Taylor et al. 2005), and the six-year federal statute of limitations, which would preclude forcing habitat designations for hundreds of species listed in the early 1990s.

Chapter 7. Critical Habitat and Recovery

1. The U.S. Fish and Wildlife Service lists thirteen recovered species, but we also include *Astragalus yoder-williamsii*, which was listed with critical habitat on an emergency basis in 1980 (USFWS 1980). This species is absent from most U.S. Fish and Wildlife Service databases.
2. We exclude four species that were extinct prior to being listed.
3. There is some argument about the 1978 regulation on this point. Bean and Rowland (1997) and Senatore et al. (2003) argue that the 1978 regulation is substantially the same as the 1986 regulation. Hicks (2000) argues that it is not. As a legal theory, the issue is irresolvable as both camps present a reasonable argument for how the regulation could have been applied. To see how it was applied, we reviewed biological opinions and critical habitat rules from 1978 to 1983. The USFWS did apply a recovery standard during this period. Also, the "need" to create the 1986 regulation suggests that implementation of the 1978 regulation did not satisfy the Reagan administration.
4. The sample size was erroneously reported as 171 (Jon Hoeskstra, pers. comm.).

Chapter 9. Managing the Working Landscape

1. Federal law requires the U.S. Fish and Wildlife Service to publish notice of each application for an incidental take permit in the *Federal Register* (ESA sec. 10(a)(2)(B)). Although publishing notice of permits actually issued by the USFWS would better reflect actual governmental policy, the law does not require notice of permit approvals or denials, and thus some are never noticed (Thompson 1997).
2. The total number of applications, including those issued in Texas, actually declined, but this is solely because of the large number of applications received in the mid-1990s for single-family residences in the Balcones Canyonlands of Texas.

Chapter 10. The Dynamic Urban Landscape

1. A species need not be present in every area of land being developed to trigger section 9, but it is possible to avoid section 9 liability by proving that a species never occupied the land being developed (*Defenders of Wildlife v. Bernal* 2000).
2. At least some courts appear to be adopting a more lenient standard (*Conservation Council v. Roseboro Lumber Co.* [1995]) ("imminent threat" sufficient to invoke harm rule despite a lack of showing of past or current injury).
3. Section 9.16 of the City of San Diego Guidelines for Environmentally Sensitive Land Regulations specifies that once the city or third-party beneficiary has imposed a mitigation remedy, neither the city nor the third party will be required to provide additional mitigation for any growth-inducing impacts that the project may have on the covered species (The Implementing Agreement). The agreement limits the power of cities to exercise police power in the future, and courts have consistently said that cities may not contract away their police power. California enacted legislation authorizing development agreements in 1979; the legislation

allows agreements for the permitted uses, density, height, and provisions for the dedication or reservation of land for public purposes. Agreements may be negotiated both for property within the city and property being annexed, if it is annexed within the time frame specified in the agreement. These agreements have time limitations and are subject to modification by the local government so long as the modifications do not prevent the development from being completed. They are also subject to subsequent state or federal laws or regulations. The quid pro quo is that the developer may proceed under the land use rules in force when the development is executed. The long history of the post–World War II judicial validation of conditional zoning and other developer-municipal agreements suggest that there is no per se prohibition against a local government agreeing to limit the future exercise of the police power but that courts will review municipal forbearance for both procedural and substantive fairness.

4. The statute authorizes any person or governmental agency to prepare a natural community conservation plan (NCCP) pursuant to an agreement with, and guidelines written by, the California Department of Fish and Game. (Natural Community Conservation Act secs. 2820, 2810, 2815). The purpose of each plan is to promote "protection and perpetuation of natural wildlife diversity while allowing compatible and appropriate development and growth" (Natural Community Conservation Act sec. 2805). Once the Department of Fish and Game approves an NCCP, it may authorize developments, which might otherwise be found to adversely impact listed or candidate species, if they are consistent with the NCCP (Natural Community Conservation Act secs. 2801, 2825(c), 2835).

5. Landowners possess the surface of the earth and all flora growing on the surface of the land, as well as the exploitable subsurface and air space above the surface (*County of Westchester v. Town of Greenwich* 1990). Courts have long held that the state owns wildlife in trust for the public, and thus property owners have no expectation of ownership of wildlife found on their land (*Betchart v. California State Department of Fish and Game* 1984).

6. Federal liability is suggested by Justice Black's dissent in *Griggs*. One runway of the new Pittsburgh airport required very low flights over a residential area. The residents sued the airport operator for the imposition of a servitude that diminished the value of their property, and the county argued that it was immune from liability because it operated the runways pursuant to federal authority. The Pennsylvania Supreme Court held that if there were a taking, both the United States and the county were liable. Justice Douglas's majority opinion held that the county had no federal immunity because it was responsible for runway and approach pattern acquisition. Justice Black dissented because the county was executing a federal policy when it used the Civil Aviation Authority–mandated approach zone; thus, the county should be immune and the United States held liable for damages (Dunham 1962).

Chapter 11. Reality Check from Florida

1. This species list was compiled by the U.S. Fish and Wildlife Service and can be viewed on the Threatened and Endangered Species System Web site at

http://ecos.fws.gov/tess_public/TESSWebpageUsaLists?usMap=1&status=listed&
state=FL.

2. Florida Natural Areas Inventory databases can be viewed online at http://
www.fnai.org/.

3. Stewardship America, a private conservation and rural development organization,
promotes market-based solutions to conservation. See http://privatelands.org/.

Chapter 14. Indian Tribes

1. The bison's strong immune system may protect animals exposed to brucellosis
from carrying the infection. Steve Torbit, senior staff scientist at the National
Wildlife Federation's Rocky Mountain Natural Resource Center in Colorado, has
stated that "there is no evidence that Yellowstone bison are as severely affected by
brucellosis as cattle and there has never been a documented case of a park bison
having passed the microbe to cattle." Torbit also questions how a purge of bison
could be justified while overlooking thousands of elk that migrate out of Yellowstone each year. He adds that the focus on bison "seems even less justified in light
of the [Intertribal Bison Cooperatives'] standing offer to take the refugee bison,
quarantine them, remove any that test positive for brucellosis and use the remainder to restock reservations" (Chadwick 1998; see National Research Council 1998,
5; Keiter and Froelicher 1993; Thorne et al. 1991). Nonetheless, brucellosis has
been transmitted to cattle by elk in Wyoming and informed scientific opinion does
not assume zero risk for transmission from bison (Gordon Orians, pers. comm.).

2. This account is borrowed from a talk by Sylvia Cates (2003).

Chapter 16. Lessons Learned

1. The protections of the Endangered Species Act are unavailable only to insect pests
"whose protection . . . would present an overwhelming and overriding risk to
man" (ESA sec. 3(6)).

2. In 2003, Congress amended the act to exclude from critical habitat designation
lands owned or controlled by the U.S. Department of Defense and subject to a
management plan that benefits the species (Act of November 24, 2003).

3. Canada, for example, closely examined the U.S. experience with the Endangered
Species Act before enacting its Species at Risk Act, S.C. ch. 29 in 2002. It has been
suggested that the ESA's extensive list of endangered and threatened species worldwide may serve as a strong example for implementation of the global Convention
on International Trade in Endangered Species (Karno 1991, 998).

4. It is far from certain that the Idaho plan is sufficient to protect the gray wolf in
Idaho, but it is clear that the plan is more generous to the wolf than state management would be without the threat of federal intervention under the ESA.

5. In fiscal years 1998 through 2000, roughly half of direct expenditures on endangered species by federal and state governments went to about 10 of the more than
1,200 listed domestic species (USFWS 2001g).

6. The U.S. Environmental Protection Agency has, for example, consistently refused
to require permits for pesticide treatments that, intentionally or incidentally,

involve discharges to waterways. The federal courts have rejected the EPA's argument that such actions do not require permits (*League of Wilderness Defenders v. Forsgren* 2002 (holding that the Clean Water Act permit was required for aerial pesticide spraying); *Headwaters, Inc. v. Talent Irrigation District* 2001 (holding that a permit is required for spraying pesticides into irrigation ditches). Recently, wildlife agencies proposed rules intended to streamline ESA consultation on uses of pesticides that might affect listed species (USFWS and NOAA 2004).

7. For example, despite substantial support, the 106th Congress failed to pass the proposed Conservation and Reinvestment Act, which would have automatically appropriated revenues from offshore energy development for conservation purposes.

8. A quick search of a legal database in October 2003 turned up some fifty-two reported judicial decisions dealing substantively in some respect with the science of ESA decisions. Of those, more than 50 percent had been issued since the beginning of 2000, and fully 20 percent in the first ten months of 2003.

9. At one time, regulations implementing the Endangered Species Act adopted precisely this view, but they have since been softened (Doremus 2004).

10. Too often, data are collected but then gather dust somewhere because agency personnel, constantly responding to the latest crisis, do not make the time to analyze them. In order to be useful for management, data must be systematically analyzed and made available for review and reanalysis by the scientific community.

References

Abbitt, R. J. F., and J. M. Scott. 2001. Examining differences between recovered and declining endangered species. *Conservation Biology* 15:1274–84.

Abramsky, Z., M. L. Rosenzweig, B. Pinshow, J. S. Brown, B. Kotler, and W. A. Mitchell. 1990. Habitat selection: An experimental field test with two gerbil species. *Ecology* 71:2358–69.

Act of May 25, 1900 (Lacey Act). Chapter 553, 31 *U.S. Statutes at Large* 187 (currently codified as amended at 16 U.S.C. secs. 42, 701).

Act of July 3, 1918 (Migratory Bird Treaty Act). Chapter 128, 40 *U.S. Statutes at Large* 755 (currently codified as amended at 16 U.S.C. secs. 703–4).

Act of February 18, 1929 (Migratory Bird Conservation Act). Chapter 257, 45 *U.S. Statutes at Large* 1222 (currently codified at 16 U.S.C. secs. 715–715r).

Act of June 8, 1940 (Bald Eagle Protection Act). Chapter 278, 54 *U.S. Statutes at Large* 250 (currently codified as amended at 16 U.S.C. secs. 668–668d).

Act of June 30, 1948 (Water Pollution Prevention and Control Act [Clean Water Act]). Chapter 758, 62 *U.S. Statutes at Large* 1155 (codified as amended at 33 U.S.C. secs. 1251–1387).

Act of July 14, 1955 (Air Pollution and Control Act [Clean Air Act]). Chapter 360, 69 *U.S. Statutes at Large* 322 (codified as amended at 42 U.S.C. secs. 7401–7671q).

Act of May 28, 1963 (Land and Water Conservation Fund Act). Public Law No. 88-29, 77 *U.S. Statutes at Large* 49 (currently codified as amended at 16 U.S.C. secs. 460*l* through 460*l*-11).

Act of October 15, 1966 (National Historic Preservation Act). Public Law No. 89-665, 80 *U.S. Statutes at Large* 915 (codified as amended at 16 U.S.C. secs. 470–470x-6).

Act of January 1, 1970 (National Environmental Policy Act). Public Law No. 91-190, 83 *U.S. Statutes at Large* 852 (codified as amended at 42 U.S.C. secs. 4321, 4331–35).

Act of October 21, 1972 (Marine Mammal Protection Act). Public Law No. 95-522, 86 *U.S. Statutes at Large* 1027 (codified as amended at 16 U.S.C. secs. 1361–1407).

Act of November 10, 1986 (Emergency Wetlands Resources Act). Public Law No. 99-485, 100 *U.S. Statutes at Large* 3582 (codified at 16 U.S.C. secs. 3901–32).

Act of December 13, 1989 (North American Wetlands Conservation Act). Public Law No. 101-233, 103 *U.S. Statutes at Large* 1969 (codified at 16 U.S.C. secs. 4401–14).

Act of October 23, 1992 (Wild Bird Conservation Act). Public Law No. 102-440, 106 *U.S. Statutes at Large* 2224 (codified at 16 U.S.C. secs. 4901–16).

Act of April 10, 1995 (Emergency Supplemental Appropriations and Rescissions for the Department of Defense to Preserve and Enhance Military Readiness Act). Public Law No. 104-6, 109 *U.S. Statutes at Large* 73, 86.

Act of October 11, 1996 (Sustainable Fisheries Act). Public Law No. 104-297, 110 *U.S. Statutes at Large* 3559 (amending the Magnuson Fisheries Conservation and Management Act, codified at 16 U.S.C. secs. 1801–83).

Act of October 9, 1997 (National Wildlife Refuge System Improvement Act). Public Law No. 105-57, 111 *U.S. Statutes at Large* 1252 (codified at 16 U.S.C. secs. 668dd–668ee).

Act of November 24, 2003 (National Defense Authorization Act for Fiscal Year 2004). Public Law No. 108-136, 117 *U.S. Statutes at Large* 1392.

Aengst, P., J. Anderson, J. Chamberlin, C. Grunewald, S. Loucks, and E. Wheatley. 1998. *Balancing public trust and private interest: Public participation in habitat conservation planning.* Ann Arbor: School of Natural Resources and Environment, University of Michigan. http://www.snre.umich.edu/emi/pubs/hcp.pdf.

Allen, R. P. 1952. *The whooping crane.* New York: National Audubon Society.

Anderson, I. 1999. Protecting the salmon: An implied right of habitat protection in the Stevens Treaties, and its impact on the Columbia River Basin. *Vermont Law Review* 24:143–68.

Ando, A. W. 1999. Waiting to be protected under the Endangered Species Act: The political economy of regulatory delay. *Journal of Law and Economics* 42:29–60.

Annett, A. F. 1998. *Reforming the Endangered Species Act to protect species and property rights.* Washington, D.C.: Heritage Foundation. Also available at http://www.heritage.org/Research/EnergyandEnvironment/BG1234.cfm.

Arizona Cattle Growers Association v. U.S. Fish and Wildlife Service. 2001. 273 F.3d 1229. U.S. Court of Appeals for the 9th Judicial Circuit.

Arizona Republic. 2002. Bureau of Reclamation wants to flood Grand Canyon to save native fish. April 26.

Armstrong, A. 2002. Critical habitat designations under the Endangered Species Act: Giving meaning to the requirements for habitat protection. *South Carolina Environmental Law Journal* 10:53–86.

Armsworth, P. R., C. V. Kappel, F. Micheli, and E. Bjorkstedt. Forthcoming. Working seascapes. In *The Endangered Species Act at thirty: Conserving biodiversity in human-dominated landscapes*, ed. J. M. Scott, D. D. Goble, and F. W. Davis. Washington, D.C.: Island Press.

Arnold, C. A. 1991. Conserving habitats and building habitats: The emerging impact of the Endangered Species Act on land use development. *Stanford Environmental Law Journal* 10:1–43.

Ashley, M. V., M. F. Willson, O. R. W. Pergams, D. J. O'Dowd, S. M. Gende, and J. S. Brown. 2003. Evolutionarily enlightened management. *Biological Conservation* 111:115–23.

Babbitt v. Sweet Home. 1995. 515 U.S. 687. U.S. Supreme Court.

Babcock, R., and J. Keesing. 1999. Fertilization biology of the abalone *Haliotis laevigata*: Laboratory and field studies. *Canadian Journal of Fisheries and Aquatic Sciences* 56:1668–78.

Bangs, E. E., and S. H. Fritts. 1996. Reintroducing the gray wolf to central Idaho and Yellowstone National Park. *Wildlife Society Bulletin* 24:402–13.

————. 1998. Status of gray wolf restoration in Montana, Idaho, and Wyoming. *Wildlife Society Bulletin* 26:785–98.

Barrow, M. V., Jr. 1998. *A passion for birds: American ornithology after Audubon.* Princeton: Princeton University Press.

Barry, D. J. 1991. Amending the Endangered Species Act, the ransom of the red chief, and other related topics. *Environmental Law* 21:587–604.

————. 1998. Keynote speech—opportunity in the face of danger: The pragmatic development of habitat conservation plans. *Hastings West-Northwest Journal of Environmental Law and Policy* 4:129–33.

Bart, J. 2003. Development of a coordinated bird monitoring plan for Canada and the United States. Unpublished report to the North American Bird Conservation Initiative. Arlington, Va.

Bean, M. J. 1998. The Endangered Species Act and private land: Four lessons learned from the past quarter century. *Environmental Law Reporter* 28:10701–10.

————. 2001. Major Endangered Species Act developments in 2000. *Environmental Law Reporter* 31:10283–90.

————. 2004. The agony of critical habitat. *Environmental Forum* 21 (6): 18–26.

Bean, M. J., S. G. Fitzgerald, and M. A. O'Connell. 1991. *Reconciling conflicts under Endangered Species Act: The habitat conservation planning experience.* Washington, D.C.: World Wildlife Fund.

Bean, M. J., and M. J. Rowland. 1997. *The evolution of national wildlife law.* 3rd ed. Westport, Conn.: Praeger.

Bean, M. J., and D. S. Wilcove. 1997. The private-land problem. *Conservation Biology* 11:1–2.

Beard, D., F. C. Lincoln, V. H. Cahalane, H. H. T. Jackson, and B. H. Thomson. 1942. *Fading trails: The story of endangered American wildlife.* New York: Macmillan.

Beatley, T. Forthcoming. Cities. In *The Endangered Species Act at thirty: Conserving biodiversity in human-dominated landscapes,* ed. J. M. Scott, D. D. Goble, and F. W. Davis. Washington, D.C.: Island Press.

Belsky, M. H. 1996. Indian fishing rights: A lost opportunity for ecosystem management. *Journal of Land Use and Environmental Law* 12:45–62.

Benson, M. H. 2002a. The Tulare case: Water rights, the Endangered Species Act, and the Fifth Amendment. *Environmental Law* 32:551–87.

————. 2002b. Giving suckers (and salmon) an even break: Klamath Basin water and the Endangered Species Act. *Tulane Environmental Law Journal* 15:197–238.

Betchart v. California State Department of Fish and Game. 1984. 205 *California Reporter* 135. California Court of Appeals.

Biggins, D., B. J. Miller, T. W. Clark, and R. P. Reading. 1997. Management of an endangered species: The black-footed ferret. In *Principles of conservation biology,* ed. G. K. Meffe and C. R. Carrol, 420–26. Sunderland, Mass.: Sinauer Associates.

Billings Gazette. 2003. Bison group wants more say in management. July 24.

Black, S. H., M. Shephard, and M. M. Allen. 2001. Endangered invertebrates: The case for greater attention to invertebrate conservation. *Endangered Species Update* 2 (7): 42–50.

BLM (Bureau of Land Management). 1980a. Letter from R. J. Neary, acting Winnemucca district manager, Bureau of Land Management, to L. Greenwalt, director, U.S. Fish and Wildlife Service. July 1.

————. 1980b. Letter from E. F. Spang, Nevada state director, Bureau of Land Management, to Boise area manager, U.S. Fish and Wildlife Service. October 24.

———. 2001. BLM to implement additional interim measures to protect endangered species. Press release. Sacramento. January 18.

Blumm, M. C., and B. M. Swift. 1998. The Indian treaty piscary profit and habitat protection in the Pacific Northwest: A property rights approach. *University of Colorado Law Review* 69:407–502.

Boal, C. W., and R. W. Mannan. 1999. Comparative breeding ecology of Cooper's hawks in urban and exurban environments. *Journal of Wildlife Management* 62:864–71.

Boersma, P. D., P. Kareiva, W. F. Fagan, J. A. Clark, and J. M. Hoekstra. 2001. How good are endangered species recovery plans? *BioScience* 51:643–49.

Boffey, P. 1975. *The brain bank of America: An inquiry into the politics of science.* New York: McGraw-Hill.

Boice, L. P. 1996. Managing endangered species on military lands. *Endangered Species Update* 13 (7-8): 1–6.

Bosselman, F. 1992. Planning to prevent species endangerment. *Land Use Law and Zoning Digest* 44 (3): 3–8.

Boyd, J. K., K. Caballero, and R. D. Simpson. 1999. *The law and economics of habitat conservation: Lessons from an analysis of easement acquisitions.* Washington, D.C.: Resources for the Future.

Brailovskaya, T. 1998. Obstacles to protecting marine biodiversity through marine wilderness preservation: Examples from the New England region. *Conservation Biology* 12:1236–40.

Brewer, G. D., and T. W. Clark. 1994. A policy sciences perspective: Improving implementation. In *Endangered species recovery: Finding the lessons, improving the process,* ed. T. W. Clark, R. P. Reading, and A. L. Clark. Washington, D.C.: Island Press.

Brook, A., M. Zint, and R. D. Young. 2003. Landowners responses to an Endangered Species Act listing and implications for encouraging conservation. *Conservation Biology* 17:1638–49.

Brosi, B. B., G. C. Daily, and F. W. Davis. Forthcoming. Agricultural and urban landscapes. In *The Endangered Species Act at thirty: Conserving biodiversity in human-dominated landscapes,* ed. J. M. Scott, D. D. Goble, and F. W. Davis. Washington, D.C.: Island Press.

Brown, P. 1999. Tools for ecological stewardship. In *Ecological stewardship: A common reference for ecosystem management,* ed. W. T. Sexton, A. J. Malk, R. C. Szaro, and N. C. Johnson. Oxford: Elsevier Science.

Brush, M., A. Hance, K. Judd, and E. Rettenmaier. 2000. Recent trends in ecosystem management. Master's thesis, School of Natural Resources and Environment, University of Michigan. http://www.snre.umich.edu/emi/pubs/trends.pdf.

Brussard, P. F., D. D. Murphy, and C. R. Tracy. 1994. Cattle and conservation biology: Another view. *Conservation Biology* 8:919–21.

Buchman, S. L., and G. P. Nabhan. 1996. *The forgotten pollinators.* Washington, D.C.: Island Press.

Buffalo Field Campaign. 2003. Honor the Earth: March 31 Press Advisory. http://honorearth.com/ (accessed April 23, 2003).

Burgess, P. M., and L. L. Slonaker. 1978. *The decision seminar: A strategy for problem solving.* Columbus: Merschon Center, Ohio State University.

Burnham, W. 2003. Peregrine falcon restoration in the Rocky Mountains/Northwest. In *Return of the peregrine, a North American saga of tenacity and teamwork,* ed. T. J. Cade and W. Burnham. Boise, Idaho: Peregrine Fund.

Burnham, W., and T. J. Cade. 2003. The Endangered Species Act, the U.S. Fish and Wildlife Service, and peregrine falcon restoration. In *Return of the peregrine, a North American saga of tenacity and teamwork*, ed. T. J. Cade and W. Burnham. Boise, Idaho: Peregrine Fund.

Burnham, W. A. 1997. *A fascination with falcons*. Blaine, Wash.: Hancock House.

Burnham, W. A., and T. J. Cade. 1995. Raptor populations: The basis for their management. *Transactions of the 60th North American Wildlife and Natural Resources Conference* 60:115–30.

Butcher, R. D., 2003. *America's national wildlife refuges: A complete guide*. Lanham, Md.: Roberts Rinehart.

Cade, T. J. 1998. Delisting the peregrine falcon: Management and mismanagement under the Endangered Species Act. *Transactions of the 63rd North American Wildlife and Natural Resources Conference* 63:475–85.

———. 2003. Starting the Peregrine Fund at Cornell University and eastern reintroduction. In *Return of the peregrine, a North American saga of tenacity and teamwork*, ed. T. J. Cade and W. Burnham. Boise, Idaho: Peregrine Fund.

Cade, T. J., J. L. Lincer, C. M. White, D. G. Roseneau, and L. G. Swartz. 1971. DDE residues and eggshell changes in Alaska falcons and hawks. *Science* 172:955–57.

Cade, T. J., S. A. H. Osborn, W. G. Hunt, and C. P. Woods. 2004. Commentary on released California condors, *Gymnogyps californianus*, in Arizona. In *Worldwide raptors*, ed. R. D. Chancellor and B. U. Meyburg. Proceedings conference 6 of the World Working Group on Birds of Prey and Owls. Budapest, Hungary.

CALFED Bay-Delta Program. 2003. *About CALFED*. http://calwater.ca.gov/About-Calfed/CALFEDProgram.shtml (accessed July 5, 2005).

California Coastal Conservancy. 2000a. About the Coastal Conservancy. http://www.coastalconservancy.ca.gov/About/about.htm (accessed August 4, 2000).

———. 2000b. Coastal Conservancy programs. http://www.coastalconservancy.ca.gov/Programs/pandp.htm (accessed August 4, 2000).

California Department of Fish and Game. 2003. *Klamath River fish kill: Preliminary analysis of contributing factors*. Redding: California Department of Fish and Game, Northern California–North Coast Region.

California Native Plant Society v. Lujan. 1991. Civ. S 91-0038 EJG-JFM (U.S. District Court for the Eastern District of California).

California Resources Agency. 1999. *Private land programs and incentives*. Sacramento: California Department of Fish and Game. See also http://www.dfg.ca.gov/ (accessed December 1999).

———. 2000. *Timber tax fish (related) incentives for sustainable habitat*. http://www.dfg.ca.gov/timbertax/ttcp_2.html (last visited Nov. 7, 2003).

Callahan, K. 1993. Bioregionalism: Wiser planning for the environment. *Land Use Law and Zoning Digest* 45 (8): 3–9.

Callenbach, E. 1996. *Bring back the buffalo! A sustainable future for America's Great Plains*. Washington, D.C.: Island Press.

Callicott, B. Forthcoming. Explicit and implicit values. In *The Endangered Species Act at thirty: Conserving biodiversity in human-dominated landscapes*, ed. J. M. Scott, D. D. Goble, and F. W. Davis. Washington, D.C.: Island Press.

Carlton, J. T., G. J. Vermeij, D. R. Lindberg, D. A. Carlton, and E. C. Dudley. 1991. The first historical extinction of a marine invertebrate in an ocean basin: The demise of the eelgrass limpet. *Biological Bulletin* 180:72–80.

Carpenter, S. L., and W. J. D. Kennedy. 1988. *Managing public disputes: A practical guide for handling conflict and reaching agreements.* San Francisco: Jossey-Bass.

Carter, J. 1977. Presidential directive on critical habitat. In House Committee on Merchant Marine and Fisheries, Hearings, Endangered species part 1, 95th Congress, 2nd Session. 95–96.

Casey, F. S., S. Schmitz, S. Swinton, and D. Zilberman, eds. 1999. *Flexible incentives for the adoption of environmental technologies in agriculture.* Norwell, Mass.: Kluwer.

Cates, S. A. 1998. Agreements with the U.S. Fish and Wildlife Service and other agencies: Creative approaches to addressing endangered species issues on Indian lands and meeting tribal resource management priorities. Tucson, Ariz.: CLE International.

———. 2003. White Mountain Apache and the ESA. University of Washington, School of Law, May 25.

Cawley, R. M. 1993. *Federal land, western anger: The sagebrush rebellion and environmental politics.* Lawrence: University of Kansas Press.

Cebellos, G., and P. R. Ehrlich. 2002. Mammal population losses and the extinction crisis. *Science* 296:904–7.

Census Bureau. 2000. *Historical national population estimates: July 1, 1900 to July 1, 1999.* http://www.census.gov/popest/archives/1990s/popclockest.txt.

———. 2004a. Home page. http://www.census.gov/ (accessed March 5, 2004).

———. 2004b. *U.S. interim projections by age, sex, race, and Hispanic origin.* http://www.census.gov/ipc/www/usinterimproj/.

Center for Biological Diversity. 2004. *ESA listing petition database.* Tucson, Ariz.

Center for Biological Diversity v. Bureau of Land Management. 2004. CV 03-02509 SI. U.S. District Court for the Northern District of California.

Center for Biological Diversity v. Norton. 2001. CIV 01-2063-JR. U.S. District Court for the District of Columbia.

———. 2003. 240 F. Supp. 2d 1090. U.S. District Court for the District of Arizona.

Center for Biological Diversity v. Sprague. 1998. CV 98-2434 SC. U.S. District Court for the Northern District of California.

Center for Wildlife Law and Defenders of Wildlife. 1996. *Saving biodiversity: A status report on state laws, policies and programs.* Albuquerque: Center for Wildlife Law and Defenders of Wildlife.

———. 1998. *State endangered species acts: Past, present and future.* Albuquerque: Center for Wildlife Law and Defenders of Wildlife.

Cervero, R. 2003. Road expansion, urban growth, and induced travel: A path analysis. *Journal of the American Planning Association* 69:145–63.

Chadwick, D. 1998. Rebirth on the Great Plains. *National Wildlife* 36 (3): 20–29.

Channell, R., and M. V. Lomolino. 2000. Dynamic biogeography and conservation of endangered species. *Nature* 403:84–86.

Cheyenne River Sioux Tribe and National Wildlife Federation. 2001. *Restoring the Prairie, mending the sacred hoop: Prairie conservation and restoration on the Cheyenne River Reservation.* http://216.109.89.116/resourceLibrary/getData.cfm?officeID=F8811202-65BF-0A01-0E19343752DAF7F5&catID=3941FE41-65BF-1173-569E0E2AE7628C6F&pageID=A5D893E9-65BF-1173-5F2C6C9C17946E45.

Chicago Wilderness. 2004. Home page. http://www.chicagowilderness.org/.

Cicin-Sain, B., and R. W. Knecht. 2000. *The future of U.S. ocean policy: Choices for the new century.* Washington, D.C.: Island Press.

CITES (Convention on International Trade in Endangered Species of Wild Fauna and Flora). 1973. 27 U.S.T. 1087, T.I.A.S. No. 8249.

City of San Diego. 2005. *Multiple species conservation program: Plan summary.* http://www.ci.san-diego.ca.us/mscp/plansum.shtml.

Clark, J. A., and E. Harvey. 2002. Assessing multi-species recovery plans under the Endangered Species Act. *Ecological Applications* 12:655–62.

Clark, J. A., J. M. Hoekstra, P. D. Boersma, and P. Kareiva. 2002. Improving U.S. Endangered Species Act recovery plans: Key findings and recommendations of the SCB recovery plan project. *Conservation Biology* 16:1510–19.

Clark, J. R. 1999. Testimony before the Senate Committee on Environment and Public Works, Subcommittee on Fisheries, Wildlife, and Drinking Water on S.1100. Washington, D.C.

Clark, T. W. 1993. Creating and using knowledge for species and ecosystem conservation: Science, organizations, and policy. *Perspectives in Biology and Medicine* 36:497–525.

———. 1996. Appraising threatened species recovery efforts: Practical recommendations. In *Back from the brink: Refining the threatened species recovery process,* ed. S. Stephens and S. Maxwell. New South Wales: Australia Nature Conservation Agency.

———. 1997. *Averting extinction: Reconstructing endangered species recovery.* New Haven, Conn.: Yale University Press.

———. 2001. A course on species and ecosystem conservation: An interdisciplinary approach. In *Species and ecosystem conservation: An interdisciplinary approach,* ed. T. W. Clark, M. Stevenson, K. Ziegelmayer, and M. Rutherford. Bulletin Series 105. New Haven, Conn.: Yale School of Forestry and Environmental Studies.

———. 2002. *The policy process: A practical guide for natural resources professionals.* New Haven, Conn.: Yale University Press.

Clark, T. W., G. N. Backhouse, and R. P. Reading. 1995. Prototyping in endangered species recovery programmes: The eastern barred bandicoot experience. In *People and nature conservation: Perspectives on private land use and endangered species recovery,* ed. A. Bennett, G. N. Backhouse, and T. W. Clark. New South Wales: Australia Nature Conservation Agency.

Clark, T. W., and R. D. Brunner. 1996. Making partnerships work in endangered species conservation: An introduction to the decision process. *Endangered Species Update* 13 (9): 1–5.

Clark, T. W., D. Hinckley, and T. Rich. 1989. *The prairie dog ecosystem: Managing for biological diversity.* Wildlife Technical Bulletin No. 2. Montana Bureau of Land Management.

Clark, T. W., and R. P. Reading. 1994. A professional perspective: Improving problem solving, communication, and effectiveness. In *Endangered species recovery: Finding the lessons, improving the process,* ed. T. W. Clark, R. P. Reading, and A. L. Clarke. Washington, D.C.: Island Press.

Clark, T. W., M. Stevenson, K. Ziegelmayer, and M. B. Rutherford, eds. 2001. *Species and ecosystem conservation: An interdisciplinary approach.* Bulletin Series 105. New Haven, Conn.: Yale School of Forestry and Environmental Studies.

Clark, T. W., and R. L. Wallace. 2002. The dynamics of value interactions in endangered species conservation. In *An interdisciplinary approach to endangered species recovery,* ed. R. Wallace, T. W. Clark, and R. P. Reading. *Endangered Species Update* 19 (4): 1–202.

Clark, T. W., A. R. Willard, and C. M. Cromley, eds. 2000. *Foundations of natural resources policy and management.* New Haven, Conn.: Yale University Press.

Clarren, R. 2004. Dams will stand, salmon be damned. *High Country News.* Oct. 11.

Clifford, F. 1995. Coalition's olive branch saves economy, forest. *Los Angeles Times.* Nov. 15.

Code of Federal Regulations. 50:17.22. Permits for scientific purposes, enhancement of propagation or survival, or for incidental taking.

Coggins, G. C. 1998. Of californicators, quiblings and crazies: Some perils of devolved collaboration. *Chronicle of Community* 2:27–31.

Cohn, J. P., and J. A. Lerner. 2003. *Integrating land use planning and biodiversity.* Washington, D.C.: Defenders of Wildlife.

Cold Mountain v. Garber. 2004. 375 F.3d 884. U.S. Court of Appeals for the 9th Judicial Circuit.

Committee on Rare and Endangered Wildlife Species. 1966. *Rare and endangered fish and wildlife of the United States.* Resource Publication No. 34. Washington, D.C.: Department of the Interior.

Community-Based Collaboratives Research Consortium. 2004. Home page. http://www.cbcrc.org/ (accessed January 4, 2004).

Congressional Research Service. 2003. *South Florida ecosystem restoration and the comprehensive Everglades restoration plan.* Washington, D.C.

Conservation Council for Hawaii v. Lujan. 1990. Civ. 89-953 (ACK) (U.S. District Court for the District of Hawaii).

Conservation Council v. Roseboro Lumber Co. 1995. 50 F.3d 781. U.S. Court of Appeals for the 9th Judicial Circuit.

Convention with Great Britain for the Protection of Migratory Birds. 1916. 39 Stat. 1702, T.S. No. 628.

Conway, W. 1986. The practical difficulties and financial implications of endangered species breeding programs. *International Zoo Yearbook* 24/25:210–19.

Coonan, T. J. 2001. *Recovery plan for island foxes (Urocyon littoralis) on the northern Channel Islands.* Ventura, Calif.: National Park Service, Channel Islands National Park.

Coonan, T. J., and K. Rutz 2003. *Island fox captive breeding program 2002 annual report.* Ventura, Calif.: National Park Service, Channel Islands National Park.

Coope, G. R. 1987. The response of late Quaternary insect communities to sudden climatic changes. In *Organization of communities past and present,* ed. J. H. R. Gee and P. S. Giller. Oxford: Blackwell Scientific.

Coughlin, C., M. Hoben, D. Manskopf, S. Quesada, and J. Wondolleck. 1999. *A systematic assessment of collaborative resource management partnerships.* Ann Arbor: University of Michigan. Also available at http://www.snre.umich.edu/ecomgt/pubs/crmp.htm.

County of San Diego. 2000. Multiple species conservation program. http://www.sandiego.gov/mscp/ (accessed July).

County of Westchester v. Town of Greenwich. 1990. 745 F. Supp. 951. U.S. District Court for the Southern District of New York.

Cowling, R. M., and D. Richardson 1995. *Fynbos: South Africa's unique floral kingdom.* Vlaeberg, South Africa: Fernwood Press.

Cowling, R. M., G. E. Russell, M. T. Hoffman, and C. Hilton-Taylor. 1989. Patterns of plant species diversity in southern Africa. In *Biotic diversity in southern Africa:*

Concepts and conservation, ed. B. J. Huntley. Cape Town, South Africa: Oxford University Press.

Cox, C., R. Kautz, M. MacLaughlin, and T. Gilbert. 1994. *Closing the gaps in Florida's wildlife habitat conservation system.* Tallahassee: Florida Game and Freshwater Fish Commission.

Cox, G. W. 1999. *Alien species in North America and Hawaii: Impacts on natural systems.* Washington, D.C.: Island Press.

Cunningham, L. L. 1981. Applying Lasswell's concepts in field situations: Diagnostic and prescriptive values. *Educational Administrative Quarterly* 17:24–37.

Curtin, C. G. 1993. The evolution of the U.S. National Wildlife Refuge System and the doctrine of compatibility. *Conservation Biology* 7:29–38.

Czech, B. Forthcoming. The capacity of the national wildlife refuge system to conserve animal species in the United States. *Conservation Biology.*

Czech, B., P. R. Krausman, and R. Borkhataria. 1998. Social construction, political power, and the allocation of benefits to endangered species. *Conservation Biology* 12:1103–12.

Daft, R. L. 2003. *Organization theory and design.* 8th ed. Saint Paul: South-Western College Publishing.

Dail v. York County. 2000. 528 S.E.2d 447. Virginia Supreme Court.

Daily, G. C. 1997. *Nature's services: Societal dependence on natural ecosystems.* Washington, D.C.: Island Press.

Darrin, T. F. 2000. Designating critical habitat under the Endangered Species Act: Habitat protection versus agency discretion. *Harvard Environmental Law Review* 24:209–35.

Davis, M. B. 1983. Holocene vegetational history of the eastern United States. In *Late-quaternary environments of the United States*, ed. H. E. Wright Jr. Minneapolis: University of Minnesota Press.

Davis, T. 2001. Healing the Gila. *High Country News.* 1, 8–10. October 22.

Davis, W. H., and P. Roca. 1995. *Bluebirds and their survival.* Lexington: University Press of Kentucky.

Dawn Chorus. 2001. Letters to the editor. 46:12. http://www.123.co.nz/tiri/Newsletters/Newsletter46.pdf.

DeBonis, C., Jr. 2000. Development approvals within critical habitat and cactus ferruginous pygmy-owl Survey Zone 1. Pima County Public Works Development Service: Tucson, AZ. December 15.

Defenders of Wildlife. 1998. *Oregon's living landscape: Strategies and opportunities to conserve biodiversity.* Lake Oswego, Ore.

———. 2002. *Conservation in America: State government incentives for habitat conservation.* Status report. Lake Oswego, Ore.

Defenders of Wildlife v. Ballard. 1999. CV 97-794 TUC ACM. U.S. District Court for the District of Arizona.

Defenders of Wildlife v. Bernal. 2000. 204 F.3d 920. U.S. Court of Appeals for the 9th Judicial Circuit.

Defenders of Wildlife v. Secretary. 2005. 354 F. Supp. 2d 1156. U.S. District Court for the District of Oregon.

Denton, J. S., S. P. Hitchings, T. J. C. Beebee, and A. Gent. 1997. A recovery program for the natterjack toad (*Bufo calamita*) in Britain. *Conservation Biology* 11:1329–38.

DeShazo, J. R., and J. Freeman. 2003. The congressional competition to control delegated power. *Texas Law Review* 81:1443–520.

Dinerstein, E. 1998. It takes a village. *Zoogoer.* http://natzoo.si.edu/Publications/Zoo Goer/1998/2/ittakesavillage.cfm.

———. 2002. *The return of the unicorns: A success story in the conservation of Asian rhinoceros.* New York: Columbia University Press.

Dingell, J. 1973. Statement. *Congressional Record* 119:30162–3. Reprinted in Senate Committee on Environment and Public Works, 97th Congress, 2d Session, *A legislative history of the Endangered Species Act of 1973, as amended in 1976, 1977, 1978, 1979, and 1980.* Committee Print, 1982.

Dolan v. City of Tigard. 1994. 512 U.S. 374. U.S. Supreme Court.

Doremus, H. 2000a. Delisting endangered species: An aspirational goal, not a realistic expectation. *Environmental Law Reporter* 30:10434–54.

———. 2000b. The rhetoric and reality of nature protection: Toward a new discourse. *Washington and Lee Law Review* 57:11–73.

———. 2001. Adaptive management, the Endangered Species Act, and the institutional challenges of "new age" environmental protection. *Washburn Law Journal* 41:50–89.

———. 2002. Biodiversity and the challenge of saving the ordinary. *Idaho Law Review* 38:325–54.

———. 2004. The purposes, effects, and future of the Endangered Species Act's best available science mandate. *Environmental Law* 34:397–450.

Doremus, H., and J. E. Pagel. 2001. Why listing may be forever: Perspectives on delisting under the U.S. Endangered Species Act. *Conservation Biology* 15:1258–68.

Doremus, H., and A. D. Tarlock. 2003. Fish, farms, and the clash of cultures in the Klamath Basin. *Ecology Law Quarterly* 30:279–350.

Doremus, H. Forthcoming. "Science and the Endangered Species Act." In *The Endangered Species Act at thirty: Conserving biodiversity in the human-dominated landscapes,* ed. J. M. Scott, D. D. Goble, and F. W. Davis. Washington, D.C.: Island Press.

Dorsey, K. 1998. *The dawn of conservation diplomacy: U.S.-Canadian wildlife protection in the progressive era.* Seattle: University of Washington Press.

Doughty, R. 1975. *Feather fashions and bird preservation.* Berkeley: University of California Press.

Dulvy, N. K., Y. Sadovy, and J. D. Reynolds. 2003. Extinction vulnerability in marine populations. *Fish and Fisheries* 4:25–64.

Dunham, A. 1962. *Griggs v. Allegheny County* in perspective: Thirty years of Supreme Court expropriation law. *Supreme Court Review* 63–106.

Dunlap, T. R. 1988. Sport hunting and conservation, 1880–1920. *Environmental History* 12:51–56.

East Contra Costa County Habitat Conservation Plan Association. 2003. Conservation Strategy. Chapter 6 in *Preliminary Draft Conservation Strategy and Alternatives.* http://www.cocohcp.org/downloads/chapter6/Chapter6_1-16-03_final.pdf.

Echeverria, J. D. 2001. No success like failure: The Platte River collaborative watershed planning process. *William and Mary Environmental Law and Policy Review* 25:559–604.

Elliot, W. R. 2000. Conservation of North America cave and karst biota. In *Ecosystems of the world: Subterranean ecosystems,* ed. H. Wilkens, D. C. Culver, and W. F. Humphreys, 665–89. Amsterdam: Elsevier.

Environmental Defense. 1999. *Mitigation banking as an endangered species conservation tool.* November. http://www.environmentaldefense.org/documents/146_mb.pdf.

———. 2004. Safe harbor agreements by date. http://www.environmentaldefense.org/article.cfm?ContentID=403.

Epstein, R. A. 1996. A conceptual approach to zoning: What's wrong with Euclid. *New York University Environmental Law Journal* 5:277–91.

ESA (Endangered Species Act). 1973. Public Law No. 93-205, 87 *U.S. Statutes at Large* 884 (Dec. 23, 1973) (codified as amended at 16 U.S.C. secs. 1531–43).

ESCA (Endangered Species Conservation Act). 1969. Public Law No. 91-135, 83 *U.S. Statutes at Large* 275 (repealed by ESA sec. 14).

ESPA (Endangered Species Preservation Act). 1966. Public Law No. 89-669, 80 *U.S. Statutes at Large* 926 (repealed by ESA sec. 14).

Estes, J. A., and B. B. Hatfield. 1998. *Population status of the California sea otter.* Ventura, Calif.: Biological Resources Division, U.S. Geological Survey/U.S. Fish and Wildlife Service.

Estes, J. A., and G. R. VanBlaricom. 1985. Sea otters and shellfisheries. In *Marine mammals and fisheries*, ed. R. Beverton, D. Lavigne, and J. Beddington. London: Allen and Unwin.

Executive Order 12291. 1981. *Federal Register* 46:13193–98.

Farber, D. A. 1999. Taking slippage seriously: Noncompliance and creative compliance in environmental law. *Harvard Environmental Law Review* 23:297–326.

Fausold, C. J., and R. L. Lilieholm. 1999. The economic value of open space: A review and synthesis. *Environmental Management* 23:307–20.

Field Talk. 2000. *Habitat conservation plan is no-win for Kern farmers.* http://www.rinconpublishing.com/white_papers/Valley_Floor_HCP.htm.

Fischer, H. 1995. *Wolf wars: The remarkable inside story of the restoration of wolves to Yellowstone.* Helena, Mont.: Falcon Press.

Fischer, H., and W. Hudson, eds. 1993. *Building economic incentives into the Endangered Species Act.* Washington, D.C.: Defenders of Wildlife.

Fischman, R. L. 2003. *The national wildlife refuges: Coordinating a conservation system through law.* Washington, D.C.: Island Press.

Fischman, R. L., and J. Hall-Rivera. 2002. A lesson for conservation from pollution control law: Cooperative federalism for recovery under the Endangered Species Act. *Columbia Journal of Environmental Law* 27:45–172.

Fisher, R., W. Ury, and B. Patton. 1991. *Getting to yes: Negotiating agreement without giving in.* 2nd ed. New York: Penguin Books.

Fjetland, C. A. 1999. Native trout in a native land. Unpublished report.

Florida Natural Areas Inventory. 2004. *Summary of Florida conservation lands.* Tallahassee, Fla.

———. 2005. Home page. http://www.fnai.org/.

Fordham, S. 2001. Editorial. *Dawn Chorus* 45:2. http://www.123.co.nz/tiri/Newsletters/Newsletter45.pdf.

Forest Guardians v. U.S. Forest Service. 1997. CV 97-2562-PHX-SMM. U.S. District Court for the District of Arizona.

Forman, R. T. T., D. Sperling, J. A. Bissonette, A. P. Clevenger, C. D. Cutshall, V. H. Dale, L. Fahrig, R. France, C. R. Goldman, K. Heanue, J. A. Jones, F. J. Swanson, T. Turrentine, and T. C. Winter. 2003. *Road ecology: Science and solutions.* Washington, D.C.: Island Press.

Foster Creek Conservation District. 2000. *Habitat conservation plan.* http://www.fostercreek.net/hcpmissn.html.

Fox, J., A. Davis, B. Thompson, G. C. Daily, and A. Nino-Murcia. Forthcoming. Conservation banking. In *The Endangered Species Act at thirty: Conserving biodiversity in human-dominated landscapes*, ed. J. M. Scott, D. D. Goble, and F. W. Davis. Washington, D.C.: Island Press.

Frazer, G. 2003. Affidavit of Assistant Director for Endangered Species, U.S. Fish and Wildlife Service. In *Defenders of Wildlife v. Norton.* CIV 02-00165-M-DWM. U.S. District Court for the District of Columbia.

Freyfogle, E. T. 1993. Ownership and ecology. *Case Western Reserve Law Review* 43:1269–97.

———. 2004. *Battling for Leopold's legacy*. Washington, D.C.: Georgetown Environmental Law and Policy Institute.

Friends of the Swainson's Hawk. 2003. *Proposed 2003 Natomas Basin habitat conservation plan: A plan to eliminate endangered species in Natomas Basin*. May 7. http://www.swainsonshawk.org/nbhcp5.7.pdf.

Fund for Animals v. Clark. 1998. 27 F. Supp. 2d 8. U.S. District Court for the District of Columbia.

Fund for Animals v. Lujan. 1991. 794 F. Supp. 1015. U.S. District Court for the District of Montana. *Affirmed*. 1992, 962 F.2d 1391. U.S. Court of Appeals for the 9th Judicial Circuit.

———. 1992. Civ. No. 92-800 (GAG). U.S. District Court for the District of Columbia.

Gaby, R., M. P. McMahon, F. J. Mazzoti, W. N. Gillies, and J. R. Wilcox. 1985. Ecology of a population of *Crocodylus acutus* at a power plant site in Florida. *Journal of Herpetology* 19:189–98.

Gallagher, T. 2005. *The grail bird*. New York: Houghton Mifflin.

GAO (U.S. General Accounting Office). 1979. *Endangered species: A controversial issue needing resolution*. Report no. CED-79-65. Washington, D.C.

———. 1993. *Endangered species: Factors associated with delayed listing decisions*. Report no. GAO/RCED-93-152. Washington, D.C.

———. 1994a. *National Wildlife Refuge System contributions being made to endangered species recovery*. Report no. GAO/RCED-95-7. Washington, D.C.

———. 1994b. *Endangered Species Act: Information on species protection on nonfederal lands*. Report no. GAO/RCED-95-16. Washington, D.C.

———. 2000. *Comprehensive Everglades restoration plan: Additional water quality projects may be needed and could increase costs*. Report no. RCED-00-235. Washington, D.C.

———. 2002. *Columbia River Basin salmon and steelhead: Federal agencies' recovery responsibilities, expenditures, and actions*. Report no. GAO-02-612. Washington, D.C.

———. 2003. *Endangered species: Fish and Wildlife Service uses best available science to make listing decisions, but additional guidance needed for critical habitat designations*. Report no. GAO-03-803. Washington, D.C.

GDF Realty Investments Ltd v. Department of Interior. 2003. 326 F.3d 622. U.S. Court of Appeals for the 5th Judicial Circuit.

Gergely, K., J. M. Scott, and D. D. Goble. 2000. A new direction for the U.S. national wildlife refuges: The National Wildlife Refuge System Improvement Act of 1997. *Natural Areas Journal* 20:107–18.

Germano, D. J., G. B. Rathbun, and L. R. Saslaw. 2001. Managing exotic grasses and conserving declining species. *Wildlife Society Bulletin* 29:551–59.

Getches, D. H. 1997. Colorado River governance: Sharing federal authority as an incentive to create a new institution. *University of Colorado Law Review* 68:573–658.

————. 2001. The metamorphosis of western water policy: Have federal laws and local decisions eclipsed the states' role? *Stanford Environmental Law Journal* 20:3–72.

Gibbs v. Babbitt. 2001. 214 F.3d 483. U.S. Court of Appeals for the 4th Judicial Circuit. *certiorari denied sub nomine, Gibbs v. Norton.* 532 U.S. 1145. U.S. Supreme Court.

Gifford Pinchot Task Force v. United States Fish and Wildlife Service. 2004. 378 F.3d 1059. U.S. Court of Appeals for the 9th Judicial Circuit.

Goble, D. D. 1992. Of wolves and welfare ranching. *Harvard Environmental Law Review* 16:101–27.

————. 2002. Experimental populations: Reintroducing the missing parts. In *Endangered Species Act: Law, policy, and perspectives*, ed. D. C. Baur and W. R. Irvin, 379–99. Chicago: ABA.

————. Forthcoming. Protection of at-risk species. In *The Endangered Species Act at thirty: Conserving biodiversity in human-dominated landscapes*, ed. J. M. Scott, D. D. Goble, and F. W. Davis. Washington, D.C.: Island Press.

Goble, D. D., and E. T. Freyfogle. 2002. *Wildlife law: Cases and materials.* New York: Foundation Press.

Goble, D. D., S. M. George, K. Mazaika, J. M. Scott, and J. Karl. 1999. Local and national protection of endangered species: An assessment. *Environmental Science and Policy* 2:43–59.

Goldstein, B. D., and R. S. Carruth. 2003. Implications of the precautionary principle for environmental regulation in the United States: Examples from the control of hazardous air pollutants in the 1990 Clean Air Amendments. *Law and Contemporary Problems* 66:247–61.

Goodman, E. 2000. Protecting habitat for off-reservation tribal hunting fishing rights: Tribal co-management as a reserved right. *Environmental Law* 30:279–361.

Gray, B. 1989. *Collaborating: Finding common ground for multiparty problems.* San Francisco: Jossey-Bass.

Greenpeace v. National Marine Fisheries Service. 2002. CIV 98-492Z. U.S. District Court for the Western District of Washington.

Greenwald, N. D. 1998. *Betrayal of an endangered species: Status and management of the southwestern willow flycatcher.* Tucson, Ariz.: Center for Biological Diversity. http://www.biologicaldiversity.org/swcbd/Programs/science/swwfr1.htm.

Griggs v. Allegheny County. 1962. 369 U.S. 84. U.S. Supreme Court.

Groombridge, B., and M. D. Jenkins. 2002. *World atlas of biodiversity: Earth's living resources in the 21st century.* Berkeley: University of California Press.

Groves, C. R. 2003. *Drafting a conservation blueprint: A practitioner's guide to planning for biodiversity.* Washington, D.C.: Island Press.

Groves, C. R., D. B. Jensen, L. L. Valutis, R. H. Redford, M. L. Shaffer, J. M. Scott, J. V. Baumgartner, J. V. Higgins, M. W. Beck, and M. G. Anderson. 2002. Planning for biodiversity conservation: Putting conservation science into practice. *BioScience* 52:499–512.

Groves, C. R., L. S. Kutner, D. M. Stoms, M. Murray, J. M. Scott, M. Schafale, A. S. Weakley, and R. L. Pressey. 2000. Owning up to our responsibilities: Who owns lands important for biodiversity? In *Precious heritage: The status of biodiversity in the United States*, ed. B. A. Stein, L. S. Kutner, and J. S. Adams. New York: Oxford University Press.

Grumbine, R. E. 1994. What is ecosystem management? *Conservation Biology* 8:1–12.

Gunderson, L. H., C. S. Holling, and S. S. Light. 1994. *Barriers and bridges to the renewal of ecosystems and institutions.* New York: Columbia University Press.

Gustaitis, R. 2001. Secrets of San Bruno Mountain. *California Coast and Ocean* 17 (1). See also http://www.coastalconservancy.ca.gov/coast&ocean/spring2001/pages/two.htm.

Hagen, D. A., J. W. Vincent, and P. G. Welle. 1992. Benefits of preserving old-growth forests and the spotted owl. *Contemporary Economic Policy* 10:13–26.

Hanley, N., J. F. Shogren, and B. White. 1997. *Environmental economics: In theory and practice*. New York: Oxford University Press.

Harding, E. K., E. E. Crone, B. D. Elderd, J. M. Hoekstra, A. J. McKerrow, J. D. Perrine, J. Regetz, L. J. Rissler, A. G. Stanley, E. L. Walters, and NCEAS Habitat Conservation Plan Working Group. 2001. The scientific foundations of habitat conservation plans: A quantitative assessment. *Conservation Biology* 15:488–500.

Hardy, R., and F. Wendell. 1982. A status report on California shellfish fisheries. In *Social science perspectives of managing conflicts between marine mammals and fisheries*, ed. B. Cicin-Sain, P. M. Griffin, and J. B. Richards. Santa Barbara: Marine Science Institute, University of California.

Headwaters, Inc. v. Talent Irrigation District. 2001. 243 F.3d 526. U.S. Court of Appeals for the 9th Judicial Circuit.

Heal, G. Forthcoming. Arbitrage and options. In *The Endangered Species Act at thirty: Conserving biodiversity in human-dominated landscapes*, ed. J. M. Scott, D. D. Goble, and F. W. Davis. Washington, D.C.: Island Press.

Henderson, E. 1982. *United States v. Washington II*: Toward a judicial standard of tribal status. *Arizona Law Review* 24:179–94.

Hicks, E. P. 2000. Designation without conservation: The conflict between the Endangered Species Act and its implementing regulations. *Virginia Environmental Law Journal* 2000:491–523.

Hobday, A. J., and M. J. Tegner. 2000. *Status review of white abalone (Haliotis sorenseni) throughout its range in California and Mexico.* Silver Spring, Md.: NOAA.

Hoben, M. 1999. Clark County habitat conservation planning process. Chapter 7 in *A systematic assessment of collaborative resource management partnerships.* http://www.snre.umich.edu/ecomgt//pubs/crmp/clarkcounty.PDF.

Hodel v. Virginia Surface Mining and Reclamation Association. 1981. 452 U.S. 314. U.S. Supreme Court.

Hoekstra, J. M., J. A. Clark, W. F. Fagan, and P. D. Boersma. 2002a. A comprehensive review of Endangered Species Act recovery plans. *Ecological Applications* 12:630–40.

Hoekstra, J. M., W. F. Fagan, and J. E. Bradley. 2002b. A critical role for critical habitat in the recovery planning process? Not yet. *Ecological Applications* 12:701–7.

Holling, C. S. 1978. *Adaptive environmental assessment and management.* London: John Wiley.

Hood, L. C. 1998. *Frayed safety-nets: Conservation planning under the Endangered Species Act.* Washington, D.C.: Defenders of Wildlife.

Hoogland, J. L. 1995. *The black-tailed prairie dog: Social life of a burrowing mammal.* Chicago: University of Chicago Press.

Hornaday, W. T. 1889. *The extermination of the American bison.* Repr., Washington, D.C.: Smithsonian Institution Press, 2002.

Hornstein, D. T. 1982. Indian fishing rights return to spawn: Toward environmental protection of treaty fisheries. *Oregon Law Review* 61:93–122.

Houck, O. A. 1993. The Endangered Species Act and its implementation by the U.S. Departments of Interior and Commerce. *University of Colorado Law Review* 64:277–370.

Hughes, J. B., G. C. Daily, and P. R. Ehrlich. 1997. Population diversity: Its extent and extinction. *Science* 278:689–92.

Hutchings, J. A. 2001. Conservation biology of marine fishes: Perceptions and caveats regarding assignment of extinction risk. *Canadian Journal of Fisheries and Aquatic Sciences* 58:108–21.

———. 2002. Life histories of fish. In *Handbook of Fish and Fisheries*, vol. 1., ed. P. J. B. Hart and J. D. Reynolds, 149–74. Oxford: Blackwell.

Idaho Code. 2005. Albany, N.Y.: Mathew Bender.

Idaho House Bill 294. 2003. http://www3.state.id.us/oasis/2003/H0294.html (accessed September 12, 2004).

Idaho Legislative Wolf Oversight Committee. 2002. *Idaho wolf conservation and management plan.* March. http://fishandgame.idaho.gov/cms/wildlife/wolves/wolf_plan.pdf.

Innes, R. 2000. Takings and compensation for private lands. *Land Economics* 76:195–212.

Innes, R., S. Polasky, and J. Tschirhart. 1998. Takings, compensation and endangered species protection on private lands. *Journal of Economic Perspectives* 12 (3): 35–52.

In re Kisiel. 2001. 772 A.2d 135. Vermont Supreme Court.

Intertribal Bison Cooperative. 2003. Home page. http://www.intertribalbison.org/ (accessed June 10, 2003).

IUCN (International Union for the Conservation of Nature). 2003. *2003 IUCN Red List of Threatened Species.* http://www.redlist.org/ (accessed October 2003).

Jackson, J. B. C., M. X. Kirby, W. H. Berger, K. A. Bjorndal, L. W. Botsford, B. J. Bourque, R. H. Bradbury, R. Cooke, J. Erlandson, J. A. Estes, T. P. Hughes, S. Kidwell, C. B. Lange, H. S. Lenihan, J. M. Pandolfi, C. H. Peterson, R. S. Steneck, M. J. Tegner, and R. R. Warner. 2001. Historical overfishing and the recent collapse of coastal ecosystems. *Science* 293:629–38.

Jenny, J. P. 2003. Turning away from extinction. *Privatization Watch* 319:4–5.

Jenny, J. P., W. Heinrich, A. Montoya, B. Mutch, C. Sandfort, and G. Hunt. 2004. Progress in restoring the aplomado falcon to southern Texas. *Wildlife Society Bulletin* 32:276–85.

Jewell, S. 2000. Multi-species recovery plans. *Endangered Species Bulletin* 25:30–31.

Kareiva, P., S. Andelman, D. Doak, B. Elderd, M. Groom, J. Hoekstra, L. Hood, F. James, J. Lamoreux, G. LeBuhn, C. McCulloch, J. Regetz, L. Savage, M. Ruckelshaus, D. Skelly, H. Wilbur, K. Zamudio, and the Habitat Conservation Plan Working Group of the National Center for Ecological Analysis and Synthesis (NCEAS). 1998. *Using science in habitat conservation plans.* Report of the American Institute of Biological Sciences, Washington, D.C., and the NCEAS, Santa Barbara, Calif..

Karno, V. 1991. Protection of endangered gorillas and chimpanzees in international trade: Can CITES help? *Hastings International and Comparative Law Review* 14:989–1016.

Katzen, P. E. 2000. Tribal rights to protect the fishery habitat necessary to exercise the treaty right of taking fish: A case law overview. 13th Annual Western Regional Indian Law Symposium. Seattle. September 14–15.

Kautz, R. S., and J. A. Cox. 2001. Strategic habitats for biodiversity conservation in Florida. *Conservation Biology* 15:55–77.

Keiter, R. B., and P. H. Froelicher. 1993. Bison, brucellosis and law in the greater Yellowstone ecosystem. *Land and Water Law Review* 28:1–75.

Kepler, C. B., and J. M. Scott. 1990. Notes on distribution of the endangered Hawaiian hoary bat, 1964–1983. *Elepio* 50:59–64.

Keystone Center. 1995. *Dialogue on incentives to protect endangered species on private lands*. Keystone, Colo.

Kiff, L. F. 1980. Historical changes in resident populations of California islands raptors. In *The California islands: Proceedings of a multidisciplinary symposium*, ed. D. M. Power. Santa Barbara, Calif.: Santa Barbara Museum of Natural History.

Kiff, L. F., D. B. Peakall, and S. R. Wilbur. 1979. Recent changes in California condor eggshells. *Condor* 81:166–72.

Koch, E. D. 2002. The practice of endangered species conservation on private lands: One federal biologist's experiences. *Idaho Law Review* 38:505–20.

Kohm, K. A., and J. F. Franklin. 1997. Introduction. In *Creating a forestry for the 21st century: The science of ecosystem management*. Washington, D.C.: Island Press.

Kostyack, J. 2001. *NWF v. Babbitt*: Victory for smart growth and imperiled wildlife. *Environmental Law Reporter* 31:10712–18.

Kuehler, C., P. Harrity, A. Lieberman, and M. Kuhn. 1995. Reintroduction of hand-reared 'alala (*Corvus hawaiiensis*) in Hawaii. *Oryx* 29:261–65.

Kuehler, C., M. Kuhn, J. Kuhn, A. Lieberman, N. Harvey, and B. Rideout. 1996. Artificial incubation, hand-rearing, behavior and release of common amakihi (*Hemignathus virens virens*): Surrogate research for restoration of endangered Hawaiian forest birds. *Zoo Biology* 15:541–53.

Kuehler, C., A. Lieberman, P. Harrity, M. Kuhn, J. Kuhn, B. McIlraith, and J. Turner. 2001. Restoration techniques for Hawaiian forest birds: collection of eggs, artificial incubation and hand-rearing of chicks, and release to the wild. *Studies in Avian Biology* 22:354–58.

Kuehler, C., A. Lieberman, P. Oesterle, T. Powers, M. Kuhn, J. Kuhn, J. Y. Nelson, T. Snetsinger, C. Herrman, P. Harrity, E. Tweed, S. Fancy, B. Woodworth, and T. Telfer. 2000. Development of restoration techniques for Hawaiian thrushes: collection of wild eggs, artificial incubation, hand-rearing, captive-breeding and reintroduction to the wild. *Zoo Biology* 19:263–77.

Kysar, D. A., and J. Salzman. 2003. Environmental tribalism. *Minnesota Law Review* 87:1099–138.

Land Trust Alliance. 1998. *Summary of data from the 1998 national land trust census*. Washington, D.C. See also http://www.lta.org/aboutlt/censum.htm.

———. 2005. Home page. http://www.lta.org/.

Lasswell, H. D. 1971. *A pre-view of policy sciences*. New York: American Elsevier Press.

Lasswell, H. D., and M. S. McDougal. 1992. *Jurisprudence for a free society*. The Hague, Netherlands: Kluwer Law International.

Lavender, D. 1992. *Let me be free: The Nez Perce tragedy*. New York: HarperCollins.

League of Wilderness Defenders v. Forsgren. 2002. 309 F.3d 1181. U.S. Court of Appeals for the 9th Judicial Circuit.

Leighton, D. L. 1972. Laboratory observations on the early growth of abalone Haliotis sorenseni and the effect of temperature on larval development and settling success. *U.S. National Marine Fisheries Service Fishery Bulletin* 70:373–81.

Leopold, A. 1936. Threatened species: A proposal to the Wildlife Conference for an inventory of the needs of near-extinct birds and animals. *American Forests* 42:116–19. Reprinted in *The River of the Mother of God and Other Essays*, ed. S. L. Flader and J. B. Callicott. Madison: University of Wisconsin Press. 1991.

————. 1949. The land ethic. In *A Sand County Almanac* 201–26. New York: Oxford University Press.

Leshy, J. D. 2001. The Babbitt legacy at the Department of the Interior: A preliminary view. *Environmental Law* 31:199–227.

Lester, J. P. 1990. A new federalism: Environmental policy in the states. In *Environmental policy in the 1990s: Toward a new agenda*, ed. N. J. Vig, and M. E. Draft, 59–79. Washington, D.C.: CQ Press.

Levinson, A. 1996. Why oppose TDRs?: Transferable developmental rights can increase overall development. *Regional Science and Urban Economics* 27:283–96.

Lewis, J. C. 1995. Whooping crane (*Grus americana*). In *The birds of North America*, No. 153, ed. A. Poole and F. Gill. Philadelphia: Academy of Natural Sciences and American Ornithologists Union.

Lewiston Morning Tribune. 1999. Nez Perce honored for gray wolf recovery. October 9.

Libby, L., ed. 1998. *The performance of state programs for farmland retention: Proceedings*. Columbus: Ohio State University Press.

Lindholm, J., and B. Barr. 2001. Comparison of marine and terrestrial protected areas under federal jurisdiction in the United States. *Conservation Biology* 15:1441–44.

Lomolino, M. Forthcoming. Space-time and conservation biogeography. In *The Endangered Species Act at thirty: Conserving biodiversity in human-dominated landscapes*, ed. J. M. Scott, D. D. Goble, and F. W. Davis. Washington, D.C.: Island Press.

Lomolino, M. V., and R. Channell. 1995. Splendid isolation: Patterns of range collapse in endangered mammals. *Journal of Mammalogy* 76:335–47.

Loomis, J. B., and D. S. White. 1996. Economic benefits of rare and endangered species: Summary and meta-analysis. *Ecological Economics* 18:197–206.

Loretto v. Teleprompter Manhattan CATV Corp. 1982. 458 U.S. 419. U.S. Supreme Court.

Loucks, B. 2003. *Testimony for field hearing*. http://epw.senate.gov/108th/Loucks_082603.htm.

Love, M. S., M. Yoklavich, and L. K. Thorsteinson. 2002. *The rockfishes of the northeast Pacific*. Berkeley: University of California Press.

Lucas v. South Carolina Coastal Council. 1992. 505 U.S. 1003. U.S. Supreme Court. *On remand*, 1992. 424 S.E.2d 484. South Carolina Supreme Court.

Luce, R. J. 2003. A multi-state conservation plan for the black-tailed prairie dog, *Cynomys ludovicianus*, in the United States, an addendum to the black-tailed prairie dog conservation assessment and strategy. Sierra Vista, Ariz.: Prairie Dog Conservation Team.

MacArthur, R. H., and E. O. Wilson. 1963. An equilibrium theory of insular zoogeography. *Evolution* 17:373–87.

————. 1967. *The theory of island biogeography*. Princeton, N.J.: Princeton University Press.

MacCall, A. D., and X. He. 2002. *Status review of the southern stock of Bocaccio (*Sebastes paucispinis*)*. Santa Cruz, Calif.: NOAA.

Mace, G. M., and R. Lande. 1991. Assessing extinction threats: Towards a reevaluation of IUCN threatened species categories. *Conservation Biology* 5:148–57.

Mack, C. M., and J. Holyan. 2003. *Idaho wolf recovery program: Restoration and management of gray wolves in central Idaho: Progress Report 2002*. Lapwai, Idaho: Nez Perce Tribe, Department of Wildlife Management.

MacNaughton, A. L., and J. Folk-Williams. 2003. Engaging stakeholders for sustainable water resource solutions. *Natural Resources and Environment* 19 (3): 36–40.

Malakoff, D. 1997. Extinction on the high seas. *Science* 277:486–88.

Mank, B. C. 2002. Protecting intrastate threatened species: Does the Endangered Species Act encroach on traditional state authority and exceed the outer limits of the commerce clause? *Georgia Law Review* 36:723–95.

Mann, C., and M. Plummer. 1995. *Noah's choice: The future of endangered species.* New York: Knopf.

Mannan, R. W., and C. W. Boal. 2000. Home range characteristics and habitat selection of male Cooper's hawks in an urban environment. *Wilson Bulletin* 112:21–27.

Marbled Murrelet v. Babbitt. 1996. 83 F.3d 1060. U.S. Court of Appeals for the 9th Judicial Circuit.

Margules, C. R., and R. L. Pressey. 2000. Systematic conservation planning. *Nature* 405:243–52.

Massachusetts Division of Fisheries and Wildlife. 2001. *BioMap: Guiding land conservation for biodiversity in Massachusetts.* Westborough, Mass.: Commonwealth of Massachusetts.

Master, L. L., B. A. Stein, L. S. Kutner, and G. A. Hammerson. 2000. Vanishing assets: Conservation status of U.S. species. In *Precious heritage: The status of biodiversity in the United States*, ed. B. A. Stein, L. S. Kutner, and J. S. Adams. New York: Oxford University Press.

Mathews, A. 1992. *Where the buffalo roam.* New York: Grove Weidenfeld.

May, R. M. 1994. Biological diversity: Differences between land and sea. *Philosophical Transactions of the Royal Society of London Biological Sciences* 343:105–11.

McCloskey, M. 1996. The skeptic: Collaboration has its limits. *High Country News.* May.

McHenry, M. G. 2003. The worst of times: A tale of two fishes in the Klamath Basin. *Environmental Law* 33:1019–58.

McKinney, M. L. 1999. High rates of extinction and threat in poorly studied taxa. *Conservation Biology* 13:1273–81.

McMillan, M., and D. Wilcove. 1994. Gone but not forgotten: Why have species protected by the Endangered Species Act become extinct? *Endangered Species UPDATE* 11(11):5–6.

McNamee, T. 1997. *The return of the wolf to Yellowstone.* New York: Henry Holt.

McNulty, F. 1966. *The whooping crane: The bird that defies extinction.* New York: E. P. Dutton.

Metrick, A., and M. L. Weitzman. 1996. Patterns of behavior in endangered species preservation. *Land Economics* 72:1–16.

Meyer, S. M. 1998. The economic impact of the Endangered Species Act on the housing and real estate markets. *New York University Environmental Law Journal* 6:450–79.

Meyers, G. D. 1988. *United States v. Washington* (Phase II) revisited: Establishing an environmental servitude protecting treaty fishing rights. *Oregon Law Review* 67:771–97.

Miccosukee Indian Tribe. 2003. Miccosukee Tribe of Indians of Florida. http://www.miccosukee.com/tribe.html (accessed June 18, 2003).

Michigan Compiled Laws Annotated. Eagan, MN: West Group.

Miller, A. J. 1999. Transferable development rights in the constitutional landscape: Has *Penn Central* failed to weather the storm? *Natural Resources Journal* 39:459–516.

Miller, B., R. P. Reading, and S. Forrest. 1996. *Prairie night: Black-footed ferrets and the recovery of endangered species.* Washington, D.C.: Smithsonian Institution Press.

Miller, J. K., J. M. Scott, C. R. Miller, and L. P. Waits. 2002. The Endangered Species Act: Dollars and sense. *BioScience* 52:163–68.

Minot Daily News. 2003. Region in focus: Three affiliated tribes to sell bison products in the area. Oct. 13.

Missoulian 2003. Tribal control of National Bison Range unlikely. October 17.

Monson, P.C. 1982. *United States v. Washington* (phase II): The Indian fishing conflict moves upstream. *Environmental Law* 12:469–503.

Montoya, A. B., P. J. Zwank, and M. Cardenas. 1997. Breeding biology of aplomado falcons in desert grasslands of Chihuahua, Mexico. *Journal of Field Ornithology* 68:135–43.

Moore, C. 1996. *The mediation process: Practical strategies for managing conflict.* San Francisco: Jossey-Bass.

Moreno, P., and D. Lentz. 2003. *Affirming the effectiveness of outreach, education and voluntary participation in the Wisconsin Karner blue butterfly habitat conservation plan: A 3-year review report to the Fish and Wildlife Service.* Madison: Bureau of Forestry, Wisconsin Department of Natural Resources. See also http://dnr.wi.gov/org/land/forestry/karner/.

Musick, J. A., M. M. Harbin, S. A. Berkeley, G. H. Burgess, A. Eklund, L. Findley, R. G. Gilmore, J. T. Golden, D. S. Ha, G. R. Huntsman, J. C. McGovern, S. J. Parker, S. G. Poss, E. Sala, T. W. Schmidt, G. R. Sedberry, H. Weeks, and S. G. Wright. 2000. Marine, estuarine, and diadromous fish stocks at risk of extinction in North America (exclusive of Pacific salmonids). *Fisheries* 25:6–30.

Muth, R., and J. M. Bolland. 1983. Social context: A key to effective problem solving. *Planning and Change* 14:214–25.

Myers, R. A., K. G. Bowen, and N. J. Barrowman. 1999. Maximum reproductive rate of fish at low population sizes. *Canadian Journal of Fisheries and Aquatic Sciences* 56:2404–19.

Naeem, S., and C. Jouseau. Forthcoming. Preserving ecosystem functions. In *The Endangered Species Act at thirty: Conserving biodiversity in human-dominated landscapes,* ed. J. M. Scott, D. D. Goble, and F. W. Davis. Washington, D.C.: Island Press.

Naeem, S., C. Moritz, and R. Waples. Forthcoming. Preserving nature. In *The Endangered Species Act at thirty: Conserving biodiversity in human-dominated landscapes,* ed. J. M. Scott, D. D. Goble, and F. W. Davis. Washington, D.C.: Island Press.

Nagle, J. C. 1998a. Playing Noah. *Minnesota Law Review* 82:1171–260.

———. 1998b. The commerce clause meets the Delhi Sands flower-loving fly. *Michigan Law Review* 97:174–215.

Nagle, J .C., and J. B. Ruhl. 2002. *The law of biodiversity and ecosystem management.* New York: Foundation Press.

National Association of Home Builders v. Babbitt. 1997. 130 F.3d 1041. U.S. Court of Appeals for the District of Columbia Circuit. *certiorari denied,* 1998. 524 U.S. 937. U.S. Supreme Court.

National Association of Home Builders v. Norton. 2003. 340 F.3d 835. U.S. Court of Appeals for the 9th Judicial Circuit.

National Governors Association. 2001. *Private lands, public benefits: Principles for advancing working lands conservation.* Washington, D.C.: National Governers Association, Center for Best Practices. Also available at http://www.nga.org/cda/files/01022PRIVATELANDS.pdf.

National Research Council. 1993. *Setting priorities for land conservation.* Washington, D.C.: National Academy Press.

———. 1995. *Science and the Endangered Species Act.* Washington, D.C.: National Academy Press.

———. 1998. *Brucellosis in the greater Yellowstone area.* Washington, D.C.: National Academy Press.

———. 2002. *Interim report on scientific evaluation of biological opinions on endangered and threatened fishes in the Klamath River Basin.* Washington, D.C.: National Academy Press.

———. 2003. *Endangered and threatened fishes in the Klamath River Basin: Causes of decline and strategies for recovery.* Prepublication copy. Washington, D.C.: National Academy Press.

———. 2004a. *Endangered and threatened fishes in the Klamath River Basin: Causes of decline and strategies for recovery.* Washington, D.C.: National Academy Press.

———. 2004b. *Endangered and threatened species of the Platte River.* Washington, D.C.: National Academy Press.

———. 2004c. *Atlantic salmon in Maine.* Washington, D.C.: National Academy Press.

———. 2004d. *Managing the Columbia River: Instream flows, water withdrawals, and salmon survival.* Washington, D.C.: National Academy Press.

National Wilderness Institute. 1994. Endangered species blueprint. *NWI Resource* 5 (1): 1–20.

National Wildlife Federation. 1998a. Wolf spirit NWF priority: Nez Perce Indians saving gray wolves. *National Wildlife.* August.

———. 1998b. Petition for rule listing the black-tailed prairie dog (*Cynomys ludovicianus*) as threatened throughout its range. Denver: USFWS, Region 6.

———. 2004. *Backyard wildlife habitat.* http://www.nwf.org/backyardwildlifehabitat/.

National Wildlife Federation v. Babbitt. 2001. 128 F. Supp. 2d 1274. U.S. District Court for the Eastern District of California.

Natural Community Conservation Act. 1991. Currently codified at *California Fish and Game Code,* secs. 2800–40.

Natural Resources Defense Council, Center for Biological Diversity, and Center for Marine Conservation. 2001. *A petition to list the central/southern population of bocaccio (Sebastes paucispinis) as a threatened species.*

Nature Conservancy, The. 2003a. *Santa Cruz Island: Foxes, pigs, and eagles.* http://nature.org/wherewework/northamerica/states/california/preserves/art9827.html.

———. 2003b. *Santa Cruz Island: Relocating golden eagles.* http://nature.org/wherewework/northamerica/states/california/preserves/art9829.html.

———. 2003c. *Santa Cruz Island: Bringing back the bald eagle.* http://nature.org/wherewework/northamerica/states/california/preserves/art9830.html.

———. 2004. Big Darby Creek Watershed. http://www.bigdarby.org/.

———. 2005. *Island Fox recovery project.* http://nature.org/wherewework/northamerica/states/California/Features/sci_overview.html.

NatureServe. 2003. *NatureServe explorer: An online encyclopedia of life.* Version 1.8. Arlington, Va. http://www.natureserve.org/explorer/.

Newton, I. 2003. The contribution of peregrine research and restoration to a better understanding of peregrines and other raptors. In *Return of the peregrine, a North*

American saga of tenacity and teamwork, ed. T. J. Cade and W. Burnham. Boise, Idaho: Peregrine Fund.

New York Times. 1979. Interior Department assailed on missing a deadline for species. November 7.

———. 2004. Washington proposes to remove a wolf from endangered list. July 17.

Nijhuis, M. 2000. A land-trust toolbox. *High Country News*, February 28.

Nixon, Richard. 1972. The president's 1972 environmental program. *Weekly Compilation of Presidential Documents* 8:218–24.

NMFS (National Marine Fisheries Service). 2002. *Biennial Report to Congress on the Recovery Program for Threatened and Endangered Species*. Silver Spring, Md.: U.S. Department of Commerce, Office of Protected Resources.

———. 2003. *Annual report to Congress on the status of U.S. fisheries—2002*. Silver Spring, Md.: U.S. Department of Commerce.

NOAA (National Oceanic and Atmospheric Administration). 2001. Endangered and threatened species: Endangered status for white abalone. *Federal Register* 66:29046–55.

———. 2002. Endangered and threatened wildlife and plants: 12-month finding on a petition to list bocaccio as threatened. *Federal Register* 67:69704–8.

Nollan v. California Coastal Commission. 1987. 483 U.S. 825. U.S. Supreme Court.

Nolon, J. R. 2003. *New ground: The advent of local environmental law*. Washington, D.C.: Environmental Law Institute.

North American Bluebird Society. 2004. Home page. http://www.nabluebirdsociety.org/.

Northeastern Nevada Stewardship Group. 2004. About us. http://www.nnsg.org/info. (accessed January 12, 2004).

Northern Spotted Owl v. Lujan. 1991. 758 F. Supp. 621. U.S. District Court for the Western District of Washington.

Northwest Indian Fisheries Commission. 2005. Salmon recovery. http://www.nwifc.wa. gov/recovery/index.asp (visited September 7, 2005).

Norton, B. Forthcoming. A policy-relevant definition of biodiversity. In *The Endangered Species Act at thirty: Conserving biodiversity in human-dominated landscapes*, ed. J. M. Scott, D. D. Goble, and F. W. Davis. Washington, D.C.: Island Press.

Noss, R. F., E. T. LaRoe, and J. M. Scott. 1995. *Endangered ecosystems of the United States: A preliminary assessment of loss and degradation*. Biological Report 28. Washington, D.C.: U.S. Department of the Interior, National Biological Service.

Noss, R., R. Amundson, M. Barbour, R. Bugg, B. Cypher, R. Grosberg, T. Hanes, R. Hansen, B. Pavlik, P. Trenham, K. Rice, B. Shaffer, and B. Weir. 2002. Report of science advisors for the Eastern Merced County Natural Community Conservation Plan Habitat Conservation Plan, part 1: General review of approach, methods, and planning principles, and responses to initial questions. http://www.dfg.ca.gov/ nccp/mercedsciadvrpt.pdf.

NPS (National Park Service), USFS (U.S. Forest Service), and APHIS (Animal and Plant Health Inspection Service). 2000a. *Summary final environmental impact statement for the interagency bison management plan for the state of Montana and Yellowstone National Park*. http://www.nps.gov/yell/technical/planning/bison%20eis// main2.htm (accessed June 10, 2003).

———. 2000b. *Record of decision for final environmental impact statement and bison management plan for the state of Montana and Yellowstone National Park*. Dec. 20. http:// www.planning.nps.gov/document/yellbisonrod%2Epdf (accessed June 10, 2003).

Oakleaf, R., and G. R. Craig. 2003. Peregrine falcon restoration from a state biologist's perspective. In *Return of the peregrine, a North American saga of tenacity and teamwork*, ed. T. J. Cade and W. Burnham. Boise, Idaho: Peregrine Fund.

Odell, R. 2002. Northwest braces itself for wolves. *High Country News*. December 23.

Olliver, Narena. 2002. Tiritiri Matangi: New Zealand birding. http://nzbirds.com/TiriTiriMatangi.html.

OMB (Office of Management and Budget). 2003. Budget of the United States government, fiscal year 2003. Appendix: Detailed budget estimates by agency submitted to Congress. Washington, D.C.

Opiela, E. 2002. The rule of capture in Texas. *University of Denver Water Law Review* 6:87–115.

Orians, G. 2003. Abstract. Politics and the national academies. *Environmental Review*. 10 (11): 13. http://www.environmentalreview.org/vol10/Orians%20abstract.html (accessed September 7, 2004).

Ortiz, F. 1999. Candidate conservation agreements as a devolutionary response to extinction. *Georgia Law Review* 33:413–511.

Pagel, J., T. W. Clark, and D. Rohlf. Forthcoming. Recovery and the United States Endangered Species Act: Overview, experience, and recommendations. In *Endangered species conservation: Lessons*, ed. I. Jimenz and M. Delibes. Conference proceedings. Valencia, Spain. December, 2002.

Palila v. Hawaii Department of Land and Natural Resources. 1979. 47 F. Supp. 985. U.S. District Court for the District of Hawai'i. *affirmed*, 1981. 639 F.2d 495. U.S. Court of Appeals for the 9th Judicial Circuit. *subsequent decision* 1986. 649 F. Supp. 1070. U.S. District Court for the District of Hawai'i. *affirmed*, 1988. 852 F. 2d 1106. U.S. Court of Appeals for the 9th Judicial Circuit.

Parkhurst, G. M., and J. F. Shogren. 2004. An evaluation of incentive mechanisms for conserving habitat. *Natural Resources Journal* 43:1093–149.

Patlis, J. M. 2001. Paying tribute to Joseph Heller with the Endangered Species Act: When critical habitat isn't. *Stanford Environmental Law Journal* 20:133–217.

Pattee, O. H., P. H. Bloom, J. M. Scott, and M. R. Smith. 1990. Lead hazards within the range of the California condor. *Condor* 92:931–37.

Pauli, W. 1999. Statement of the American Farm Bureau Federation to the Committee on Environment and Public Works: Habitat conservation planning and the Endangered Species Act. October 19.

Paulson, D. A. 2003. No endangered species left behind: Correcting the inequity in critical habitat designation for pre-1978-amendment listed species. *Hawaii Law Review* 25:525–59.

Pauly, D. 1995. Anecdotes and the shifting baseline syndrome of fisheries. *Trends in Ecology and Evolution* 10:430.

Perkins, B. 2002. *Habitat conservation plans impose unnecessary new burdens on land owners without corresponding benefits.* http://www.montereycountyfarmbureau.org/Habitat%20conservation%20planning.htm.

Peters, R. L., and J. D. S. Darling. 1985. The greenhouse effect and nature reserves. *BioScience* 35:707–17.

Pew Oceans Commission. 2003. *America's living oceans: Charting a course for sea change.* Arlington, Va.

Phelps, M. F. 1997. Candidate conservation agreements under the Endangered Species Act: Prospects and perils of an administrative experiment. *Boston College Environmental Affairs Law Review* 25:175–212.

Pickrell, J. 2004. Are U.S. landowners inhospitable to rare species to avoid regulation? *National Geographic News.* http://news.nationalgeographic.com/news/2003/12/1224_031229_jumpingmouse.html.

Pima County. 2001. Sonoran Desert Conservation and Comprehensive Land Use Plan. Pima County, Tucson, AZ.

Pimentel, D., U. Stachow, D. A. Takacs, H. W. Brubaker, A. R. Dumas, J. J. Meaney, J. O'Neil, D. E. Onsi, and D. B. Corzilius. 1992. Conserving biological diversity in agricultural/forestry systems. *BioScience* 42:354–62.

Pimm, S. L., M. L. Rosenzweig, and W. Mitchell. 1985. Competition and food selection: Field tests of a theory. *Ecology* 66:798–807.

Powles, H., M. J. Bradford, R. G. Bradford, W. G. Doubleday, S. Innes, and C. D. Levings. 2000. Assessing and protecting endangered marine species. *ICES Journal of Marine Science* 57:669–76.

Predator Conservation Alliance. 2001. Restoring the prairie dog ecosystem of the Great Plains: Learning from the past to ensure the prairie dog's future. Bozeman, Mont.

Preston, F. W. 1960. Time and space and the variation of species. *Ecology* 41:785–90.

Rachlinski, J. J. 1997. Noah by the numbers: An empirical evaluation of the Endangered Species Act. *Cornell Law Review* 82:356–89.

Rancho Viejo, LLC v. Norton. 2003. 323 F.3d 1062. U.S. Circuit Court of Appeals for the District of Columbia.

Reading, R. P., T. W. Clark, L. McCain, and B. J. Miller. 2002. Black-tailed prairie dog conservation: A new approach for the 21st century challenge. In *An interdisciplinary approach to endangered species recovery,* ed. R. Wallace, T. W. Clark, and R. P. Reading. Special issue of *Endangered Species Update.* 19 (4): 162–70.

Reaka-Kudla, M. L. 1997. The global biodiversity of coral reefs: A comparison with rain forests. In *Biodiversity II: Understanding and protecting our biological resources,* ed. M. L. Reaka-Kudla, D. E. Wilson, and E. O. Wilson, 83–108. Washington, D.C.: National Academies Press, Joseph Henry Press.

Redford, K. H., P. Coppolillo, E. W. Sanderson, G. A. B. DaFonseca, E. Dinnerstein, C. Groves, G. Mace, S. Maginnis, R. A. Mittermeier, R. Noss, D. Olson, J. G. Robinson, A. Vedder, and M. Wright. 2003. Mapping the conservation landscape. *Conservation Biology* 17:116–31.

Reed, J. M., H. R. Akcakaya, M. Burgman, D. Bender, S. R. Beissinger, and J. M. Scott. Forthcoming. Critical habitat. In *The Endangered Species Act at thirty: Conserving biodiversity in human-dominated landscapes,* ed. J. M. Scott, D. D. Goble, and F. W. Davis. Washington, D.C.: Island Press.

Restani, M., and J. M. Marzluff. 2002. Funding extinction? Biological needs and political realities in the allocation of resources to endangered species recovery. *BioScience* 52:169–77.

Richie, D., and J. Holmes. 1999. *State wildlife diversity program funding: A 1998 survey.* Washington, D.C.: International Association of Fish and Wildlife Agencies.

Rieke, E. A. 1996. The bay-delta accord: A stride toward sustainability. *University of Colorado Law Review* 67:341–69.

Riverside County Integrated Project. 2003. MSHCP final documents. June 17. http://rcip.org/conservation.htm.

Roberts, C. M., and J. P. Hawkins. 1999. Extinction risk in the sea. *Trends in Ecology and Evolution* 14:241–46.

Rodgers, W., Jr. 2000. The myth of win-win: Misdiagnosis in the business of reassembling nature. *Arizona Law Review* 42:297–306.

————. 2001. The Miccosukee Indians and environmental law: A confederacy of hope. *Environmental Law Reporter* 31:10918–27.

Roemer, G. W., T. J. Coonan, D. K. Garcelon, J. Bascompte, and L. Laughrin. 2001. Feral pigs facilitate hyperpredation by golden eagles and indirectly cause the decline of the island fox. *Animal Conservation* 4:307–18.

Roemer, G. W., and C. J. Donlan. 2004. Biology, policy and law in endangered species conservation: I. The case history of the island fox on the northern Channel Islands. *Endangered Species Update* 21:23–31.

Rogers-Bennett, L., P. L. Haaker, T. O. Huff, and P. K. Dayton. 2002. Estimating baseline abundances of abalone in California for restoration. *California Cooperative Oceanic Fisheries Investigations* 43:97–111.

Root, T. L., J. T. Price, K. R. Hall, S. H. Schneider, C. Rosenzweig, and A. Pounds. 2003. Fingerprints of global warming on wild animals and plants. *Nature* 421:57–60.

Rosenzweig, M. L. 1973. Habitat selection experiments with a pair of coexisting heteromyid rodent species. *Ecology* 54:111–17.

————. 1981. A theory of habitat selection. *Ecology* 62:327–35.

————. 1991. Habitat selection and population interactions: The search for mechanism. *American Naturalist* 137:S5–28.

————. 1995. *Species diversity in space and time.* New York: Cambridge University Press.

————. 1999a. Heeding the warning in biodiversity's basic law. *Science* 284:276–77.

————. 1999b. Species diversity. In *Advanced theoretical ecology: Principles and applications,* ed. J. McGlade. Oxford, UK: Blackwell Science.

————. 2001. Loss of speciation rate will impoverish future diversity. *Proceedings of the National Academy of Sciences of the United States of America* 98:5404–10. http://www.pnas.org/cgi/reprint/98/10/5404.pdf.

————. 2003a. *Win-win ecology: How the earth's species can survive in the midst of human enterprise.* New York: Oxford University Press.

————. 2003b. Reconciliation ecology and the future of species diversity. *Oryx* 37: 194–205.

————. 2003c. *The careful foot.* http://www.reconciliationecology.com/.

Rosenzweig, M. L., and E. A. Sandlin. 1997. Species diversity and latitudes: Listening to area's signal. *Oikos* 80:172–76.

Ruckelshaus, M., and D. Darm. Forthcoming. Science and implementation. In *The Endangered Species Act at thirty: Conserving biodiversity in human-dominated landscapes,* ed. J. M. Scott, D. D. Goble, and F. W. Davis. Washington, D.C.: Island Press.

Ruhl, J. B. 1998. Who needs Congress? An agenda for administrative reform of the Endangered Species Act. *New York University Environmental Law Journal* 6:367–410.

————. 1999. How to kill endangered species, legally: The nuts and bolts of Endangered Species Act "HCP" permits for real estate development. *Environmental Lawyer* 5:345–405.

Sacramento and Sutter Counties. 2002. Draft Natomas Basin habitat conservation plan. Sacramento. July 25.

Sagoff, M. 1982. We have met the enemy and he is us—or conflict and contradiction in environmental law. *Environmental Law* 12:283–315.

Sanders, A. H. 1996. Damaging Indian treaty fisheries: A violation of tribal property rights. *Public Land and Resources Law Review* 17:153–75.

Save the Pine Bush, Inc. v. Planning Board. 2002. 749 N.Y.S.2d 318. New York Supreme Court.

Sax, J. L. 1993. Property rights and the economy of nature: Understanding *Lucas v. South Carolina Coastal Council. Stanford Law Review* 45:1433–55.

———. 2000. Environmental law at the turn of the century: A reportorial fragment of contemporary history. *California Law Review* 88:2375–402.

Schemske, D. W., B. C. Husband, M. H. Ruckelshaus, C. Goodwillie, I. M. Parker, and J. Bishop. 1994. Evaluating approaches to the conservation of rare and endangered plants. *Ecology* 75:584–606.

Schön, D. A. 1983. *The reflective practitioner: How professionals think in action.* New York: Basic Books.

Schorger, A. W. 1955. *The passenger pigeon: Its natural history and extinction.* Madison: University of Wisconsin Press.

Schultz, C. B., and L. R. Gerber. 2002. Are recovery plans improving with practice? *Ecological Applications* 12:641–47.

Schwartz, M. W. 1999. Choosing the appropriate scale of reserve for conservation. *Annual Review of Ecology and Systematics* 30:83–108.

Scott, J. M., R. J. F. Abbitt, and C. R. Groves. 2001a. What are we protecting? *Conservation Biology in Practice* 2 (1): 18–19.

Scott, J. M., B. Csuti, J. D. Jacobi, and J. E. Estes. 1988. Species richness: A geographic approach to protecting future biological diversity. *BioScience* 37:782–88.

Scott, J. M., F. W. Davis, R. G. McGhie, R. G. Wright, C. Groves, and J. Estes. 2001b. Nature reserves: Do they capture the full range of America's biological diversity? *Ecological Applications* 11:999–1007.

Scott, J. M., D. D. Goble, J. A. Wiens, D. S. Wilcove, M. Bean, and T. Male. Forthcoming. Recovery of imperiled species under the Endangered Species Act: The need for a new approach. *Frontiers in Ecology and the Environment.*

Scott, J. M., T. Loveland, K. Gergely, J. Strittholt, and N. Staus. 2004. National Wildlife Refuge System: Ecological context and integrity. *Natural Resources Journal* 44 (4): 1041–66.

Scott, J. M., S. Mountainspring, F. L. Ramsey, and C. B. Kepler. 1986. Forest bird communities of the Hawaiian Islands: Their dynamics, ecology, and conservation. *Studies in Avian Biology* no. 9. A publication of the Cooper Ornithological Society. Lawrence, Kans.: Allen Press.

Scott, J. M., T. H. Tear, and L. S. Mills. 1995. Socioeconomics and the recovery of endangered species: Biological assessment in a political world. *Conservation Biology* 9:214–16.

Scott, T., L. Fernandez, and M. Allen. Forthcoming. Land use planning. In *The Endangered Species Act at thirty: Conserving biodiversity in human-dominated landscapes,* ed. J. M. Scott, D. D. Goble, and F. W. Davis. Washington, D.C.: Island Press.

Sea Grant Law Center. 2004. *Governing the oceans.* U.S. Commission on Ocean Policy, appendix 6.

Senatore, M., J. Kostyack, and A. Wetzler. 2003. Critical habitat at the crossroads: Responding to the G. W. Bush administration's attacks on critical habitat designation under the ESA. *Golden Gate University Law Review* 33:447–71.

Shaffer, M. L., J. M. Scott, and F. Casey. 2002a. Noah's options: Initial cost estimates of a national system of habitat conservation areas in the United States. *BioScience* 52:439–43.

Shaffer, M. L., and B. A. Stein. 2000. Safeguarding our precious heritage. In *Precious heritage: The status of biodiversity in the United States*, ed. B. A. Stein, L. S. Kutner, and J. S. Adams. New York: Oxford University Press.

Shaffer, M. L., L. H. Watchman, W. J. Snape III, and I. Latchis. 2002b. Population viability analysis and conservation policy. In *Population viability analysis*, ed. S. R. Beissinger and D. R. McCullough. Chicago: University of Chicago Press.

Shogren, J. Forthcoming. Benefits and costs. In *The Endangered Species Act at thirty: Conserving biodiversity in human-dominated landscapes*, ed. J. M. Scott, D. D. Goble, and F. W. Davis. Washington, D.C.: Island Press.

Shogren J., J. Tschirhart, T. Anderson, A. Whritenour, S. Beissinger, D. Brookshire, G. Brown, D. Coursey, R. Innes, S. Meyer, and S. Polasky. 1999. Why economics matters for endangered species protection. *Conservation Biology* 13:1257–61.

Shore, D., and S. Packard. 2000. A green vision for Chicago. *Chicago Wilderness Magazine*. http://chicagowildernessmag.org/issues/spring2000/greenchicago.html.

Sidle, J. G. 1998. Arbitrary and capricious species conservation. *Conservation Biology* 12:248–49.

Sierra Club v. California Coastal Commission. 2003. 133 *California Reporter* 2d 182. California Court of Appeals.

Skorupa, J. 2003. Review of "Critical habitat significantly enhances endangered species recovery." Washington, D.C.: U.S. Fish and Wildlife Service.

Small, S. J. 1998. *Preserving family lands: Book 1, essential tax strategies for the landowner.* Boston: Landowner Planning Center.

———. 2000. An obscure tax code provision takes private land protection into the twenty-first century. In *Protecting the land: Conservation easements past, present, and future*, ed. J. A. Gustanski and R. H. Squires, 55–66. Washington, D.C.: Island Press.

Smith, R. B., and J. F. Shogren. 2001. Protecting species on private land. In *Protecting species in the United States: Biological needs, political realities, economic choices*, ed. J. Shogren and J. Tschirhart. New York: Cambridge University Press.

———. 2002. Voluntary incentive design for endangered species protection. *Journal of Environmental Economics and Management* 43:169–87.

Smithsonian Institution. 1974. *Report on endangered and threatened plant species of the United States.* Washington, D.C.

Snape, W. J., III, M. S. Senatore, K. Gillon, S. George, C. Muffett, L. Anderson, and R. Kondor. 2001. Protecting ecosystems under the ESA: A Sonoran Desert example. *Washburn Law Journal* 41:14–49.

Solid Waste Agency of Northern Cook County v. U.S. Army Corps of Engineers. 2001. 531 U.S. 159. U.S. Supreme Court.

Southwest Center for Biological Diversity v. U.S. Forest Service. 1997. CV 97-666-TUC-JMR. U.S. District Court for the District of Arizona.

Spirit of the Sage Council v. Norton. 2003. 294 F. Supp. 2d 67. U.S. District Court for the District of Columbia.

Stanfield, R. B. 2002. *The workshop book: From individual creativity to group action.* Gabriola Island, British Columbia: New Society.

Stein, B. A., L. S. Kutner, and J. S. Adams. 2000. *Precious heritage: The status of biodiversity in the United States.* New York: Oxford University Press.

Steinhart, P. 1995. *The company of wolves.* New York: Knopf.

Strahan, R. 1983. *The Australian Museum complete book of Australian mammals.* North Ryde, New South Wales: Angus and Robertson.

Strahan v. Coxe. 1997. 127 F.3d 155. U.S. Court of Appeals for the 1st Judicial Circuit.

Suckling, K. F., B. Nowicki, and R. Slack. In preparation. Extinction and the Endangered Species Act.

Suckling, K. F., R. Slack, and B. Nowicki. 2004. *Extinction and the Endangered Species Act.* May 1. Tucson, Ariz.: Center for Biological Diversity. http://www.biological-diversity.org/swcbd/Programs/policy/esa/eesa.html.

Sunding, D. Forthcoming. Economic impacts. In *The Endangered Species Act at thirty: Conserving biodiversity in human-dominated landscapes,* ed. J. M. Scott, D. D. Goble, and F. W. Davis. Washington, D.C.: Island Press.

Susskind, L., S. McKearnan, and J. Thomas-Larmer, ed. 1999. *The consensus-building handbook: A comprehensive guide to reaching agreement.* Thousand Oaks, Calif.: Sage.

Symposium. 1997. The ecosystem approach: New departures for land and water. *Ecology Law Quarterly* 24:619–33.

Takacs, D. 1996. The idea of biodiversity: Philosophies in paradise. Baltimore, Md.: John Hopkins Press.

Tarlock, A. D. 1993. Local government protection of biodiversity: What is its niche? *University of Chicago Law Review* 60:574–86.

———. 1994. Bioregionalism: What is its niche? *Land Use Law and Zoning Digest* 46(4):3–10.

Taylor, M. S., and M. E. Hellberg. 2003. Genetic evidence for local retention of pelagic larvae in a Caribbean reef fish. *Science* 299:107–9.

Taylor, M. T., K. F. Suckling, and J. R. Rachlinski. 2003. Critical habitat significantly enhances endangered species recovery: Analysis of the three most recent U.S. Fish and Wildlife Service biennial reports to congress on the recovery of threatened and endangered species. Tucson, Ariz.: Center for Biological Diversity.

———. 2005. The effectiveness of the Endangered Species Act: A quantitative analysis. *BioScience* 55:360–67.

Tear, T. H., J. M. Scott, P. Hayward, and B. Griffith. 1993. Status and prospects for the Endangered Species Act: A look at recovery plans. *Science* 262:976–77.

Tear, T. H., J. M. Scott, P. H. Hayward, and B. Griffith. 1995. Recovery plans and the Endangered Species Act: Are criticisms supported by data? *Conservation Biology* 9:182–95.

Tennessee Valley Authority v. Hill. 1978. 437 U.S. 153. U.S. Supreme Court.

Terman, M. R. 1997. Natural links: Naturalistic golf courses as wildlife habitat. *Landscape and Urban Planning* 38:183–97.

Thomas, C. D., A. Cameron, R. R. Green, M. Bakkenes, L. J. Beaumont, Y. C. Collingham, B. F. N. Erasmus, M. F. de Siqueira, A. Grainger, L. Hannah, L. Hughes, B. Huntley, A. S. van Jaarsveld, G. F. Midgley, L. Miles, M. A. Ortega-Huerta, A. T. Peterson, O. L. Phillips, and S. E. Williams. 2004. Extinction risk from climate change. *Nature* 427:145–48.

Thompson, B. H., Jr. 1997. The Endangered Species Act: A case study in takings and incentives. *Stanford Law Review* 49:305–80.

———. 1999. People or prairie chickens: The uncertain search for optimal biodiversity. *Stanford Law Review* 51:1127–85.

———. 2002a. Providing biodiversity through policy diversity. *Idaho Law Review* 38:355–84.

———. 2002b. Conservation options: Toward a greater private role. *Virginia Environmental Law Journal* 21:245–315.

Thorne, E. T., M. Meagher, and R. Hillman. 1991. Brucellosis in free-ranging bison: Three perspectives. In *The greater Yellowstone ecosystem: Redefining America's wilderness heritage*, ed. R. N. Keiter and M. S. Boyce, 275–87. New Haven, Conn.: Yale University Press.

Tobin, R. 1990. *The expendable future: U.S. politics and the protection of biological diversity*. Durham, N.C.: Duke University Press.

Tripp, J. T. B., and D. J. Dudek. 1989. Institutional guidelines for developing transferable rights programs. *Yale Journal on Regulation* 6:369–91.

Trust for Public Land. 2003. *LandVote 2003*. San Francisco.

Tufts, C., and P. Loewer. 1995. *Gardening for wildlife*. Emmaus, Pa.: Rodale Press.

United States v. Morrison. 2002. 529 U.S. 598. U.S. Supreme Court.

United States v. Town of Plymouth. 1998. 6 F. Supp. 2d 81. U.S. District Court for the District of Massachusetts.

United States v. Washington. 1980. 506 F. Supp. 187. U.S. District Court for the Western District of Washington.

———. 2001. Civil No. C70-9213, Sub-Proceeding No. 01-01 (Phase II: Culverts), Request for Determination, 3.2 (filed Jan. 2001).

United States v. West Coast Forest Resources Limited Partnership. 2000. No. 96-1575-MO. U.S. District Court for the District of Oregon.

U.S. Commission on Ocean Policy. 2002. *Developing a national ocean policy: Mid-term report of the U.S. Commission on Ocean Policy*. Washington, D.C. http://www.oceancommission.gov/documents/midterm_report/midterm_report.html.

———. 2004. *Preliminary report of the U.S. Commission on Ocean Policy: Governor's draft*. Washington, D.C. Also available at http://oceancommission.gov/documents/prelimreport/welcome.html.

U.S. Congress. 1973. House of Representatives. Report no. 412, 93d Congress, 1st Session.

———. 1975. House of Representatives. Committee on Merchant Marine and Fisheries, hearings, Endangered Species Oversight, 94th Congress, 1st Session.

———. 1976. House of Representatives. Report no. 887, 94th Congress, 2nd Session.

———. 1982a. House of Representatives. Conference Report no. 835, 97th Congress, 2d Session. Reprinted in *United States Code Congressional and Administrative News* 1982:2860–76.

———. 1982b. House of Representatives. Report no. 567, 97th Congress, 2d Session. Reprinted in *United States Code Congressional and Administrative News* 1982: 2807–59.

———. 1982c. Senate. Report no. 418, 97th Congress, 2d Session.

———. 2003. Senate. *Designation of critical habitat under the Endangered Species Act: Hearing before the Subcommittee on Fisheries, Wildlife, and Water of the Senate Committee on Environment and Public Works*, 108th Congress (Testimony of Craig Manson, assistant secretary for fish and wildlife and parks, Department of the Interior, before the Subcommittee on Fisheries, Wildlife and Water of the Senate Committee on Environment and Public Works, regarding the designation of critical habitat under the Endangered Species Act.) http://laws.fws.gov/TESTIMON/2003/2003april10.html.

U.S. Department of Agriculture. 2004. *Percent change in developed land area, 1982–1997*. Natural Resources Conservation Service. http://www.nrcs.usda.gov/technical/land/lgif/m5008l.gif.

U.S. Department of Energy. 2000. Memorandum of agreement between the U.S.

Department of the Interior and the U.S. Department of Energy for the *A. grandiflora* reserve at Lawrence Livermore National Laboratory Site 300 Experimental Test Facility, San Joaquin and Alameda Counties, California. Livermore, CA.

U.S. Department of the Interior. 1967. Native fish and wildlife: Endangered species. *Federal Register* 32:4001.

———. 1978. Endangered and threatened wildlife and plants: Interagency cooperation. *Federal Register* 43:870–76.

———. 2003. Critical habitat disclaimer. Washington, D.C. May 1.

———. 2004. Letter from J. Laws, Freedom of Information Act, Appeals Officer, Department of Interior, to B. Plater, Center for Biological Diversity. July 22.

U.S. Department of the Interior Inspector General. 1990. Report no. 90-98. Washington, D.C.

U.S. Department of the Interior and U.S. Department of Commerce. 1986. Endangered and threatened wildlife and plants: Interagency cooperation. *Federal Register* 51:19926–63.

———. 1997. Secretarial order no. 3206. June 5. Reprinted in the *Washington Law Review* 72:1089–107.

USFS (U.S. Forest Service). 2001. Letter from L. Beck, U.S. Forest Service, Pacific Southwest Regional Office, to the Wellman Family Trust. February 9.

USFWS (U.S. Fish and Wildlife Service). 1976. *Guidelines to assist federal agencies in complying with section 7 of the Endangered Species Act.* April 22.

———. 1977a. Endangered and threatened wildlife and plants: Review of the status of 10 species of amphibians. *Federal Register* 42:39121–22.

———. 1977b. Determination of critical habitat for six endangered species. *Federal Register* 42:40685–90.

———. 1979. Endangered and threatened wildlife and plants: Notice of withdrawal of five expired proposals for listing of 1,876 species, and intent to revise 1975 plant notice which includes most of these species. *Federal Register* 44:70796–97.

———. 1980. Emergency determination of endangered status and designation of critical habitat for *Astragalus yoder-williamsii*. *Federal Register* 45:53968–70.

———. 1981. Endangered and threatened wildlife and plants: Final redefinition of "harm." *Federal Register* 46:54748–50.

———. 1982a. Endangered and threatened wildlife and plants: Review of vertebrate wildlife for listing as endangered or threatened species. *Federal Register* 47:58454–60.

———. 1982b. Box score. *Endangered Species Technical Bulletin* 7 (9): 12.

———. 1983. Endangered and threatened wildlife and plants: Deregulation of the longjaw cisco and the blue pike. *Federal Register* 48:39941–43.

———. 1987a. Endangered and threatened wildlife and plants: Establishment of an experimental population of southern sea otters. *Federal Register* 52:29754–76.

———. 1987b. *Administration of the Marine Mammal Protection Act of 1972, January 1, 1986 to December 31, 1986.* Washington, D.C.

———. 1990a. Memorandum from director of FWS to regional director, Region 1. Subject: Cluster listing packages.

———. 1990b. *Recovery plan for the interior population of the le⁺ tern (Sterna antillarum).* Twin Cities, Minn.

———. 1990c. *Northern aplomado falcon recovery plan.* Albuquerque, N.Mex.

———. 1991a. *American burying beetle (Nicrophorus americanus) recovery plan.* Newton Corner, Mass.

———. 1991b. *Administration of the Marine Mammal Protection Act of 1972, January 1, 1990, to December 31, 1990.* Washington, D.C.

———. 1991c. *Annual report: Southern sea otter translocation to San Nicolas Island August 1990–July 1991.* Ventura, Calif.

———. 1992a. Determination of critical habitat for the northern spotted owl. *Federal Register* 57:01796–834.

———. 1992b. *Recovery plan for the northern spotted owl.* Washington, D.C.: Government Printing Office.

———. 1993a. Endangered and threatened wildlife and plants: Determination of threatened status for the coastal California gnatcatcher. *Federal Register* 58:16742–57.

———. 1993b. *Annual report southern sea otter translocation to San Nicolas Island August 1992–July 1993.* Ventura, Calif.

———. 1994. *Biological opinion for the Bureau of Land Management's interim livestock grazing program in Mojave desert tortoise critical habitat.* 1-5-94-F-107. Portland, Ore.

———. 1995a. Memorandum from the director of USFWS to regional directors. Policy on candidate assessment and petition management under the Endangered Species Act. July 19. Washington, D.C.

———. 1995b. Endangered and threatened wildlife and plants: Withdrawal of proposed rule to list the plant *Salix arizonica* (Arizona willow) as endangered with critical habitat. *Federal Register* 60:20951–52.

———. 1995c. *Federal and state endangered species expenditures: Fiscal year 1995.* Washington, D.C.

———. 1996a. *Piping plover (Charadnus melodus), Atlantic coast population, revised recovery plan.* Hadley, Mass.

———. 1996b. Availability of an environmental assessment/habitat conservation plan and receipt of application for incidental take permit for construction of one single family residence on 201 Lowell Land, Lot 65, Block B, Rob Roy on the Lake, Section 2, Austin, Travis County, Texas. *Federal Register* 61:15507.

———. 1996c. Golden-cheeked warbler, etc., Travis County et al., TX; Incidental take permits; Availability of an environmental assessment/habitat conservation plan and receipt of application for incidental take permit for construction of one single family residence on 201 Lowell Land, Lot 65, Block B, Rob Roy on the Lake, Section 2, Austin, Travis County, Texas. *Federal Register* 61:15507.

———. 1996d. Availability of an environmental assessment/habitat conservation plan and receipt of application for an incidental take permit for construction of one single family residence at Yucca Mountain Road (across from 9206 Yucca Mountain Road), Austin, Travis County, Texas. *Federal Register* 61:22071.

———. 1996e. *Draft southern sea otter recovery plan.* Revised. Portland, Ore.: Southern Sea Otter Recovery Team for the U.S. Fish and Wildlife Service.

———. 1997. *Biological and conference opinion on lower Colorado River operations and maintenance: Lake Mead to southerly international boundary.* R2/ES-SE. Albuquerque, N.Mex.

———. 1998a. Availability of a habitat conservation plan and receipt of an application for an incidental take permit for the Newhall Land and Farming Project on the Santa Clara River, California. *Federal Register* 63:13062–63.

———. 1998b. Endangered and threatened wildlife and plants; Reopening of comment period for availability of an environmental assessment/habitat conservation plan and receipt of application for incidental take permit for ranching and related activities on El Coronado Ranch (PRT-837858), Cochise County, Arizona. *Federal Register* 63:11690.

———. 1998c. *Recovery plan for the Hawaiian hoary bat.* Portland, Ore.

———. 1999a. Safe harbor agreements and candidate conservation agreements with assurances. *Federal Register* 64:32706–16.

———. 1999b. Boxscore. *Endangered Species Bulletin,* 24 (6): 28.

———. 1999c. Endangered and threatened species: Final listing priority guidance for fiscal year 2000. *Federal Register* 64:57114–19.

———. 1999d. Endangered and threatened wildlife and plants: Notice of intent to clarify the role of habitat in endangered species conservation. *Federal Register* 64:31871–74.

———. 1999e. *90-day finding for a petition to list the black-tailed prairie dog as threatened.* Washington, D.C.

———. 1999f. *Draft biological opinion on reinitiation of formal consultation on the containment program for the southern sea otter.* Report no. 1-8-99-FW-38R. Ventura, Calif.

———. 1999g. *Draft evaluation of the southern sea otter translocation program.* Ventura, Calif.

———. 1999h. *South Florida multi-species recovery plan.* Atlanta, Ga.

———. 2000a. Endangered and threatened wildlife and plants: Determination of whether designation of critical habitat is prudent for 81 plants and proposed designations for 76 plants from the islands of Kauai and Niihau, Hawaii. *Federal Register* 65:66808–85.

———. 2000b. Memo from U.S. Fish and Wildlife Service Colorado field supervisor, L. Carlson. Jan. 10.

———. 2001a. Endangered and threatened wildlife and plants: Final rule to remove the Aleutian Canada goose from the federal list of endangered and threatened wildlife. *Federal Register* 66:15643–56.

———. 2001b. Developing an endangered species listing action priority system. Working draft. Nov. 16. Washington, D.C.

———. 2001c. Final determination of critical habitat for Peninsular bighorn sheep. *Federal Register* 66:8649–77.

———. 2001d. Environmental statements: Availability, etc: Incidental take permits—Travis County, TX; Golden cheeked warbler. *Federal Register* 66:20675.

———. 2001e. Notice of intent to hold a 30-day scoping period to solicit public comments for a National Environmental Policy Act (NEPA) decision on a proposed habitat conservation plan for the Lake Erie water snake. *Federal Register* 66: 39052–53.

———. 2001f. Final environmental impact statement for the proposed issuance of an incidental take permit for the Metro Air Park Habitat Conservation Plan, Sacramento County, CA. *Federal Register* 66:43265–67.

———. 2001g. *Three-year summary of federal and state endangered and threatened species expenditures, fiscal years 1998–2000.*

———. 2002a. Removal of *Potentilla robbinsiana* (Robbins' cinquefoil) from the federal list of endangered and threatened plants. *Federal Register* 67:54968–75.

———. 2002b. Box score. *Endangered Species Bulletin* 27 (3): 32.

———. 2002c. Receipt of a permit application (Sultan and Kahn Amendment #1) for incidental take of the bone cave harvestman. *Federal Register* 67:3907–8.

———. 2002d. Receipt of an application for an incidental take permit for the Lenox Village development site, Nashville, Davidson County, Tennessee. *Federal Register* 67:13185–87.

———. 2002e. Proposed habitat conservation plan for the northern spotted owl, Napa County, CA. *Federal Register* 67:65998–99.

———. 2002f. *Safe harbor agreements for private landowners.* http://endangered.fws.gov/recovery/harborqa.pdf.

———. 2003a. Box score. *Endangered Species Bulletin* 28 (4): 44.

———. 2003b. *Testimony of Craig Manson, assistant secretary for fish and wildlife and parks, Department of the Interior, before the Subcommittee on Fisheries, Wildlife and Water of the Senate Committee on Environment and Public Works, regarding the designation of critical habitat under the Endangered Species Act.* http://laws.fws.gov/TESTIMON/2003/2003april10.html.

———. 2003c. *Recovery report to Congress: Fiscal years 1997–98 and 1999–2000.* Washington, D.C.

———. 2003d. *Draft revised recovery plan for Hawaiian forest birds.* Portland, Ore.

———. 2003e. Notice of availability of a draft environmental assessment/habitat conservation plan related to application for an incidental take permit for the long point homeowner's association development. *Federal Register* 68:12711–12.

———. 2003f. Endangered and threatened wildlife and plants; Final rule to reclassify and remove the gray wolf from the list of endangered and threatened wildlife in portions of the conterminous United States; Establishment of two special regulations for threatened gray wolves. *Federal Register* 68:15804–75.

———. 2003g. Endangered and threatened wildlife and plants: Removing the western distinct population segment of gray wolf from the list of endangered and threatened wildlife. *Federal Register* 68:15879–82.

———. 2003h. *Final revised recovery plan for the southern sea otter.* Washington, D.C.: U.S. Department of the Interior.

———. 2003i. Amendment to the 2000 biological opinion on the operation of the Missouri River main stem reservoir system, operation and maintenance of the Missouri River bank stabilization and navigation project, and operation of the Kansas River reservoir system. December 16. http://www.nwd-mr.usace.army.mil/mmanual/FinalBO2003.pdf.

———. 2003j. Environmental conservation online system (ECOS). http://ecos.fws.gov/ecos/index.do.

———. 2004a. *Threatened and endangered species system (TESS).* http://ecos.fws.gov/tess_public/TESSWebpage (accessed April 1, 2004).

———. 2004b. ECOS: Environmental conservation online system. http://ecos.fws.gov/ecos/index.do (accessed April 1, 2004).

———. 2004c. *Recovery report to Congress: Fiscal years 2001–2002.* Washington, D.C.

———. 2004d. The endangered species program. http://endangered.fws.gov/ (accessed June 15, 2004).

———. 2004e. Endangered and threatened wildlife and plants: Removing the eastern distinct population segment of the gray wolf from the list of endangered and threatened wildlife. *Federal Register* 69:43664–92.

———. 2004f. Endangered and threatened wildlife and plants: Withdrawal of proposed rule to list *Lepidium papilliferum* (slickspot peppergrass) as endangered. *Federal Register* 69:3094–116.

———. 2004g. *Service withdraws proposal to list slickspot peppergrass.* Regional office press release. January 22.

———. 2004h. *The number of species listed as threatened or endangered.* http://endangered.fws.gov/wildlife.html#Species.

———. 2004i. *Recovery of upper Colorado River basin fish.* http://mountain-prairie.fws.gov/coloradoriver/Crrpovvu.htm (accessed January 6, 2004).

———. 2004j. Notice of availability of a safe harbor agreement for topminnow and pupfish in Arizona and receipt of application for incidental take permit for the Arizona Game and Fish Department. *Federal Register* 69:15362.

———. 2005. *Massasoit National Wildlife Refuge.* http://refuges.fws.gov/profiles/index.cfm?id=53517 (accessed February 17, 2005).

USFWS (U.S. Fish and Wildlife Service) and NMFS (National Marine Fisheries Service). 1975. Endangered and threatened species: Notice on critical habitat areas. *Federal Register* 40:17764–65.

———. 1978. *Critical habitat priorities.* Washington, D.C.

———. 1998. *Consultation handbook: Procedures for conducting consultation and conference activities under section 7 of the Endangered Species Act.* Washington, D.C.

USFWS (U.S. Fish and Wildlife Service) and NOAA (National Oceanic and Atmospheric Administration). 1994a. Endangered and threatened wildlife and plants: Final rule to remove the eastern North Pacific population of the gray whale from the list of endangered wildlife. *Federal Register* 59:31094–95.

———. 1994b. Endangered and threatened wildlife and plants: Notice of interagency cooperative policy on recovery plan participation and implementation under the Endangered Species Act. *Federal Register* 59:34272–73.

———. 1996. Notice of availability of final habitat conservation planning and incidental take permitting process. *Federal Register* 61:63854–57.

———. 1998. Habitat conservation plan assurances ("no surprises") rule. *Federal Register* 63:8859.

———. 1999. Announcement of final policy for candidate conservation agreements with assurances. *Federal Register* 64:32726.

———. 2004. Joint counterpart Endangered Species Act section 7 consultation regulations. *Federal Register* 69:4465–80.

Utah Critical Lands Conservation Committee. 1997. *Land conservation in Utah: Tools, techniques, and initiatives.* http://governor.utah.gov/planning/CriticalLands/white.htm.

Vickerman, S. 1998a. *National stewardship incentives: Conservation strategies for U.S. landowners.* Lake Oswego, Ore.: Defenders of Wildlife.

———. 1998b. *Stewardship incentives: Conservation strategies for Oregon's working landscape.* Lake Oswego, Ore.: Defenders of Wildlife.

Vuilleumier, F. 1970. Insular biogeography in continental regions. I. The northern Andes of South America. *American Naturalist* 104:373–88.

Wagner, W. E. 2003. The "bad science" fiction: Reclaiming the debate over the role of science in public health and environmental regulation. *Law and Contemporary Problems* 66:63–133.

Wallace, R. L. 1994. The Florida manatee: Organizational learning and a model for improving recovery programs. In *Endangered species recovery: Finding the lessons, improving the process*, ed. T. W. Clark, R. P. Reading, and A. L. Clarke. Washington, D.C.: Island Press.

———. 2000. Marine mammal recovery: The human dimensions. Ph.D. diss. Yale University.

———. 2003. Social influences on conservation: Lessons from U.S. recovery programs for marine mammals. *Conservation Biology* 17:104–15.

Wallace, R. L., and T. W. Clark. 2002. Decision seminars in endangered species conservation: Making realistic, timely, and cooperative decisions. In *An interdisciplinary approach to endangered species recovery*, ed. R. Wallace, T. W. Clark, and R. P. Reading (Special Issue of *Endangered Species Update*) 19 (4): 130–35.

Wallace, R. L., T. W. Clark, and R. P. Reading. 2002a. Interdisciplinary endangered species conservation: A new approach for a new century. In *An interdisciplinary approach to endangered species recovery*, ed. R. Wallace, T. W. Clark, and R. P. Reading. Special issue of *Endangered Species Update* 19 (4): 70–73.

———. 2002b. *An interdisciplinary approach to endangered species recovery*. ed. R. Wallace, T. W. Clark, and R. P. Reading. Special issue of *Endangered Species Update* 19(4):1–202.

Wall Street Journal. 1995. Caught in a trap: Democrats get snared by GOP pact on list of endangered species—A Bush-era "critter quota" boosts animal protection—and antiregulatory ire. Feb. 17.

Walters, C. J. 1986. *Adaptive management of renewable resources*. New York: Macmillan.

Walters, M. J. 1992. *A Shadow and a Song*. White River Junction, VT: Chelsea Green.

Waples, R. S. Forthcoming. Conservation units. In *The Endangered Species Act at thirty: Conserving biodiversity in human-dominated landscapes*, ed. J. M. Scott, D. D. Goble, and F. W. Davis. Washington, D.C.: Island Press.

Washington v. Washington State Commercial Passenger Fishing Vessel Association. 1979. 443 U.S. 658. U.S. Supreme Court.

Watchman, L. H., M. Groom, and J. D. Perrine. 2001. Science and uncertainty in habitat conservation planning. *American Scientist* 89:351–59.

Wells, J., B. Robertson, K. V. Rosenberg, and D. W. Mehlman. 2004. Looking in or looking out: How the scale of state political boundaries impacts avian biodiversity conservation within the United States. Unpublished manuscript.

Western Ecological Research Center. 2002. *White abalone restoration*. Sacramento, Calif.: U.S. Geological Survey.

White Mountain Apache Tribe. 1994. Resolution No. 02-94-060. Feb. 24.

White, R. 1991. *"It's your misfortune and none of my own": A history of the American west*. Norman: University of Oklahoma Press.

Wiebe, K., A. Tegene, and B. Kuhn. 1996. Partial interests in land: Policy tools for resource use and conservation. Agricultural Economic Report 744. Washington, D.C.: Economic Research Service, U.S. Department of Agriculture.

Wilcove, D. S., M. J. Bean, R. Bonnie, and M. McMillan. 1996. *Rebuilding the ark: Toward a more effective Endangered Species Act for private land*. Washington, D.C.: Environmental Defense Fund.

Wilcove, D. S., M. McMillan, and K. C. Winston. 1993. What exactly is an endangered species? An analysis of the U.S. endangered species list: 1985–1991. *Conservation Biology* 7:87–93.

Wilcove, D. S., D. Rothstein, J. Dubow, A. Phillips, and E. Losos. 1998. Quantifying threats to imperiled species in the United States: Assessing the relative importance of habitat destruction, alien species, pollution, overexploitation, and disease. *BioScience* 48:607–15.

———. 2000. Leading threats to biodiversity: What's imperiling U.S. species. In *Precious heritage: The status of biodiversity in the United States*, ed. B. A. Stein, L. S. Kutner, and J. S. Adams. New York: Oxford University Press.

Wilkinson, C. 1997. The role of bilateralism in fulfilling the federal-tribal relationship: The tribal rights-endangered species secretarial order. *Washington Law Review* 72:1063–107.

Wilkinson, J. B. 1999. The state role in biodiversity conservation. *Issues in Science and Technology* 15:71–77.

Wilkinson, T. 1998. *Science under siege: The politician's war on nature and truth*. Boulder: Johnson Books.

Williams, J. E., and C. A. Macdonald. 2003. *A review of the conservation status of the Borax Lake chub, an endangered species*. Portland, Ore.: U.S. Fish and Wildlife Service.

Williams, S. E., E. E. Bolitho, and S. Fox. 2003. Climate change in Australian tropical rainforests: An impending environmental catastrophe. *Proceedings of the Royal Society of London* 270:1887–92.

Williams, W. 2001. Identifying critical habitat in the halls of Congress. *BioScience* 51:432.

Wilson, E. O., and E. O. Willis 1975. Applied biogeography. In *Ecology and evolution of communities*, ed. by M. L. Cody and J. M. Diamond, 522–34. Cambridge, Mass.: Harvard University Press, Belknap Press.

Wilson, P. I. 1999. Wolves, politics, and the Nez Perce: Wolf recovery in central Idaho and the role of native tribes. *Natural Resources Journal* 39:543–64.

Wisconsin Department of Natural Resources. 2002. Wisconsin karner blue butterfly habitat conservation plan. http://dnr.wi.gov/org/land/forestry/karner/.

Wondolleck, J., and C. Ryan. 1999. What hat do I wear now? An examination of agency roles in collaborative processes. *Negotiation Journal* 15:117–34.

Wondolleck, J., and S. Yaffee. 2000. *Making collaboration work: Lessons from innovation in natural resource management*. Washington, D.C.: Island Press.

Woods, J. 2001. Idaho's underdogs. *Defenders*. Fall.

Wyoming Farm Bureau Federation v. Babbitt. 2000. 199 F.3d 1224. U.S. Court of Appeals for the 10th Judicial Circuit.

Yaffee, S. L. 1982. *Prohibitive policy: Implementing the federal Endangered Species Act*. Cambridge: MIT Press.

———. 1994. *The wisdom of the spotted owl: Policy lessons for a new century*. Washington, D.C.: Island Press.

Yaffee, S. L., A. Phillips, I. Frentz, P. Hardy, S. Maleki, and B. Thorpe. 1996. *Ecosystem management in the United States: An assessment of current experience*. Washington, D.C.: Island Press.

Yaffee, S. L., J. M. Wondolleck, and S. Lippman. 1997. *Factors that promote and constrain bridging: A summary and analysis of the literature*. Ann Arbor: University of Michigan. http://www.snre.umich.edu/emi/collaboration/Factors_that_Promote_and_Contrain_Bridging.pdf.

Zabel, R. W., C. J. Harvey, S. L. Katz, T. P. Good, and P. S. Levin. 2003. Ecologically sustainable yield. *American Scientist* 91:150–57.

Zellmer, S. B. 1998. Indian lands as critical habitat for Indian nations and endangered species: Tribal survival and sovereignty come first. *South Dakota Law Review* 43:381–437.

Zuccotti, J. A. 1995. A native returns: The Endangered Species Act and wolf reintroduction to the northern Rocky Mountains. *Columbia Journal of Environmental Law* 20:329–60.

Contributors

PAUL R. ARMSWORTH recently joined the University of Sheffield as Lecturer in Biodiversity and Conservation. Previously, he was a postdoctoral fellow in the Center for Conservation Biology at Stanford University. A theoretical ecologist, he holds Ph.D.s in mathematics and biology. His recent research examines the consequences of dispersal and recruitment dynamics in shaping reef fish populations and the economic efficiency of management alternatives for highly migratory stocks.

MICHAEL J. BEAN is Chair of the Wildlife Program of Environmental Defense, a position he has held since 1977. He is coauthor with Melanie Rowland of *The Evolution of National Wildlife Law* and has written on conservation topics for numerous scientific, legal, and popular journals. His recent work focuses on efforts to engage private landowners in endangered species conservation efforts and policies to foster such efforts. He helped conceive and design the nation's first endangered species safe harbor agreements.

MAEVEEN BEHAN is project director and primary drafter of the Sonoran Desert Conservation and Comprehensive Land Use Plan. She received a law degree from the University of Alabama and is a member of the Arizona State Bar Association. She is currently completing a Ph.D. in the Arid Lands Resource Sciences interdisciplinary program at the University of Arizona.

ERIC P. BJORKSTEDT is a research scientist with NOAA's National Marine Fisheries Service and an adjunct professor at Humboldt State University. His research focuses on biological and physical processes that influence recruitment and spatial structure of fish and invertebrate populations in coastal marine systems, and on the population dynamics and structure of anadromous salmonids.

His recent work contributes to the scientific foundation of recovery planning for Pacific salmon and steelhead.

MICHELLE L. BROWN is a conservation planner for the Eastern New York Chapter of the Nature Conservancy. Her interests include enhancing the relationship between regional and local-scale conservation efforts, and the application of ecosystem ecology to conservation planning.

WILLIAM BURNHAM is President of the Peregrine Fund. He has worked for the organization since 1974 and has been instrumental in developing and implementing its many national and international programs. He holds a Ph.D. from Colorado State University and has authored over ninety technical and popular articles. He has conducted research on peregrine falcons for over forty years.

TOM J. CADE is Professor Emeritus of Cornell University and Founding Chairman of the Peregrine Fund. He holds a Ph.D. from the University of California, Los Angeles. Birds of prey have been his lifelong interest, and for the past forty years he has bred falcons in captivity and reintroduced them to the wild.

FRANK CASEY is a natural resources economist and Director of the Defenders of Wildlife Conservation Economics Program. He holds an M.S. in agricultural economics from Cornell University and a Ph.D. in food and resource economics from the University of Florida. His research focuses on analyzing economic incentive policies for biodiversity conservation on public and private lands. He is currently involved in several projects that estimate market and nonmarket benefits of wildlife habitat conservation.

TIM W. CLARK is the Joseph F. Cullman 3rd Adjunct Professor of Wildlife Ecology and Policy in the School of Forestry and Environmental Studies and Fellow in the Institution for Social and Policy Studies, Yale University. He has written over 350 papers, many on interdisciplinary problem solving. He is currently working on large carnivore conservation in western North America and other projects. For over thirty years, he has dedicated himself to endangered species conservation.

FRANK W. DAVIS is Professor in the Donald Bren School of Environmental Science and Management at the University of California, Santa Barbara, where he teaches and conducts research in landscape ecology and conservation planning. He holds a Ph.D. in geography and environmental engineering from the

Johns Hopkins University. He is a Fellow in the Aldo Leopold Leadership Program and member of the board of trustees of the Nature Conservancy of California.

ROBERT P. DAVISON is Northwest Field Representative for the Wildlife Management Institute. He is a former deputy assistant secretary of the interior for fish and wildlife and parks and a professional staff member on the Senate Committee on Environment and Public Works responsible for fisheries, wildlife, endangered species, and wetlands issues and legislation. He holds a Ph.D. in wildlife science from Utah State University.

J. R. DESHAZO is Assistant Professor in the School of Public Policy and Social Research at the University of California, Los Angeles. He holds an M.Sc. from Oxford University, where he was a Rhodes Scholar, and a Ph.D. from Harvard University. He was a faculty associate at the Harvard Institute for International Development from 1997 to 2000 and is currently Associate Director of the Lewis Center for Regional Studies at UCLA. Trained as an economist, his research focuses on models of decision making and choice, positive political economy, devolution, nonmarket valuation, and several areas of policy analysis.

ROBERT DEWEY is Vice President for Government Relations and External Affairs for Defenders of Wildlife. He oversees federal issues and relations with other national environmental organizations and collaborative initiatives. From 1994 to 2000, he directed Defender of Wildlife's work on habitat and public lands, advocating wildlife protection on federal refuges and forests and promoting transportation planning and conservation initiatives in Florida and Alaska.

HOLLY DOREMUS is Professor of Law and Chancellor's Fellow at the University of California, Davis. She is a Member Scholar of the Center for Progressive Regulation. She earned a Ph.D. in plant physiology from Cornell University and J.D. from the University of California, Berkeley, Boalt Hall. She has written extensively about endangered species and biodiversity protection as well as the intersection of science and natural resources policy.

ALESSANDRA FALCUCCI is an associate researcher at the University of Rome and is currently working on her Ph.D. at the University of Idaho. Her primary interests are ecological modeling for wildlife habitat and protected areas efficacy using GIS (geographic information system) and remote-sensing technologies. She has also worked for the Institute of Applied Ecology, in Rome, since 1998.

ROBERT M. FERRIS is Executive Director of the Community Environmental Council in Santa Barbara, Calif., focusing on renewable energy and watershed restoration. He has worked for more than a decade on national conservation policy and the restoration of imperiled predators in North America, most recently as Vice President for Species Conservation for Defenders of Wildlife.

DALE D. GOBLE is the Margaret Wilson Schimke Distinguished Professor of Law at the University of Idaho, where his teaching and research focus on the intersection of natural resource law and policy, constitutional law, and history. He has written numerous articles and essays and is coauthor with Eric Freyfogle of two books, *Wildlife Law: Cases and Materials* and *Federal Wildlife Statutes: Texts and Contexts*.

D. NOAH GREENWALD is a conservation biologist with the Center for Biological Diversity. His work focuses on protection for imperiled species under the Endangered Species Act. He earned an M.S. in forest ecology and conservation in 1997 from the University of Washington.

WILLIAM R. HEINRICH is Species Restoration Manager for the Peregrine Fund. He oversees release programs for the peregrine falcon, aplomado falcon, and California condor throughout the western United States. He has worked with birds of prey for forty-two years and has studied raptors internationally in nine countries including Bahrain, Mexico, Colombia, Greenland, Guatemala, Italy, Panama, United Kingdom, and Zimbabwe.

J. PETER JENNY is Vice President of the Peregrine Fund. He has been instrumental in developing and implementing a 1.6-million-acre safe harbor agreement to facilitate the recovery of the endangered aplomado falcon on private property. He divides his time between the management of species restoration efforts and overall program development.

CARRIE V. KAPPEL is a graduate student in ecology at Stanford University's Hopkins Marine Station. Her research focuses on rare marine species, including spatial patterns in coral species diversity and rarity and its implications for reserve network design to the threats, as well as management of vulnerable marine species and habitats worldwide. She has also studied Caribbean coral reefs, California kelp forests, and rocky intertidal habitats.

PETER KAREIVA is Lead Scientist for the Nature Conservancy's Pacific Western Conservation Region. He earned a Ph.D. from Cornell University in 1981. After a twenty-year academic career in ecology and mathematical biology, he worked for National Marine Fisheries Service, providing scientific input in support of federally listed salmon species. He has been a Guggenheim Fellow and served on the editorial boards of numerous scientific journals. His current projects emphasize the interplay of human land use and biodiversity, resilience in the face of global change, and marine conservation.

KIMBERLY KORTH is Private Lands Zoologist for the New Jersey Division of Fish and Wildlife's Endangered and Nongame Species Program. Her primary responsibility is coordinating the Landowner Incentive Program, where her focus is habitat restoration.

ALAN LIEBERMAN is Avian Conservation Coordinator for the Zoological Society of San Diego and Program Director for the Hawaii Endangered Bird Conservation Program. His focus is on developing the role of captive propagation for reintroduction and recovery of endangered species.

LUIGI MAIORANO is a Ph.D. student at the University of Idaho in the College of Natural Resources. His research focuses on the efficiency of the Italian protected areas network for the conservation of the Italian biodiversity. His research interests are GIS and remote sensing applied to wildlife habitat modeling and conservation biology. He works for the University of Rome as associate researcher and for the Institute of Applied Ecology.

MARGARET MCMILLAN is an endangered species specialist for Environmental Defense, in Washington, D.C. She works for the organization's Center for Conservation Incentives, which focuses on policy initiatives and on-the-ground projects that use voluntary financial, technical, and regulatory incentives to encourage private landowners to maintain and restore habitat for rare species. She is editor of a newsletter, *Conservation Incentives*.

FIORENZA MICHELI is Assistant Professor of Biological Sciences at Stanford University, Hopkins Marine Station. She studies species interactions and species-habitat relationships in marine communities and the applications of community ecology to the conservation of marine ecosystems. Dr. Micheli is a Fellow of the Aldo Leopold Leadership Program, a member of the Monterey Bay National Marine Sanctuary research activity panel, and serves on the editorial board of *Conservation Biology*.

LAWRENCE NILES is Chief of the Endangered and Nongame Species Program in the New Jersey Division of Fish and Wildlife. He is project leader for the Shorebird Project, conducting research on Red Knots in the Arctic, South

America, and Delaware Bay. His focus is protecting endangered species habitat at a landscape level using a GIS-based mapping system and species models.

GREGORY M. PARKHURST is Assistant Professor of Economics in the Department of Agricultural Economics at Mississippi State University. His research focuses on the behavior underpinnings of the private provision of spatially allocated public goods.

ANNA PIDGORNA is a Ph.D. student in the Environmental Science Program at the University of Idaho. Her doctoral research focuses on analysis of U.S. conservation policy pertaining to national wildlife refuges.

WILLIAM H. RODGERS JR. is Stimson Bullitt Professor of Environmental Law at the University of Washington. He specializes in natural resource law and is recognized as one of the founders of environmental law. He is author of numerous essays on environmental law and of several books, including *Handbook of Environmental Law, Energy and Natural Resources Law*, and a four-volume treatise on environmental law. A fifth volume, *Environmental Law in Indian Country*, is forthcoming.

MICHAEL L. ROSENZWEIG is Professor of Ecology and Evolutionary Biology at the University of Arizona. He has worked with mathematical theories of predation dynamics, foraging choice, and species diversity, as well as the ecology of small desert mammals. He holds a Ph.D. from the University of Pennsylvania. He is author of *Species Diversity in Space and Time* and *Win-Win Ecology*. He is publisher and editor in chief of the journal *Evolutionary Ecology Research*, which he founded in 1998.

J. MICHAEL SCOTT is Professor of Wildlife Biology at the University of Idaho, a research biologist with the U.S. Geological Survey, and Leader of the Idaho Cooperative Fish and Wildlife Research Unit. He first worked with endangered species in 1974 in Hawaii where he studied distribution, abundance, and limiting factors of endangered birds. He has served as Director of the Condor Research Center for two years, and since 1986 has conducted research on endangered species and reserve identification, selection, and design.

MARK L. SHAFFER is Program Director for the Environment at the Doris Duke Charitable Foundation. Previously, he was Senior Vice President of Programs for Defenders of Wildlife and has also worked with the Nature Conservancy, the Wilderness Society, and the U.S. Fish and Wildlife Service. He holds a Ph.D. from Duke University School of Forestry and Environmental Studies.

His doctoral research on grizzly bears helped to pioneer population viability analysis in conservation biology.

JASON F. SHOGREN is the Stroock Distinguished Professor of Natural Resource Conservation and Management at the University of Wyoming. His research focuses on the behavioral underpinnings of private choice and public policy, especially for environmental and natural resources. Before returning to his alma mater, he taught at Iowa State and Yale universities. In 1997, he served as the senior economist for environmental and natural resource policy on the Council of Economic Advisers in the White House.

WILLIAM J. SNAPE III is Chairman of the Board for the Endangered Species Coalition and a lawyer in private practice in Washington, D.C., where his clients include environmental organizations, private landowners with natural resource issues, and Gallaudet University. From 1994 to 2004, he was chief counsel for Defenders of Wildlife, where he directed all domestic and international program legal policy and supervised the organization's litigation docket. He is editor and author of *Biodiversity and the Law*, published by Island Press.

LEONARDO SOTOMAYOR is a GIS and data manager for the Nature Conservancy. Born and raised in Quito, Ecuador, he earned an M.A. in GIS and International Development from Clark University in 1999. He is currently working on the development of ecoregional assessments tools, such as those used for portfolio assembly, data management, and data standards.

KIERAN F. SUCKLING is Policy and Biodiversity Program Director for the Center for Biological Diversity, which he founded in 1989. A philosopher by training and linguist by inclination, he has won awards for his work in philosophy, literary criticism, and conservation. His work at the Center focuses on assessing and improving strategies to protect and recover imperiled species. He lives outside Tucson, Ariz., with his novelist wife, Lydia Millet, and their daughter, Nola.

LEONA K. SVANCARA received her M.S. degree in wildlife resources from University of Idaho and is currently working on a Ph.D. in natural resources. She is a spatial ecologist and data manager for the Inventory and Monitoring Program of the Upper Columbia Basin Network for the National Park Service.

A. DAN TARLOCK, LL.B., Stanford University, is Distinguished Professor at the Chicago-Kent College of Law, Illinois Institute of Technology. Among his numerous publications, he is coauthor of *Environmental Protection: Law and*

Policy and Water Resources Management. He served as Special Counsel to the State of California in the development of a multispecies habitat conservation plan for Orange County.

MARTIN TAYLOR trained in environmental studies in Australia and researched and taught biology at Princeton University and the University of Arizona before taking up the study of conservation biology in 1999. He has conducted Endangered Species Act–related research on the northern goshawk, southern resident killer whale, and Arizona bald eagle, and on the impacts of livestock grazing on U.S. public lands. He has been an invited participant at scientific meetings of the International Whaling Commission and the Convention on International Trade in Endangered Species.

TIMOTHY H. TEAR is Director of Conservation Science for the Eastern New York Chapter of the Nature Conservancy. His work focuses on the use of science to inform conservation actions at local and regional scales, evaluating goal-setting in conservation, and strengthening the link between conservation science and planning.

BARTON H. THOMPSON JR. is Director of the Stanford Institute for the Environment and the Robert E. Paradise Professor of Natural Resources Law at Stanford Law School. He is author of *Environmental Law and Policy: Concepts and Insights* and of numerous articles on biodiversity policy and other environmental issues. Professor Thompson holds M.B.A. and J.D. degrees from Stanford University. Following law school, he clerked for Chief Justice William H. Rehnquist of the United States Supreme Court.

SARA VICKERMAN is Senior Director of Biodiversity Partnerships for Defenders of Wildlife and manages the organization's northwest office in Oregon. She initiated the Oregon Biodiversity Project, a collaborative effort that included a statewide biodiversity assessment and conservation strategy. The project has served as a model for other programs around the country that focus on preventing additional species from becoming endangered. Her work has emphasized the need for more effective incentives for landowners to encourage the conservation of habitat on private land.

RICHARD L. WALLACE is Director of the Environmental Studies Program at Ursinus College. He is formerly a senior staff member at the Marine Mammal Commission, where he analyzed programs for the conservation of marine mammals and their habitats. He has written numerous papers applying social science analytical methods to conservation biology. In his current research he evaluates individual and organizational behavior in programs authorized under the U.S. Endangered Species Act and the Marine Mammal Protection Act.

LAURA HOOD WATCHMAN is Senior Manager of Land Use Programs at Defenders of Wildlife in Washington, D.C. She has worked to promote large-scale conservation planning and prioritizing land conservation and has researched habitat conservation plans under the Endangered Species Act and developed a certification program for green development. She earned a bachelor of science degree in ecology and evolutionary biology from Princeton University and master's degree in zoology from the University of Washington.

DAVID S. WILCOVE is Professor of Ecology and Evolutionary Biology and Public Affairs at Princeton University. Previously, he has worked for Environmental Defense, the Wilderness Society, and the Nature Conservancy. He has authored numerous technical and popular articles in the fields of conservation biology, ornithology, and endangered species protection. He has served on the boards of directors of the Society for Conservation Biology, Rare Center for Tropical Conservation, American Bird Conservancy, and the Natural Areas Association.

STEVEN L. YAFFEE is the Theodore Roosevelt Professor of Ecosystem Management and Professor of Natural Resource and Environmental Policy at the University of Michigan. He has worked for more than twenty-five years on federal endangered species, public lands, and ecosystem management policy, and is the author or coauthor of *Making Collaboration Work, The Wisdom of the Spotted Owl,* and *Ecosystem Management in the United States,* all published by Island Press. He holds a doctorate from the Massachusetts Institute of Technology.

CHRISTOPHER YUAN-FARRELL is a landscape ecologist for the Nature Conservancy. He works on issues of land transformation and developing strategies for biodiversity protection. His research focuses on the effectiveness of conservation easements as a strategy for long-term land protection.

Index

Italicized page numbers refer to boxes, figures, and tables.